13

THE ORTHODOX CHURCHES AND THE WEST

THE ORTHODOX CHURCHES AND THE WEST

PAPERS READ AT
THE FOURTEENTH SUMMER MEETING AND
THE FIFTEENTH WINTER MEETING
OF THE
ECCLESIASTICAL HISTORY SOCIETY

EDITED BY
DEREK BAKER

PUBLISHED FOR
THE ECCLESIASTICAL HISTORY SOCIETY
BY
BASIL BLACKWELL · OXFORD
1976

PREFACE

The present volume of *Studies in Church History* is the thirteenth to be produced by the Ecclesiastical History Society and the fourth to be published by the Society itself in collaboration with Basil Blackwell. 'The Orthodox Churches and the West' was the theme of the fourteenth summer meeting of the Society, held at the University of Lancaster, and of the fifteenth winter meeting. The twenty papers included in this volume are a selection from those read at these two meetings.

The Society is grateful to the British Academy for generous financial assistance in the production of this volume.

Derek Baker

CONTENTS

CONTENTS

CONTRIBUTORS

DONALD M. NICOL *(President)*
Koraës Professor of Byzantine and Modern Greek History, Language and Literature, University of London, King's College

PETER BROWN
Professor of History, University of London, Royal Holloway College

RICHARD R. M. CLOGG
Lecturer in Modern Greek History, University of London, King's College and School of Slavonic and East European Studies

DENO J. GEANAKOPLOS
Professor of History and Religious Studies, Yale University

E. AMAND DE MENDIETA
Canon Residentiary, Winchester Cathedral

ERIC D. TAPPE
Professor of Rumanian, University of London, School of Slavonic and East European Studies

NICOLAS ZERNOV
Warden of St Gregory and St Macrina Houses, Oxford; formerly Spalding Lecturer in Eastern Orthodox Culture, University of Oxford

DEREK BAKER
Lecturer in History, University of Edinburgh

BRENDA BOLTON
Lecturer in History, University of London, Westfield College

AVERIL CAMERON
Reader in Ancient History, University of London, King's College

G. J. CUMING
Lecturer in Liturgical Studies, University of London, King's College

W. H. C. FREND
Professor of Ecclesiastical History, University of Glasgow

CONTRIBUTORS

MURIEL HEPPELL
Lecturer in the Medieval History of Orthodox Eastern Europe, University of London, School of Slavonic and East European Studies

KATHRYN D. HILL
University of London, Bedford College

ROSALIND M. T. HILL
Professor of History, University of London, Westfield College

STUART P. MEWS
Lecturer in Sociology of Religion, University of Lancaster

JANET L. NELSON
Lecturer in History, University of London, King's College

JOAN M. PETERSEN
Formerly Editor, SPCK, London

HENRY R. SEFTON
Lecturer in Church History, University of Aberdeen

KALLISTOS WARE
Fellow of Pembroke College, Oxford; Spalding Lecturer in Eastern Orthodox Studies, University of Oxford

INTRODUCTION

As the studies included in this volume make clear there is more to Orthodoxy than Byzantium and the Byzantine church, and for medievalists in particular it is salutary to be reminded not simply of the immensity of the Orthodox world, but of those mutations of Orthodoxy which find all too little space in this volume, or in other recent studies of relations between east and west. In a further detailed study of the Acacian schism, and an examination of the visit of archbishop Arsenios to Scotland in the eighteenth century, there are hints of these wider perspectives, but for the most part, and inevitably, these studies deal with aspects of the mainstream topics in this area of discussion. Western knowledge, and misunderstanding, of the Greeks and their language in the age of Gregory the Great, Grosseteste and the first and fourth crusades are the subjects of four particular studies; the influence of the east in the west, in political matters, ritual, liturgy and spirituality, the themes of five more. The Orthodox world, however, received as well as donated, and papers on the council of Constance and the election of an archbishop in the twentieth century demonstrate in microcosm the external political, ecclesiastico-political and, latterly, secular pressures to which Orthodoxy was subjected in the years of its material weakness and subjugation. These are matters which are considered at greater length in the medieval contributions of the president and professor Geanakoplos, and in Dr Zernov's emotive discussion of the contemporary diaspora from holy Russia, that successor third Rome.

Professor Tappe's study of Orthodoxy in Rumania is a further reminder that there was a Byzantine family of churches which was long to outlast its counterpart and initial condition, the imperial commonwealth of peoples, and to become willy-nilly its secular and political heir. The possibilities and dangers of such a situation are admirably indicated in a major reconsideration of the church in pre-independence Greece. But for all this political involvement it is as well not to forget that the strength of Orthodoxy has always lain in its spirituality: the president has remarked that the Byzantines were obsessively theological, while Dr Ware's sympathetic portrayal of the fifth earl of Guilford gives an insight into those spiritual qualities and attractions which could convert a peer of the age of George III to Orthodoxy. Frederick North was renowned as a romantic philhellene, but as Dr Amand de Mendieta has shown in his magisterial account of

xi

Basil of Caesarea, Christian hellenism was an uncertain amalgam of the teachings of Christ and the philosophers, and the contradictions evident in the Cappadocian can be paralleled at many points in later Byzantine centuries—and in non-Byzantine lands and societies, for, as professor Brown has provocatively emphasised, in contrast to Dr Zernov, there was a mediterranean *koine* which blurs the distinctions so often made between east and west, and suggests, rather, a horizontal, north-south divide.

Whatever the distinctions made, however, and however the differences are categorised, it remains true that for the medieval west the Byzantine east was a world apart. There had indeed been 'a parting of the ways', and to westerners, then as later, the tale has appeared one of decline, and apparently inevitable fall. How far the fortunes of the empire comprehend those of the church, however, is a different matter. Auden succinctly defined the dilemma of the early Christians,

> Knowing that as their hopes grew less
> So would their heavenly worldliness,
> Their early agape decline
> To a late lunch with Constantine.[1]

The compromised attitudes and policies which proceeded from this concordat are too well-known to need rehearsing here. But the compromises necessary for the survival of an established church took different forms in east and west. For the Byzantines their empire and their church were coterminous. The one could not exist without the other. This myth was sustained to the bitter end, and it was not until the fifteenth century, during and after the collapse of their material world, that the Orthodox were left to live solely upon the resources of their spiritual capital. The Orthodox church none the less has shown a phenomenal talent for survival. It is the contention of the president that it developed some of that talent through its encounters with the Christians of the west and its resistance to those of its own emperors who wished to submit to the claims of the papacy in order to ensure the material security of their empire. The view that the Orthodox church has consistently gained strength through oppression and suffering is endorsed for the twentieth century by Dr Zernov, and empirically demonstrated by his first-hand account of the renaissance of Orthodoxy in his lifetime. Whatever the qualifications and caveats then, the basic theme of this volume is, as professor Nicol has declared, 'the survival and the living continuity of the Orthodox tradition'.

[1] *New Year Letter* (London 1941) lines 645–8.

EASTERN AND WESTERN CHRISTENDOM
IN LATE ANTIQUITY:
A PARTING OF THE WAYS

by PETER BROWN

I must begin with the words of the clergyman: 'My short sermon for today is divided into three parts. One: God. Two: Man. Three: The Universe.' It will be impossible to do justice to the subject in hand in the short span of one lecture. This is not only because of the vast range of time and space involved in any consideration of the parting of the ways between eastern and western Christianity in the late antique period. To embark on such a theme involves holding up for scrutiny the very nature of ecclesiastical history. For what we have to deal with is not merely *what* happened in the relations between east and west, but *why* what happened happened as it did. Once the ecclesiastical historian asks why, he will find himself sooner or later forced to grapple with the whole quality of men's lives in the past— that is, with how they lived the full twenty-four hours of the day, not only in their books, but in their churches, not only in their churches, but in the most intimate and most monotonous rhythms of their life.

For one thing can be said with certainty. The parting of the ways between east and west in Christianity cannot be reduced to a few formulae. It cannot be explained in terms of a map of the division of the Roman empire between its Greek and Latin-speaking halves. Still less can the later alienation of the churches be blamed on the delinquencies of interpreters and the surprising inability of so many great Latin minds to reach 'A' level in Greek. Tempting though this course may be, it cannot be compressed into brilliant juxtapositions between representative early Christian authors. Merely to contrast Tertullian and Clement of Alexandria, Augustine and Basil of Caesarea, as if by this comparison alone it were possible to trace the divergent trajectories of two great Christian regions, may be a device of considerable didactic power, and revealing when skilfully exploited, but it has little explanatory value.

At this juncture in scholarship, a sense of perspective is worth more than any so-called 'explanation' of the division of east and west. So I would like to begin with a dictum of Edward Gibbon: 'The distinction of North and South is real and intelligible . . . But the difference between East and West is arbitrary and shifts round the globe'.[1]

In the present state of late antique studies, Gibbon's point needs to be stressed. Some of the most interesting work in late Roman history in the past generations has been carried out in terms of the east-west division of Graeco-Roman civilisation. The tendency of the two *partes* of the Roman empire to grow apart in the fourth century has received very great prominence as one of the main factors of late antique history. The alienation of east and west has been accepted as one of the principal causes of the ruin of the Roman empire in the west. On the short time-scale, in the crisis that followed the death of Theodosius in 395 and the first official division of the empire between his sons, the inability of the two parts of the empire to collaborate against barbarian invasion has been explained in terms of a deep-seated difference in aims and outlook.[2] On a longer time-scale, the alienation of the two *partes*, the emergence in each of a distinctive culture and social structure, has been fruitfully invoked to account for the sinister ease with which western Roman society settled down to life without an empire.[3] Instances of misunderstanding and conflict in the history of church and empire tend, nowadays, to be seen as no more than symptomatic of a deeper alienation: they are mere foam on a sea furrowed by ineluctable currents.

I would like to step outside this perspective for a moment, not necessarily to exclude it altogether, but to seek a different vantage-point from which to take a new look at our subject. I would like to suggest that the history of the Christian church in late antiquity and in the early middle ages is far more a part of the history of the mediterranean and its neighbours than it is part of the history of the division of the mediterranean itself between east and west. I would like therefore to hark back to the perspective of Henri Pirenne, in his *Mahomet et Charlemagne*.[4] Whatever the weaknesses of Pirenne's

1 Edward Gibbon, *The History of the Decline and Fall of the Roman Empire*, notes to the second edition, introduction, p xxxvi.
2 S. Mazzarino, *Stilicone e la crisi imperiale dopo Teodosio* (Rome 1942) and E. Demougeot, *De l'unité à la division de l'empire romain* (Paris 1951).
3 M. Wes, *Das Ende des Kaisertums im Westen des römischen Reichs* (The Hague 1967) and W. Goffart, 'Zosimus, the first historian of Rome's fall', *AHR* 76 (1971) pp 412–41; see [P.] Brown, *Religion and Society [in the Age of Saint Augustine]* (London 1972) pp 229–30.
4 See Peter Brown, 'Mohammed and Charlemagne by Henri Pirenne', *Daedalus* 102 (Cambridge, Mass., 1973) pp 25–33.

thesis from the point of view of the commercial and maritime history of the mediterranean, his intuition of the basic homogeneity of mediterranean civilisation deep into the early middle ages still holds good. The history of the Christian church is a history of *Romania à la Pirenne*. It is the history of a religion which identified itself almost from its origins with a mediterranean-wide style of urban civilisation; that penetrated the sprawling countryside of western Europe along trade routes that linked it to the boom towns of Asia Minor. It fed its imagination on Palestine and Syria; its intellectual powerhouse in the Latin world was North Africa, and in this Africa Carthage, 'Rome in Africa', remained, like Rome, a great mediterranean town, moving to rhythms strangely similar to those of Alexandria, Antioch and Constantinople.

It is important to stress this, the horizontal, unity of the mediterranean. Any divergence along the east-west spectrum of the mediterranean was always dwarfed by the immensity of the gulf which separated the mediterranean itself from the alien societies which flanked it.

Let us look east for a moment: Seen from the point of view of the near east, the most crucial parting of the ways was not between east and west in the mediterranean, but between the mediterranean itself and the exuberant hinterland that stretched eastwards across the fertile crescent. If Christ had lived in the hellenistic rather than in the Roman period, or in the third century AD rather than in the first, then we could imagine a very different Christianity—a Christianity whose missionaries would not have been drawn into the unitary civilisation of the mediterranean at a time of its maximum gravitational pull, but who would have wandered in a more random manner into the great caravan cities and sprawling villages of eastern Syria and Mesopotamia. The beautiful new book of Robert Murray, *Symbols of Church and Kingdom. A Study in Early Syrian Tradition* and the forthcoming study by Roberta Chesnut on the monophysite Christologies of three Syriac authors are reminders of a whole third world of Christian experience, whose rich voice is too often drowned by the articulate and bustling mediterranean.[5] Yet, as Gregory Dix wrote of the early

---

[5] Robert Murray, *Symbols of Church and Kingdom. A Study in the Early Syrian Tradition* (Cambridge 1975) and Roberta Chesnut, *Three Monophysite Christologies: Severus of Antioch, Philoxenus of Mabbug, and Jacob of Sarug* (Oxford 1975). See also, José Grosdidier de Matons, *Romanos le Mélode et les origines de l'hymnographie byzantine* (Lille 1974) pp 23–43.

Syrian liturgies—these allow us to penetrate 'behind the divergence of Greek and Western Christianity generally to that oriental world to which the Galilaean apostles had belonged'.[6]

It is the same when we look to the north of Europe. Once again, the divergence of east and west along the mediterranean was dwarfed by the rise in north-western Europe of Christian societies which were seen to differ *toto caelo* from the ancient Christianity of the mediterranean. In the early middle ages we have to deal with a 'mediterranean chauvinism' whose force is too often underrated. As Maurice Chevalier said: 'Old age is not so bad if you consider the alternative'. Nothing was better calculated to shrink the distance between Rome and Constantinople than the contemplation of the alien alternative across the Alps. Generalisations to the effect that the papacy served as a rallying point of western consciousness against the east assume that there was a west to be conscious. As long as the mediterranean remained the heart of *Romania*, the division that was 'real and intelligible' to every early medieval man was that between north and south. Listen to a Roman on his northern co-religionists: 'For the transalpine voices . . . roaring deep with their thunderous throats . . . cannot bring forth the proper sweetness of the melody, because the savage barbarity of their drunken throats, while endeavouring to utter this gentle strain, through its natural noisiness, proffers only unmodulated sounds, like unto farm carts clumsily creeping up a rutted hill.'[7] Listen to a northerner on a representative of *Romania*: 'There was a certain deacon who followed the habits of the Italians in that he was perpetually trying to resist nature. He used to take baths, he had his head very closely shaved, he polished his skin, he cleaned his nails, he had his hair cut short as if it had been turned on a lathe, and he wore linen underclothes . . .'[8]

I would suggest that we abandon a model of relations between east and west based on the assumption of deep alienation. It is not enough that we should pile up detailed studies of those persons, moments or milieux where the shores of the mediterranean appear to have drawn closer together. Such studies have proved invaluable, ranging as they do from consideration of the Greek culture of the early Christian communities of Carthage,[9] from the figures of Augustine,

[6] [Gregory] Dix, [*The Shape of the Liturgy*] (London 1945) p 178.
[7] Johannes Diaconus, *Vita Gregorii* II, 7, *PL* 75, col 91.
[8] Notker, *Life of Charlemagne* cap 32, transl Lewis Thorpe, *Two Lives of Charlemagne* (Pelican, Harmondsworth 1969) p 130.
[9] [T. D.] Barnes, [*Tertullian*] (Oxford 1971) pp 67–9.

Pelagius,[10] and John Cassian,[11] to the popes of the early middle ages,[12] from the missions of Constantine and Methodius[13] to that extraordinary galaxy of holy men at the court of Otto III[14] and in the monastery of Sant' Alessio on the Aventine.[15] But these studies might be mis-interpreted if they were seen as so many incidents of east-west relations, if by 'relations' we mean the interchange between two separate, free-standing worlds.

For this is precisely what may not have happened. Nothing has done more to handicap our understanding of mediterranean history in the medieval period than the tendency of scholars to treat Byzantium as a world apart, standing aside and above the destinies of an 'under-developed' western Europe. Once this view is accepted, the east tends to be treated as a distinct and enclosed reservoir of superior culture, from which the occasional stream is released, to pour down hill—by some obscure law of cultural hydraulics—to water the lower reaches of the west. Relations between east and west, therefore, tend to be treated as so many 'releases' of Byzantine 'influence'; and the 'eastern' features of early medieval art and piety are ascribed to 'borrowings' from a superior Byzantine model. Nothing has been more conducive to confusion in the study of art and religion in the dark ages than such an assumption.[16]

When seen in this way, also, undue attention is given to those obvious 'sluice-gates' that would facilitate the downhill flow of culture from east to west. To take one example: I suspect that we will soon

---

[10] Peter Brown, 'The Patrons of Pelagius', *JTS* ns 21 (1970) pp 56–72 in *Religion and Society* pp 208–26.

[11] Philip Rousseau, 'Cassian, Contemplation and the Coenobitic Life', *JEH* 26 (1975) pp 113–26.

[12] Peter Llewellyn, 'The Roman Church in the Seventh Century: the Legacy of Gregory I', *JEH* 25 (1974) pp 363–80 and Evelyne Patlagean, 'Les armes et la cité à Rome du viième au ixème siécle', *Mèlanges de l'École francaise de Rome* 86 (Rome 1974) pp 25–62.

[13] Imre Boba, *Moravia's History Reconsidered* (The Hague 1971). If the author is right in placing Moravia in the region of Sirmium, then the mission of Constantine and Methodius took place not in the depths of eastern central Europe, but within the traditional orbit of *Romania*.

[14] K. Leyser, 'The Tenth Century in Byzantine-Western Relations', *Relations between East and West in the Middle Ages*, ed Derek Baker (Edinburgh 1973) pp 29–63, at pp 44–5.

[15] B. Hamilton, 'The Monastery of S. Alessio and the Religious and Intellectual Renaissance in 10th century Rome' *Studies in Medieval and Renaissance History* (1965) pp 265–310.

[16] J. Hubert, 'Les relations artistiques entre les diverses parties de l'ancien empire romain pendant de haut moyen âge,' *Settimane di Studi sull'Alto Medio Evo* 11 (Spoleto 1964) pp 453–77.

no longer be as concerned as we have been with the question of whether or not Gregory the Great spoke Greek. For a theory of cultural interchange that treats the build-up of a culture—especially of a religious culture—in terms of so many discrete acts of 'reception' tends to overlook the inarticulate familiarities of a shared landscape. Throughout late antiquity vital areas of culture were transmitted by a mediterranean-wide process of osmosis. The ideology of the Byzantine state is inconceivable without generations of Byzantines who could 'think Latin' even when they could not read it.[17] Life, in late antiquity was wider and more embracing than any knowledge of the right classical languages. The spread of the feast of kalends of January in the late Roman period is an astonishing example of this. A feast that had been limited to Rome in the high empire suddenly becomes a mediterranean wide phenomenon in late antiquity.[18] Plainly, when the city-dwellers of late antiquity wanted to say something important about the way life was lived, and find ceremonial expression for it, they said the same thing all over the mediterranean, in whatever language came to hand. Christianity, which grew out of precisely that milieu, was exceptionally sensitive to the same mediterranean-wide rhythms. Furthermore, adoption by osmosis came easily to a group in which oral methods of transmission had always played a great part in its religious culture: the Christian faith was passed on by oral catechesis, Christian spiritual direction was carried out in terms of a fund of monastic *apophthegmata*.

In this situation I would like to introduce the concept of a mediterranean *koiné*. To take a few examples from the end of our period. The history of monasticism in the fifth and sixth centuries is not a history of an 'oriental' monasticism penetrating the west: in the simple phrase of P. Riché, we are dealing with *un monachisme méditerrenéen*.[19] The new edition of a Latin translation of the *Apophthegmata* by Paschasius of Dumio shows this Christian Mediterranean *koiné* at work. Paschasius is unlocalisable; and the apophthegamatic literature that he handles has become as thickly

[17] Brown, *Religion and Society* p 230. H. G. Beck, '*Res Publica Romana* Vom Staatsdenken der Byzantinern', *ABAW*, *PhK* (1970) pp 7–41, in *Das Byzantinische Herrscherbild*, *Wege der Forschung* 341 (Darmstadt 1975) pp 379–414. E. Rosenthal, *The Illumination of the Virgilius Romanus* (Zurich, 1972) p 98, assumes an east Roman origin for a Vergil manuscript of the sixth century.

[18] M. Meslin, *La fête des kalendes de janvier dans l'empire romain*, Collection Latomus 115 (Brussels 1970).

[19] P. Riché, *Education et culture dans l'Occident barbare* (Paris 1962) p 149.

matted as a bed of reeds, bridging the mediterranean with a single monastic folklore.[20] To take another example: often in the history of early medieval piety, where the unwary might acclaim a direct 'eastern' influence, it is possible to sense 'a breath of the warm south'. A stylite hermit established outside Cologne—Wulfilach, a Lombard, from a north Italy heavy with the *koiné* of *Romania*.[21] A miracle connected with an icon, the only one in the *Libri Miraculorum* of Gregory of Tours—a story by Venantius Fortunatus, straight from Ravenna.[22]

There is therefore no shortcut to the problem of the parting of the ways between east and west. It would be a serious mistake to import into the history of the Christian church supposed contrasts whose outlines have been sketched *grosso modo* by previous generations of late Roman historians of society and culture. The ecclesiastical historian cannot ignore the intimate dependence of the Christian church on its social and cultural environment. But it is vital that he should offer a differentiated and up-to-date explanation of how such an environment was experienced in the church, and precisely what this environment was. It is not enough to compound his own generalisations by importing the generalisations of others.

Alas, such remarks are only a preface to the main task. For now we come to the most delicate part of our undertaking. We cannot subsume the explanation of the parting of the ways between east and west beneath any overwhelming antithesis of two societies: the unity of a mediterranean civilisation exerts a constant, discreet pressure to blur such stark and convenient contrasts. If there is a divergence between the eastern and western churches, we must look for it within the churches themselves; and if we do this we must begin at the beginning —we must have a clear idea of the implications of the rise of Christianity in the Roman world.

Here it is a pleasure to pay tribute to a great tradition of English scholarship, well known in its representatives. W. H. C. Frend in his *Martyrdom and Persecution in the Early Church*[23] and R. A. Markus in a

[20] J. G. Freire, *A versão latina por Pascasio de Dume dos Apophthegmata Patrum* (Coimbra 1971) 1 p 17.

[21] Gregory of Tours, *Lib[ri] Hist[oriarum]* VIII, 15, ed B. Krusch, *MGH, SRM*, 1, 2, p 380.

[22] Gregory of Tours, *de virt[utibus sancti] Mart[ini]* I, 15a, ed. B. Krusch, *MGH, SRM* 1, 1, p 147.

[23] W. H. C. Frend, *Martyrdom and Persecution in the Early Church* (Oxford 1965). See Peter Brown, 'Approaches to the Religious Crisis of the Third Century A.D.' *EHR* 83 (1968) pp 542–58 in *Religion and Society* esp pp 91–3.

characteristically distinguished slim volume, *Christianity in the Roman World*,[24] have made clear that the parting of the ways between east and west springs from the ways in which Christianity adapted itself to its Roman environment. The parting of the ways between east and west was implied at the joining of the ways of Christianity and classical culture. Christianity took up a different stance in east and west to the state, to society, to classical culture. In the west, the church maintained its 'twice-born' attitudes. It stood to one side of the *saeculum*. West Roman society and culture, first shunned as demonic, was firmly *entzaubert* by Augustine: no mystique but the most sinister was allowed to rest upon it. Later, when this society was in the hands of barbarians, it sank to the status of a passive and potentially refractory laity dominated by a clearly defined clerical élite. The contrast with eastern Christianity, whose apologists had early acclaimed a harmony between Christianity and Greek culture, and whose emperors, from Constantine onwards, had negotiated endlessly for the unanimity of church and state, stands out in pointed contrast to that situation.

As a result of such studies, the contrast of east and west has become firmly rooted in 'the history of Christian self-awareness in the Roman world'; and this is a history which, as we all know, has been pursued with quite exceptional insight into the social and cultural environment of the classical and late antique world. Such studies are the meeting point par excellence of all that is best in the full range of late Roman studies. It is in this tradition, rather than in the more pragmatic side of late Roman economic and administrative history, that it is possible to catch the full significance of the late antique revolution and to seize most clearly its implications for the medievalist.

I would like to end by adding to this perspective rather than by challenging it. I feel obscurely that the social and cultural historians of the relations of Christianity and the classical world have had their say and have said it very well. It is now time for the strictly religious historian to take up his cue. I would like to suggest that we trace some features of the divergence between east and west in terms of diverging attitudes to the idea of the *holy* in the two churches. Far from proposing an alternative explanation, I would like to bring this approach to bear like an ultra-violet light which enables us to see differing structures in one and the same crystal.

In late antiquity attitudes to culture and society were inextricably intertwined with attitudes to the holy. The religious revolution of

[24] R. A. Markus, *Christianity in the Roman World* (London 1975).

A parting of the ways

late antiquity did not only see the rise of the Christian church as a society within a society and a culture within a culture. Hence the study of the Christian church in east and west cannot be reduced to its stances towards culture and society. The rise itself was intimately connected with a drastic redistribution and re-definition of those points at which the holy was thought to impinge on human affairs.

Unlike paganism and much of Judaism, the Christian communities were prepared to invest individual human beings with supernatural powers or with the ability to exercise power on behalf of the super-natural. It was as precisely identifiable bearers of the holy, and as the heirs of an imagined genealogy of similar bearers of the holy—apostles, martyrs, prophets—that the Christian leaders were able to form the Christian communities. The groups that took up a stance to the society and culture of their times were formed around known and revered *loci* of the holy—and these *loci* tended to be human beings. As the rabbis told Justin Martyr: 'but as for you, who have forsaken God and put your trust in a man, what salvation can await you?'[25]

The early Christians lived down to these strictures. Small details of their behaviour, revealed in passing in the acts of the martyrs, speak volumes: 'Polycarp took off all his clothing, loosed his belt and even tried to take off his sandals, although he had never had to do this before: for all the Christians were always eager to be the first to touch his flesh'.[26] In this respect, Christianity added a radical twist to a tide in late antique sensibility. Pagan biographies of θεῖοι ἄνδρες and later rabbinic literature show a common search for heroes who would sum up in their persons the values of the group.[27] Ideals that had been allowed to float free, available to any member of an educated or religious class but attached to no-one in particular, come to be given 'an earthly habitation and a name', and so a power that is best caught in some of the masterpieces of third and fourth century portrait sculpture.[28] Throughout the mediterranean world, face and halo tend to come together in late antiquity.

[25] Justin, *Dialogus cum Tryphone* viii, 4, *PG* 6, col 493B.

[26] *Martyrium Polycarpi*, 13 3d, and transl. H. Musurillo, *The Acts of the Christian Martyrs* (Oxford 1972) p 13.

[27] L. Bieler, ΘΕΙΟΣ ΑΝΗΡ *Das Bild des 'göttlichen Menschen' in Spätantike und Frühchristentum* (Vienna 1935) and J. Neusner, *A History of the Jews in Babylonia*, 4 (Leiden 1969) pp 297–402. See now E. Urbach, *Ḥazal: pirqe emunoth we de 'oth* [*The Sages: Their concepts and beliefs*] (Jerusalem 1969).

[28] H. P. L'Orange, *Apotheosis in Ancient Portraiture* (Oslo 1947) and H. von Heintze, 'Vir gravis et sanctus. Bildniskopf eines spätantiken Philosphen', *JAC* 6 (1963) pp 35–53.

PETER BROWN

Pagans who might have taken more kindly to divine men than did their Jewish contemporaries, were appalled by what the Christians did to their heroes when dead—they brought the stench of death into the preserve of the holy. This was new. For all his intimacy with the goddess Artemis, in dying Hippolytus was cut off by the unbridgeable chasm which the fact of death itself had opened between himself and his goddess: ἐμοὶ γὰρ οὐ θέμις φθιτοὺς ὁρᾶν οὐδ᾽ ὄμμα χραίνειν θανασίμοισιν ἐκπνοαῖς.[29]

In Eunapius of Sardis' account of the Christianisation of the great temples of Egypt we can catch the charnel horror of the rise of Christianity: 'For they collected the bones and skulls of criminals who had been put to death for numerous crimes . . . made them out to be gods, haunted their sepulchres, and thought that they became better by defiling themselves at their graves. "Martyrs" the dead men were called, and "ministers" of a sort, and "ambassadors" with the gods to carry men's prayers.'[30] Yet much of medieval history is inconceivable without this preliminary decision to allow the dead into a central position in worship:[31] 'Male fecit ergo Romanus episcopus qui super mortuorum hominum Petri et Pauli, secundum nos ossa venerabilia, secundum te vilem pulvisculum, offert Domino sacrificia et tumulos eorum Christi arbitrantur altaria.'[32]

Yet it is precisely around such idealised objects that Christianity succeeded in crystallising lasting pyramids of dependence. In the Roman world of the third and fourth centuries the old forms of power and dependence were being transformed and re-articulated with abrasive vigour: we need only think on the one hand of the elaboration of the imperial ceremonial,[33] and on the other on the tightening and the rendering more explicit of the links of patronage in town and

---

[29] Euripides, *Hippolytus*, lines 1437–8.

[30] Eunapius of Sardis, *Lives of the Sophists* 472, ed and transl W. C. Wright, Loeb Classical Library (London 1961) p 425.

[31] T. Klauser, 'Christliche Märtyrerkult, heidnische Heroenkult und spätjüdische Heiligenverehrung', *Gesammelte Arbeiten zur Liturgiegeschichte, Kunstegeschichte und christlichen Archäologie*, ed E. Dassmann, *JAC* Ergänzungsband 3 (1974) pp 221–9.

[32] Jerome, *Contra Vigilantium* 8, *PL* 23, col 346.

[33] see now the important studies of [Sabine G.] MacCormack, ['Change and Continuity in Late Antiquity]: the Ceremony of Adventus', *Historia* 31 (Wiesbaden 1972) pp 721–52; 'Latin Prose Panegyrics' *Empire and Aftermath*. Silver Latin 2, ed T. A. Dorey (London 1975) pp 143–205; 'Latin Prose Panegyrics: Tradition and Discontinuity in the Later Roman Empire,' *Revue des études augustiniennes* (Paris 1975) pp 1–49; 'Roma, Constantinopolis, [the Emperor and his Genius,'] *C[lassical] Q[uarterly]* 25 (London 1975) pp 131–50.

A parting of the ways

countryside.[34] In this situation, the pyramids of idealised dependence erected by the Christian church around men and objects thought of as 'holy' stand with uncanny congruence in a society constantly experimenting with forms of power and social influence.

It is in this region that I would like to look for a parting of the ways between east and west. Even if we cannot reach an explanation of the phenomenon, I would like to suggest that we are dealing with a phenomenon to explain.

In the west the precise *locus* of the supernatural power associated with the holy was fixed with increasing precision. Cyprian of Carthage, in his astute handling of the *confessores* and in his statements on the position of the bishop,[35] has a bafflingly 'medieval' ring about him: this may well be because no serious doubt as to the precise nature and location of spiritual power and the means by which it was exercised in ritual actions troubled his own mind or those of most of his successors.[36] At the same time, the eastern church had entered on to what came to strike early medieval western observers as a baffling 'crisis of overproduction' of the holy. More men were accepted as bearers or agents of the supernatural on earth, and in a far greater variety of situations, than came to be tolerated in western Europe. As a result, the precise *locus* of spiritual power in Byzantium remained, by western standards, tantalisingly ambiguous,[37] and Byzantine attitudes to sanctity, and hence to the world in general against which the holy was placed, were shot through with paradox. By the end of late

---

[34] [Peter] Brown, ['The Rise and Function of the] Holy Man', *JRS* 61 (1971) pp 80–101 at pp 85–7.

[35] J. Speigl, 'Cyprian über das judicium bei der Bischofseinsetzung', *Römische Quartalschrift* 69 (Rome/Freiburg/Vienna) (1974) pp 30–45.

[36] Dix p 116 on Cyprian and the consecration of the eucharist: 'that sort of logical directness and unity which has always appealed to Western theologians'. For the possible influence of Roman pagan attitudes to religion, the most suggestive treatment is by A. D. Nock, 'A Feature of Roman Religion' *HTR* 32 (1939) p 96 in *Essays [on Religion and the Ancient World]*, ed Zeph Stewart (Oxford 1972) 1 pp 491–2. To go further by ascribing to classical Roman attitudes and to the study of Roman law a 'legalism' which distinguished western Christianity, is to import into our understanding of men of whose background we know little—see Barnes pp 22–9 ('Still less can "Tertullian the jurist" be invoked to explain the later development of Latin Christendom'), and G. W. Clarke, 'The Secular Profession of Saint Cyprian of Carthage', *Latomus* 24 (Brussels 1965) pp 633–8—writing in a late classical milieu of uncertain nature, a dizzy continuity with the world of Cicero. I have no head for such heights; but they must be considered, more especially on points of religious practise: for one example, see F. Dölger, *Der Exorzismus im altchristliche Taufritual* (Paderborn 1906) p 97.

[37] Brown, 'Holy Man' pp 95–6.

antiquity, this contrast was clear, and it was all the clearer for being seen not as an inevitable contrast, but rather as the cumulative result of mutations within a single *koiné—a koiné* which, by the end of this period had already spilled far from the shores of the mediterranean, to the Nestorian hagiography of Sassanian Iran[38] and the Celtic holy men of Northumbria.

I think it would be best to move from two clear examples, briefly sketched, to the implications of these examples.

The rise and function of the holy man in the sixth century eastern mediterranean as revealed in the work of John of Ephesus stands in marked contrast to the world of religious experience—mainly crystallised around relics—revealed in the works of John's contemporary, Gregory of Tours.[39] The contrast is all the greater for having become crystallised from a mediterranean-wide *koiné*. For Gregory can embrace *Romania*.[40] His gaze pierces to Edessa, where a miraculous annual rainstorm washes clean the dunged-up *souk* after the great fair of saint Thomas.[41] It even reaches as far as Sergiopolis (Resafa), where saint Sergius is known as a stern protector of ex-voto offerings to his shrine: so stern, indeed, is he that chickens dedicated to him, if stolen, emerge from the cooking-pot even tougher than when they went in![42] (This was a fact known also to the shahanshah of Iran himself, none other than Khusro II Aparwez, who, in a great silver ex-voto dish, had proclaimed to saint Sergius his gratitude for success and had reported on the exceptional favours enjoyed by his Christian wife, the beautiful Shirin.[43] This inscription is the last great address of a near eastern ruler to his gods, of which the first, by Khusro's predecessor Darius, looks out from the cliffs of Bisutun, to be read only by gods and rock-climbers. Nevertheless, with Gregory we can trace the direction of a mutation that would finally weaken the hold of the mediterranean *koiné* on Gaul, and consequently on the emergent

---

[38] G. Wiessner, 'Christlicher Heiligenkult im umkreis eines sassanisischen Grosskönigs' *Festgabe deutscher Iranisten zum 2500 Jahrfeier Irans*, ed W. Eilers (Stuttgart 1971) pp 141–55, esp p 149.

[39] John of Ephesus, [*Lives of the Eastern Saints*] ed and transl E. W. Brooks, PO 17, pp 1–304, 18, pp 513–697, 19, pp 153–273, and *HE*, transl E. W. Brooks, CSCO, *Script Syr* 55 (Louvain 1936). A strictly religious commentary exists neither for Gregory nor John.

[40] Gregory's isolation from the eastern mediterranean has been exaggerated by N. H. Baynes, 'M. Pirenne and the Unity of the Mediterranean', *Byzantine Studies* (London 1960) pp 310–14.

[41] Gregory of Tours, *de gloria martyrum*, cap 32, pp 57–8.

[42] *Ibid* cap 96, p 103.

[43] P. Peeters, 'L'*ex voto* de Khusro Aparwez à Sergiopolis', *An Bol* 65 (1947) pp 5–56.

societies of north western Europe, in such a way as to bring about a final confrontation of east and west.

In the eastern mediterranean, the holy man had been forced to the fore by those exuberant and abrasive developments by which new classes came to compete for control of the countryside.[44] The position of holy men in Syria is a paradigm of the need of eastern Christians to consider as 'holy' ascetic figures on whom they could place their hopes for a 'holy', that is for an idealised, patronage, in a world over-shadowed by an 'unholy', that is, by an only too real, patronage. This aspect of east Roman social and spiritual life is well summed up by Thomas Hobbes in chapter ten of his *Leviathan*: 'Reputation of power is power: because it draweth with it the adherence of those that need protection.' The saints described by John of Ephesus had no doubts on that score: 'Neither yet think that this power of the saints before whom these people come and groan is a void thing, lest it be roused against you and your house perish.'[45]

All this is striking and well-known, yet let us look for a moment at the precise basis of this power. Here we must enter deeply into the materials from which east Romans framed their expectations of the holy, and how they combined these in such a way not only to facilitate the exercise of 'reputation and power' but tacitly, to delimit this same exercise.

The Christian *koiné* was articulated in the eastern mediterranean not to place the holy man above human society, but outside it. The holy man lived a life that was an imitation of the angels.[46] He gained his powers from retiring to the desert, that is, to the antithesis of human life, where Christ had been served by the angels,[47] and where the angels had invested John the Baptist with the first monk's cloak.[48] The holy, therefore, was at its most holy when least connected with that conflict of human interests which it was constantly called upon to palliate.

---

[44] Brown, 'Holy Man' pp 85–91. These views have been modified and placed in a wider context by R. M. Price, 'The Role of Military Men in Syria and Egypt from Constantine to Theodosius II', unpublished Oxford D Phil thesis 1974.

[45] John of Ephesus, *PO* 17, p 72.

[46] P. Nagel, *Die Motivierung der Askese, Texte und Untersuchungen* 95 (Berlin 1966) pp 34–48.

[47] G. Kittel, see under ἔρημος, *Theologisches Wörterbuch zum Neuen Testament*, 2 (Stuttgart 1935) pp 634–57 and Philipp Vielhauer, 'Tracht und Speise Johannes des Täufers', *Aufsätze zum Neuen Testament* (Munich 1965) pp 47–54.

[48] This became a prominent issue in the iconoclastic controversy: Peter Brown, 'A Dark Age Crisis: aspects of the Iconoclastic Controversy' *EHR* 88 (1973) pp 1–34 at p 21.

The east Roman holy man, as we observe him in both the fourth and fifth centuries, and in the age of Gregory and John, preserved his reputation, therefore, by an exacting ritual of de-solidarisation and even of social inversion.[49] He wielded his 'idealised' power in society by adopting stances that were the exact inverse of those connected with the exercise of real power. Where the patron was inaccessible, the holy man was open to all comers: of Habib it was said, 'he did not, as a man of high reputation, refuse to go, but, in order to satisfy him, would go with him at once without delay'.[50] Where the patron flaunted his status and his immunity, the holy man was 'an afflicted one', and often carried chains, associated in the near east not with physical discomfort so much as with the status of a political prisoner fallen from his high estate. Thus, in few societies outside the *sanyasi* culture of Hindu India, has 'reputation of power' within a society been exercised on so strict a tacit understanding that those who exercised it should be seen to stand outside this society.[51]

I feel that we touch here on something more revealing than merely the social strategies of a charismatic *ombudsman*. We are dealing with a society which accepts such strategies because they could be associated with other basic ideas about the nature of the holy and its impingement on human affairs. Here I would risk a suggestion. The holy escaped social definition—or, rather, its absence of social definition became intelligible—because it was thought of principally as a power that 'manifested' itself in a manner that was as vivid as it was discontinuous with normal human expectations. If this is so, then we are in a very ancient world indeed. It is the world of the *epiphaneia*, of the sudden appearances of the gods. It is not enough that the divine should exist, it must be seen to exist, in the occasional flash of clear vision.[52] Such moments of *epiphaneia* were significantly widely-distributed throughout the whole range of east Roman religious experience. They could suddenly highlight any moment of east Roman religious life

---

[49] Brown, 'The Holy Man' pp 91–2.
[50] John of Ephesus, *PO* 17 p 9.
[51] L. Dumont, 'World Renunciation in Indian Religions' *Religion, Politics and History in India* (Paris and the Hague 1970) pp 33–60, *ASR* 7 (1959) pp 45–69.
[52] A. J. Festugière, *La révélation d'Hermès Trismégiste* (Paris 1950) pp 33–7 and 44–66, A. D. Nock, 'A Vision of Mandulis Aion,' *HTR* 27 (1934) pp 68–74 in *Essays* I, pp 368–74. See J. Kirchmeyr, under 'Grecque ('Eglise)', *Dictionnaire de la spiritualité* 6 (Paris 1965) col 848. In the sixth century a pagan at the shrine of saints Cosmas and Damian in Constantinople knew exactly what he wanted: ἀξιῶσαι αὐτὸν ὀπτασίας τινὸς καὶ θείας ἐκλάμψεως. A. Deubner, *Kosmas and Damian* (Leipzig 1907) 10, 22–23, p 118.

A parting of the ways

and can penetrate into any corner of east Roman Christian society. *Epiphaneia* might occur in the waking dream;[53] liturgical expectations were articulated in terms of potential *epiphaneia*—trembling, in many sources, on the edge of breaking forth[54]—with the presence of the angel at the altar[55] and the *epidemia*, the *adventus*, of the divine in the eucharist.[56] Hagiography was read as so many unpredictable manifestations in diverse times and places of men of every possible social status. At a slightly later time, icons rose to prominence as so many visions frozen in encaustic and mosaic.[57]

Such an idea of the holy, so strictly defined as all that was non-human in any situation and all that could be suddenly 'manifested' from beyond human consciousness, tended to erode rather than to reinforce those institutional structures in which it might have found a nesting place. Sanctity, for east Romans, always bordered on the paradoxical. For what we have are men with 'reputation of power'; yet this power was thought of to have been drawn from outside any apparent niche in the power-structure of society. It was gained in the desert, beyond human sight, and depended upon a freedom to speak to God, the exact extent of which lay beyond human power to gauge. A woman dreamed that her daughter would be cured at a certain monastery. The monks brought her the abbot. No, said she, this is not the man I dreamed of. Bring me the red-faced one, with warts on his knees. Byzantine monastic folk-lore toyed lovingly with the possibilities of this situation. For at any one time, the man who enjoyed most favour with God in Heaven might be, not saint Antony, but a doctor in Alexandria, not saint Macarius, but a farmer in an Egyptian village, and even, who knows, an imperial inspector of brothels in Monemvasia.[58] There is nothing in the sixth and seventh century west to equal the *Life* of saint Symeon the Holy Fool.[59] In this

[53] E. R. Dodds, *Pagan and Christian in an Age of Anxiety* (Cambridge 1965) pp 38–9. For a later period, the patriarch Germanus confesses his debt to icons for αἱ καθ᾽ ὕπνους πολλάκις τῶν γεγραμμένων ἐπιφάνειαι Mansi, 13, col 125A.

[54] John Moschus, *Pratum Spirituale*, 25, PG 87, cols 3, 2872.

[55] Well expressed by A. Veilleux, *La liturgie dans le cénobitisme pachômien au ivème siècle* (Rome 1968) pp 203–4 and esp p 363: 'Dans la pensée orientale, il s'agit plutôt d'une descente, d'une manifestation et d'une présence de choses célestes à travers les sacrements'.

[56] Dix pp 163, 168: for the same ideas surrounding the arrival of the emperor, see MacCormack, 'the Ceremony of Adventus', pp 727–8.

[57] Peter Brown and Sabine MacCormack, 'Artifices of Eternity', *New York Review of Books*, 22 (2 February 1975) pp 19–32.

[58] Brown, 'The Holy Man' p 95 for this and further evidence.

[59] *Vita Symeonis ASB* July I (Paris/Rome 1865) cols 121–51.

seventh-century masterpiece, the paradoxes of sanctity are explored with exemplary thoroughness. Here the dogged role-inversion of those hardworked Syrian cursers has spilled over into a delightful study of a man who, because he fulfils no overt social function, can enjoy to the full the position of the 'outsider' allotted to the bearer of the holy—*ut novellus pazzus*. In Emesa you could go to the tavern of the mad monk and watch Symeon dancing the jig with the people of the town.[60]

Paradox, after all, is a device of inclusion. The paradox of sanctity enabled the holy to scatter itself widely throughout Byzantine society. At the top, the touch of the hand of God gave an inexhaustible reservoir of initiative to the Byzantine emperors.[61] At the bottom, it fell heavily on prostitutes as it never fell on the equally whore-laden towns of Italy.[62] In between, it ratified the anomalous position of the soldier, and did so to such an extent that, when, in the eleventh century, the chaplain Hugh of Avranches attempted to reassure the Norman knights with examples of warriors pleasing to God, he could only find a catalogue dominated by *Byzantine* saints.[63]

Let us now see what Gregory of Tours does *not* share with this world. I have been struck by the following features:

First: there is the obvious feature of a marked shortage of living holy men. A society which knew all about Symeon Stylites[64] somehow did not want one of its own: our Wulfilach was told in no uncertain terms to get down off his column.[65] The appearance of itinerant holy men in Tours are recounted by Gregory in tones of 'While the cat's away, the mice do play.'[66] Now this is easier said than understood. I would like to posit a climate of opinion that actively withheld enthusiasm from all but the most well-tried bearers of the holy. 'Call no man holy until he be dead' is the motto of Gregory's writings. While in Syria the hillsides on which the stylites perched their columns would be ominously ringed by brand new, empty

---

[60] *Vita Symeonis* 33, col 136E.

[61] John of Nikiu, *Chronicle,* transl R. H. Charles (London 1916) p 89 and the commentary of S. MacCormack, 'Roma, Constantinopolis' p 146.

[62] F. Graus, *Volk, Herrscher and Heiliger im Reich der Merowinger* (Prague 1965) pp 103–4.

[63] Ordericus Vitalis, *HE* 6, 2, ed and transl M. Chibnall, *The Ecclesiastical History of Ordericus Vitalis* 3 (Oxford 1972) p 217.

[64] V. H. Albern, 'HIC SCS SYMION. Eine vorkarolingische Kultstatue des Symeons Stylites in Poitiers,' *CA* 16 (1966) pp 23–38.

[65] Gregory of Tours, *Lib Hist* VIII, 15, p 381.

[66] *Ibid* IX, 6, p 417.

martyria, waiting to receive their guaranteed holy occupants,[67] with the world of Gregory even death marks only the beginning of long and acrimonious hagiographical manoeuvres. Was Nicetius of Lyon, who died in 573, and whose tomb lay in the basilica of the apostle at Lyon, a saint? This was decidedly not the opinion of his successor, Priscus, nor of Priscus' wife, Susanna, nor of any of their friends and dependents. One of Priscus' deacons used the late bishop's chasuble, among other things, as a dressing-gown—'A robe from whose very hems, if one was to believe aright, healing would have come to the sick—and, when challenged, threatened to make a pair of bedroom slippers out of it.[68] Priscus and Nicetius rest together in the same church. Maybe the inscription of Priscus contains a tacit dig at his hated neighbour.[69] But time heals even sixth-century feuds. In 1308 both tombs were examined and both occupants declared saints. Only readers of Gregory can guess from this one clear example the febrile and insecure accumulation and dispersal of reputation that went to make up what too often strikes the unwary as the marmoreal facade of western episcopal sanctity.

A governing class carried the tensions of a governing class as well as exercising its power.[70] Here we are dealing with oligarchies of bishops powerful enough to overshadow any other bearers of the holy, but who were themselves locked in such bitter competition to remain equal as to deny holiness to any but the most well-tried, that is, the most safely-dead figure. The patriarchate of Constantinople in the late sixth century is the only milieu that can offer an analogy to Gregory. Here we have the remarkable *Life* of saint Eutychius,[71] a 'saint' on whom John of Ephesus had his own opinions.[72] But this is nothing compared with the convergence of hagiography and

---

[67] See the evidence in H. Delehaye, *Sanctus* (Brussels 1927) p 114.

[68] Gregory of Tours, *Vitae Patrum* 8, 5, p 246; compare *Lib Hist* IV, 36, p 169.

[69] In the epitaph of Priscus, *iurgia conponens more serenifero* (*Corpus 1, Scriptionum Latinarum* 13, 2399, 8) may echo the *iurgia despiciens suscipiensque Deum* of Nicetius (ibid 2400, 20).

[70] There is room for a reconsideration of the structure of the sixth century aristocracy of Gaul. Its tensions and areas of fragility have received less attention than its supposed homogeneity and continuity with the Roman past. Peter Brown, 'Sorcery, Demons and the Rise of Christianity,' *Witchcraft Confessions and Accusations, Association of Social Anthropologists Monographs,* 9 (London 1970) p 27, in *Religion and Society* p 131 certainly exaggerates: 'In the West, the triumph of the great landowners ensured that senatorial blood, episcopal office and sanctity presented a formidable united front.' Such exaggeration is widespread.

[71] Eustathius, *Vita Eutychii, PG* 86, 2, cols 2273–402.

[72] John of Ephesus, *HE* II, 31–7 pp 71–4 and III, 18, p 107.

propaganda that marked the *Adelsheilige* of the sub-Roman west.[73]

Second: the contact with the holy itself, in the form of the relic, is fraught with an open ended quality lacking in the piety of the eastern empire. The *locus* of the holy might be ambiguous in the east; but its *epiphaneia* was an unambivalently good event. In the work of Gregory, by contrast, we come across an element which strikes me as quite remarkable. Contact with the supernatural is fraught with all the open ended quality of an ordeal. It is a searing light, that can throw the *merita* of the recipient into high relief.[74] The theme runs through Gregory's works. At Bazas, the relic in a cross—a crystallised drop of the divine mercy that had once fallen on the altar from the vault (where, as at Ravenna, the Lamb of God may have stood among the stars of heaven)—'when it is adored, will appear crystal clear to a man free of sin; but if, as often happens, some evil is attached to the frail human nature of the beholder, appears totally obscure.'[75]

Therefore, a holy relic does not only enhance the status of a church or a locality, giving its favours indiscriminately to all connected with the site. There is nothing in Gregory of the universal franchise on the favours granted by saint Thecla to all citizens of Seleucia,[76] nor to the open handed, consular *sparsio* of protection which the inhabitants of Thessalonica saw in their saint Demetrius.[77] Nor is there any of that informal access to the holy across the frontier that any man may pass when he goes to sleep. The right to dream in the presence of the holy is denied. There is no incubation in Gaul. Again when there is no incubation, the 'holy' is denied a chance to express itself at its most paradoxical. The shrine of saint Martin of Tours never witnessed the *psychodrames* that were played out regularly in the *iatriké skéné* of the great incubatory shrine of saints Cosmas and Damian in Constantinople. No paralytic was emboldened by the saint to make love to

[73] F. Prinz, *Frühes Mönchtum im Frankenreich* (Munich 1965) pp 489–502. The function of such hagiography is already clearly adumbrated in Gregory; there is therefore less discontinuity between the hagiography of the sixth and that of the seventh century than Prinz would allow.

[74] Gregory of Tours, *de gloria martyrum* 1, p 38; 5, p 4; 27, p 54; 31, p 56; 54, p 76; 85, pp 95–6.

[75] Gregory of Tours, *de gloria martyrum* 12, p 46.

[76] *Miracula Sanctae Theclae* 18 *PG* 85, cols 597AB: ἐφ' ὑψηλοῦ τινος καὶ χρυσηλάτου καὶ ἐπηρμένου θρόνου· διανέμειν δὲ ἑκάστῳ τῶν συνεληλυθότων κατὰ τὴν πανήγυριν τὰ ὑπὲρ αὐτῆς τῆς πανηγύρεως δῶρα λαμπρά τε κα πολλά, καὶ αὐτῆς τῆς παρεχούσης ἄξια. This power extends to 'the poor and artisans': cap 7, col 576B.

[77] *Miracula Sancti Demetrii*, *PG* 116, col 1232A: ὡς τινα ὕπατον παρὰ βασιλέως ἐξουσίαν λαβόντα, διανεῖμαι τῷ δήμῳ τὰς χάριτας ἐρχόμενον.

a dumb lady.[78] No hulking butcher was told to shave a touchy senator.[79]

Rather, the contact with the holy is used to mark out unambiguously those individual members of the community who enjoyed a permanent status different from the rest. We meet in Gregory's works a whole gallery of individuals clearly designated as those who enjoyed greater intimacy with the supernatural because their *merita* were declared acceptable by the 'ordeal of the holy'.[80] From a Christian *koiné* that linked sin and miracle, Gregory has drawn sharper conclusions. The blessing of the relic falls most heavily on those vested protectors and agents of the relic, and that, in Gregory's case is almost invariably the bishop. The cult of the relic reaches its annual climax in a ceremony modelled on the old fashioned imperial *adventus* ceremony of the western provinces;[81] but it is a ceremony where the elements of heady enthusiasm and ideal concord are acted out in such a way as to re-create and so re-embellish the precarious concord of the Christian community around its bishop. Idealised *consensus* around Martin re-lives the far from ideal *consensus* on which every Gallic bishop depended for his own position.[82] In that way the ceremonial of the martyrs differs *toto caelo* from the *panygyreis* of east Rome. It is a ceremony of the bishop and his shrine; it is not the ceremony of a town. At a time when the Byzantine town had sucked the churches on its periphery into its traditional urban centre,[83] and the mosaics of the church at Qasr el-Lebya contain reference to the *Tyche* of the city,[84] the western towns were already being pulled out of shape around their peripheral shrines.[85] Somehow, as in the case of Nicetius

[78] Deubner, *Kosmas und Damian*, 24, pp 162–4.   [79] *Ibid* 34, pp 184–7.

[80] *de gloria martyrum* 41, p 66—on Aredius of Limoges. For the reverse, see *Lib Hist* VII, 31, p 351: 'and Mummolus taking one of them [a fragment of the relic of saint Sergius], departed, though not with the favour of the martyr, as the sequel shall declare.'

[81] MacCormack, 'the Ceremony of Aventus' pp 721–39, 'Latin Prose Panegyric' pp 154 seq, 178 seq and 184, and *'Adventus and Consecratio*: Roman Imperial Art and Panegyric from the Late Third to the Sixth Century', unpublished Oxford D Phil thesis 1974. The *adventus* of relics is shown for Vienne: *Bulletin de la Société des amis de Vienne* 67 (1971) pl 2 on p 31. See Gregory of Tours, *de virt Mart* II, 25, p 167, II, 28, p 169, and *de gloria martyrum* 89, pp 97–8.

[82] D. Claude, 'Die Bestellung der Bischöfe im merowingischen Reiche', *ZRG* 80, KA 49 (1963) pp 1–75, esp p 23.

[83] D. Claude, *Die byzantinische Stadt im 6 Jahrhundert*, *Byzantinisches Archiv* 13 (Munich 1969) p 95.

[84] A. Grabar, 'La mosaïque de pavement de Qasr el-Lebya,' *Comptes rendus de l'Académie d'Inscriptions et de Belles Lettres* (June 1969) pp 264–82.

[85] J. Hubert. 'Evolution de la topographie et de l'aspect des villes de Gaule de vème aux xème siècle, *Settimane di Studio sull'Alto Medio Evo* 6 (Spoleto 1959) pp 529–58.

of Lyon, the holy shrine carried with it the associations of the aristocratic family grave: it was a 'fine and private place'.[86]

Third: Much of this is intelligible in terms of a streak in Gregory
which defines the holy very strictly in terms of individual salvation.
The Christian *koiné* by which the miracle is meaningful as a
deliverance from sin bears a very heavy weight in Gregory: 'O if
only the blessed confessor [Martin] would have deigned to make himself known in such an act of power to me, in loosing the fetters of my
sins in the same way as he smashed the vast weight of the chains that
held that man.'[87]

Holiness is possible only after death, because only after death can
salvation be secure. Gregory's hagiography is an illustration of the
deep roots of an Augustinian doctrine of predestination. A chill
breath blows through Gregory's works when he contemplates the
vast anonymity of cemeteries. The silence of the Polyandrion—the
place of the great majority—at Autun is broken only by a few
mysterious echoes of chanted psalms, betraying the presence, among
so many thousands, 'of a few tombs of faithful souls worthy of God.'[88]
Gregory was oppressed by how infinitesimally small the number of
such tombs must be. For these were the tombs of the predestinate;
they belonged to the 'snow white number of the elect.'[89]

I must repeat that all this is easier said than explained. It would be
facile to reduce it to a contrast between the exuberant and basically
optimistic world of east Rome and the grim and depleted Gaul of
Gregory. To do this would be to ignore the *koiné* of basic attitudes
which ran from one end of the mediterranean to the other: John and
Gregory, for instance, both write history under the shadow of the
approaching end of the world.[90] In some respects, admittedly, the
parting of the ways is a parting in two styles of urban life. The holy
tended, in the west, to be increasingly confined to the rhythms of the
great basilica-shrine and the monastery, while in the Byzantine empire
it could spill out unself-consciously to join the vast ceremoniousness
of Byzantine urban life. Styles of liturgy and preaching show how

[86] Gregory of Tours, *Vitae Patrum* 8, 5, p 245—Nicetius had been expected to leave a
legacy to the basilica in which his tomb lay. See also *Lib Hist* X, 12, p 495 on Ingytrudis:
'Haec vero cum filia discordiam tenens, pro eo quod res suas ei abstulerit,
obtestaretque, ut neque in monasterio, quod instituit, neque super sepulchrum eius
permitteretur orare.'
[87] Gregory of Tours, *de virt Mart* I, 23, p 150.
[88] Gregory of Tours, *de gloria confessorum* 72, p 341.
[89] Gregory of Tours, *Vitae Patrum* I, praef p 213.
[90] John of Ephesus, *HE* I, 3, p 1; Gregory of Tours, *Lib Hist* I, praef p 2.

easily the street flowed into the basilica; and the receding tide brought out much of the holy into the street.[91] When the straitlaced carolingian divines attacked the Byzantine cult of icons, they thought they saw in it a disastrous 'over-production' of the holy, strictly connected with a blurring of the boundaries between basilica and street:

> Si ergo vulgus partim laetitiae bachatu effrenis, partim saecularis pompae novitate arcessitus, partim ventosi honoris inflatione cupidus, partim adolationis vitio stimulatus, partim publicae securis metu perterritus imperatorum imagines vanis et perniciosis laudibus honorat, quid ad nos . . .?[92]

Yet much more needs to be said, especially by an ecclesiastical historian. I would like to return to the definition of the holy in east Rome as what is *outside* human society. This is not a definition which Gregory accepts in the way in which it was meant by a Byzantine. The holy, in the west, could be defined as it was in the east, in terms of a stark discontinuity between the human and the non-human: the drop of divine mercy at Bazas caused the jewels to fall out of the frame into which it was first inserted—there was no *consortium caelestibus cum terrenis*.[93] And yet this discontinuous holy is deeply inserted into human society. In the most poker-faced and unparadoxical manner it makes clear who has received grace in its sight and who has not. This declaration is held to have immediate social consequences: slaves healed by saint Martin are automatically emancipated.[94] Its blessing is clear and covers a narrower range: it rests heavily on bishops of predictable *merita*. And this blessing is thought of as the intrusion into human life of those dead men and women who had persevered in clear roles within the human community rather than in the desert.

I would risk the suggestion that these phenomena reveal a mentality where the holy plays a more permanent role in law and in politics than it would ever play in east Rome. Gregory's world is one in which men worry much about perjury: Claudius, riding to Tours to bring Eberulf, dead or live, from the sanctuary of saint Martin, is one

[91] G. La Piana, *Le rappresentazioni sacre nella letteratura bizantina* (Grottaferrata 1912, Variorum Reprints 1971); T. F. Mathews, *The Early Churches of Constantinople: Architecture and Liturgy* (Pennsylvania 1971); and Sabine MacCormack, *EHR* 88 (1973) pp 366–8.

[92] *Libri Carolini*, I, 19 ed H. Bastgen, *MGH Leg* sectio III, concilia ii (Berlin 1924) p 79.

[93] Gregory of Tours, *de gloria martyrum* 12, p 46. See [Peter] Brown, 'Society and the Supernatural[: a Medieval Change]', *Daedalus* 104 (1975) pp 133–51 at p 141.

[94] For example Gregory of Tours, *de virt Mart* II, 4, p 161; II, 58, p 178; II, 59, p 179; III, 46, p 193; IV, 46, p 211; *de gloria confessorum* 67, p 338.

example among many in the pages of Gregory—'Upon his way, after the custom of the barbarians, he began to take notice of omens, and to find them unfavourable. At the same time he enquired of many whether the power of the holy martyr had of late been made manifest against breakers of oaths . . .'[95] We are touching on a world where many of the human relations basic to the working of society are made subject to sacred law.[96] The use of the holy in day to day affairs in this manner is parallelled, in east Rome, only in villages in the forbidding hinterland of Asia Minor.[97]

In Gregory's works, the mediterranean *koiné*—which had always linked oaths with the holy and treated the drama of exorcism as an informal law-court, in which public judgement was passed on those sins that plainly disrupted society[98]—is hardened to take the strain of permanent government. In the mediterranean world of late antiquity this coalescence had never quite happened. A glance at the *Dialogues* of Gregory's namesake, Gregory the Great, shows this. We are still in the world of *le monachisme méditerrenéen* which is a world of mild paradoxes. There are tame bears and salad-gardens—warm memories of a mediterranean-wide monastic anecdotage. Nor do we have the same phenomenon even among the stern heroes of John of Ephesus. These knew how to exercise the 'power of the saints' in society. Occasionally, among the loose-knit inhabitants of the mountains, the mirage of a theocracy founded around a holy man, where excommunication from the company of the believers replaced the blood feud, flickers a good century before Islam:[99] but the Djebel Izala was no Mecca, and Simon the Mountaindweller left no *Koran*. For the 'power of the saints' in Syria was based upon a dizzy ritual of social inversion; it existed for occasional, dramatic application to a society that was normally accustomed to looking after itself. The social use of the holy was delimited to those moments when a normative legal and social structure had broken down. With Gregory, the holy is losing its function as an emergency surrogate for justice. It is securely vested in men who knew what it was to rule, and who lived in a society where few men were prepared to rule as they were. The path towards the position of the early medieval bishop, whose social and

---

[95] Gregory of Tours, *Lib Hist* VII, 29, p 347.

[96] For example Gregory of Tours, *Lib Hist* VII, 6, p 329 and VII, 14, p 336.

[97] F. Steinleitner, *Die Beicht im Zusammenhang mit der sakralen Rechtsgang in der Antike* (Leipzig 1913), p 99 and L. Robert, *Nouvelles Inscriptions des Sardes* (Paris 1964) p 26.

[98] Brown, 'The Holy Man' p 89.

[99] John of Ephesus, *PO* 17, pp 229–47.

sacred functions interlocked around an invincible sense of *das Tremendum*, may be slower than some exegetes of Gregory would have us believe:[100] the relation of the bishop to his town, for instance, still has an untidiness that belongs to late antique *Romania*—even in Tours, acclamation by the people can be as deadly a political weapon as it was in Edessa or Constantinople; and Gregory could be threatened by it.[101] Nevertheless, Gregory's works take us to the crest of a watershed: the manner in which he assumes a linking of law and the holy makes him look north rather than south, to the middle ages rather than to late antiquity, and therefore, away from the east. He is the first Auvergnat as Michelet described them: 'on dirait une race méridionale grelottante au vent du nord, et comme reserrée, durcie sous ce ciel étranger.'[102]

A perceptive if unsympathetic western thinker put his finger on this contrast: in his *Philosophy of History* Hegel wrote—'The history of the highly civilised Eastern Empire—where as we might suppose, the Spirit of Christianity could be taken up in its truth and purity—exhibits to us a millennial series of uninterrupted crimes, weaknesses, basenesses and want of principle . . . It is evident here how Christianity may be abstract, and how as such it is powerless, on account of its very purity and intrinsic spirituality . . . Light shining in darkness may perhaps give colour, but not a picture animated by Spirit. The Byzantine Empire is a grand example of how the Christian religion may maintain an abstract character among a cultivated people, if the whole organisation of the State and of the Laws is not reconstructed in harmony with its principle'.[103]

This contrast of east and west does exist. But it need not be interpreted in so harsh a manner. I hope that a historical examination of the late antique phase of the parting of the ways of east and west may make plain part of the Byzantine answer. Byzantine society could take the strain of life on its own, frankly secular, terms.[104] Ringed, in the

[100] H. Prinz, 'Die bischöfliche Stadtherrshaft im Frankenreich', *HZ* 217 (1973) pp 1–35 exaggerates for the sixth century.

[101] Gregory of Tours, *Lib Hist* V, 18, p 219. On the use of acclamations, see W. Liebeschütz, *Antioch* (Oxford 1972) pp 209–13.

[102] J. Michelet, *Tableau de la France* (Paris 1949) p 29.

[103] G. W. F. Hegel, *Philosophy of History*, transl J. Sibree, (New York 1944) p 338.

[104] N. H. Baynes, 'Some Aspects of Byzantine Civilisation', *Byzantine Studies* (London 1960) p 75 'The law of Islam was fashioned by the religious consciousness of Islam: religion and law were inextricably intertwined . . . But the Christian Church, professing a creed of altruism, accepted a code of law which, as Mitteis has shown, is logically so completely satisfying because consistently based on the pre-

early middle ages, on one side by Islam, where religion and law fused, and on the other by a western Europe where religion blew through gaping cracks in the structure of society, Byzantines could keep the holy where they needed it—and in so doing, they preserved a vital part of its meaning—it was an unexpected wellspring of delight in the scorching summer of mediterranean life.

University of London
Royal Holloway College

suppositions of an egoism untroubled by humanitarian scruples'. For the ordeal in western Europe and the conditions under which sacred and profane were mingled and later disentangled, see Brown, 'Society and the Supernatural' pp 135–43 and Rebecca V. Colman, 'Reason and Unreason in Early Medieval Law', *JIntH* 4 (1974) pp 571–91.

THE OFFICIAL ATTITUDE OF BASIL OF CAESAREA AS A CHRISTIAN BISHOP TOWARDS GREEK PHILOSOPHY AND SCIENCE

by EMMANUEL AMAND DE MENDIETA

IN this paper[1] I wish to deal with a rather specialised topic. But this specialised topic may partly explain what was in fact the official attitude of the Byzantine Church, of its patriarchs, bishops and monks, over the centuries, towards Greek philosophy and science. May I suggest that Greek philosophy and science were, and still are indeed, one of the component factors and inspirations of our renaissance and post-renaissance western civilisation?

In order to avoid misunderstanding, I must explain the title of this paper, so that the limitations or strict boundaries of this paper, and also its precise contents, its scope or design may be fully realised.

I intend to give some factual information about the official attitude of Basil of Caesarea as a bishop towards Greek philosophy and science. Basil expressed his official attitude neither in his private or personal letters, nor in his theological treatises *Against Eunomius* and *On the Holy Spirit*, which are mainly addressed to bishops, theologians and cultivated Christian laymen, nor in his genuine ascetic and monastic writings, because 'perfect Christians' were not supposed to be very interested in the profane wisdom of the Greek philosophers. On the other hand, we may find the expression of the official attitude of Basil, as a priest or as bishop preaching to a Christian congregation, towards Greek philosophy and science, in his official and public homilies or sermons. In these homilies he speaks, as an official representative of the orthodox and catholic church, explaining and defending the faith proclaimed by the fathers at Nicaea, in the first ecumenical council (AD 325).

Among his homilies, there is a short work, which is really not a homily or sermon, but a finely polished essay, the so-called *Address* or

---

[1] I wish to express my deep and friendly gratitude to Miss J. E. Bickersteth, MA, DPhil, university lecturer at the university of Hull, who carefully read this paper, kindly corrected my ungrammatical English prose, and suggested many useful and constructive criticisms. To her, my colleague in patristic studies, I am especially grateful.

Warning to Young Men, on how they might derive benefit from Greek Literature.[1a] But we cannot find in this charming but short and superficial treatise, addressed by the bishop of Caesarea to his nephews or first cousins, an expression of his official attitude towards Greek philosophy and science. This essay is too short and too element-ary to allow us to assert that it sums up all Basil's ideas, towards the end of a life of wide experience, on a question much-mooted in this period in Christian circles. This question was: should the study of the so-called pagan classics of Greek literature form an important part of a system of Christian education? In the *Address*, Basil's main point was that the reading and the study of Greek literature (including of course the philosophers) involved a *grave moral danger*. When the Greek writers teach vice and immorality, they must be avoided and condemned; but, when they teach what is morally good, noble and true, they should be read and studied, because in this case young Christians may reap moral advantage from their writings. But Basil always made it a strict condition that Christian teachers of young Christian pupils must make a choice and selection for them from works of Greek literature, and must omit and condemn everything which might poison their souls. After a careful expurgation and a removal of many immoral books or passages, Greek classical literature remained useful, even necessary, for a full and liberal education or παιδεία, but it was merely a preparation and an introduction to the study of divinely inspired scriptures, the only fount of full truth. We must therefore not exaggerate the so-called liberalism and Erasmian humanism of this gentle *causerie*. In this warning written in attic style, the severe and very biblical bishop tried to adapt himself to the minds of his nephews, and to put them on their guard against the moral dangers which they would find in classical Greek writers, even in the works of Plato.[2]

In this homely address, which is not a homily or sermon, Basil

[1a] *PG* 31, cols 563C–90A, the Greek printed text is the text of the edition of C. A. F. Fremion (Paris 1819), published, with notes and a French translation. There is a good edition by Fernand Boulenger, *Saint Basile. Aux jeunes gens sur la manière de tirer profit des lettres helléniques*, Texte établi et traduit (Paris 1935) 75 pages. Photographic repro-duction in 1952 (*Collection des Universités de France* publiée sous le patronage de l'Association Guillaume Budé).

[2] A fair appreciation of this familiar address in: Aimé Puech, *Histoire de la littérature grecque chrétienne*, 3 (Paris 1930) pp 276–8.

On the many allusions to the *Dialogues* of Plato, especially to the *Republic*, see the *Introduction* of F. Boulenger to his edition of this essay (Paris 1935) p 31, and also the footnotes and the *notes complémentaires*, pp 63–71.

mentioned many Greek poets, orators, historians and philosophers, but he never stated his own formal and official attitude, as a Christian bishop, towards Greek philosophy and science. He confined himself to describing, in a true platonic phraseology, what kind of moral life all Christians, and in particular young men, must lead: to take care of their immortal soul and to have only contempt for the body, freeing it from all bodily passions, and giving to it only what is strictly necessary for the maintenance of physical life.[3]

I have made a check on Basil's *homilies on the Psalms* and on his so-called *moral* or *diverse homilies*. Nowhere have I found a passage in which Basil, as a priest or as a bishop, explains at any length his official attitude towards Greek philosophy and science. Of course, sometimes, he repeated Paul's condemnation of the profane and foolish wisdom of Greek philosophers and scientists, in the first chapter of his letter to the Romans: *So they are without excuse; for, although they knew God, they did not honour him as God or give thanks to him, but they became futile in their thinking, and their senseless minds were darkened. Claiming to be wise, they became fools* (Rom., 1: 20–2). There are some partial quotations of this text (or allusions to it), but they are not very frequent and are never developed into an articulate statement.

But there are, happily, other homilies or sermons preached by the bishop of Caesarea, in which he stated, plainly and systematically, his official attitude, as a Christian bishop, towards Greek philosophy and science. We shall find these statements in the *corpus* of his nine genuine or authentic *homilies on the Hexaemeron* (namely the creation of the universe in six days).

In the second and longer part of this paper, I shall study some of the important passages or texts in these *homilies on the Hexaemeron*, where Basil expressed his official attitude, as a Christian bishop, towards Greek philosophy and science. But before I attempt to show, from these texts or passages in the *homilies on the Hexaemeron*, what was the official and public attitude of Basil towards Greek philosophy and science, I should like to make it crystal clear that I do not intend to deal at all with the problem of the personal, real and practical attitude of Basil towards Greek philosophy and science, which is a quite different question. I shall confine myself to the plain affirmation that the personal, real and practical attitude of Basil towards Greek philosophy

---

[3] A characteristic quotation from this address (in French translation) is to be found in my book: David Amand, *L'ascèse monastique de saint Basile. Essai historique* (Maredsous 1949) pp 194–8 (the contempt for the body).

and science, is clearly evident on almost every page of his theological and homiletic writings, and in his genuine letters, but not formally in his ascetic rules and treatises. Every reader of the genuine works of Basil will realise how greatly indebted he really was to Greek culture, especially to philosophy, eloquence and science. He became hellenised *ad unguem*, and he gladly and abundantly used the Greek philosophers and even scientists, in spite of what he said officially, and in spite of his public and perhaps conventional attitude of contempt.[4]

II

In this second and more developed part of my paper, I intend to keep to the following procedure in the presentation of the passages or texts, all taken, as I have explained, from the nine *homilies on the Hexaemeron*.[5] I shall, of course, only select the passages in which the Cappadocian bishop deals with Greek philosophy and science, expressing publicly his official viewpoint. Therefore I shall not quote the numerous passages or texts in which the Christian bishop attacks Christian heretics, such as the Christian gnostics and the anomeans. I shall also omit the passages in which he disputes with the Jews and in particular with Philo, and the passages in which he rejects the allegorical exegesis of his master Origen, and tries to reply to the objections raised by some critical intellectuals among the hearers of his homilies.

In order to make a fair and factual presentation of the main passages or texts in which Basil criticises Greek philosophy and science, my procedure will be as follows. Each passage will be quoted in translation, and followed by a short commentary. To avoid wearying the reader, the texts or passages themselves will be placed in some kind of logical order, under headings, with references to Migne's *Patrologia Graeca*, volume twenty-nine,[6] and to the good, but not critical, edition of Stanislas Giet.[7] A critical edition of these homilies, which Stig Y.

---

[4] For a first orientation in this difficult and subtle matter, I may refer the reader to pages 384-9 of my book *Fatalisme et liberté dans l'antiquité grecque*, David Amand (Louvain 1945).

[5] I have good reasons to believe that Basil delivered these homilies during Lent 378, namely the last year of his life. He died on 1 January 379.

[6] *PG* 29 (1857) cols 3A-208C; accurate reproduction of the in-folio edition of Julien Garnier, 1 (Paris 1721) pp 1-88.

[7] [Stanislas] Giet, [Basile de Césarée, *Homélies sur l'Hexaéméron*], texte grec, introduction et traduction (Paris 1950) = *SCR* 26. A second revised edition (with complementary notes) was published in 1968, *SCR* 26b; in both volumes, the pagination is the same for text and translation.

Rudberg and I have prepared, is virtually achieved, and will be eventually published in the *Berlin Corpus (GCS)*.

One word may summarise the official attitude of Basil of Caesarea towards Greek philosophy and science as it is revealed in these homilies. It is an attitude of contempt, a very severe and exaggerated judgement of complete condemnation of a philosophy and science, which are held up to ridicule, because they are useless, foolish, insane, and full of vain curiosity. Against this frivolous and insane curiosity, Basil emphasised the solidity and infallibility of the Christian faith, based on holy scripture. This simple Christian faith must be preferred to the arrogant demonstrations of human reason. This was the official attitude of Basil in his *homilies on the Hexaemeron*. On the other hand, I do not suggest at all that this official scornful attitude towards Greek philosophy and science was the real, personal and practical attitude of Basil in this matter. There was a very strange dichotomy between his official and his personal and practical attitude.

I. THE TRADITIONAL ARGUMENT OF THE EARLY CHRISTIAN THEOLOGIANS AGAINST GREEK PHILOSOPHY: THE MUTUAL CONTRADICTIONS BETWEEN PHILOSO-PHERS AND THEIR SYSTEMS.

(1) *The first text: Homily 1, chapter 2.*[8]

What shall I say first? Where shall I begin my explanation of the creation of the universe? Shall I show forth the vanity of the pagan philosophers? Shall I exalt the truth of our Christian faith?

The philosophers of Greece have written many treatises about the nature of things, but not one of their systems has remained firm and unshaken: always each of them is overturned by the opinions of his successor. There is no need to refute them by our reasonings; they are sufficient in themselves to destroy one another.

Here we have the first text in which the bishop expressed, officially and explicitly, his contempt for the vanity of the authors who are strangers to us, that is of the Greek philosophers and scientists. Not one of their δόξαι or systems has remained firm and unshaken. We do not need to refute their contradictory opinions, which destroy one another.

[8] *PG* 29, cols 5C–8A; Giet p 92, translation. I refer only to the Greek text in Giet's edition, not to the French translation which is printed on the opposite page.

I shall not discuss the question whether Basil expressed here a personal contempt for the Greek philosophy and science, or whether he was only repeating, almost mechanically, a kind of traditional argument among Christians, an argument of a very dubious efficacy and of sceptic origin. I am inclined to adopt the second hypothesis.

From the apologists onwards, most Christian theologians used this argument, either with personal conviction, or simply because they took the customary stance in this matter. Even the theologians, who seem to us to be rather 'humanist' and broad-minded, such as Clement of Alexandria, Origen and Gregory of Nyssa, did not escape from the tyranny of this Christian custom and convention.

(2) *The second text: homily 1, chapter 11.*[9]

Owing to these so-called logical necessities, these philosophers [namely Aristotle and his disciples][9a] reject the arguments of their predecessors about the four elements, and have recourse to their own hypothesis. They suppose that the existence of a fifth kind of bodily substance or element, is necessary to the genesis of the heaven and of the stars therein.

But another fine speaker, skilful in the arts of persuasion [namely Zeno or Chrysippus], arises, and disperses and destroys this peripatetic theory, to give predominance to an opinion of his own invention.

Do not let us undertake to discuss these matters and to follow them, for fear of falling into like frivolities; let them refute each other, and, without disquieting ourselves about the essence of things, let us rather say with Moses: *God created the Heaven and the Earth* (Gen., 1:1).

In chapters ten and eleven of this homily, Basil discussed at length Aristotle's theory about the immobility and the centrality of the earth in the very midst of the universe, and also the theory of Aristotle, or Theophrastus and other peripatetics, about the aether (αἰθήρ) which was called after Aristotle's time 'the fifth body' or 'the fifth essence or οὐσία'.

Owing to so-called logical necessities, Aristotle and his disciples rejected the arguments of their presocratic and platonic predecessors

[9] PG 29, cols 25D–8A; Giet pp 132, 134.

[9a] The names in parentheses (Aristotle and his disciples, and further: Zenon or Chrysippus) are not in the Greek. I have added them for the sake of clarity.

about the four classic elements, and had recourse to their own hypothesis. They suppose the existence of an additional fifth kind of bodily
substance or element: the fifth element, or the fifth οὐσία.

But Basil was happy to stress again the mutual contradictions of
the Greek philosophers: Aristotle and his disciples against Plato and
his disciples, the stoic philosophers against the peripatetics' notion of
the 'fifth body' or *ousia*.

Of these stoic philosophers, he gave to his hearers a very vague and
wholly negative idea. He said only that another fine speaker, skilful in
the art of persuasion, arose (he means the founder of the Stoa, Zeno of
Citium, or rather the second founder of the Stoa, the very prolific
Chrysippus) who dispersed and destroyed the peripatetic theory on
the fifth body or substance, and propounded a new theory of his own
invention.

Basil advised his hearers not to follow the reasonings of these stoic
philosophers, for fear of falling into like frivolities, and he asked them
to see the Greek philosophers contradicting and refuting each other.
This is a wretched commonplace which Christian theologians of the
first centuries abused too much. By means of this traditional and not
very honest mockery, they tried to disparage the Greek philosophers,
and to inspire in their fellow Christians a sense of greater security in the
profession of their faith.

(3) *The third text: homily 3, chapter 8.*[10]

> But why should we torment ourselves by refuting the errors
> or rather the lies of the Greek philosophers, when it is sufficient to
> produce and compare their mutually contradictory books, and,
> as quiet spectators, to watch their internecine war?
>
> For those thinkers [Basil means the stoics] are no less numerous,
> nor less celebrated, nor more sober in speech in fighting their
> adversaries than the other [he means the peripatetics]. These
> [stoic] philosophers say that the universe will be consumed by
> fire, and that, from the seeds which remain in the ashes of the
> burnt world, the universe will be brought to life again. Hence in
> the world, there will be destruction and palingenesis or rebirth
> without end.

[10] *PG* 29, cols 73BC; Giet p 234. Compare also another text on the same subject: homily
III, cap 3. *PG* 29, cols 57AB; Giet p 198 (the Greek philosophers who assert that it is
only one heaven and no other; and other philosophers who assert that there are many or
innumerable heavens).

All these philosophers are equally far from the truth, and on either side they find paths and by-ways which lead them to error.

In this passage, Basil renewed for his hearers, in a childish and even insulting manner, the traditional Christian attack against the errors or the lies of the philosophers who contradict each other. This time, he raised the most serious and unjust charge: these Greek philosophers, who do not recognise the true God, are only liars. It must be said that sometimes the Cappadocian bishop did not shrink from intolerable rhetorical exaggeration. Why torment ourselves by refuting the lies of these Greek philosophers? It is better for us to enjoy their mutual contradictions, and to watch quietly their internecine war.

We may regret that Basil, who was not, in any case, a Christian humanist, publicly pronounced such unjust and offensive words against the Greek philosophers. In this passage, his irony is very heavy and unpleasant.

At the end of this text, he stated that peripatetics and stoics were equally far from the truth, and that, in their contradictory opinions, only ways which led to error were to be found.

II. THE FOLLY OF THE GREEK PHILOSOPHERS CONCERNING THE COSMOS, THE HEAVEN AND METEMPSYCHOSIS.

(1) *The first text: homily 1, chapter 3.*[11]
The folly and insanity of the Greek philosophers concerning the eternity and the divinity of the κόσμος.

That which was begun in time is condemned to come to an end in time. If there has been a beginning of the universe, do not doubt of its end. Of what use then are geometry, the calculations of arithmetic, the study of solids and the much renowned astronomy, all this laborious vanity? Of what use are these sciences, if those who pursue them imagine that this visible world is co-eternal with the Creator of all things, with God himself; if they attribute to this limited world, which has a material body, the same glory as to the incomprehensible and invisible divine nature; if they cannot conceive that a whole, of which the parts

[11] *PG* 29, cols 9C–12A; Giet pp 98, 100. Compare also another text or passage on the same subject: homily I, cap 7. *PG* 29, col 17BC; Giet pp 114, 116. Among those who have imagined that the world co-exists with God from all eternity, many have denied that it was created by God, but have said that God is only the involuntary cause of it, as the body is the cause of its own shadow.

are subject to corruption and change, must of necessity end by itself, submitting to the fate of its parts? *But they became futile in their thinking, and their senseless minds were darkened. Claiming to be wise, they became fools* (Rom., 1: 22). Some have affirmed that heaven (τὸν οὐρανόν) co-exists with God from all eternity; others that heaven is God himself without beginning or end, and the cause of the particular arrangement of all things.

In commenting briefly on this passage, in which Basil held up to ridicule the folly and insanity of the Greek philosophers and scientists who professed the eternity and the divinity of the cosmos, I shall, first of all, stress the fact that he did not hesitate to consider the Greek sciences of geometry, mathematics and astronomy, these positive sciences in which Greek scientists attained such an excellency, as laborious vanities. He heaped up scornful expressions, and spoke with the heaviest irony of the men of genius who, in ancient Greece, laid the firm foundations of geometry, mathematics and astronomy as exact and positive sciences. According to Basil, their research revealed these miserable scientists as foolish, insane and deprived of all understanding. This is polemical language indeed.

The real reason for the foolishness of the Greek scientists was that they imagined that the visible world was co-eternal with the Creator of all things, with God himself, and that they attributed to this limited and material world or cosmos the same glory as to the invisible and divine nature.

Imbued with a strictly monotheistic and biblical faith, Basil was merely following a deeply rooted tradition in patristic literature: he upbraided Greek philosophers and scientists for what he judged to be a form of practical atheism. They hold the view of the eternity of the cosmos, and also of its divinity; they think that the cosmos should receive the honour which must be exclusively reserved to the invisible and transcendent or supreme Creator. Basil castigated them severely, applying to them the scornful and condemnatory words of Paul: claiming to be wise, Greek philosophers and scientists became fools (Rom., 1: 22).

In order to understand this insistence of Basil in calling the Greek philosophers and scientists fools and insane, it must be realised that these insulting words were not written as part of a theological treatise, but pronounced in the course of homilies or sermons. This particular *genre littéraire* seemed to demand that the Christian orator should display both his own orthodoxy, and his passionate fondness for the litteralist interpretation of the bible, especially for the most severe Pauline condemnation of pagan intellectuals.

(2) *The second text: homily 3, chapter 3.*[12]
The folly and insanity of the Greek philosophers concerning the uniqueness of the Heaven: most of them are bitterly opposed to the plurality of heavens.

In the second place, does the firmament (τὸ στερέωμα) that is called heaven, differ from the heaven (ὁ οὐρανός) that God created in the beginning? Are these two heavens?

The philosophers, who have dealt with the problem of heaven, would rather lose their tongues than grant this. There is only one heaven, they claim; and it is of the nature of heaven neither to admit of a second, nor of a third, nor of several others. They say that all the essence or substance of the celestial body was used to produce this vast unity of the unique heaven. Because, they say, every body which has a circular motion is one and is finite. And if this body is used in the construction of the first heaven, there will be nothing left for the formation of a second or a third heaven.

Here we see that those who imagine these reasons are precisely those philosophers who bring in uncreated matter for the *demiourgos* to use, a lie that follows from the first fable. But we ask the Greek sages not to mock us, before they are agreed among themselves, because there are among them some philosophers who say that there are innumerable and infinite heavens and worlds.

When those who use more decisive demonstrations will have upset the foolish system of the upholders of the innumerable heavens and worlds, when they will establish by laws of geometry that, according to the nature of heaven, it is impossible that there should be two heavens, we, Christians, shall only laugh the more at this vanity of their linear and artificial imaginations. These learned men see not merely one bubble but several bubbles formed by the same cause, and they doubt the power of creative wisdom to bring several heavens into being! We, Christians, find, however, if we raise our eyes towards the omnipotence of God, that the strength and immensity of the heavens do not differ at all from the drops of water bubbling on the surface of a fountain. How ridiculous, then, is the argument of impossibility raised by the Greek philosophers!

[12] PG 29, cols 56C–7B; Giet pp 196, 198.

Basil of Caesarea and Greek philosophy and science

I shall not comment, line by line, on this long passage, in which Basil emphasised the folly and insanity of the Greek philosophers who held the 'dogma' of the uniqueness of heaven. I shall restrict myself to stating three facts which may explain the preceding passage.

First, according to his litteralist (if I may say: fundamentalist) exegesis of the bible, Basil believed that there were at least three heavens: the heaven that God made in the beginning, the firmament which the scriptures also call 'heaven', and a third heaven, the heaven whereon Paul the apostle was found worthy to gaze. For Basil, the plurality of heavens was clearly taught by the infallible bible, and this plurality was absolutely true. Plato and Aristotle were wrong when they said that there was only one heaven.

Secondly, Basil summarised the arguments which Aristotle used in his *De caelo* to prove this uniqueness of the heaven, but, immediately afterwards, said that these arguments were silly because they presupposed the existence of uncreated matter. He added that this foolish system of Plato and Aristotle was in blatant contradiction to the affirmations of many other philosophers who professed the multiplicity, or rather the infinity, of heavens and worlds. We, Christians, we shall only laugh the more at this elaborate scientific trifling of Plato and Aristotle.

Thirdly, there was Basil's recourse to the facile argument of the omnipotence of the divine Creator. For Almighty God, there was no difference at all between producing drops of water bubbling on a surface of a fountain, and creating three or more heavens. How ridiculous then was the philosophical argument of the impossibility of more than one heaven!

(3) *The third text: homily 3, chapter 3.*[13]
The folly and insanity of the Greek philosophers who profess the harmonious music of the seven planetary spheres.

> Is the plurality of heavens stranger than the seven circles through which nearly all the philosophers agree that the seven planets are passing? These philosophers represent to us these spheres as placed each within another, like casks fitting the one into the other.
>
> These spheres, they say, are carried away in a direction contrary to that of the universe, and, striking the aether, they make

[13] PG 29, cols 57BD; Giet pp 200, 202.

sweet and harmonious sounds, unequalled by our sweetest melodies.

But, if we ask these philosophers for the witness of the senses to this sidereal music, what do they say? That we are accustomed to this noise from our birth, and, on account of hearing it always, we have lost the sense of it, like men in smithies with their ears incessantly dinned.

But, if I were to refute this ingenious and sophistical frivolity, the untruth of which is evident from the first word, it would seem as though I did not know the value of time, and as though I mistrusted the intelligence of such an audience. But we are now leaving the vanity of outsiders to those who are without, and we return to the doctrine of the church.

There are many factual errors in this passage. It was not true that almost all Greek philosophers and astronomers accepted the existence of the seven astral homocentrical spheres of Plato's system. Besides, Plato's description of the seven homocentrical planetary spheres and orbits is included in a very mythological account in book ten, chapter three of the *Republic*.[14]

Also it was not true that all the Greek philosophers and astronomers who accepted the hypothesis of the planetary spheres and orbits, also accepted the Pythagorean idea of the harmonious music of the planets. Plato speaks of it, but only in a very mythical and poetical context. Aristotle expressly rejects this childish theory.

The so-called explanation of this sidereal music and symphony, which Basil wrongly attributed to nearly all the Greek philosophers (our ears are accustomed to this music from our birth), was held only by Pythagoreans and, some centuries after, by neo-Pythagoreans. In *De Caelo* (II, 9), Aristotle expounded this Pythagorean invention and rejected it very strongly.[15] This 'explanation' of the planetary symphony was not held at all by other Greek philosophers. Admittedly Aristotle did report this Pythagorean explanation of the lack of audibility of this music, but only to refute the theory and its childish justification.

Basil's errors may be explained by his probable use of a philosophical manual or doxographical collection, but, even though we may perhaps concede that he was misled by a not very reliable handbook, there was no reason for him to pour such contempt on almost all the

[14] Plato, *Republic*, X, 3, 616C–17D.   [15] Aristotle, *De Caelo*, bk II, cap 3, 290 b 12–29.

Greek philosophers and astronomers, who were, in his opinion, the upholders of 'this ingenious and sophistical frivolity, the untruth of which is evident from the first word'.

(4) *The fourth text: homily 8, chapter 2.*[16]
The folly and insanity of the Greek philosophers who believed in metempsychosis.

> Do not suppose that the soul of beasts is older than the substance of their body, nor that their soul survives the dissolution of the flesh. Let us avoid the nonsense of those arrogant philosophers who do not blush to liken their own soul to the soul of a dog; who say that they have been formerly themselves women, shrubs, fishes.
>
> Have they ever been fishes? I do not know; but I do not fear to affirm very strongly that in their writings they show themselves more irrational and more nonsensical than fishes.

This attack against the doctrine of the metempsychosis which was upheld by Pythagoras, Empedocles and especially by Plato (*Timaeus*, 91 D, 92 AC) and the later Platonists, was of course a much used piece of Christian apologetics against the pagan Greeks, and mainly against Greek philosophers. Basil of Caesarea, Gregory of Nyssa, Augustine of Hippo, for instance, were fiery adversaries of a doctrine which was fundamentally at variance with the Christian doctrine of the resurrection of the body.

What is notable in this passage is the bitterness of Basil's attack against the nonsense of those arrogant philosophers. Plato, in fact, said in the *Timaeus* that it was probable that men who were dastardly and unjust might be changed into women, that light, naive and frivolous men might be changed into birds, that un-philosophical and passionate men might be changed into four-footed animals, and that very stupid and ignorant men might be changed into fishes.

III. THE VANITY, THE USELESSNESS AND THE SIN OF THE GREEK PHILOSOPHERS AND ASTRONOMERS: THEY ARE CLEVER BUT IMPIOUS.

(1) *The first text: homily 1, chapter 4.*[17]
The sinful vanity of profane wisdom is clearly showed in the voluntary blindness of Greek philosophers and astronomers: they refuse to recognise God as creator and supreme judge.

[16] PG 29, cols 168AB; Giet p 436.   [17] PG 29, cols 12AC; Giet p 102.

EMMANUEL AMAND DE MENDIETA

One day, surely, on account of the richness and super-abundance of their wordly wisdom, the terrible condemnation that God will pronounce against the philosophers and astronomers will be very heavy. The reason is that, seeing so clearly into the vain objects of their investigations, they have wilfully and voluntarily blinded themselves to the knowledge of the truth.

These men have measured the distances between the stars, and they have described the constellations, both those of the north, which always shine brilliantly in our view, and those of the southern pole which are only visible to the inhabitants of the south, but unknown to us. These men have divided the northern zone and the circle of the zodiac into an infinity of parts. They have observed with great accuracy the course of the planets, their risings, their standings and fixed positions, their declensions or their passings away from the normal course, the movement which pushes all of them onwards, and the time which is necessary for each planet to make its revolution.

These men, I say, have, in their cleverness, discovered everything, except one thing: they have not discovered the fact that God is the Creator of the universe, and the just Judge who will reward all the actions of our life according to their merit. They have not known how to raise themselves to the idea of the consummation of all things, which is the consequence of the doctrine of judgement, and they were unable to see that the world must change, if our souls pass from this life to a new life.

In this passage, Basil, the Christian bishop, cast against Eudoxus, Hipparchus, Eratosthenes, Ptolemy, and their competitors and disciples, an unfounded and atrocious accusation. They have blinded themselves wilfully and voluntarily to the knowledge of the truth. The Cappadocian bishop was not tender-hearted towards people who did not profess his Christian faith. His unjust and fanatical condemnation of Greek astronomy, and his ostentatious contempt for the futile studies of the astronomers, put in a clear light the fact that Basil did not possess what we would call the scientific mind at all, and that he was not really interested in scientific research, and in particular in the progress of the positive sciences. He was a Christian theologian who seems to have been interested only in theological matters, such as God, Christ, the Spirit, man, and specifically the man who is a member of the church.

38

Basil of Caesarea and Greek philosophy and science

Just after his severe verdict on the superfluity and uselessness of Greek astronomy, he gave his hearers a striking specimen of his knowledge, certainly of very recent date, of astronomical terminology. The good people in the cathedral were probably very much impressed by the enormous display that their bishop was making of his astronomical learning. But Basil was quite certain that, at the day of the great and universal judgement, God would send all those astronomers to the eternal punishment of hell.

(2) *The second text: homily 9, chapter 1.*[18]
The vanity, uselessness and mutual contradictions of the opinions of Greek philosophers and astronomers compared with the real utility and perfect truth of the holy scripture.

The philosophers who have written treatises about the nature of the universe, have propounded at length many opinions about the shape of the earth. They have said that it is a sphere or a cylinder, that it resembles a disc and is equally rounded in all parts, or that it has the form of a winnowing basket and is hollow in the middle. All these conjectures have been suggested by the philosophers who have written about the cosmos; each of them has upset the system of his predecessor.

But all these philosophical opinions will not lead me to speak with contempt about our biblical account of the creation, on the pretext that Moses, the servant of God, is silent as to the shapes of the earth.

He has not said, as the Greek astronomers did, that the earth is a hundred and eighty thousand stades (στάδια) in perimeter or circumference. Moses has not measured how far into the air the shadow of the earth is projected, while the sun revolves underneath it, nor stated how this shadow, when cast upon the moon, produces eclipses. He has passed over in silence, as useless, all the facts which are unimportant for us, Christians.

Shall I then prefer the foolish wisdom of this world to the oracles of the Holy Spirit? Shall I not rather exalt our God who, not wishing to divert our minds with these vanities, has regulated all the economy of Scripture in view of the edification, of the salvation and of the making perfect of our souls?

[18] PG 29, cols 188C–9A; Giet pp 480, 482.

Basil emphasised, with ironical contempt, the vanity and uselessness of the conflicting opinions of Greek philosophers about the shape of the earth. Its spherical shape was upheld, among others by Plato and Aristotle. For Anaximander, its shape was that of a cylinder or column; for Leucippus, of a disc or a tambourine; for Democritus, of a flat winnowing-basket. All these opinions seem to have been taken by Basil from a doxographical collection of philosophical δόγματα. He showed very clearly his scorn for this kind of problem, and again he repeated his favourite tag of the mutual contradictions of the Greek philosophers, with the same lack of sympathy and understanding for what philosophy is.

Instead, he was full of praise for Moses and his account of the creation in six days. Moses did not waste his time by describing the shape of the earth, or, as the Greek astronomers did, its perimeter, its enormous shadow during the night and during eclipses of the moon. All these astronomical matters are foolish and frivolous. Of course, the Christian bishop preferred to the foolish wisdom of this world the infallible oracles (please note this word: τὰ λόγια) of the Holy Spirit.

Expressing his purely religious and pragmatic viewpoint, Basil repeated his firm belief that God had regulated all the economy of holy writ, with a view to the edification and salvation of our Christian souls.

IV. THE FRIVOLOUS AND USELESS CURIOSITY OF THE GREEK PHILOSOPHERS ABOUT THE ESSENCE OF HEAVEN AND EARTH.

(1) *The first text: homily 1, chapter 8.*[19]
The futile curiosity of Greek philosophers about the essence of Heaven.

If we Christians were to try to discover the essence or nature of everything in existence which is offered for our contemplation, or comes under our senses, we should be drawn away into long digressions, and the solution of these problems would require extensive arguments out of all proportion to the arguments which are necessary for the specific questions concerning our exegesis of the Mosaic account. Moreover to spend much time on such research about the essence of things, would not be useful to the edification of the church.

[19] PG 29, cols 20C–1A; Giet pp 118, 120.

About the essence or nature of the heaven, it is enough for us to be content with what Isaiah says. In simple and plain language, he gives us a sufficient idea of the nature of the heaven when he writes: *He established the heaven like smoke* (Isa., 51:6, LXX), that is to say: he created a subtle substance, without solidity and density, from which to form the heaven.

As to the form or the shape of the heaven, we should again content ourselves with the words of the same prophet when he praised God saying: *He stretched the heaven as a vault* (Isa., 40:22, LXX).

To the philosophical problem: What is the essence or the nature or the substance (ἡ οὐσία) of the heaven, Basil refused to propound any scientific solution, partly on account of the sociological composition of his audience, in which craftsmen, workers and their wives made up the majority. Also, he said, to try to reply to a such philosophical question would mean that he would be drawn away into disproportionately long digressions.

But the main reason for Basil's refusal was a pastoral one: it is quite useless to trouble and torment ourselves about this philosophical question, because the answer would be quite irrelevant to the edification of the church. For Basil acting and speaking as a bishop, the main concern was always to consolidate the orthodox faith of his people, and to nourish their Christian piety and devotion. In this passage, he implicitly warned his hearers that, for the faithful members of the Christian church, it was quite useless to make inquisitive investigations beyond what was clearly revealed in holy scripture. The infallible oracles of the Holy Spirit, which were written down in the books of holy writ, must be sufficient for them. This is a declaration and an exhortation which was frequently repeated in the *homilies on the Hexaemeron*, and in the other homilies. Sometimes Basil seems to be very near to the fideist position.

For instance, he said that we, Christians, must be satisfied by the very plain and ordinary descriptions which the prophet Isaiah gave of the essence or substance of the heaven, and of the shape of heaven. They are indeed very simple and indeed poetic, but they are quite insufficient at the intellectual level.

Moreover Basil here again confused the heaven in the philosophical sense, and the heaven as synonymous with the biblical firmament (τὸ στερέωμα).

(2) *The second text: homily 1, chapter 8.*[20]
The futile curiosity of the Greek philosophers about the essence or substance of the earth, and its foundations.

> In the same way, as concerns the earth, let us persuade ourselves not to torment ourselves by trying to discover, as the philosophers do, its essence or substance, devoting ourselves to indiscreet and inquisitive researches. Let us not wear ourselves out by seeking by our reasonings what is the essence or the substance of the earth, which is hidden behind the appearances. Do not let us seek for any nature or substance devoid of qualities by the conditions of its existence. . . .
> If I ask you to leave these vain questions, I do not advise you to try to find out what is the support or the foundations of the earth. Your mind would reel on beholding your reasonings, which lose themselves without end and lead to no secure conclusion.

The commentary which I have just given of the first text of this fourth section, will dispense me from a long explanation: here Basil advised his hearers not to worry about the essence or substance of the earth, and about its foundations. He again upbraided the Greek philosophers for their futile curiosity about these purely speculative matters. Towards these two problems, he took the same agnostic and deeply sceptical attitude, which seems to be almost a fideist one. *Vana curiositas. Et quid ad aeternitatem?*

Concerning the οὐσία of the earth, let us resolve, he said, not to weary ourselves by indiscreet and useless researches (πολυπραγμονεῖν).

But, after a rather short discussion about the philosophical problem of the non-existence of the *materia prima*, Basil went on to discuss at length, probably with the help of a philosophical manual, the problem (or rather the false problem) of the foundations of the immobile earth. Before embarking on this extensive and complex debate, he repeated his advice to his hearers to leave such vain questions, and in particular the question about the support or the foundations of the earth.

The bishop, who had just warned his hearers against this vain problem, then expatiated at length upon the doubtful and contradictory theories which Greek philosophers had propounded to explain, if possible, what was the fulcrum or the foundation upon which the earth rested. Was it a bed of air on which the earth reposed? Or, alternatively, was it water which was its foundation? Or was it a

[20] *PG* 29, cols 21AB; Giet pp 120, 122.

heavier body which prevented the earth from falling into the abyss?

(3) The third text: homily 1, chapter 9.[21]
Christians must put a limit to their curiosity in exploring the incomprehensible. They must not imitate the frivolous philosophers, and they must be satisfied with the plain, secure and profitable doctrine of holy scripture.

And the further we advance on this reasoning about a heavier body supporting the earth, the greater the power we are obliged to give to this basis, so that it may be able to support all the mass weighing upon it.

Put a limit to your thought then, so that your inordinate curiosity in investigating the incomprehensible may not incur the reproaches which God addressed to Job, and you may be not asked by the Lord: *Whereupon are fastened the foundations of the earth?* (Job, 38:6, **LXX**). If ever you hear in the Psalms: *I bear up the pillars of it* (Ps., 74:4, LXX), see in these pillars the power which sustains it. Because what does the other passage mean: *He has founded it upon the seas* (Ps., 23:2, LXX), if not that the water is spread all around the earth? . . .

But let us admit that the earth rests upon itself, or let us say that it rides on the waters. We must still remain absolutely faithful to the beliefs of true religion, and we must recognise that all the universe is sustained by the Creator's power. Let us then reply to ourselves, and let us reply to those who ask us upon what support this enormous mass of the earth is resting: *In his hands are the ends of the earth* (Ps., 94:4, LXX). This scriptural doctrine is more trustworthy for our mind, and more profitable for our hearers.

When Basil said: 'Put a limit to your thought . . .', I think that he was addressing himself rhetorically to a member of this small minority of scientifically minded intellectuals, who were surely Christians. He asked him and any other members of this small minority to put a limit to their too inquisitive thought, and not to carry on their curious and useless research (ἡ πολυπραγμοσύνη), as they were to investigate depths which were incomprehensible.

In his homilies, Basil kept repeating over and over again that Christians, all Christians, must, of necessity, renounce all such

[21] *PG* 29, cols 21D, 24AB; Giet pp 124, 126.

speculative, curious and vain studies, because they will find everything which they really need by reading and meditating on the divinely inspired scriptures. This was an Origenist theme, to which Basil frequently had recourse in his treatises and mainly in his homilies.

As a conclusion to his long philosophical discussion about the diverse hypotheses concerning the foundations of the earth, the bishop of Caesarea declared that while we may accept one of these hypotheses, all of us must still remain absolutely faithful to the beliefs of true religion. We must recognise that all the universe is sustained by the Creator's power. The spiritual doctrine that in God's hands are the ends of the earth, is more profitable for the hearers. This was a specifically religious answer to philosophical difficulties.

V. THE SIMPLICITY AND CERTAINTY OF HOLY SCRIPTURE AND OF THE CHRISTIAN FAITH ARE TO BE PREFERRED TO THE DEMONSTRATIONS OF REASON AND TO THE POLISHED PERIODS OF THE PHILOSOPHERS AND SOPHISTS.

(1) *The first text: homily 1, chapter 10.*[22]
The theories which attempt to explain the immobility and the centrality of the earth may seem probable or improbable. In any case, the simplicity of our faith is to be preferred to the demonstrations of reason.

> Do not then be surprised that the earth never falls on one side or on the other side, because it occupies the very centre of the universe, its natural place. By all necessity, the earth is obliged to remain in its place, unless a movement contrary to its nature should displace it.
>
> If there is anything in these systems or theories which might appear probable to you, transfer your admiration to the source of such perfect order, to the wisdom of God himself. The greatest phenomena do not strike us the less, when we have discovered something of their wonderful mechanism. Is it otherwise here? At all events, let us Christians prefer the simplicity of our faith, which is stronger, to the demonstrations of human reason.

Without naming Anaximander, Plato and Aristotle, Basil expounded at length their systems to explain the immobility and the centrality of

[22] *PG* 29, cols 24D–5A; Giet pp 128, 130.

the earth in the very centre of the universe. In particular, probably following very closely the account of his literary source (probably a philosophical manual), he has well summarised chapters thirteen and fourteen of book II of Aristotle's *De caelo*.

Addressing himself again to the minority of philosophically minded intellectuals in his audience, the Cappadocian bishop gave them fatherly advice. If one of these philosophical hypotheses should appear probable to you, transfer your admiration to the personal source of such perfect order, to the wisdom of God himself.

Finally he turned to the people who made up the majority of his hearers: craftsmen, workers, shopkeepers, their wives and children. He tried to obtain from them forgiveness for the boredom which he has inflicted on them, during his extensive philosophical expositions, which they could not have understood at all. If you cannot, he said, make a selection among these hypotheses concerning the immobility of the earth, do not be dismayed. At all events, let us, Christians, prefer the simplicity of our faith, which is stronger, to the demonstrations of human reason.

This firm affirmation of the superiority of Christian faith to the vain curiosity of philosophers, is one of the main themes which recurs very often in the *homilies on the Hexaemeron*.

(2) *The second text: homily 3, chapter 8.*[23]
The simplicity and certainty of scripture and of our Christian faith are highly superior to the indiscreet curiosity of the Greek philosophers.

And do not let any one compare with the indiscreet curiosity of the philosophers discussing the unique heaven, the simplicity and the unartificial character of the utterances of the Spirit in holy scripture. As the beauty of chaste women surpasses that of harlots, so our teachings borrowed from scripture are different from the arguments of our adversaries outside the church. These philosophers only seek to persuade by forced reasonings. But with us, Christians, truth, that is to say biblical truth, presents itself naked and without any artifice.

But why torment ourselves to refute the errors, or rather the lies, of the Greek philosophers, when it is sufficient to produce and compare their mutually contradictory books, and, as quiet spectators, to watch their internecine war.

[23] PG 29, col 73B; Giet pp 232, 234.

The audience of Basil's nine *homilies on the Hexaemeron* was mainly composed of workers, craftsmen and their wives. One of the main concerns of the bishop was to put them on their guard against the vain and indiscreet curiosity (ἡ περιεργία) of the Greek philosophers who drew up treatises on the heaven. On the other hand, he extolled the simplicity and the unartificial character of the utterances of the Holy Spirit in divinely inspired scripture. He applied to Greek philosophy and to inerrant scripture a comparison frequently found in ancient literature between the dignified and natural beauty of chaste women and mothers, and the artificial and painted beauty of prostitutes. This was, in the mouth of a monk and bishop, a comparison which was not very courteous, and it smacks too much of sophistic exaggeration.

Basil made his unfavourable appreciation even more explicit, when he said that Greek philosophers and scientists did violence to the probabilities, in order to introduce dubious and unsound reasonings. This was a very summary condemnation of the most eminent of philosophers, such as Plato and Aristotle, and of scientists, such as Aristarchus of Samos and Posidonius.

On the other hand, Basil, who was a prudent disciple of Origen, did not cease to proclaim, in all his genuine works, that holy scripture (and for him the holy scripture of the old testament was, in fact, the Greek translation of the septuagint) was divinely inspired in all its parts, inerrant and infallible. Only in holy writ, did the truth which was really useful to men present itself to us, Christians, naked and without any artifice. This proclamation of the perfect and inerrant truth of holy scripture, which was really useful to our souls, was one of the most crucial doctrines which Basil taught in all his writings, and that with full conviction.

After this enthusiastic praise of the pure, clear, useful and infallible truth of divinely inspired scripture, the Christian bishop repeated again the old and rather childish Christian argument about the mutual contradictions of the Greek philosophers.

(3) *The third text: homily IV, chapter 2.*[24]
We, Christians, are not interested in polished periods and in sophistic and sonorous expressions. To rhetorical sentences, we prefer clear sentences and clear words.

    Light was already created before the sun; so why does scripture say that the sun was created to give light or to illuminate (εἰς φαῦσιν)?

[24] *PG* 29, cols 120D–1A; Giet pp 332, 334.

Basil of Caesarea and Greek philosophy and science

And, first do not laugh at the strangeness of this expression (εἰς φαῦσιν). We, Christians, we do not follow your subtlety about the artistic selection of words, and we trouble ourselves but little to give them a harmonious disposition. Our writers do not amuse themselves by polishing their periods and chiselling their words. Everywhere, we prefer clear meaning in the words to sonorous and musical expressions.

See then, if, by this expression (εἰς φαῦσιν), the sacred writer made his thought sufficiently understood.

I do not think that this short but violent attack of Basil against the oratorical subtleties of contemporary rhetors (and by implication against the too rhetorical presentation of some philosophical treatises) should be understood as a kind of solemn literary manifesto, as a peremptory and one-sided condemnation which Basil would have pronounced against every concern for a literary and eloquent presentation of ideas. Doubtless he reproached the Greek rhetors and philosophers of his time who were at great pains to give rhythmical and harmonious expression to ideas, at the expense of seriousness of thought.

Basil repeated here a traditional protest among the Christians against τὸ εὔηχον τῶν φωνῶν, this vain and ridiculous purpose of the pagan rhetors and philosophers. On the other hand, he affirmed that Christian writers, theologians and preachers were not polishers of words and periods, but asserted that they always preferred words with a clear and plain meaning. They were not sophists at all.

It is quite possible to imagine that this traditional attack by Basil against the superficiality and artificiality of the Second Sophistic, was a kind of literary precaution which he and many other Greek and Latin patristic preachers used, in order to protect themselves against the complaints and accusations of those who had a very simple faith, or a not well enlightened one.

But the fact is that Basil, who was a sober disciple of the Second Sophistic, affected in his *homilies on the Hexaemeron*, to unite under the same condemnation, contempt for the rhetorical art of the Greeks and contempt for their philosophy and science. In these homilies, Basil frequently expressed his official attitude about the radical opposition which, in his opinion, existed between the wonderful simplicity of the Christian faith, based upon holy scripture, and the vanity, frivolity and mutual contradictions of the Greek philosophers and, by implication, of the sophists. Later, Ambrose of Milan would show

47

himself still more bitter than Basil, in his sermons and in his exegetical treatises based on his sermons.

III

In this last and shortest part of my paper, I shall draw general conclusions from the texts or passages which I have translated from Greek, and to which I have added some words of commentary, to put them in their historical and literary context.

First of all, I give a concise summary of the main ideas which, in different passages of the *homilies on the Hexaemeron*, Basil developed concerning his official and public attitude, as a Christian bishop, towards Greek philosophy and science. Not all the relevant passages have been quoted: merely a sufficiently large selection from them to elucidate his formal attitude.

Basil did not shrink from repeating, almost *ad nauseam*, the traditional but not very fair argument of the early Christian theologians against Greek philosophy, the argument of the mutual contradictions between philosophers and their systems or opinions.[25] This topic was extensively developed by Tertullian in his *Apologeticum*, chapter forty-seven,[26] and by Augustine in his *De civitate Dei*, book XVIII, chapter forty-one.[27]

But, more specifically, Basil delighted in condemning, sometimes with very heavy irony, the folly and insanity of the Greek philosophers concerning the eternity and the divinity of the cosmos, the uniqueness of the heaven, the so-called harmonious music of the seven planetary spheres, and the ridiculous belief in metempsychosis.

Another theme of Basil's bitter criticism was the vanity, the uselessness and the voluntary blindness of Greek philosophers and astronomers: they refused to recognise God as Creator and supreme Judge. They were certainly very clever, but they were impious. They ignored the real utility and perfect truth of holy scripture.

But the reproach that Basil levelled most often, and with polemical eagerness, at Greek philosophers and scientists, was surely their frivolous and useless curiosity (ἡ περιεργία). Their curiosity explored, without avail, difficult philosophical problems,[28] such as the essence or

[25] I have omitted many other passages and allusions.
[26] Tertullian, *Apologeticum*, ed crit H. Hoppe, *CSEL*, 69 (1939) pp 109–12.
[27] Augustine, *De civitate Dei*, ed crit E. Hoffmann, *CSEL*, 40 (1900) pp 331–5.
[28] This topic is extensively developed by Augustine, *De Genesi ad litteram liber secundus*, cap X: ed crit by I. Zycha, *CSEL*, 28 (1894) pp 47–8. *De caeli motu*, PL 34, cols 271–2.

substance of heaven and of the earth, and the real nature or substance of the foundations of the earth. Christians instead must put a limit to their own curiosity, and be satisfied with the plain, secure and profitable doctrine of holy scripture.

Here is another theme which was central in Basil's theological thought: that of the simplicity and the certainty of holy scripture and of the Christian faith. Both are to be preferred by Christians to the demonstrations of human reason, and to the polished periods of philosophers and sophists. Basil was never tired of extolling in his writings, and especially in his homilies, this simplicity and certainty of scripture and of the orthodox faith. We, Christians, are not interested in artistic periods and in sophistic expressions. In everything, we always prefer the truth and clear and plain sentences. We do not chisel our words and sentences; we seek only the truth.

Finally there remains a particular problem which cannot be solved here. This problem is to attempt to explain the appreciable difference which existed between the official and public attitude of Basil of Caesarea towards Greek philosophy and science, and his personal, practical and real attitude towards the same subjects, and discrimination between the two attitudes is made more difficult because Basil himself often inserted, among his immoderate and sometimes absurd declamations of contempt and scorn for Greek philosophy and science, ideas expressing his deepest convictions, concerning for instance divinely inspired scripture and the biblical and orthodox faith of Christians.

Very little has been said about the personal, practical and real attitude of Basil towards Greek philosophy. It appears, as I have said, on almost every page of his works, with the possible and partial exception of his ascetic rules and treatises. Though he might scold Plato, Aristotle, the stoics and Plotinus the natural milieu in which his mind easily operated was the climate of Greek and Roman civilisation, in particular the Attic atmosphere which he had breathed with rapture, when, for four or five years, he had been a student at the university at Athens. He always kept unaltered his mind, his sensibility, and his aesthetic sense, formed and refined when he was reading the works of Homer and Plato, and contemplating the masterpieces of Phidias and Praxiteles.

Winchester

THE EARLY RELIGIOUS POLICIES
OF JUSTIN II

by AVERIL CAMERON

ON 14 November AD 565, Justinian died and his nephew Justin was raised to the throne in a well managed senatorial coup.[1] He was already of middle age and had spent the latter part of his life building up useful connections at court which served him well when the critical moment came: his rival, cousin and homonym was far more glamorous, being a military man, but he was not on the spot and Justin was easily able to have him removed.[2] We are told that the murder was engineered by Justin's empress, Sophia, the niece of Theodora, a lady who emerges as a figure as powerful and in many ways more interesting than her aunt.[3] From the first the reign was a partnership; Sophia is shown in a novel way together with her husband on Justin's coins, and is named with him in the headings to decrees preserved on papyri.[4] So Justin at least acquiesced in her prominence, even if he did not like it, and it was natural for poets and historians to give as much attention to the empress as to the emperor. When the loss of the Mesopotamian border fortress of Dara to the Persians in 573 drove Justin out of his wits Sophia very naturally took control, even though nominally the government had to be put into the hands of a man (Tiberius, appointed caesar in AD 574 and augustus in 578); yet her influence had been strong from the beginning, and we shall see that if it is right to see her driving force behind the harsh persecutions of monophysites in the 570s, we must also seek her initiative in the religious policy of the late 560s.

Very little modern work has been done on this reign.[5] It is passed

---

[1] Evagrius, *HE* ed J. Bidez and L. Parmentier (London 1898) bk V cap 1; Victor of Tunnuna, *Chronicle*, ed Th. Mommsen, *Chronica Minora* II, *MGH AA* 11 (1894) a. 567 (sic); Corippus, *In laudem Iustini*, ed Partsch, *MGH AA*, 11 (1892), bk I line 1 seq.

[2] Joh[n of] Biclar[o], *Chronicle*, ed Th. Mommsen, *Chronica Minora* II, *MGH AA*, 11 (1894) a 568 (?); Evagrius, *HE* bk V caps 1-2; Agathias, *Hist[ory]*, *CSHByz* 1 (1828) IV. 22.

[3] Joh Biclar, a. 568 (?). See my article, 'The Empress Sophia', *B* 45 (1975) pp 5-21.

[4] See [Flavius Cresconius Corippus, *In laudem Iustini minoris*, ed with commentary and translation by Averil] Cameron (London 1976) note on *Pan Anast* 23.

[5] The only two detailed studies are [K.] Groh, [*Geschichte des oströmischen Kaisers Justin II nebst den Quellen*], Diss. Halle (Leipzig 1889) and [E.] Stein, [*Studien zur Geschichte des*

over briefly in the general histories, and Justin is usually portrayed unsparingly and unsympathetically as a fool who got his deserts by going mad; on this reading his two main initiatives were equally disastrous—the renewal of the war with Persia ('megalomaniac and irresponsible'[6]) led to long years of struggle and defeat, while the reopening of persecution against the monophysites contributed to the eventual development of monophysite separatism. I am not suggesting that there is very much that can be said in Justin's favour. But at least we might pay him the compliment of studying the sources for his reign fully and critically. They may not be good enough to allow a full 'internal history' of the period,[7] but there is very varied material available, from which a rather more subtle narrative can be reconstructed.

Justin's religious policy between 565 and 572 is a case in point. If we read Frend's account of these years[8] we view Justin as mainly concerned with the east. 'The empire was becoming "Greek" rather than "Roman", and the concentration of Monophysitism in Egypt and astride the vital frontier area with Persia urged, as always, the need for compromise.'[9] Further, 'the new emperor and his consort were well-disposed towards Monophysite theology';[10] accordingly Justin made immediate efforts towards conciliation, and when the first attempt ended in failure he returned to the task with a second *Henotikon*.[11] Only when this too failed did he become 'exasperated' and turn to persecution. I do not question the general outlines of this portrayal of Justin's relations with the monophysites in his early years. As we shall see, he does seem to have tried conciliation before force; but as an overall picture of Justin's religious policies this version has serious omissions, simply because it is based only on one section of the sources, the eastern rather than the western, and then mainly on the twelfth-century monophysite chronicle of Michael the Syrian. A statement affirming Sophia's monophysitism based solely on Michael's biased

---

byzantinischen Reiches, vornehmlich unter den Kaisern Justinus II und Tiberius Constantinus] (Stuttgart 1919).
[6] A. H. M. Jones, *The Later Roman Empire 284–602* (Oxford 1964) 1, p 306.
[7] Stein p 1.
[8] [W. H. C.] Frend [*The Rise of the Monophysite Movement*] (Cambridge 1972) pp 317 seq.
[9] *Ibid* p 320.
[10] *Ibid* p 319.
[11] *Ibid* pp 321–2. See Evagrius *HE* bk V cap 4; Nicephorus Callistus, *HE* bk XVII cap 35 (*PG* 146) col 308; John of Ephesus, *HE*, trans R. Payne Smith (Oxford 1860) bk I caps 19 seq; Michael the Syrian, [*Chronicle*], ed J-B. Chabot, I-III (Paris 1899–1905) bk X cap 4.

account must be regarded as dubious, when Michael's main source, the contemporary and equally monophysite John of Ephesus, explicitly says that she gave it up so as not to impede Justin's chances of getting the throne.[12] We cannot then say without qualification that Justin's attitude in 565 was wholly favourable to monophysitism, even if it is true (although again we owe the information to Michael alone) that one of his first actions was to receive the exiled monophysite patriarch of Alexandria, Theodosius, and, when he died in June 566, to allow a funeral oration which condemned Chalcedon.[13] When we turn back to the first edition of J. B. Bury's *History of the Later Roman Empire* (still a very useful account of this period), we find a very different emphasis.[14] Justin's accession is said to mark a reaction in the direction of orthodoxy; he issued an edict enforcing orthodoxy on all his subjects and expressly excluding monophysites from the designation 'orthodox'.[15] Now it is true that as it happens (if we believe Michael the Syrian, with Frend) Bury was wrong on both the interpretation and the dating of Justin's edict,[16] but his general impression of the opening of Justin's reign was not hopelessly out, as we shall see if we look at another group of sources altogether. I shall argue that (as one would expect) the western sources and the eastern sources for Justin emphasise quite opposite tendencies in his policies—policies which (again as one would expect) were themselves in any case ambiguous. Consequently any reconstruction of these policies based only on one sector of the sources must be at best misleading; the truth must be more complex than has hitherto been allowed.

There is then an apparent conflict in the sources, with attendant problems of dating. Even so, some sort of coherent narrative can be pieced together to show that Justin and Sophia by no means confined their religious activities to the east. In one quarter of the west at least they appeared in a totally orthodox guise.

Our first reference for Justin's religious activity comes from the Spanish chronicler John of Biclar, who, though then still a boy, had actually been living in Constantinople at the time of these events.[17] In the first year of Justin's reign, he says, *ea quae contra synodum*

---

[12] Michael the Syrian, bk X cap 7; John of Ephesus *HE* bk II cap 10.
[13] Michael the Syrian, bk X cap 1.
[14] [J. B.] Bury, [*History of the Later Roman Empire from Arcadius to Irene*] (London 1889) 2, p 72.
[15] *Ibid.* For the edict see n 11 above and pp 62-5 below.
[16] Below p 62.
[17] Joh Biclar a. 567 (?).

Chalcedonensem fuerant commentata destruxit ('he destroyed what had been written in opposition to the council of Chalcedon'). Whatever this means, it indicates a very early action against monophysites. John puts this notice before the murder of Justin and the conspiracy of Aetherius and Addaeus, both of which took place in 566.[18] Then he says that Justin ordered the creed of Constantinople to be recited in all catholic churches before the Lord's Prayer. This could only be taken, to use Bury's misapplied phrase, as an orthodox manifesto. If at the same time Justin was honouring the monophysite patriarch Theodosius and restoring monophysite bishops from exile,[19] he was walking a tightrope, trying to present himself simultaneously as fully Chalcedonian. He did not restore Eutychius, the exiled patriarch of Constantinople, at this time, but for reasons of prudence retained the violently anti-monophysite John Scholasticus who had crowned him; it is to John's influence that John of Ephesus attributes much of the later persecutions.[20] At the same time again his *quaestor* was already that Anastasius who was to be the other great persecutor, and was accused of being a Samaritan.[21] Justin's motive in ordering the inclusion of the creed was surely indeed what Bury suspected his aim must be—the desire to reestablish the concern of the imperial government for orthodoxy after Justinian's final lapse into heresy. The patriarch Eutychius had gone into exile rather than accept Justinian's heretical edict; John Scholasticus had been more accommodating on that point, but where monophysitism was concerned he was an unrelenting Chalcedonian.

The decree recorded by John of Biclar explains the point of allusions made by two contemporary Latin poets, both writing in the late 560s and both depicting Justin as completely orthodox. Only one was really a westerner—Venantius Fortunatus, writing on behalf of Radegund at Poitiers—and he will need fuller discussion, but the other must be dealt with first. This is Corippus, an African by birth who had achieved literary success with a Latin epic nearly twenty years before, had come to Constantinople and now wrote a panegyric on the accession of

---

[18] The execution of Aetherius and Addaeus was in October: Eustratius, *Vita Eutychii*, PG 86, col 2361; Evagrius *HE* bk V cap 3; Joh Biclar a. 568 (?); Theophanes, [*Chronographia*], ed de Boor (Leipzig 1883–5) 1 p 242. See Cameron, note on Corippus *In laudem Iustini* bk I lines 60–1.

[19] Michael the Syrian bk X cap 1; Joh Biclar a. 567 (?); Venantius Fortunatus, *Appendix Carminum* 2, lines 39–46, ed F. Leo, *MGH AA*, IV. 1 (1881).

[20] See Cameron, note on Corippus, *In laudem Iustini*, bk II line 160. John Scholasticus is John of Ephesus's chief villain: see especially *HE* bk II cap 17.

[21] John of Ephesus *HE* bk II cap 29; on Samaritans see Justin's *Novel* 144 (a. 572).

Justin which he dedicated to the *quaestor* Anastasius.[22] The poem was written before 568; books I–III perhaps belong to 566 and book IV to 567.[23] Into book IV Corippus inserts a very unwieldly digression in praise of the church of St Sophia,[24] of which part[25] is virtually a paraphrase of the creed, said to be symbolised by the physical appearance of the church.[26] The only point in interposing this quite untypical and 'unclassical' section in the middle of a description of Justin's consular inauguration on 1 January 566 is surely to compliment the emperor's recent decree ordering the inclusion of the creed in the liturgy. This is not a religious poem as such, except insofar as the imperial ideology had a religious content; but stress is laid throughout on Justin's position as God-given and his own role as the imitator of God, and in this work dedicated to the hyper-orthodox Anastasius there is nothing that is not itself completely orthodox. Book IV was added shortly after the first three books, and seems to have a defensive air about it—the speech attributed to the dying Justinian is an obvious defence of Justin's execution of Aetherius and Addaeus in 566[27]—so that it would be quite in keeping for Corippus to attempt to support Justin's religious policies by lending them the prestige of a link with St Sophia; in the same passage he drags in a reference to Justin's new palace called the Sophianae[28] and attempts a forced connection between the name of the church and the name of the new empress.[29] This creed passage is then no mere rhetorical flourish, but a tendentious allusion to a decree which had surely given rise to opposition in eastern quarters.

The same decree lies behind the allusions to Justin's restoration of orthodoxy in the poem which Venantius Fortunatus wrote to thank Justin and Sophia for their gift to the convent at Poitiers of a fragment

---

[22] *In laudem Iustini minoris.* See note 4 above.

[23] Cameron, intro, (i). See also [Averil] Cameron 'Notes [on the Sophiae, the Sophianae and the Harbour of Sophia'], *B* 37 (1967) pp 15 seq.

[24] Bk IV lines 264–325.

[25] Bk IV lines 290–311.

[26] Bk IV lines 292–4: 'internis oculis illic pia cernitur esse indivisa manens patris genitique potestas spiritus et sanctus . . .' *Internis oculis* (line 292) proves that lines 293–311 refer to the symbolism of the church and not to a real mosaic decoration—so A. Heisenberg, 'Die alten Mosaiken der Apostelkirche und der Hagia Sophia', Ξένια. *Hommage international à l'université nationale de Grèce* (Athens 1912) pp 121 seq, 143 seq.

[27] Bk IV lines 348 seq; see Cameron, notes *ad loc.*

[28] Bk IV lines 285–90, esp 287: *Sophianarum splendentia tecta novarum.* For the palace see Cameron, 'Notes'.

[29] Bk IV lines 264–73. The name of the church foretold the accession of Justin and Sophia —line 273, 'sceptri fuerant ea signa futuri'.

of the true cross.[30] The circumstances of Venantius's life are well known from his own poems and especially his metrical *Life* of Saint Martin;[31] born about 530, he came from Treviso, near Venice, studied in Ravenna, undertook a pilgrimage to the shrine of St Martin at Tours after a cure for an eye disease, reached the court of Sigibert of Austrasia in 565, where he wrote many poems including an epithalamium for Sigibert's marriage in 566, went on to Tours and thence reached Poitiers in 567, where he was so captivated by the romantic figures of Radegund, queen turned nun and ascetic, and Agnes, her young abbess, that he stayed there for the rest of his life, being ordained presbyter and indeed ending as bishop of Poitiers. During those years at Poitiers he had a considerable poetic output, largely occasional poetry, but including some more serious pieces, among them two of the great hymns of the catholic church, *Vexilla regis prodeunt* and *Pange lingua*, both written for the very occasion when Justin sent the relic of the holy cross. We are equally well informed about the life of Radegund herself, from the prose *Life* which Venantius wrote soon after her death in 587, from Gregory of Tours, a close friend of both, and from the secondary *Life* written by a nun of the convent in 609.[32] Through the foundation of her convent at Poitiers, when she had eventually prevailed upon her husband Lothar I to allow it, and her subsequent life there in a nominally subservient position (but drawing attention to herself by frequent ascetic seclusions) she became an important figure in the development of western monasticism, while the poems of Venantius to herself and Agnes set an early pattern for courtly literature.[33] She never forgot that she was a queen, and it was this that enabled her to exploit the accession of a new emperor in Byzantium in 565 by sending a messenger to ask for relics. Her first step was to turn to Sigibert for aid; he sent

---

[30] *Appendix carminum.* 2 *Ad Iustinum et Sophiam Augustos.*

[31] Compare also Paulus Diaconus, *H[istoria] L[angobardorum]*, ed Bethmann and Waitz, *MGH SRL* (1878) bk II cap 13. See in particular [W.] Meyer, ['Der Gelegenheitsdichter Venantius Fortunatus'], *AAWG* PhK, NF, band IV. 5 (1901); [R.] Koebner, [*Venantius Fortunatus. Seine Persönlichkeit und seine Stellung in der geistigen Kultur des Merowinger-Reiches*] (Leipzig/Berlin 1915).

[32] The *Lives* by Fortunatus and Baudonivia are edited by B. Krusch, *MGH, SRM*, 2 (1888). For Radegund's life see [R.] Aigran, [*Sainte Radegonde*] (Paris 1918, 2 ed Poitiers 1952). F. Graus, *Volk, Herrsche und Heiliger im Reich der Merowinger* (Prague 1965) pp 407 seq and [F.] Prinz, [*Frühes Mönchtum in Frankenreich*] (Munich/Vienna 1965) pp 157 seq, give some idea of the bibliography.

[33] [R.] Bezzola, [*Les origines et la formation de la littérature courtoise en Occident (500-1200)*], *BEHE* 286, 1 (1944) pp 55 seq.

letters in her support which her envoys took to Constantinople.[34] But she was also concerned with the political relations between Sigibert and Byzantium;[35] we know that some time later Sigibert himself sent two ambassadors to Justin,[36] and Radegund saw further than the convent walls at Poitiers. She also appealed to her cousin Amalafrid in Constantinople.[37] He had been there since the capture of Ravenna in 540 with his mother and family and had served as a general in the Byzantine army.[38] With this support Radegund's request for relics was successful. Her envoys returned with a fragment of the true cross set in a reliquary, together with other relics of the apostles and martyrs and a beautiful gospel book.[39] The relic of the cross is still preserved in the convent of the Holy Cross at Poitiers (when the relic arrived the convent took its name from it); it is contained in a partially preserved reliquary of enamel work which some scholars believe is the original Byzantine reliquary sent by Justin and Sophia.[40] But the reception of the relic was not without incident; in this mysterious and hothouse community of aristocrats, to become the scene of shameful scandals after the death of Radegund,[41] there was already dissension. Maroveus, the then bishop of Poitiers, refused to receive the relics into the convent, and, as Gregory puts it, 'mounted his horse and went off to a country estate';[42] Sigibert's aid had to be called for again, and the ceremony was performed by Euphronius, bishop of Tours. This then was the occasion of Venantius's great hymns, and the background to the poem of thanks which he wrote in Radegund's name to be sent to Justin and Sophia in Constantinople.[43]

---

[34] Gregory [of Tours], H[istoria] F[rancorum], ed B. Krusch and W. Levison, MGH SRM I. 1 (2 ed 1951) bk IX cap 40; Vita Radegundis (see note 32) bk II cap 16.

[35] Compare Vita Radegundis, bk II cap 16 'pro totius patriae salute et eius regni stabilitate'.

[36] Gregory, HF bk IV cap 40. For the date (? 571) see Stein, p 34 n 18; [W.] Goffart, ['Byzantine Policy in the West under Tiberius II and Maurice'], Traditio 13 (1957) p 77 seq.

[37] Venantius, App[endix] carm[inum] 1, De excidio Thoringae.

[38] Bezzola, pp 55 seq. Compare Procopius, [De] B[ello] G[othico], ed Haury-Wirth (Leipzig 1963) bk IV cap 25, Venantius, App carm 1, lines 97 seq.

[39] Gregory, HF bk IX cap 40; Vita Radegundis bk II cap 16. For the reliquary see Sir M. Conway, 'St. Radegund's Reliquary at Poitiers', The Antiquaries' Journal 3 (London 1923) pp 1–12. [E.] Mâle, [Le Fin du paganisme en Gaule et les plus anciennes basiliques chrétiennes] (Paris 1950) pp 294–5.

[40] Mâle, p 295.

[41] Gregory, HF bk IX caps 40–3.

[42] Ibid bk IX cap 40.

[43] App carm 2. For the hymns see J. Szöverffy, 'Venantius Fortunatus and the earliest hymns to the Holy Cross', Classical Folia 20 (New York 1966) pp 107–22.

The poems written at this time and collected at the beginning of Venantius's second book are sufficient testimony to the veneration of the holy cross which immediately centred on the relic at Poitiers;[44] in particular the two hymns are still in use today. But it is the poem to Justin and Sophia that is of direct interest to our present theme. Its importance in relation to Justin's religious policies is obvious, yet it has hardly been used so far. The poem divides into two sections, addressed to Justin and Sophia respectively[45] and throughout the emperor and empress are treated as a pair, each peerless—*ecce pari voto, Augusti, certatis utrimque*; | *ipsa tuum sexum subrigis, ille suum* (lines 56–66). Justin is a Constantine, Sophia a Helena (line 67). Above all, the request of Radegund was granted on Sophia's initiative (lines 55 following), and Sophia is given equal space with Justin. But the opening of the poem is the most interesting: it consists of an address to the Trinity, with ten lines of orthodox theological definition, very closely reminiscent of Corippus's creed section. There are even certain verbal similarities, though perhaps derived from the close similarity of subject matter rather than from direct acquaintance.[46] After this trinitarian opening Venantius explicitly praises Justin for his conformity to catholic doctrine: 'how rightly Rome and the Roman world is ruled by him who follows the doctrine voiced by the chair of Peter!' (lines 15–16). Then again, 'the faith of the church, once shaken, is strengthened and shines out anew, and venerable law returns to its former position. Give thanks to God, that the new emperor (*nova purpura*) holds to what the council of Chalcedon decided' (lines 23–6). All the west is said to rejoice at the fact that Christ and the emperor are now united (lines 27 following). And witness to that are the exiled bishops restored to their sees on Justin's accession (lines 39 following, especially line 40, *tunc rediere sibi, cum diadema tibi*). No less than Corippus, Venantius is celebrating a specific event, and it seems obvious that the demonstration of catholic faith given by Justin consisted in his decree about the creed. Like Corippus, Venantius commemorated the decree in his poem with a trinitarian section which would otherwise seem oddly inappropriate. Michael the Syrian tells us that on his accession Justin was anxious to secure church unity,[47] and it seems that he convinced both sides at first. The monophysites saw

---

[44] *Carm* II 1–6. Bks I-VIII were published by Venantius in 576 or soon after—Meyer p 24. For the holy cross see Prinz pp 157 seq; John of Ephesus *HE* bk II cap 29.
[45] Lines 1–50, 51–100.
[46] *App carm* 2. 1–8; Corippus. *In laudem Iustini* bk IV lines 293–7.
[47] Michael the Syrian bk X cap 1.

Theodosius honoured and negotiations opened with their bishops, while Chalcedonians and westerners looked to Justin for support of their own point of view. By their action in sending the relic to Poitiers Justin and Sophia created a centre of catholic devotion for centuries to come.

The dates of Venantius's poem and of the sending of the relic can be fixed to within a year or so, if not absolutely precisely. *Nova purpura* (line 25) suggests a time near Justin's accession. But Venantius did not reach Poitiers until 567,[48] nor did Charibert die and Sigibert's authority over Poitiers begin before the end of that year. Radegund sent first to Sigibert, and then her envoys would have taken some considerable time over their journey (Sigibert's ambassadors were away for a year).[49] It seems that the expedition to Constantinople left during 568, was rewarded without delay by the emperor and empress, and that Venantius's poem of thanks belongs to the following year, 569, after the formal reception ceremony had taken place;[50] during this interval Maroveus of Poitiers had become estranged from the queen.[51] The poem certainly antedates 573, when Euphronius of Tours died and Gregory became bishop,[52] and there is every reason to suppose that the reception ceremony and the composition of Venantius's poems took place as soon as possible after the arrival of the relics. In 568, therefore, it was in Justin's interest to appear as cooperative as possible to western religious sensibilities. Perhaps it was about now that Justin and Sophia sent their famous cross to Rome, now in the Vatican treasury.[53] Like the Poitiers relic, this was a joint gift; it bears the portraits of Justin and Sophia on the arms of the cross, with the Lamb of God in between and an incription on the back.

Venantius represents the motives of Justin and Sophia as wholly religious, but there must have been a strongly political slant to the gift. The Franks after all were catholic, unlike most of the Germanic world; they stood out from the rest of the barbarian peoples as obvious potential allies for Byzantium, and this is how the Byzantines had

[48] Meyer pp 9 seq; Koebner pp 39 seq.
[49] Gregory *HF* bk IV cap 40.
[50] Aigran, first edition p 102. Radegund sent Reovalis back to Constantinople with thanks for Justin—presumably Venantius' poem (*Vita Radegundis* bk II cap 17).
[51] Gregory *HF* bk IX cap 40.
[52] *Ibid* bk X cap 31.
[53] H. Pierce and R. Tyler, *L'Art byzantin* (Paris 1932) 2, plates 136, 199b; D. Talbot Rice, *The Art of Byzantium* (London 1959) no 71; J. Beckwith, *The Art of Constantinople* (2 ed London 1968) plate 55. For the importance of this imperial gift see A. Grabar, *L'Iconoclasme byzantin* (Paris 1957) pp 19, 25.

optimistically viewed them in the Italian wars of Justinian.[54] Theudebert's invasion of Italy in 539 had given the lie to an idealistic idea of the Franks (hence Procopius's hostility),[55] yet such a view persisted in Byzantium. The historian, Agathias, writing in the early 570s, and of an expedition when the Byzantines and the Franks were on opposite sides, included a striking eulogy of them.[56] It is partly, and indeed, explicitly, based on religious considerations, but I have argued elsewhere that political motives enter also.[57] Agathias could have derived his information from those ambassadors of Sigibert already mentioned, from Radegund's own envoys, from Reovalis, who carried Venantius's poem to Constantinople, or indeed from Amalafrid and his family. The late 570s were the years when Byzantine hopes for the west centred on trying to persuade the Franks to drive out the Arian Lombards from Italy (especially after 575, when the Byzantines made an ill-fated attempt to do the job themselves).[58] But it is far too cavalier to say, as does the standard work on the subject, that Justin II was not interested in the west.[59] We have seen, through Venantius, that he was. It was a simple gesture to send the relic in response to Radegund's request; yet it made a deep impression and had the advantage of simultaneously complimenting Radegund's patron, Sigibert. Agathias's eulogy of the Franks, Sigibert's embassy, Radegund's request and her attempt to enlist the support of Amalafrid (whom she at least thought influential at the Byzantine court)—all these show that Byzantine interest in the Franks never waned, even though in the shadowy years of the 560s and 570s little positive could be done. The Poitiers relic demonstrated that both sides were alive to the possibilities.

This is an opportunity to put forward another sign of the fruits of Radegund's mission to Constantinople. It so happens that Venantius is one of the few writers to show possible knowledge of the poems of

[54] Procopius *BG* bk I cap 5.

[55] *Ibid* bk IV cap 34.18, compare 24.11. See [Averil] Cameron, 'Agathias [on the Early Merovingians]', *Annali della Scuola Normale Superiore di Pisa*, ser. 2, 37 (1968) pp 122, 136 seq.

[56] Agathias *Hist* I. 2–7.

[57] Cameron 'Agathias', pp 136 seq. On the orthodoxy of the Franks compare Agathias, *Hist* I.2, p 17.7 f. Bonn.

[58] Joh Biclar, a. 576; Agnellus, *liber pontificalis*, ed Holder-Egger, *MGHS RL* (1878) p 51, Paulus Diaconus, *HL* bk II cap 32; see Goffart p 80. The Byzantine army, under Justin's son-in-law Baduarius, was totally defeated.

[59] P. Goubert, *Byzance avant l'Islam II.1: Byzance et les Francs* (Paris 1956) p 9. See however Goffart pp 74 seq, Stein pp 16–7.

Corippus.[60] The two poems of Corippus are each preserved in only one manuscript, in each case from Spain, and it seems that the panegyric at least had reached Spain at an early date.[61] It is tempting to believe that Venantius actually acquired a copy of Corippus directly from Radegund's envoy, on this very occasion. We have seen that Corippus cannot have completed the panegyric on Justin later than 567, while Radegund's envoys were in Constantinople in the very next year and Reovalis in 569. So Venantius's trinitarian section in his poem to Justin and Sophia (composed in 569) *could* have been written with Corippus's creed paraphrase immediately before him. We have to suppose in any case that Corippus's poems reached Venantius in Poitiers very soon after their completion, and it seems far more likely that they were transmitted by the envoys from Poitiers when the panegyric was still topical and fresh.[62] So we have an intriguing connection between two of our main sources so far, and a further sign of interest in Byzantium evinced from Poitiers. Corippus's panegyric is an interesting production for its milieu: a complex Latin poem written in the surroundings of the Greek culture of Constantinople and wholly concerned with Byzantine imperial ideology and ceremonial. But there is a further bonus. Among the poems labelled *spuria* in Leo's edition of Venantius is one *In laudem Mariae*, in praise of the Virgin Mary. It so happens that Corippus's poem includes a prayer to the Virgin spoken by the empress Sophia.[63] Numerous verbal parallels have been adduced between the prayer and Venantius's poem,[64] and while some certainly belong to the genre in general, there could well be a connection between the two.[65] If this were so, it would be very tempting to believe what seems very likely on other grounds—namely that Venantius is indeed the writer of the *In laudem Mariae*.[66] From these tenuous threads a fuller picture gradually emerges, showing on the one hand the interest of a western community and a western poet in

[60] M. Manitius, '*Zu spätlateinischen Dichtern*', ZOG (1886) pp 250 seq.

[61] For the *Iust*, see Cameron intro, (x).

[62] It would have lost its relevance very quickly; compare the loss of the many panegyrics honouring Justinian.

[63] *Iust* bk II lines 52–69. For Sophia and the Virgin see also Michael the Syrian bk X cap 7.

[64] See Cameron comm. *ad loc.*

[65] I hope to investigate this elsewhere, as part of a general study of Mariological developments in the later sixth century.

[66] So Koebner pp 143 seq; D. Tardi, *Fortunat* (Paris 1927) pp 167 seq; S. Blomgren, *Studia Fortunatiana 2, De carmine in laudem Sanctae Mariae composito Venantio Fortunato recte attribuendo*, Uppsala Universitets Årsskrift 1934. 2, Diss. Uppsala (1934) (full treatment with bibliography to date). Most arguments adduced so far have been linguistic; a different approach may also prove helpful.

eastern affairs and on the other a possible explanation of how a Byzantine poem came only to survive in the west.

To return to Justin's policies. It is in no way surprising to find that while Justin was thus doing his best to meet western expectations, he also sought to conciliate the eastern bishops. We saw that Michael the Syrian said that his aim at his accession was the peace of the church,[67] and he tried to achieve it by doing his best to please both sides. It would be naive to suppose that emperors necessarily had a consistent 'religious policy' or, if they had, that they enforced it unswervingly throughout. Rather, each emperor was surrounded by individuals and groups with divergent interests; he had to attempt to strike some sort of balance between them—a balance that would change as circumstances changed. It is probable enough that Justin's first aim was in fact to restore unity after Justinian's final lapse into heresy, but he would only be likely to achieve it through compromise and apparent inconsistencies, as different interests came to the fore. The claims for monophysite sympathies in the imperial couple made by the monophysite historians must be approached with some caution, therefore. All parties in the religious disputes tried to claim imperial support[68] and no doubt Justin and Sophia were glad enough to have it so. We happen to know that Justin was in fact a devotee of the orthodox saint Symeon the Younger—though after Sophia had called in a sorcerer to cure Justin's madness the intercession of the saint could do no good.[69]

It is not easy to be certain about the sequence of events which led to the publication of Justin's edict addressed to monophysites. The final edict is given in detail by the orthodox Evagrius[70] and the monophysite Michael the Syrian.[71] But historians have been misled by Evagrius's dating, which telescopes the happenings in these years and appears to put the edict immediately after the conspiracy of Aetherius and Addaeus in 566.[72] Evagrius was writing more than twenty years later; but the contemporary John of Ephesus was himself one of the leaders of the monophysite bishops who were, as he tells us in great detail,

---

[67] Michael the Syrian, bk X cap 1.

[68] The patriarch Eutychius—*Vita Eutychii*, PG 86 col 2349; John Scholasticus—*Vita S. Symeoni Iunioris*, ed P. Van den Ven, *Subsidia Hagiographica* 32.1 (Brussels 1962) caps 202 seq.

[69] *Vita S. Symeoni Iunioris*, cap 208.

[70] *HE* bk V cap 4, translated by Frend pp 366–8. Evagrius is very hostile to Justin; compare *HE* bk V caps 1, 2.

[71] Michael the Syrian bk X cap 4.

[72] Compare Frend p 319, n 2; so Bury.

imprisoned in the patriarchal palace. The framing of the edict resulted from the inclusion of corrections made after discussion by these bishops, together with other clauses deriving from an attempt to please the opposing party (whom John calls Nestorians). The result pleased no-one, and was rejected by the monophysite bishops.[73] No date emerges from John's passionate and anecdotal account—which gives a vivid picture of the warring factions trying to influence the emperor, with Anastasius the *quaestor* and the patriarch John already at the head of the Chalcedonians—but the account of Michael the Syrian, though heavily dependent on John, gives more information. According to this Justin opened negotiations immediately, calling an assembly of monophysite bishops in Constantinople and then holding a series of further meetings. All this resulted in a first edict presented to the monophysites by John Scholasticus at Callinicum on the Persian border.[74] This was thrown out by the monks; but negotiations continued in the capital, culminating in the formulation of a second edict, that now recorded by Michael and by Evagrius. This must also be the edict which John of Ephesus tells us was given such a rough ride; neither he nor Evagrius mention the earlier one.[74a] John makes the rejection of the ?second edict the cause of the monophysite persecution which began in 572; he refers to the six years during which Justin was merciful to the monophysites,[75] and Michael seems to set the edict in the sixth year of Justin.[76] Hence 571—though Michael makes Justin's reign start in 568, not 565. But the dating of the earlier dealings with the monophysites are less clear; the edict of Callinicum could date from 567 or 568, the year of Radegund's mission. But Michael's narrative is not without its problems. The edict reported in book X chapter 4 is not set in a clear historical context. Justin is said to have threatened persecution to all who refused to accept it, and its rejection did indeed lead to persecution and the repeated exiling of the monophysite bishops. John of Ephesus is very clear that persecution began in 572. Yet Michael tells us that Justin gave up his concern for the peace of the church and turned to persecution after

[73] The edict—John of Ephesus *HE* bk I cap 19 seq; John was imprisoned himself—*ibid* bk I cap 22; bk II cap 4 seq; Michael the Syrian bk X cap 6. The sufferings of the bishops—John of Ephesus *HE* bk I cap 23. The circumstances of the composition of the *History*—John of Ephesus, *HE* bk II cap 50.

[74] Michael the Syrian bk X cap 2.

[74a] But John refers to preliminary discussions: John of Ephesus *HE* bk I cap 17.

[75] *Ibid* bk I cap 3; bk III cap 1.

[76] Michael the Syrian bk X cap 6.

Callinicum and, apparently, before the second edict, which is indeed presented as an ultimatum.[77] Brute force was used to compel monophysites to take orthodox communion, a general persecution was announced and the monophysite bishops were compelled to accept the emperor's edict and take communion in the presence of all the people in St Sophia.[78] There is certainly confusion in Michael's chronology, such as it is, and we are forced to conclude that he is not as sure a guide as has been supposed. The narrative of John of Ephesus, which he expressly follows at this point, has been elaborated and its main articulation (the connection of the edict with the opening of persecution after six years of Justin's reign) has been destroyed. Whether this is Michael's doing is not clear. We can say nothing as to the value of his possible other source, Cyrus of Batna, who wrote a Syriac history of Justin II and Tiberius, perhaps not long after the latter's death.[79] But even as it stands, Michael's account does not bear out Frend's picture of Justin turning to persecution in desperation only after the rejection of the edict.[80] With some hesitation I conclude that the edict which we now have does probably belong to 571, and that despite Michael's statements persecution did not seriously break out until after then. John was not merely a contemporary, but one of the main participants in the drama, and the story of Justin's persecution and the madness which he saw as a punishment for it was the *raison d'être* of this part of his history; we must stick closely to it and regard Michael as what he was—a late chronicler with no real understanding of the sequence of events.

It seems clear that the general tone of the final edict, again despite what Michael says, was as far as possible conciliatory towards the monophysites.[81] But it represented 'an attempt by the emperor to restore peace by a general formula without meeting the specific

---

[77] *Ibid* bk X caps 2 and 3.

[78] *Ibid* bk X cap 3. John of Ephesus *HE* bk I caps 23 seq. seems rather to suggest that this followed the second edict. The persecution was vigorous and harsh (John of Ephesus *HE* bk II caps 9 and 25).

[79] J. B. Chabot, *Chronique de Michel le Syrien*, I (Paris 1924) p 31.

[80] Frend pp 321–3.

[81] *Ibid* p 322. Dr Philip Sherrard kindly confirmed for me that in his opinion the edict as reported by Evagrius 'left a door open' to the monophysite position, without itself lapsing from orthodoxy. Despite his low opinion of Justin (n 70 above) Evagrius seems to have reported the edict fairly; but it is significant that he includes the pro-Chalcedonian final clause omitted by Michael the Syrian (pointed out to me by Pauline Allen).

monophysite demands'.[82] It was inevitably rejected, and John of Ephesus tells us why: the Nestorians, the bishops thought,

> had confused and mutilated it according to their own fancy: and though they had not ventured, through fear of the king, to expunge those expressions of his which were opposed to the two natures, yet they had managed to insert in it so much of their own, that while some parts were against the synod, others were strongly in its favour, and plainly were borrowed from it and on its side. . . . if it were to be proclaimed in the church, not a thousand such edicts, though fixed up in all parts and in every quarter, would bring about a unity, but produce rather schisms.[83]

Both John and Michael imply that Justin's aim was to achieve unity;[84] after the rejection of the edict the patriarch John tells the monophysite bishops 'it is you who prevent and hinder the unity of the church of God'. And until 571 it seems that Justin and Sophia pursued a moderate religious policy, steering a middle course between the various extremist views. The conciliation of the monophysites was only one part—though perhaps the most important part—of that policy.

We can in fact dimly discern in this reign a new sort of piety creeping over Byzantine life, the emperor setting the tone. In 574 the famous *acheiropoietos* image of Camuliana was solemnly brought to Constantinople.[85] Saint Symeon the Younger, the friend of Justin, defended icons by the analogy of imperial images.[86] Corippus stated for the first time the doctrine that Constantinople was a God-guarded city; it was soon to emerge as specially under the protection of the Mother of God.[87] Justin II's reign seems to mark a kind of apogee of imperial and Roman themes in official art, soon to be succeeded by a greater emphasis on the emperor's religious role.[88] Justin's activity as a patron of religious art was interpreted specifically as a sign of his piety.[89] Kitzinger has argued that it was the court which set the pattern and

---

[82] Frend p 322.

[83] John of Ephesus, *HE* bk I cap 20, trans Payne Smith.

[84] John of Ephesus, *HE* bk I cap 19; Michael the Syrian, bk X caps 1, 2.

[85] Cedrenus, *Historiarum compendium, CSHByz* 37–8 (1838–9) I p 685.

[86] *PG* 86 col 3215 (letter of saint Symeon to Justin II).

[87] *Iust* bk III line 333, 'res Romana dei est, terrenis non eget armis.' See N. Baynes, 'The Supernatural Defenders of Constantinople', B[*yzantine*] St[*udies*] (London 1955) pp 248–60.

[88] So A. Grabar, *L'Empereur dans l'art byzantin* (Paris 1936) pp 24–6, and see Averil Cameron 'Corippus's poem on Justin II: a terminus of antique art?', *Annali della Scuola Normale Superiore di Pisa*, 3 ser, 5.1 (1975) pp 129–65.

[89] Theophanes, ed de Boor, p 241; Zonaras, *Epitome historiarum, CSHByz* 50 (1897) bk XIV, cap 10.

officially encouraged the greater general emphasis on pietism, and in particular supported the contemporary growth of the cult of images, as a means of reinforcing the religious side of the emperor's position.[90] Perhaps it is not inappropriate to tie in the increasingly religious emphasis in imperial coronation rites which was taking place during this period, shown very clearly in the completely religious interpretation which Corippus gives to his long account of Justin's own coronation.[91] There is certainly a shift at this point in Byzantine life, which is expressed outwardly in terms of a change in the religiosity of Constantinople. Increased devotion to the *Theotokos*, the steady development of icon worship, an altered focus for imperial ideology, the coming official assumption of *basileus* as an imperial title[92]—all these lie behind the religious and political crisis posed by the Avar and Persian attack on the city in 626[93] and the changes to come in the seventh century.

As if looking through a glass darkly, we can see that the reign of Justin II was critical for these developments. Before the pathetic ravages of his illness took a hold,[94] Justin, with the help of Sophia, was energetic and ambitious. His financial measures were unpopular and earned him a bad press;[95] his foreign policy may have been ill judged.[96] But he was a most vigorous patron of the arts,[97] and in no area more conspicuously so than in that of religious art.[98] He and Sophia seem to have had a special veneration for the Virgin, building a chapel for the Virgin's robe at the great church of Blachernae and a reliquary for her

[90] E. Kitzinger, 'The Cult of Images in the Period before Iconoclasm', *DOP* 8 (1954) pp 83–150 esp 121 seq. For the early development of image worship see also N. Baynes, 'The Icons before Iconoclasm', *BSt* pp 226–39. The most subtle treatment will be found in [P.] Brown, ['A Dark-Age Crisis: aspects of the Iconoclastic Controversy'], *EHR* 88 (1973) pp 1 seq. (see esp pp 10 seq, 17 seq, for an alternative explanation of the rise of icons).

[91] *Iust* bk II lines 84 seq, with my notes.

[92] By Heraclius in 629: I. Shahid, 'The Iranian Factor in Byzantium during the Reign of Heraclius', *DOP* 26 (1972) pp 295, 317–20. Not by Maurice (Frend p 320 n 1).

[93] Brown p 14; A. Frolow, 'La dédicace de Constantinople dans la tradition byzantine', *RHR* 127 (1944) pp 61–127, esp 94 seq.

[94] John of Ephesus, *HE* bk III caps 2 seq tells some lurid stories.

[95] Evagrius, *HE* bk V cap 1; John of Ephesus, *HE* bk V caps 20, compare bk III caps II, 22; Gregory *HF* bk IV cap 40 (=Paulus Diaconus, *HL* bk III cap II). The financial policy was announced in *Novel* 148 (a. 566); compare Corippus, *In laudem Iustini* bk II lines 254 seq, 361 seq.

[96] Stein pp 4 seq.

[97] D. Talbot Rice, *The Beginnings of Christian Art* (London 1957) pp 95–6 (remarks which can be supplemented very extensively). Theophanes calls Justin φιλοκτίστης (ed de Boor, p 241.29).

[98] Compare the passages quoted in n 89.

girdle at the church of Chalcoprateia, near St Sophia.[99] Among the many churches which he is said to have 'adorned' were St Sophia and the Holy Apostles.[100] The sending of the relic and reliquary to Poitiers was then more than an isolated gesture, and had more than a passing significance. For political and religious reasons Justin was ready to honour the catholic Franks, but he and Sophia seized the opportunity presented by Radegund to do so in a typical way—reinforcing devotion to relics and the cult of the holy cross, and using an artefact produced under imperial patronage to demonstrate imperial involvement. If what survives is really Radegund's reliquary, it is the oldest western Byzantine enamel. Its iconography and style associate it with the cross sent to Rome and place it alongside the most characteristic productions of this stylistically ambiguous period.[101] Justin's gift to Radegund, the inspiration of some of Venantius's best poems and the object of devotion in the convent of the Holy Cross to this day, is one of the best testimonies to the imagination of this imperial couple who have suffered so badly from conventional historical sources.

University of London
King's College

---

[99] See R. Janin, *La Géographie ecclésiastique de l'empire byzantin I.3: Les églises et les monastères* (2 ed Paris 1969) pp 169 seq, 237 seq; M. Jugie, 'L'Église de Chalcoprateia et le culte de la ceinture de la Sainte Vierge à Constantinople', *EO* 16 (1913) pp 308 seq.

[100] Theophanes, ed de Boor pp 241 seq; see Cameron note on *Iust* IV lines 290 seq.

[101] On the iconography see Mâle p 295. For the delicate task of interpreting stylistic features in this transitional period see first E. Kitzinger, 'Byzantine Art in the Period between Justinian and Iconoclasm', *Berichte zum XI Internationalem Byzantinisten-Kongress*, (Munich 1958) pp 18 seq, with the same author's 'Mosaic Pavements in the Greek East and the question of a "Renaissance" under Justinian', *Actes du VIe Congrès international des études byzantines*, Paris 1948, 2 (Paris 1951) pp 209 seq; K. Weitzmann, 'The Mosaic in St. Catherine's Monastery on Mt. Sinai', *Proceedings of the American Philosophical Society* 110 (Philadelphia 1966) pp 392 seq; *Studies in Classical and Byzantine MSS. Illumination* (Chicago 1971) pp 126–50, 'The Classical Heritage in the Art of Constantinople'.

EASTERN ATTITUDES TO ROME
DURING THE ACACIAN SCHISM

by W. H. C. FREND

THE Acacian schism which lasted from 484 to 519 has been regarded as a bitter affair, characterised by intransigence on both sides and ending in an unqualified disaster for the Byzantine church.[1] A closer look at the evidence suggests that the rigid attitudes of popes Gelasius (494–8) and Hormisdas (514–23) were far from being reproduced on the Byzantine side even at moments of provocation, and among the populace as a whole its existence was for most of the time a matter of indifference. The eventual ending of the schism through the initiative of the emperor Justin I was not regarded in the east as involving a derogation of the rights of the eastern patriarchates and of the church at Constantinople in particular.[2]

Though differences of interpretation of the status of the council of Chalcedon and its definition of the doctrine of the Person of Christ were always in the background, the schism was caused largely by a clash of jurisdictions between Old and New Rome, and a clash of personalities between pope Simplicius and the patriarch Acacius. The quarrel was made the more intractable because neither side could envisage a permanent breach with the other. Yet if final rupture between Old and New Rome was unthinkable, the issues that divided the two were scarcely soluble. Moreover, almost equally difficult problems bedevilled the relations between Constantinople and Alexandria, and between the pro and anti-Chalcedonians within the east Roman provinces. The emperors Zeno (474–91) and Anastasius (491–518) had to weigh up their priorities. Given existing circumstances, was harmony between Constantinople and Alexandria more

[1] The element of triumph from the Roman point of view is indicated by L. Duchesne, *L'Eglise au vie siècle* (Paris 1925) p 51—'Un succès plus complet ne se peut imaginer'—and in sorrow by V. Bolotov, *Lectures in the History of the Early Church* 3, Christianskoe Chtenie (Petrograd 1915) pp 362–3 (cited from A. A. Vasiliev, *Justin the First*, pp 165–8).

[2] A. A. Vasiliev, *Justin the First, Dumbarton Oaks Studies* 1 (Cambridge, Mass., 1950) pp 161 seq. I am inclined to believe that there was a temporary collapse of the Byzantine position due perhaps to the personal weakness of the patriarch John, but that the situation was rapidly restored by the actions of Justin and his nephew Justinian. See [W. H. C.] Frend, [*The Rise of the Monophysite Movement*] (Cambridge 1972) pp 237–9.

important than harmony with Rome? After the revolt of Vitalian in 513, the question became broader. How far could the diplomatic contest with pope Hormisdas be continued without risking the loyalty of the western and Latin-speaking provinces of the empire on the one hand, and alienating the Syrian and Egyptian populations on the other? That eventually Justinian managed to retain the loyalty of both, together with the restoration of communion between Rome and the eastern patriarchates[3] represents a very considerable achievement.

The issues that resulted in the outbreak of the Acacian schism went back to the council of Chalcedon in 451 and beyond. While Rome and Constantinople had accepted the doctrinal definition of the Person of Christ subsisting in two natures inseparably united, Rome had never agreed to the twenty-eighth canon that confirmed the primatial standing of the see of Constantinople saving only the primacy of honour to Rome as 'Old Rome', contrasted with the empire's capital, 'New Rome'. Yet so long as there remained emperors in the west, Rome's main concern was with them and with the diminishing empire they controlled. Between 460 and 477 ecclesiastical diplomacy between east and west was evidently at a low ebb and no papal correspondence between Rome and Constantinople has survived. In 476, however, the situation changed. In August the emperor Zeno was restored to his throne after the eighteen month usurpation by Basiliscus, and in the same month the last of the emperors in the west, Romulus Augustulus was removed by the Herul chieftain Odoacar. The latter's followers proclaimed him king and in 477 Odoacar's envoys returned the imperial insignia to Zeno. Thenceforth, Odoacar was nominally the emperor's vice-gerent in Italy with the title of patricius. The pope like the patriarch at Constantinople therefore became a subject of the same emperor and was brought willy-nilly into the day-to-day religious politics of the empire. One of the aims, however, of Basiliscus had been the renunciation of the two-nature Christology agreed at Chalcedon. The support of the anti-Chalcedonians at Ephesus, Antioch and Alexandria had led him to neglect the interests of Acacius, the patriarch of Constantinople, against the violent and eventually successful opposition of its citizens. Once restored, Zeno had no wish to go on his travels again. On 17 December 476 the privileges of the see of Constantinople were solemnly reaffirmed.[4] It was to be regarded as 'the mother of our Piety and of all Christians of

---

[3] Though in Alexandria only with the restored melkite patriarchs after 537.
[4] Cod Just 1.2.16.

the orthodox religion'. The pope regarded this as a further unwarranted challenge to the see of Peter.

Zeno's immediate task, however, was to restore harmony between the four eastern patriarchates and dampen the fires of urban faction that threatened the security of some of the larger eastern cities. The anti-Chalcedonian leaders in Ephesus, and Antioch, were exiled, and the same fate was being prepared for Timothy the Cat at Alexandria when he died on 31 July 477. There, however, the clergy, monks and people refused to accept his Chalcedonian rival, also named Timothy and immediately consecrated another long-standing anti-Chalcedonian, Peter Mongus, in his stead. Acacius at once appealed to his colleague in Rome, pope Simplicius (468–83) for support. Peter Mongus he denounced as a 'friend of darkness' and subverter of the canons of the fathers.[5] Simplicius needed no prompting. Peter was unfit even to be a deacon. For a moment Old and New Rome were acting as one.

This was not to last. Gradually Acacius came round to the view that some accommodation must be made with the monophysite opinion in Alexandria including Peter Mongus, if another revolution was to be avoided. He found the germs of compromise in a formula proposed by the new patriarch of Jerusalem, Martyrius in 478, whereby the true faith was to be found in the decisions of the first three ecumenical councils (Nicaea, Constantinople and Ephesus 1), and anyone who accepted different doctrines whether pronounced at 'Ariminum, Serdica, Chalcedon or elsewhere' was anathema.[6]

During the next three years Acacius succeeded in holding the ring between Chalcedonian and anti-Chalcedonian in the east Roman provinces without upsetting his relations with Rome. After the patriarch Stephen had been murdered in Antioch by an anti-Chalcedonian mob in 479, Acacius himself consecrated his successor, Calendio, a firm Chalcedonian, in the capital. He informed Simplicius, and promised that the election would be confirmed by a provincial synod at Antioch, (that is, he did not intend establishing a precedent in favour of his see).[7] This undertaking was not kept. Meantime,

---

[5] *Acacii Epistula ad Simplicium*, ed E. Schwartz, C[ollectio] V[eronensis] 4, publ in P[ublizistische] S[ammlungen zum acacianischen Schisma], *ABAW* PhK, NS 10.4 (1934) no 4 pp 4–5.

[6] Text given in Zacharias Rhetor, *HE* V. 6, ed E. W. Brooks, *CSCO, Scriptores Syri*, 3, 5 (Louvain 1919) pp 153–4, the association of Chalcedon with the semi-Arian council of Ariminum is interesting.

[7] Referred to in Simplicius' letters to Zeno and Acacius in June 479, C[ollectio] A[vellana] 66 and 67, ed O. Guenther, *CSEL* 35, 1 and 2 (1895).

Acacius may have opened a correspondence with Peter Mongus. In the winter of 481–2 events played into his hands. Peter's ageing rival Timothy sent a delegation to the capital asking for his successor to be appointed. His choice, the monk John Talaia, however, became involved in political intrigues threatening the position of Zeno, and before he returned to Alexandria he was obliged to swear that he would not accept the patriarchate. However, when Timothy died in February 482, John was prevented by his supporters from keeping his promise. Acacius saw himself free to abandon the Chalcedonian minority in Alexandria and stated his terms for recognising Peter Mongus as patriarch. His rival, John Talaia, betook himself to Rome and eventually became bishop of Nola in south Italy.

The terms for the restoration of communion between Acacius and Peter Mongus were contained in a skilfully drafted letter addressed to the bishops, monks and laymen of Alexandria, Egypt and Cyrenaica. This document dated 28 July 482 and known to history as the *Henotikon* of Zeno, aimed at the complete reconciliation of the sees of Constantinople and Alexandria which had been at loggerheads almost continuously since the second council of Constantinople in 381. The only right and true faith was that pronounced by the three hundred and eighteen fathers at Nicaea and confirmed at Constantinople and Ephesus. It asserted the canonicity of Cyril's *Anathemas* (not accepted at Chalcedon). It proclaimed that Christ was 'one and not two', and concluded that 'every person who has thought or thinks anything else either now or at any time either in Chalcedon or in any other synod whatever, we anathematise'. Chalcedon was effectively dethroned as a dogmatic synod, though retained as a disciplinary body that condemned Nestorius and Eutyches; however its canons, including the famous canon 28, remained valid.[8]

This fine piece of caesaro-papism, however, was not the cause of the Acacian schism. This had already become inevitable a fortnight earlier. On 15 July, pope Simplicius sent two angry letters to Acacius accusing him of double-dealing and perfidy in recognizing Peter Mongus. 'Even if Peter were now orthodox, he should be admitted to lay communion only.'[9] He was aghast at the reports reaching him concerning the situation in Alexandria. Acacius now took care not to keep Simplicius informed of events.

[8] Zacharias Rhetor, *HE* V.8. See Frend pp 177–80 (further references).
[9] Simplicius to Acacius. *CA* 68 and 69: Miramur pariter.

Eastern attitudes to Rome during the Acacian schism

Another letter from the pope dated 6 November 482,[10] complaining of events in Alexandria (but still not of the *Henotikon*), and of Acacius's silence about them, went unanswered. Events meantime consolidated Acacius's position. The *Henotikon* and Peter Mongus were immediately accepted by Martyrius of Jerusalem and unity was restored throughout the east Roman dominions. Simplicius became ill, to die in March 483. His successor Felix (483-92) seemed in no hurry to push matters to extremes. At length, he was stirred into action by Acacius's opponents in the capital. The Sleepless Monks were strongly pro-Chalcedonian and hated the *Henotikon*. Roused by their report Felix summoned Acacius to Rome to answer for having restored Peter without his permission and accused him of claiming that he was 'head of the whole church'.[11] The wound administered by Zeno's edict six years before had not healed. A papal delegation sent to Constantinople during the summer of 483 found itself participating in a eucharist attended by Peter Mongus's representatives and at which the name of Peter Mongus was commemorated on the diptychs. At last Felix acted. On 28 July 484, just two years after the *Henotikon* a synod of twenty-seven bishops met at Rome and solemnly excommunicated Acacius 'for his many transgressions'. He was a double-dealer (*hypocrita*), had promoted known heretics, and insulted the pope's legates.[12] A Sleepless Monk from the monastery of Dius pinned the sentence to the patriarch's pallium while he was celebrating the eucharist. On 1 August 484, Felix wrote to the emperor Zeno telling him he must choose between the apostle Peter and Peter Mongus.[13]

Part of the difficulty had been caused by a simple lack of communications. Rome had not learnt from the experience of popes Celestine and Leo and had no officially accredited agent in the capital. Apart from the timelag of months for correspondence imposed by distance, the need to rely on the casual reports from groups who may have had their own reasons to oppose the patriarch, deprived the pope of regular and unbiased information about the situation in the capital and the problems that confronted its leaders. Not until the reign of Justinian was the pope to have a permanent *apocrisiarius* at court. Now, lack of accurate information exacerbated feelings in Rome and was one of the factors leading to the schism.

[10] *CV* 3, p 3-4.
[11] Felix to Acacius, Mihi crede nescio quemadmodum te ecclesiae totius asseras esse principem. Schwartz, *PS*, p 73 = C[ollectio] B[erolinensis] 21.
[12] Felix to Acacius, Multarum transgressionum. *CV* 5, pp 6-7.
[13] Felix, *Ep* 8. Schwartz, *PS*, p 81 = CB 33.

Personal rancour and frustration at their relative impotence also contributed to the angry and arrogant tone adopted by the popes, with the exception of Anastasius, to the emperor and his representatives. The doctrine established in the west of the contagion of evil was invoked by Felix and his successor Gelasius (492–6) to brand Acacius as guilty of heresy 'by association' with Peter Mongus, who was the successor of Timothy the Cat and of Dioscorus who had been condemned at Chalcedon. In this context also the *Henotikon* was not explicitly an issue, only the 'tendency of the Greeks towards heresy'— and here one discerns the contempt now being felt in Rome for the Byzantines, though the final rejection of Byzantium in favour of a Frankish empire was still over two centuries away. Above all, the popes aimed at humiliating the see of Constantinople so that never again could its patriarch claim ecumenical status, and hence, the inclusion of Acacius's successors as worthy of condemnation, and, finally, the emperors Zeno and Anastasius themselves.[14]

In face of the unrelenting hostility of the popes, the east, from the emperor and patriarch to the anti-Chalcedonian populace in Syria and Egypt reacted coolly. There was no anti-papal outburst in the provinces. Acacius, if he felt any discomfiture did not show it. He dropped Felix's name from the diptychs, but that was all. His aim as that of Zeno and his successor Anastasius (491–518) was to secure religious peace in the empire on the basis of the *Henotikon*. Relations with Rome were not neglected, but until the revolt of Vitalian in 513 showed the latent power of the Latin-speaking and pro-Chalcedonian provinces, Rome was allowed to express its anger in a void. To Zacharias Rhetor, John Talaia was a 'liar' and by implication Simplicius was foolish to write to the emperor on his behalf.[14a] Acacius died in November 488. His two successors, Fravitta (d. 489) and Euphemius (489–95) both sent letters to Rome announcing their election, only to be caustically rebuffed.[15] Macedonius (495–11) wished to include Rome among the recipients of his synodical letter, but this time the emperor vetoed the move. Chances of the restoration of union, however, were not neglected on the Byzantine side. In the short but significant reign of pope Anastasius (496–8), a great effort

[14] For an account of the attitude of the popes towards the emperor and the Byzantine church at this period, see F. Caspar, *Geschichte des Papstums*, 2 vols (Tübingen 1930–3) 2, pp 35 seq.

[14a] *HE VI* 7.

[15] Gelasius told Euphemius that he belonged to 'an alien body'. *Epp* 2 and 3. See Frend pp 192–4.

was made not only to restore harmony between Old and New Rome, but also between the former and Alexandria. Anastasius was the opposite in temperament and inclination to Gelasius. He was a Roman by birth and the son of a presbyter, very much a Christian aristocrat who looked instinctively to the emperor at Constantinople as his earthly sovereign. The reaction of the patriarch Athanasius, Peter Mongus's successor, to the chance of negotiation was surprising. In tones flattering to the pope, he emphasised the links of orthodoxy and fellowship that united the sees of Peter and of 'Mark, his imitator', and their joint guardianship of the faith. The existing sorry division had been caused by the devil. In particular, he had caused Leo's letter when translated into Greek to be susceptible to Nestorian inter-pretations. The dissension was unjustified and if the pope would accept the Alexandrian confession of faith, unity could be restored. This con-fession, of course, included the *Henotikon*, which the Alexandrians cite almost verbatim, Cyril's *Anathemas*, and acceptance of Dioscorus, Timothy the Cat and Peter Mongus as guardians of that faith. If the pope had aught against them, let him prove his case or restore them to the diptychs. For their part the Alexandrians were prepared to send a delegation to Rome to discuss the unity of the churches.[16]

This was not intended as sarcasm. The tone of the letter was firm and sincere. In the capital the pope's ambassador, the Roman senator Festus intimated that Anastasius might be prepared to sign the *Henotikon* if the hostile reference to Chalcedon was omitted and Acacius were dropped from the diptychs. Cyril's *Anathemas* had never been con-demned, and it was left to the initiative of the pope to prove charges against Dioscorus and his successors as, one hundred and fifty years before, pope Julius had demanded of the eastern bishops to prove their case against Athanasius. After the Acacian schism had ended in 519, Justin and Justinian returned to the record of the negotiations with Anastasius to impress on pope Hormisdas their view of the settlement,[17] that is, no one was to be condemned except Acacius.

The negotiations in the capital in 497 between the representatives of Rome, Constantinople and Alexandria indicate a desire on all sides to reach agreement, and the absence of ill-feeling towards Rome on the

---

[16] Cited by pope Anastasius *Ep* 5=*CA* 102, (The *Libellus* of the Alexandrian church).
[17] Justin to Hormisdas, 9 Sept 520: Anastasius palam aperteque constituerit, cum ob hoc idem scriberet negotium decessori nostro, satis esse pacem affectantibus, si nomen tan-tum reticeatur Acacii=*CA* 232, p 702.

part of the two major eastern patriarchates. As time went on the schism hardened. Anastasius, however, was prepared to ask for pope Hormisdas's mediation in 515 when Vitalian seemed to be in a position to overthrow him, but all the time he stuck to two principles: he would not impose the creed of a Latin-speaking minority on the empire as a whole and he would not make the living pay for the errors of the dead. Only in 517, when the negotiations with pope Hormisdas had dragged out to an inordinate length, did the aged emperor Anastasius lose patience, and tell the pope that he was not prepared to be insulted by him.[18] Normally, the exchanges if uncompromising in substance, were courteous in tone. On the Byzantine side the schism was a matter of regret, and in this the court and patriarchate reflected opinion outside the capital.

For the monks of Egypt Rome was venerable and far away, a place where there were aristocratic ascetics and a martyr chapel in honour of Peter.[18a] For those subjects of the emperor who supported the doctrinal definition of Chalcedon, it was also the touchstone of orthodoxy and a protection against the increasingly pro-monophysite policy of the emperor Anastasius. In the end, such real success as the pope could claim at the ending of the schism was due to the massive support his cause received from the monks in the province of Syria Secunda and the churches in the Latin-speaking provinces of the Balkans.

At the same time, opposition to Chalcedon did not imply opposition to the papacy. This can be seen on the popular level, in the *Plerophoriae* (*Witnesses*) of John of Beit Rufin. Set down about 512, there is much horrific denunciation of pope Leo and his *Tome*, 'a treasure house of all blasphemy and impiety', and an abomination.[19] There is no criticism against the see of Rome, as such. Nor is there a tendency to invoke the doctrine of the contagion of evil, popular in the west, which would have involved Leo's successors in the heresy perpetrated in the *Tome*. This, by combining doctrinal with emotional antagonism would have rendered the schism irreconcilable. The *Plerophoriae* carry no attacks on Leo's successors and, so far as they may be understood, contain no reference at all to the existence of the Acacian schism. Pope Gelasius was not answered in his own theological language. A possible explanation of this may be that western concepts of papal primacy were

[18] *CA* 138, p 565.
[18a] Palladius, *Lausiac History*, ed and tr W. K. Lowther Clarke (London 1918) caps 41, 45, 4 and 46.
[19] *Plerophoria* 89, *PO* 8.1 (Paris 1912) p 151.

of little interest to the mass of eastern Christians. It has been pointed out for instance that leaders of the early Syriac tradition, such as Aphrahat (*c* 340) and Ephrem Syrus (d. 374) had a high sense of episcopal office and its continuity from apostolic times but, within that college they had nothing to say about a Petrine primacy. Ephrem comments on Matt. 16.18 without referring to Christ founding his church on Peter. Hence the impact of Acacius's quarrel with Simplicius was muted. Individual popes might be praised or blamed, but questions relating to the status of the see of Rome had not yet impinged fully on popular consciousness.[19a]

More urbane and less strident, the writings of Severus of Antioch, the monophysite patriarch of that city between 512–18 point in the same direction. Severus was a hellenist of hellenists, a Christian philosopher in the tradition of the Cappodocian fathers, but his writings lack any systematic treatment of the papacy in the light of the Acacian schism. This applies to those written in Constantinople in 509–11, such as the *Philalethes*. Leo's disgraceful utterances in the *Tome* which appeared to vindicate Nestorius affected only himself, though he had brought discredit on his see. 'Would that he had never been bishop', is Severus's verdict.[20] For Severus, Rome was a holy see whose bishops were ordinarily worthy of respect: 'those who preside over the holy church of the city of the Romans'.[21] They are placed, however, on exactly the same footing as other leaders of major churches, such as 'the great Dionysius', of Alexandria (247–64)[22] or his own predecessors 'of this Christ-loving city of Antiochus'. Their authority is quoted as of equal weight with that of these orthodox leaders, no more and no less. When Severus cites the text Mt 16.18. it is to the church and its faith, and not to Peter personally or to his descendants, that he refers the Lord's words.[23] Allegorical interpretation applied as much to this text as to others.

One example of Severus's attitude to the bishops of Rome may be given. The touchstone of Severus's religious outlook was 'accuracy' of doctrine, which involved the acceptance, as he says of every word of Cyril of Alexandria as canonical, and the toleration of the *Henotikon* only in the sense that it annulled the definition of Chalcedon. In this

---

[19a] Thus, Robert Murray, *Symbols of Church and Kingdom* (Cambridge 1975) pp 236–8.

[20] Thus, the sixth book of the *Select Letters [of Severus Patriarch of Antioch]*, ed E. W. Brooks (London 1904) IV 3, p 258.

[21] *Ibid* bk V 6, p 296 (referring to pope Stephen and similarly bk V 3, p 284, referring to pope Julius).

[22] *Ibid* p 297.   [23] *Ibid* p 295.

respect he was almost as much opposed to his contemporary, the patriarch Macedonius, as he was to pope Leo himself. Much of his time when he was patriarch was taken up in examining and if possible reconciling the numerous waverers among his clergy who placed less emphasis on doctrinal accuracy than he. Should clergy previously pro-Chalcedonian who renounced Chalcedon be rebaptised or not?

Severus who lived in the bible and the fathers at once went back to the documents relating to the rebaptism controversy in north Africa in Cyprian's time. Cyprian he regarded as over-scrupulous, preserved from dogmatism only by his conciliatory letter to the Mauretanian bishop Quintus. The proper solutions were arrived at by pope Xystus and Dionysius of Alexandria who agreed that heretics who had been baptised in the name of the Trinity should not be rebaptised on conversion to orthodox communion. Pope Xystus was cited as an 'orthodox opinion'.[24] However, the complete validity of his views could be questioned, for those heretics who were astray on doctrinal grounds, particularly as regards the Person of Christ, should be rebaptised. Here Severus cited canon 19 of the council of Nicaea, which singled out the Paulianists (followers of Paul of Samosata) as requiring re-baptism.[25] The decree of Nicaea was all important. The pope's opinion was valuable corroboration when it was needed.

Severus was glad to have the support of the pope against anything that smacked of two-nature Christology; and to his correspondents in the monastery of Tagais in Isauria who had raised the problem of re-baptism he cited the letter of pope Julius to an alleged presbyter Dionysius in which the adherents of Paul of Samosata are called *Paulianisti*.[26] This letter is a forgery, as is another alleged letter of pope Julius, addressed to Prosdocius also condemning the two-nature Christology as 'blasphemy', and glorifying the Virgin from whom Christ took flesh and reigns for ever 'in mortal form'. This letter provided Severus with some of his favourite proof texts in support of the one nature of the incarnate Christ.[26a]

By no means all of the questions concerning these 'papal letters' have been cleared up.[27] Examination indicates a passable imitation of the

---

[24] *Ibid* bk V 1, p 279.   [25] *Ibid* bk V 6, p 298.

[26] *Ibid* bk V 3, p 285. It seems that Severus mistakenly thought Dionysius was bishop. See the note in Migne *PL* 8, col 928.

[26a] Text in Migne, *PL* 8, cols 953–9.

[27] Briefly recorded in B. Altaner/A. Stuiber, *Patrologie, Leben, Schriften und Lehre der Kirchenväter* (Freiburg 1966) p 314. It seems that no one since the editors of Migne *PL* 8 has given any exhaustive study to these documents, which would repay consideration.

indignant style of Julius' surviving letters ('I am amazed', etc.),[28] and
his recourse to 'apostolic tradition' to support his authoritative utterances.[29] The writer knew what he was about and was clever enough to
direct their attack against Arianism and Paul of Samosata and to avoid
obvious Apollinarianisms. The Virgin is not referred to as '*Theotokos*'.
The letters can hardly date later than the last quarter of the fourth
century when Arianism was still a living issue and 'Theotokos' not yet
a badge of Alexandrian orthodoxy. These letters were accepted as
genuine throughout the east from the council of Ephesus I until they
were denounced as forgeries by the monks of Syria Secunda in 514,[30]
and as such they provided a point in favour of Rome. Julius was
described by the Armenians at the council of Duin in 506 as 'the guide
of the way of life for the westerns', and his outstanding orthodoxy
could be set off against Leo.[31] The bishops of Rome might be guilty of
misunderstanding the difference between the theological terms of
ousia and *hypostasis*,[32] but there was no tradition of heresy to which the
popes were victims. Severus had no rancour against Rome, but only
against Leo as purveyor of false and indeed nonsensical doctrine, and
in this he was supported by a large proportion of eastern Christians.

In all his long and varied correspondence, Severus makes no reference
to Acacius or to the schism caused by his actions. Events at Constantinople or Rome were judged against the touchstone of doctrinal
accuracy. When in April/May 518, with the end of Anastasius's reign
in sight, a new patriarch, John, was consecrated in the capital, Severus
wrote, 'As to the man who has just been instituted and holds the
prelacy of the royal city, we have learnt that he is John . . . who is
thought to be inclined to the right opinions and holds out some
pleasing hope to the orthodox, but is more desirous of adopting a
deceitful middle course'.[33] Rome is not mentioned. It was John's
'orthodoxy' in relation to Chalcedon that mattered.

Ultimately, this unremitting zeal brought its inevitable reward.
There was a storm of protest in Severus's patriarchate led by the monks
of Syria Secunda. Late in 517 they appealed to pope Hormisdas,

---

[28] Compare the style of Julius's genuine letter to the Eusebians preserved in Athanasius
Apologia Contra Arianos, cap 35, especially in the final paragraph, with the first paragraph
of his letter to Dionysius, *Miramur cum nonnullos* . . . (*PL* 8 col 930).

[29] *Ad Prosdocium* 1, *ibid* col 953.

[30] Evagrius, *HE* bk 3, 31.

[31] Letter from the Armenians to the orthodox in Persia, cited from K. Sarkissian, *The
Council of Chalcedon and the Armenian Church* (London 1965) p 204.

[32] *Ep* 22, written *c* 520, ed E. W. Brooks, *PO* 12.2 (1916).

[33] *Select Letters* VI.1, pp 260–1.

denouncing Severus as a heretic, and declaring that 'Nestorius, Eutyches, Dioscorus, the two Peters and Acacius, and all those who defended so much as one of those heretics' should be excommunicated. The language in which they wrote to the pope was flattering in the extreme (Hormisdas was addressed as 'patriarch of the whole world'), but we should be wary of accepting this as proof that papal jurisdiction was acknowledged by the petitioners. The letter reads as though written by people at the end of their tether. Everything else had failed, including a petition at Constantinople. Now they turned to Hormisdas as 'a haven from storm and tempest' but the emphasis remained on the validity of Chalcedon. Leo was praised as a vindicator of the council and Acacius was condemned because, like Severus, he was associated in their minds with those who rejected it.[34] 'Four Councils' like 'Four Gospels' had become a slogan, and those who proclaimed them were as ready to appeal to the emperor as to the pope against Severus. In the new emperor, Justin they found a ruler who would restore the true faith, and there were no further appeals to Rome. The revolution succeeded. Severus ended his days an exile.

If for the west, the Acacian schism concerned the vindication of papal discipline and jurisdiction against the eastern patriarchates, for the east the issue was always seen against the background of the controversy over Chalcedon. In this, of course, the popes could never be left out of account permanently. The *Tome* of Leo was crucial to the credibility of the papacy as a source of authority, but even here, Leo was only one pope who could be regarded as unorthodox and against many illustrious predecessors who were models of rectitude. The two sides, however, were thinking in different terms, Rome in those of discipline and the Roman primacy, the easterners in terms of doctrine and also consensus among the 'college' of patriarchs. Mutual understanding was as far off under Justin and Justinian as it had been under Zeno and Anastasius. The ultimate power, too, remained with New Rome. The schism ended through the initiative of the Latin-speaking emperor, Justin, and not through any action by pope Hormisdas. After preliminary negotiations he was instructed by Justinian 'to hasten to the capital' so that communion could be restored between the two Romes according to the emperor's will.[35]

---

[34] CA 139. The western chronicler, Victor of Tunnuna, (*Chronicon* ad ann 516) records that the monks in Palestine and Transjordan sent a similar letter to the emperor Anastasius. *MGH, AA Chronica Minora* 2, ed T. Mommsen (Berlin 1894) p 195.

[35] CA 147: 'We expect your arrival without delay'. In case of some obstacle, the pope should send plenipotentiaries, but in any event speed was of the essence.

Eastern attitudes to Rome during the Acacian schism

The events of 28–31 March 519 were regarded by contemporaries as the ceremonial enactment of this restoration, based on the mutual acceptance of Chalcedon and agreement that Rome was an orthodox and apostolic see. Acacius could be dropped from the diptychs together with 'his associates'—variously defined—but not canon 28 of Chalcedon. The patriarch John, whatever his momentary weakness in accepting the papal *libellus* as it stood, was the first openly to use the title of ecumenical patriarch.[36] Justin and his all-powerful nephew Justinian were soon at pains to show that relations between Old and New Rome would remain precisely as they had been under their predecessors.

University of Glasgow

[36] Mansi 8, col 1038.

THEODORE OF SYKEON AND THE HISTORIANS

by DEREK BAKER

SAINT George, it was noted in the epilogue to an eleventh-century collection of his miracles, 'did not only perform his daily miracles in his own person: his gracious power was extended to those whose life accorded with his, and whose trust in him was beyond doubt or question. Sometimes he rescued them from the perils that oppressed them: sometimes he collaborated with them in the miracles and wonders which they performed. Of this there is ample testimony, but particular reference may be made to that great and famous Theodore, called the Sykeote, whom everybody knows. In all this George followed his master Christ, who gave his disciples power over demons, and sent them out to heal the sick.'[1] Of the extent of Theodore's posthumous reputation there can be no question. To the author of the brief life of Theodore preserved in a fourteenth-century manuscript[2] he was one of the most eminent of the saints of Galatia, that land of 'many great and holy men', and it seems to have been both this reputation, and a personal encounter with Theodore not long before the saint's death on 22 April 613 which led the emperor Heraklios to bring his relics to the capital as an additional protection against Persian attack. However much this may in general be representative of that 'new sort of piety'[3] then emerging in the Byzantine world, the translation, and the man, were singular enough to inspire a ninth-century encomium by Nikephoros Skeuophylax[4], based upon, and

---

[1] See [A-J.] Festugière, [*Vie de Théodore de Sykeon*], Greek text with French translation and commentary, Société des Bollandistes, *sub hag* 48, 2 vols (Brussels 1970) 1 pp xxiii-iv. For the miracles of saint George see *Miracula S. Georgii*, ed J. B. Aufhauser (Teubner 1913). The quotation, given by Festugière and taken from Paris MS Gr 1604, occurs on p 40: compare Festugière 1 pp 159–60, cap 169, lines 30–9, 52–8. For the monastery of saint George Sykeotes and the cult of saint Theodore see [R.] Janin, [*Les Eglises et les monastères de Constantinople*] (Paris 1953) pp 81–3.

[2] MS Patmos 736. See Festugière 2 pp 287, 301–10 for the text of this life, and below n 20.

[3] See above p 65, and note the comments of Brown at p 20 above.

[4] For Nikephoros Skeuophylax, monk and sacristan of the church of the Blachernae in Constantinople see Beck p 546 and the references there given. The encomium was edited by C. Kirch from a twelfth-century manuscript in *An Bol* 20 (1901) pp 249–72.

adding to, existing accounts of the saint. In more recent times the *Life* of Theodore has been chosen to represent 'life amongst the peasantry of Anatolia at the end of the sixth century', and to give an insight into 'the thought-world of those humble folk who appear so rarely in the works of writers whose interests are urban . . . and linked with the life of the capital'.[5] It is, it is claimed, 'the best picture known to us of life in Asia Minor in the Byzantine period before the Arab invasions of the Empire'.[6] In these and other respects it is a remarkable *Life*: a rare source for the rural life of the early Byzantine world, comparatively rich in topographical detail, however conventional its form. Beck remarks upon *die lebendige und kulturgeschichtlich sehr aufschlussreiche Biographie*,[7] while for Halkin it is *ce très curieux document, un des plus riches en détails concrets sur l'Asie Mineure à la fin du VIe et au début du VIIe siècle*.[8] Against this background the appearance in 1970 of the new, Bollandist edition of the *Life*, prepared and translated by one of the most eminent members of that learned society, was a major event.[9]

The *Life* of Theodore of Sykeon, by his disciple George Eleusios had appeared in a number of Latin versions before Joannu first published the Greek text in 1884.[10] This, however, like its Latin predecessors was taken *e codice lacunoso* at St Mark's, Venice.[11] It was this text, too, which formed the basis of the English translation of Dawes and Baynes.[12] M is a tenth-century menology, for the period 9 March to

---

The page references given by Halkin—*BHG*, 3 vols (3 ed Brussels 1957) 2 p 276 no 1749—refer only to the Greek text. For the dating see Ehrhard 3 pp 504–5.

[5] [*Three Byzantine Saints*, trans Elizabeth] Dawes and [N.H.] Baynes (Oxford 1948) p xiii. The *Life* of Theodore occupies pp 85–192. The translation is taken from the shorter form of the longer *Life* of Theodore (see n 11 below), and is further abbreviated. There is no adequate introduction or commentary. See also the review by F. Halkin in *An Bol* 69 (1951) pp 163–4.

[6] Dawes and Baynes p 87. See also W. E. Kaegi, Jr, 'New evidence on the early reign of Heraclius', *BZ* 66 (1973) pp 308–30. I owe this reference to Dr Michael Angold.

[7] Beck p 459.

[8] [F.] Halkin, 'Un ménologe [de Patmos (MS 254) et ses légendes inédites]', *An Bol* 72 (1954) pp 15–34, at p 30.

[9] See n 1 above.

[10] [T.] Joannu, [Μνημεῖα ἁγιολογικά] (Venice 1884) pp 361–495; emended by P. V. Nikitin, *O nyekotoruikh grecheskikh Tekstakh zhitii Svyatuikh, Mémoires de l'Académie des Sciences*, 8 series, hist-phil class, 1,1 (St Petersburgh 1895) pp 59–60. See *BHG* 2, p 276, no 1748.

[11] Venice, St Marks, MS 359, fols 193ᵛ–270ʳ = M. The lacunae occur in cap 26 (26, line 15 – 26a, line 20) and after cap 146 (147, line 36 – 169, line 58), referring to the edition of Festugière. For an account of the manuscript, and in particular for the evidence for the loss of certain gatherings, see Ehrhard 1 pp 426–30.

[12] Above n 5.

23 April, of 275 folios. The *Life* of Theodore, even in its dilapidated state, occupies rather more than a quarter of the manuscript. In 1954 attention was drawn to another text of the *Life* in an early eleventh-century Patmos manuscript.[13] Like M, P is a menology, covering the complete month of April in 320 folios: more than a third of the manuscript is taken up by the *Life* of Theodore. Though there are now folios missing from the manuscript they do not affect the *Life* of Theodore, which is written throughout in the principal one of the two contemporary hands which composed the manuscript.[14] P agrees closely with M, but supplies the lacunae in the latter, amounting to forty-two folios, making it possible to produce for the first time a complete edition of a work which was already, as Halkin remarked of Joannu's edition taken from M, *une des plus longues parmi toutes les productions de l'hagiographie byzantine*.[15] This complete text Festugière's edition has now supplied.

There remain three other versions of the *Life* of Theodore, all shorter than MP. In the national library at Athens there survives a version closely related to MP but with very substantial omissions, which include almost the whole of the second half of the text.[16] A is a dilapidated manuscript, now of 164 folios, dated to 1071, containing two saints lives: the *Life* of Theodore occupies the last third of the manuscript. Not a menology, it has been seen by Festugière as designed, and hence shortened, for private devotional reading in the monastic cell. A has been used by Festugière in collation to supply certain apparent omissions in MP, and to correct their text, for, he recognises, it has been copied *sur un exemplaire parfois meilleur que le modèle de MP*.[17] Each of the two remaining versions *constitue une rédaction particulière, un ouvrage nouveau*.[18] Both are menologies. The first, an eleventh-century manuscript from Paphos, for the period 1 March to 31 May,

[13] Patmos MS 254, fols 155^r–278^r = P. See Halkin 'Un ménologe' pp 15–19 for discussion of the manuscript, which he dates c 1000, rejecting the earlier dating suggested by R. P. Blake, who supplied the photographs from which he worked. The manuscript is described by Ehrhard, 1 pp 611–14, not at first hand, nor from photographs, but from notes supplied by friends. See BHG no 1748. Festugière, 1, p xxv, decided that *il est vain de reproduire ici ces analyses*, though he did comment on the confused and faulty Greek of P (1 pp xxxv–vi).

[14] Halkin, 'Un ménologe' p 17.

[15] *Ibid* p 30.

[16] Athens National Library MS 1014, fols 113^r–60^v = A. See Festugière 1 pp xxvii–xxix. Some not altogether adequate discussion is given of the omissions from this text of the *Life*, which are listed on p xxvii. See Ehrhard 3, 2 pp 921 *seq*, and pp 86–9 below.

[17] Festugière 1, p xxviii.

[18] *Ibid* 2 p 283.

is of 337 folios: the *Life* of Theodore occupies twelve folios.[19] The second is a fourteenth-century Patmos menology, in two distinct, but united, parts, for the months of March, April and May in 279 folios of which the *Life* of Theodore occupies eight.[20] Since these two texts of the *Life* of Theodore had been *entièrement récrits* it has been taken as axiomatic by Festugière that they were of no use in the preparation of the text of the longer life from the collation of M, P and A. In sum, then, Festugière has produced a meticulously re-edited version of M, filled out and corrected by reference to P, and in a few instances by A. This last is dismissed as a version designed for private reading and deficient by reason both of deliberate omission and of accidental loss. VB[1] and VB[2] are seen as related but essentially unassociable texts, and no account is taken of the ninth-century encomium of Theodore composed by Nikephoros Skeuophylax. All this amounts to a substantial, impressive and valuable achievement, but there still remain certain aspects of the subject which might profitably be given further consideration.

All but one of the surviving texts of the *Life* of Theodore, full or abbreviated, are to be found in menologies. The exception is A, which falls, according to the classification proposed by Ehrhard and agreed by Festugière, into that category of collections of monastic biographies prepared for edifying reading within the cloister. There can be no argument here, and the appearance of the *Life* of Theodore in A, in association with that of Andreas Salos, may be taken as a further confirmation of the extent of Theodore's reputation and cult within the empire.[21] The text of the *Life* in A, however demands further examination. It is, declares Festugière, an incomplete,

[19] Now Paris BN MS Gr 1534, fols 95vb–107rb = VB[1]. Festugière copied this text himself (2 p 283). For comment and general bibliography see 2 pp 283–7; Greek text 2 pp 288–300. See Ehrhard 1 pp 399–402; p 399 n 1 for discussion of the dating and rejection of the twelfth-century dating proposed by Omont-Delehaye.

[20] Patmos MS 736, fols 117r–24v = VB[2]. See Festugière 2 p 287, and the references there given, for composition and dating—in particular for the form of the second part of the manuscript (fols 117–279), which includes VB[2], and for its relationship to the 'imperial menologies', see Ehrhard 3, 1 pp 341–78. For the association of the terminal imperial prayers to those *Lives* with the emperor Michael IV (1034–41) see Ehrhard 3, 1, pp 394, 403–5, and F. Halkin in *An Bol* 57 (1939) pp 228–30. For the Greek text see Festugière 2 pp 301–10.

[21] This is the only manuscript in which Theodore is not directly associated with material relating to his spiritual patron saint George. In part this was a natural association resulting from the occurrence of their feasts on successive days (22 and 23 April) and strengthened by the translation of Theodore's relics to the monastery of saint George at Constantinople (later saint George Sykeotes). For further discussion see Janin pp 81–3.

text, shortened by the scribe's deliberate omission of many chapters which were alien to his purpose and *qui ne l'intéressaient pas*, and by dilapidation of the manuscript subsequent to its compilation.[22] Dilapidation would appear to be responsible for the loss of a large section, in the early part of the *Life*, from the latter part of chapter 39 to the beginning of chapter 55,[23] and of three shorter sections from the later chapters.[24] With the first of these four it is plain, as Festugière demonstrates,[25] that the text as it remains in A is incomplete. In chapter 39, concerned with the visitation, and healing, of Theodore by saints Cosmas and Damian, the A text ends abruptly before the restoration of Theodore to health, and resumes on the next folio with the last word of a biblical quotation (cap 55 line 8). Similar textual considerations apply to two of the other omissions (between fols 156 and 157, and between folios 158 and 159), and Festugière is clearly right to assume that the abrupt ending of the text of the *Life* as it remains in A, before the final moments and death of Theodore, is not intentional. This said, it is as well to be clear what Festugière has not demonstrated in connection with this loss of folios from A. If both chapters 39 and 55 are demonstrably incomplete it cannot necessarily be inferred that the manuscript has lost chapters 40–54.[26] Nor can it be assumed on the basis of the textual state of chapters 164 and 167 that chapters 165 and 166 have been lost.[27] Nor does it follow from the sudden termination of the text in A that it originally possessed all the chapters now to be found after that point in MP. It must, of course, be said that it cannot be proved either that these chapters were not there. For the moment, however, it will be as well to keep both possibilities in mind while moving to a consideration of those other

---

[22] Festugière I p xxvii.

[23] Cap 39 line 14—cap 55 line 8.

[24] Cap 164 line 70—cap 167 line 34 (not caps 163–6 as given by Festugière I p xxviii); cap 167 line 101 to the end; and cap 162 line 100—cap 164 line 4. This last is not mentioned in Festugière's introduction to the text, though it is noted elsewhere (I pp 148, 149 notes) that *folium unam excidisse videtur in Cod.A.*

[25] For this discussion see Festugière I pp xxvii–xxviii.

[26] 'Il peut y avoir amputation de quelques chapitres, mais la lacune est évident,' Festugière I p xxvii. These chapters record the construction of the church of saint Michael, the appointment of Philomenos as abbot (40–1), miracles (42–5), the careers of some of Theodore's disciples (46–9), Theodore's second visit to Jerusalem (50–1), miracles (51–3), the visit of the future emperor Maurice (54).

[27] Chapter 165, a section of comment by the biographer, George Eleusios, has some connection with the previous chapters. Chapter 166, however, describing the visit of the emperor Heraklios to Theodore, is in all essentials an entirely self-contained section, though the biographer once again features in it.

omissions from the text of the *Life* in A which Festugière labelled as deliberate.[28] These are:—all but the first seven lines of the first two chapters, which together constitute an elaborate prologue to the *Life*; the latter part of chapter 8 (visitation of demons) and the whole of chapter 9 (saint George's appearance to Theodore's family); from line 6 of chapter 15 to the end of chapter 18 (again eliminating references to demons and to Theodore's family, but also omitting his inclusion under the altar in the oratory of saint George and references to his early mortifications); chapter 25 (the entry into religion of Theodore's sister and grandmother); the eight chapters from 31–8 (the death of his grandmother and mother, miracles, encounter with the sorcerer Theodotos); chapters 60–1 (miracles at Anastasiopolis); and almost the whole of the second half of the *Life*—chapters 81–160. These chapters relate to the period of his life after his resignation of the see of Anastasiopolis,[29] and in all essentials comprise a mosaic of circumstantial miracles within the framework of three visits, by invitation, to Constantinople (caps 82–97, 128–40, 154–5) and journeys of visitation and healing to the cities of Asia Minor. The encounters with the emperors Phokas (cap 133)[30] and Heraklios (cap 152, 154–5) also occur in this section.[31] The text in A resumes with the saint's return, once more, to Sykeon (cap 161).

On any reckoning these are substantial deletions for any monastic scribe to make from the existing *Life* of an established saint, and the more closely they are examined the more facile Festugière's explanation of them appears. If there appears sound reason for abbreviating the prologue, omitting references to Theodore's family as irrelevant in an account of Theodore, and paring down the miraculous material, there is none for the excision of some of the earliest references to Theodore's inclusion and mortification (cap 17) and to the intervention of saint George (caps 8, 9). Where the miraculous material is concerned what is surprising is that the scribe, on Festugière's hypothesis, chose to retain the anonymously commonplace while discarding the extended story of the sorcerer Theodotos (caps 37–8), and the more precisely located miracles recorded in chapters 60–1. In this connection, too, it is striking indeed that none of the Constantinopolitan material and miracles, peopled as they are with emperors, patriarchs, imperial

[28] Of these, the five line omission in chapter 27, lines 23–8, is a straight-forward case of homoeoteleuton: *autoū* (line 22/3)—*autoū* (line 28).

[29] See cap 80 = cap 80a, 80b in Festugière's translation (2 pp 70–1).

[30] See too *PG* 157 (1866) cols 716–17. I owe this reference to Dr Michael Angold.

[31] See also cap 166.

officials, courtiers and the like, should have been retained. Further, it is now worth returning to the possibility that some of the material apparently lost by dilapidation from A may never have been in it at all.[32] If this was so then the construction of the church of saint Michael; the account given of Theodore's disciples; the second visit to Jerusalem; the visit of the future emperor Maurice; material relating to Theodore's biographer and the visit of Heraklios might also have been excluded by the copyist. It is of course true that no well-founded case can be established in this last respect without meticulous examination of the manuscript itself, but it may be noted here that the latest editor of Theodore's *Life* has not worked directly on the manuscript either.[33] Whatever the truth about the material which Festugière regards as lost from A, however, it remains difficult to accept that any reasonable, or spiritual, scribe would exclude so much, so arbitrarily from the text of the *Life* preserved in MP. It is worth considering, in fact, whether an alternative explanation for the differences between MP and A may be advanced, and, in particular, whether A may be taken to represent an earlier version of a *Life* of Theodore, which was later expanded into the developed form it displays in MP.

Some indication of the primitive form, or forms, of the *Life* may be found in references to himself and to his *Life* by the biographer. It is in the last of these (cap 170a) that the most explicit references are to be found. Eleusios owed his very conception to Theodore: the saint's

---

[32] See above p 87, and n 26.

[33] For as complex a text as that of the *Life* of Theodore, as in so many other cases, direct access to the manuscripts is essential. Festugière, in fact, worked directly on only one manuscript, Paris MS Gr 1534 (= VB[1]): for all the others he relied on intermediaries. For M he used Joannu's text, revised from the manuscript by Saffrey; for P he worked from photographs supplied by Halkin; for A from photographs supplied by the national library at Athens; for Patmos 736 once again from photographs. It goes without saying that Ehrhard's critical commentaries underlie the whole discussion. This is not unreasonable in cases of straight-forward transcription and collation, but where any doubt exists as to the composition of a text or manuscript it is not entirely satisfactory, and in this particular case there is real cause for concern. In the case of P Ehrhard himself had worked neither from the manuscript nor from photographs but from notes supplied to him, and Halkin remarked that 'the analysis and commentary left something to be desired' (Halkin, 'Un ménologe', p 15). The photographs from which Halkin worked, and which he supplied to Festugière, had been supplied to him by professor Blake of Harvard. These photographs were, however only *presque complète*, and, Halkin remarked, *une partie des photos de Blake est malheureusement fort difficile à dechiffrer*. Some of the doubts about the dating of this manuscript derive from this failure to consult the manuscript at first hand. With A, too, a markedly different version of the *Life* from MP, it is unfortunate that, whatever the difficulties, the manuscript itself was not examined in the preparation of the new edition of the *Life*.

benediction of his parents giving them the children they had previously lacked. In gratitude they placed him at a very young age in Theodore's care. From him Eleusios received the name George 'and such education as was necessary'. For twelve years, he remarked 'I followed the holy servant of the Lord as his disciple, and was judged worthy to participate in many of his miracles'. A comment in an earlier chapter (166) illustrates this association, Theodore remarking to George Eleusios after the departure of the emperor Heraklios that the emperor would reign for thirty years,[34] and elsewhere (cap 22) George Eleusios records that he derived a great deal of what he set down 'from the mouth of the pious and holy man himself'. At a number of points in his account George Eleusios laid stress upon his youth, and consequent inadequacy as a biographer.[35] In part, of course, this was a matter of convention, but in chapter 165, in drawing attention to his 'rusticity and youth', the biographer declared that he had 'not yet attained his eighteenth year, and possessed no great literary ability'. He was led, he says, to begin to set down some account of Theodore by his awareness that 'the moment of his [Theodore's] departure was near', and by his concern that no member of that monastic community had seen fit to make any written record of Theodore—'the actions of the holy father had been neglected by the entire community, with the result that the generation succeeding ours would be deprived of that edification which results from accounts of such spiritual value'. This, then, was a biographical account, whose purpose was edification not record, begun not long before the saint's death, and added to subsequently by George Eleusios. Some indication that there was more than one stage in the composition of George Eleusios's account may be found in what is now chapter 22. This follows Theodore's ordination as priest at the uncanonical age of eighteen, and concludes the section of the Life devoted to Theodore's early years and youth. This, said the biographer, had been written after the saint's death, but was derived, for the greater part, from Theodore's own instruction of his community, and supplemented by the testimony of the companions of his youth. The section was particularly intended for the instruction and edification of the novices of the community, but it formed part of an over-all account of the earthly life and miracles of Theodore, written by a young, inexperienced disciple

[34] If this chapter is to be regarded as part of the original Life it is of importance in dating the composition of the work, but the failure of the biographer to record the translation of the relics of Theodore to Constantinople by Heraklios may be taken to reinforce doubts about including it: see n 31 above.

[35] See the end of the conventional prologue (cap 2) and cap 170a.

who, by his own account, worked hard to supplement his own inevitably limited knowledge by reference to eye-witnesses and those who had benefited from Theodore's powers of healing, and who, in the process, 'from this mass of fact have selected but a small portion'.[36] It was, in fact, a *Life* of the type described by Dölger—inspired by 'genuine love of story-telling as well as a delight in miracles and the need to edify': most of which, as he lamented, 'no longer survive in their original homely and popular form',[37] largely as a result of the literary movement in the time of the emperor Constantine VII Porphyrogenitus (913–59), and the process of rewriting associated with the name of Symeon Metaphrastes.[38]

While the testimony of George Eleusios himself goes some way to confirm the hypothesis of the development of the *Life* of Theodore from simple, homespun beginnings to the developed form to be found in MP and the edition of Festugière, it does nothing directly to confirm or deny the priority of A as a version of the *Life* to MP. On manuscript evidence alone, of course, both M, dated to the tenth century,[39] and P, dated to the earlier eleventh century,[40] take priority over A, which bears the date 1071,[41] and in the absence of other evidence it would be unreasonable to proceed further. There are, however, the two abbreviations of the *Life* contained in the quarterly menologies from Paphos and Patmos[42] which may be taken into consideration. Both were printed by Festugière in the appendix to his edition, but since, as he rightly observed, they had been completely and separately, re-written they could be collated neither with each other, nor with MPA. An analysis of their content is, however, of some interest and relevance, though the abbreviated nature of both texts makes exact comparison of the essential contents of VB[1]/VB[2] with MPA impossible. What in, general, does emerge, however, is a broad correspondence between the major omissions from the text of MP, as recorded in A, and those evidenced by the abbreviated lives.[43] As

[36] Festugière I p 165, cap 170a.
[37] *CMH* 4 (2 ed 1967) 2 p 224.
[38] See Beck pp 570–2 and the references there given, and *passim*.
[39] See n 11 above.
[40] See n 12 above.
[41] See n 16 above.
[42] See nn 19, 20 above.
[43] Where for example, A omits most of caps 1–2 so do VB[1]/VB[2]; where A omits caps 31–8, and perhaps 40–54 VB[1] omits caps 31, 35, 46–53, 57, and VB[2] 31–3, 42, 47–53. In the second part of the *Life*, where A omits caps 81–160 VB[1] omits caps 81, 84–96, 98–9, 101, 103, 106–11, 113–18, 121–6, 129–32, 138, 140–51, 154–5, 158–60, and VB[2]

manuscripts, once again, neither can be given priority over M, though neither text is much later than P. VB^1 is dated to the eleventh century, and in VB^2, though the manuscript itself is of the fourteenth century, the textual form of the later part of the manuscript associates it with the second quarter of the eleventh century.

There remains one final piece of evidence—the encomium of the early ninth-century sacristan of the church of the Blachernai in Constantinople, Nikephoros Skeuophylax.[44] This survives in a manuscript which now appears to have been finally ascribed to the twelfth century.[45] Edited by Kirch in 1901, the encomium summarises the course of Theodore's life before describing the translation of the saint's relics to Constantinople at the command of the emperor Heraklios. Immediately before the Greek text Kirch gave a brief analysis of Nikephoros's account, relating its sections to the chapters of Theodore's *Life* as given in the incomplete text of Joannu (M). Though in some respects Kirch's cross-references between the two texts require emendation and correction, and can now be extended by reference to P, they are generally sound, and provide the opportunity to examine what a ninth-century author regarded as relevant to his purposes in Theodore's *Life*. This apart, the encomium may also be used to supply some indication as to the shape and content of the *Life* which Nikephoros used.

The thirty-eight sections, out of fifty-four, of the encomium which can be compared with the *Life* of Theodore in general demonstrate the same sequence of chapters as is to be found in the *Life*. Leaving aside, for the moment, any consideration of material omitted from the encomium, but present in the *Life*, the order in the two texts is exactly the same, with the exception of the transposition of chapters 16 and 17 (encomium chapters 11 and 12), up to chapter 30b of the *Life* (encomium chapter 19). At this point, however, the orderly sequence is disrupted, and though it retains many of the incidents recorded in the *Life* the order in the encomium is thereafter significantly different. In part, of course, this may be due to Nikephoros's regrouping of material to suit his more compact chapters, and it may be noted that

---

caps 90, 92, 105–19, 122–9, 141, 143–7, 149–51, 153, 157–61. Much of this is miraculous material of precisely the sort that a brief life might omit, but not all of it, and caps 12, 46–53, 64–8, 154–5 (VB^1), caps 7, 9, 28–9, 47–53, 59, 66, 74–7, 119, 129, 153 (VB^2) illustrate this.

[44] See n 4 above.

[45] For discussion see Ehrhard 3, pp 504–5.

much of the material from *Life* chapter 30b (encomium chapter 19) is miraculous material which lends itself to this sort of treatment. Nonetheless, Nikephoros, as his encomium demonstrates, cannot be credited with a rigorously-orderly mind and technique, and Kirch himself remarked upon the apparent displacement of material in relation to its order in the *Life*. Not until chapters 29/30 (*Life* chapters 58/61) of the encomium does an approximate correlation become re-established, and even then it cannot compare with that displayed in the first nineteen chapters of the encomium (*Life* to chapter 30b). This disruption of the correlation of the two texts is not to be ascribed to the introduction of new material into the encomium, though chapter 20 of the encomium does record an austere incident which is not part of the *Life*. The encomium, in fact, adds little to the *Life* at any point before Theodore's death, and that little is comprised of entirely commonplace edifying material relating to miracles and the saint's austerity.[46]

It is, however, when material present in the *Life* but omitted in the encomium, is considered that the most significant contrasts between the two texts emerge. From the first half of the *Life* the encomium omits chapters 5, 10, 12–15, part of 16, 22, 25–6, 31–4, 40–44, 52, 59–60, 64–7, 69–79, 80a/b. Some of these chapters can be seen as irrelevant or unnecessary in an encomium of Theodore—chapter 22, on George Eleusios; the chapters dealing with Theodore's family; some of the miraculous material; perhaps even the chapters dealing with Theodore's disciples and community (chapters 26, 40–1, 59, and the anonymous abbreviation in chapter 29 of the encomium of chapters 46–8 of the *Life*). Other omissions, however, are harder to explain. It is surprising that any reference to saint George should be omitted, given the location of Theodore's relics and the association of the two saints, yet chapters 5, 12, 15 of the *Life* do not appear. Equally it is surprising that the encomium should not contain chapters in the *Life* which relate directly to Theodore's vocation and ascetic practice (10, 12–15), to Theodore's time as bishop (73, 75, 78–9), to his pilgrimage to the shrine at Mousge, to the visit of Maurice (54), or to the second visit of Theodore to Jerusalem (50/1), though this visit, in fact, is simply a brief account of conventional miracles, and its presence in the text available to Nikephoros is implied by the reference in his thirty-first chapter to Theodore's *third* visit to Jerusalem.

It is, however, from the second half of the *Life* that the most striking

[46] See encomium caps 6, part of 19, 20.

omissions are made. In chapters 32/3 of the encomium very generalised brief references are made to Theodore's reputation at Constantinople and elsewhere, and to the desire of the great in church and state for his prayers. Such comments are too vague to relate precisely to any chapter or chapters in the *Life*. In chapter 34 of the encomium, however, there is a return to more detailed narrative, and this and the succeeding four chapters (35–8) can be related beyond any doubt to chapters 167–8 of the *Life*. There is, in fact, and apart from the superficialities of chapters 32/3 of the encomium, no reference to chapters 81–166 of the *Life*.[47] It need hardly be said how striking is the omission of, amongst other material, every reference to Theodore's visits to Constantinople from an encomium composed in the capital and designed to record the translation of Theodore's relics to the monastery of saint George there. Taken, however, with other indications and evidence, particularly in relation to A, it may suggest that in certain respects, and in particular with regard to chapters 81–166 of the *Life*, Nikephoros did not omit material, but never had it available to him. Precise and meticulous examination and collation of the manuscripts themselves would, of course, enable some of the uncertainties which surround this question to be resolved, and assist in the establishment of more definite con-clusions. Even in the absence of such an inquiry, however, it does not seem altogether unreasonable to propose certain hypotheses on the basis of the evidence at present available.

It seems likely that the *Life* of Theodore passed through several stages, and existed in a number of versions, before it achieved the finally-developed form represented by MP. Initially it was the work of a young, relatively poorly-equipped disciple of the saint, George Eleusios, designed to preserve the memory of a founding saint for a particular community, and to serve both as a memorial and as an example. In this it parallels many other hagiographical tracts, both in eastern and western tradition. Even at this early stage, however, there is some indication of sectional composition, and if the apparent testimony of the biographer may be taken at its face value then the account of the saint's earliest years and youth was composed after those sections dealing with Theodore's years of mature ministry, and in particular with the events of which the young biographer had personal experience. This need not be too formal a judgement: the absence of

---

[47] It is possible to see references to chapters 83 and 85 of the *Life* in chapter 30 of the encomium, but since these are references to standard miracles which occur more than once in the *Life* (compare caps 62, 68, 73) nothing certain can be established here.

any reference to the translation of Theodore's remains to Constantinople, for example, suggests that George Eleusios's literary labours were not too protracted. Thereafter, and the process is once again entirely commonplace, the primitive life attracted accretion, certainly from the common miraculous ground of Byzantine hagiography, and by the addition of more factual material, whether genuine or fictitious. The principal spur to the development of the *Life* into a form which places it amongst the most extended specimens of its class was undoubtedly imperial translation of the relics to Constantinople, coupled with the saint's association with saint George. It is not suggested that this development was necessarily a simple linear progression: A, the encomium, the abbreviated lives, may well hint at a variety of early forms of the *Life*, but with much in common, and to be clearly distinguished in important respects from the tradition of MP.

Textual analysis divorced from historical interpretation is arid, and it needs to be asked where such a hypothesis leaves Theodore himself. That he was a man of striking local example and developing local reputation is beyond doubt. Ascetic, healer, miracle-worker, the personal focus of the daily life of the provincial faithful, he becomes like many another of his time and type the social arbiter of his region. In more formal terms he establishes a monastic community, is ordained priest, and for a time presides over the see of Anastasiopolis: an ascetic and eccentric within the established church of the time rather than outside it. With his centre of operations placed close to one of the main highways of the empire he was likely both to have come into contact with influential travellers, and to have had his reputation spread by them. For some of his encounters, as with Phokas,[48] there is corroborative evidence elsewhere, and in view of the emperor's subsequent interest in his cult and relics it seems likely that he had come into contact with Heraklios. It was not uncommon for holy men of the time to be consulted by the great, to be called to Constantinople or to visit Jerusalem, and there is no sound reason to deny the possibility of such activities in Theodore's case: whether Theodore made three visits to each of these capitals of the Byzantine world, however, is another matter. But these more elitist aspects of Theodore's career are in a very real sense peripheral. Historians may point to 'the liturgification of public life',[49] and remark upon the bringing of

[48] See 30 above.
[49] See Nelson above p 115.

images and relics to Constantinople as part of the process of creating a new sort of piety,[50] but, as Brown has commented, what is of more significance is the use of the holy in daily life.[51] For all his asceticism Theodore does not emerge as a mystic; far from being un-, or other-, worldly he is intensely of this world: he may be reluctant to become a bishop, but it takes a hermit's advice to make him resign the office. Though no soldier, it is not without significance that Theodore's cult, and in all probability his very name, survived in conjunction with that of saint George: each in his different way epitomising the martial qualities so prized by Byzantines, in their saints as much as in their soldiers, and giving the provincial saint an 'ecumenical' significance.

Derek Baker
University of Edinburgh

[50] See Cameron above p 65.
[51] Above pp 13–15, 18, 21.

SYMBOLS IN CONTEXT:
RULERS' INAUGURATION RITUALS IN BYZANTIUM AND THE WEST IN THE EARLY MIDDLE AGES[1]

by JANET L. NELSON

HOBSBAWM[2] recently reminded young historians prone to methodologising that they would be well advised always to begin with a problem. He meant to imply—and very properly—that experimentation with methods becomes vapid and useless unless it is seen clearly for what it is: a means to an end. I propose to experiment with a method, so I want first to emphasise that I do have a problem. It is this: why, within a common framework of Christian theology, belief and practice, did the rituals for the inauguration of rulers, in early Byzantium on the one hand, and in the early medieval western kingdoms on the other, diverge as they did? What has this divergence to tell us about the differences not just between types of political power but between the two societies? These questions relate, of course, to a mere subsection of the whole vast subject of 'liturgies eastern and western' which Brightman long ago promised to survey.[3] Unfortunately, even his work was left only half-complete: the further task of systematic comparative analysis seems hardly to have been begun. But that would surely be a lifetime's work. In this paper, I confine myself to a small though significant area of the field, a single type of ritual; and I cover a limited time-span, the period down to about 1000 AD.

First, to define the size and shape of the problem, I sketch two ritual models, eastern and western, and examine what were the historical contexts in which the critical phases of their respective developments

---

[1] I am grateful for their help to my friends and colleagues Averil and Alan Cameron, who kindly let me see work in advance of publication, Johnny Parry, who advised me on the anthropological literature, and John Gillingham, who discussed with me some of the ideas in this paper.

[2] In a contribution to the discussion at the conference of the Past and Present Society at University College, London, 2 July 1975.

[3] F. E. Brightman, *Liturgies [Eastern and Western]* (Oxford 1896), a revised version of the work of C. E. Hammond (1878). Only volume 1 ever appeared.

took place. Second, and this is where the experiment comes in, I offer a provisional answer to the question: why?—both in the sense of how come? and also of what for?[4]

First then: the rituals themselves. I begin with the east. How was a Byzantine emperor made? A distinction has to be made at the outset between two sorts of emperor: the co-emperor raised as colleague by an existing senior emperor,[5] and what may be termed the 'new' emperor—a category which will include not only a usurper, would-be founder of a new dynasty, but also an emperor who did in fact succeed a member of his own family but whose succession was not formally transacted during his predecessor's lifetime. An obvious distinction between the two categories is thus that a 'new' emperor's inauguration was generally preceded by an imperial funeral, a co-emperor's never.

The inauguration of the co-emperor (and incidentally there are considerably more of these in our period than of the other kind of accession)[6] consisted basically of a coronation of the junior by the senior colleague,[7] followed by acclamations from those witnessing the ritual. The coronation of a co-emperor was final in the sense that no

---

[4] Compare E. R. Leach, 'Ritualization in man in relation to conceptual and social development.', in P[hilosophical] T[ransactions of the] R[oyal] S[ociety of] L[ondon Series B. Biological Sciences], no 772, vol 251 (London 1966) pp 403 seq. Distinguishing the 'philo-genetic question "how come?" from the functional question "what for?", ' Leach comments (p 404): 'The enormous complexity of the ritual sequences which anthropologists have to study makes any guesses of the "How come" type more or less absurd.' To a historian, the anthropologist's self-limitation appears a result, less of the complexity of his material, than of its usual lack of diachronic depth. Philogenetic questions are the historian's stock-in-trade: for him, the complexity of ritual sequences must invite rather than preclude historical investigation.

[5] For the characteristics of pre-mortem succession, see J. Goody, [Succession to High Office] (Cambridge 1966) pp 8 seq.

[6] Between 450 and 1000, there were, on my calculations, thirty-six inaugurations of co-emperors, as against twenty-seven of 'new' emperors.

[7] The dynastic element of pre-mortem succession was observed by the sixth-century chronicler Malalas, Chronographia, ed L. Dindorf (Bonn 1831) p 439: 'τὰ τέκνα αὐτῶν ἐκ παιδόθεν ἔστεφον.' For the role of the senior emperor, see the B[ook of] C[eremonies] of Constantine Porphyrogenitus, ed J. Reiske (Bonn 1829) I, 94, p 431. Ont his indispensable source, see J. B. Bury, 'The Book of Ceremonies', in EHR, 22 (1907) pp 209 seq, 418 seq. The role of crowner was sometimes delegated to the patriarch: [W.] Sickel, ['Das byzantinische Krönungsrecht bis zum 10 Jht.'], in BZ, 7 (1898) pp 511 seq, at 520, and O. Treitinger in BZ, 39 (1939) p 200, stressing that in any event the senior emperor always remained 'der auctor der Krönung.' See also P. Classen, 'Karl der Grosse, das Papsttum und Byzanz', in Karl der Grosse, 1, ed H. Beumann (Düsseldorf 1965) pp 580, 595. [Ai.] Christophilopoulou, ['Εκλογή, ἀναγόρευσις καὶ στέψις τοῦ βυζαντινοῦ αὐτοκράτορος] (Athens 1956) pp 80 seq, is needlessly over-schematic in insisting that the senior emperor always personally performed the coronation of a colleague. The events of 641 show public opinion preferring this, but

further ritual was required to legitimise him as sole or senior emperor when the existing senior colleague died.[8] The inauguration of a co-emperor until the early ninth century would regularly take place in the Hippodrome[9] or in the palace, rather than, as in the ninth and tenth centuries, in Hagia Sophia.[10]

The inauguration of a 'new' emperor was more complicated. Christophilopoulou has suggested that the procedures should be seen in terms of two originally distinct blocs,[11] and her approach is useful so long as the integration of these blocs is stressed, rather than any contradiction between them.[12] First came the *anagoreusis*, the formal proclamation of the new emperor, with ritual acclamations signifying the divinely-inspired election. All this often occurred in a military camp, and in the early period was accompanied by the shield-raising and torques-crowning appropriate to the elevation of a war-chief. Then the emperor was crowned by the patriarch and acclaimed again with laudatory hails signifying recognition of the legitimacy of the

---

equally show the possibility of delegation to the patriarch: Nicephorus, *Historia*, ed C. de Boor (Leipzig 1880) p 30. For a good instance of delegation, with the senior emperor the subject of the action, see Theophanes, *Chronographia*, ed C. de Boor (Leipzig 1883) p 426 (for the year 748): "Εστεψε Κωνσταντῖνος ὁ δυσσεβὴς βασιλεὺς τὸν ἑαυτοῦ υἱὸν Λέοντα εἰς βασιλέα δι' 'Αναστασίου τοῦ . . . . πατριάρχου.' For some further evidence, see now the important and wide-ranging article of [C.] Walter, ['Raising on a shield in Byzantine iconography'], in *REB* 33 (1975) pp 133 *seq*, especially pp 134–5. Professor D. M. Nicol very kindly drew my attention to this article.

[8] This seems true of the seventh century and later. Gregory of Tours, *Historia Francorum*, V, 30, on the accession of Tiberius II (578) seems to imply that an acclamation in the Hippodrome was 'customary' then, as it certainly was in the case of a 'new' emperor. Averil Cameron, in a forthcoming article, shows that Gregory depended on good Byzantine sources. If he can be trusted here, despite his mistaken reference to Tiberius as Caesar instead of Augustus (this Byzantine distinction may no longer have been appreciated in the west), the two forms of inauguration were not yet as clearly differentiated as they soon became. Since a senior emperor was often forced to appoint a colleague under external pressure, the difference between the political implications of the two forms should not be exaggerated.

[9] For these and other public occasions in this setting, R. Guilland, 'Études sur l'Hippo-drome [de Byzance]', in *BS*, 28 (1967) pp 262 *seq*.

[10] Full references to the data on which this and subsequent generalizations are based can be found in Christophilopoulou—a very rich collection of material.

[11] Christophilopoulou pp 58 *seq*.

[12] Christophilopoulou's exaggeration of the discreteness of the two phases is most mis-leading in regard to the early period. Still more misleading is her interpretation of the first phase as secular and constitutive, the second as religious and ancillary. For some criticisms, see below, p 105. The identification of two ritual blocs is useful for analytic purposes, but remains an artificial construct: the variability of practice, especially in the early period, needs to be remembered even when, as in the present paper, a high degree of generality is aimed at.

newly-invested ruler. From the early seventh century, the coronation was performed inside a church.

It is probably due to something more than a coincidental loss of evidence that there is so little indication of rituals associated with Roman imperial inauguration during the period from Augustus to the fourth century. At least part of the explanation lies in the persistently republican ideology of the principate, expressed in the continuing importance of the paradoxical ideal of imperial *civilitas*, the emperor being expected to act as a holder of republican office, a 'citizen amongst his fellows.'[13] The waning of the western empire fostered the revival of a very different tradition in the east, that of hellenistic monarchy.[14] The continuous history of the Byzantine imperial inauguration ritual begins in the mid-fifth century,[15] and from the outset that ritual was set in a religious, and specifically Christian, framework. What might look at first glance like a purely military affair with the shield-raising, torques-crowning and raising of the standards by the acclaiming troops was punctuated by acts of religious observance which must be treated as part of the ritual process.[16] The evolution of the Byzantine ritual down to the early seventh century was characterised by an increasingly overt religious symbolism which affected every part of the inauguration and shaped its basic structure for the whole early medieval period, as the ninth- and tenth-century sections of the *Book of Ceremonies* show.[17] The importance of a single source, Corippus, in

[13] So, Alan Cameron, 'Bread and circuses: the Roman emperor and his people', an inaugural lecture in the chair of Latin language and literature, delivered at King's College, London, 21 May 1973, p 10. Compare also A. Alföldi, 'Die Ausgestaltung des monarchischen Zeremoniells am römischen Kaiserhofe', in *Mitteilungen des deutschen archäologischen Instituts, Röm,* Abt 49 (Munich 1934), and 'Insignien und Tracht der römischen Kaiser', *ibid* 50 (1935), both now reprinted as *Die monarchische Repräsentation im römischen Kaiserreiche* (Darmstadt 1970) especially pp 25 *seq,* 45 and 127 *seq.*

[14] N. H. Baynes, 'Eusebius and the Christian Empire', in *Annuaire de l'Institut de Philologie et d'Histoire orientales,* 2 (Brussels 1934) pp 13 *seq,* reprinted in Baynes, [*Byzantine Studies and Other Essays*] (London 1955) pp 168 *seq*; [F,] Dvornik, [*Early Christian and Byzantine Political Philosophy*], 2 vols, (Washington, D.C. 1966) 2, pp 706 *seq.* On the replacement of *civilitas* by an autocratic ideal by the close of the fifth century, see cap 8 of Alan Cameron, *Circus Factions* (forthcoming.)

[15] It is no coincidence that the first of the series of protocols in *BC*, that covering Leo I's inauguration, dates from this period. See Brightman, '[Byzantine imperial] coronations', in *JTS,* 2 (1901) pp 359 *seq*; G. Ostrogorsky and E. Stein, 'Die Krönungsurkunden des Zeremonienbuches', in *B* 7 (1932) pp 185 *seq,* and the important review of this by F. Dölger in *BZ,* 36 (1936) pp 145 *seq. BC* here draws on materials collected in the mid-sixth century by Peter the Patrician. See below, n 18.

[16] This is evident already with Leo I: *BC* I, 91, p 413. See also p 425 (Anastasius) and p 430 (Justin I.)

[17] *BC* I 38, pp 191 *seq.* For the dating of the two sections of this chapter, see Dölger in

Symbols in context

illuminating the formative developments of the later sixth century has now been brilliantly demonstrated by Averil Cameron,[18] who has noted too a second critical element: the role of the demes or factions of Constantinople[19] who intervened, sometimes decisively, in the making of several emperors in the sixth and seventh centuries and came to perform various ritual functions on state occasions, most particularly that of acclaiming both 'new' emperors and co-emperors immediately after their coronations.[20] What needs to be stressed is the contemporaneity of the two main trends. The 'liturgification'[21] of the imperial inauguration, its climax the diadem-crowning by the patriarch in

---

BZ, 36 (1936) pp 149 *seq*. The originally military rituals of shield-raising and torques-crowning went out of use from the seventh century: Christophilopoulou pp 60 *seq*. Less convincing is her explanation in terms of a 'demilitarization' of ritual corresponding to the seventh-century hellenisation of Byzantine society: so also, following her almost verbatim, A. N. Stratos, *Byzantium in the Seventh Century* (Amsterdam 1968) I, pp 7, 49. But a ritual could be 'demilitarized', yet survive with other symbolic associations, as had already happened in the case of shield-raising in the sixth century and again, with its revival, in the late Byzantine period: see H. P. L'Orange, *Studies on the Iconography of Cosmic Kingship* (Oslo 1953) pp 87 *seq*; [E. H.] Kantorowicz, ['Oriens Augusti: Lever du Roi'], in *DOP*, 17 (1963) pp 152 *seq*; Ostrogorsky, 'Zur Kaisersalbung und Schilderhebung [im spätbyzantinischen Krönungszeremoniell]', in *Historia* 4 (Wiesbaden 1955) esp pp 254 *seq*. I prefer to attribute its disappearance less to conscious abandonment than to long disuse: there were no 'new' emperors between 610 and 695. For the iconographic tradition, its earliest form dating 'possibly' from the sixth century, see Walter, 'Raising on a shield', p 167 and *passim*. As for the torques-crowning, the growing importance of the diadem and the practical need to avoid an awkward 'double coronation' sufficiently account for its omission from the inauguration ritual: see [W.] Ensslin, 'Zur Torqueskrönung [und Schilderhebung bei der Kaiserwahl]', in *Klio*, 35 (Leipzig 1942) p 292.

[18] In her forthcoming edition of Corippus, [*In laudem Iustini Augusti minoris*] (London 1976), especially in section 7 of her introduction and the notes to II, lines 84 *seq* and 159 *seq*. For the increasing interest, in precisely this period, both in ritual and in the imperial ideology behind it, evidence can be found in the work of Peter the Patrician: see [A.] Pertusi, ['I principi fondamentali della concezione del potere a Bisancio. Per un commento al dialogo "Sulla scienza politica" attribuito a Pietro Patrizio (secolo VI)'] in *Bulletino del Istituto Storico Italiano per il Medio Evo*, 80 (Rome 1968) pp 1 *seq*.

[19] Corippus, notes to II, lines 308 *seq*. The forthcoming book of Alan Cameron will reassess the role of the demes in politics and ritual. See however, meanwhile, A. Maricq, 'La durée du régime des partis populaires à Constantinople', in *Bulletin de l'Académie Royale de Belgique*, Cl. des Lettres, 35 (Brussels 1949) pp 64 *seq*, and [H.-G.] Beck, 'Konstantinopel. [Zur Sozialgeschichte einer frühmittelalterlichen Hauptstadt'], in *BZ*, 63 (1965) pp 35 *seq*.

[20] *BC* I 38 especially section b: 'Ἀκτολογία τῶν δήμων ἐπὶ στεψίμῳ βασιλέως.'

[21] For this process, see Treitinger, [*Die oströmische Kaiser- und Reichsidee nach ihrer Gestaltung im höfischen Zeremoniell*] (2 ed Darmstadt 1956) pp 27–8. Treitinger presents rich illustrative material, but his analysis of the critical sixth-century development includes an identification of *Liturgisierung* with *Verkirchlichung* which, in my view, is misconceived because it presupposes a radical discontinuity between the categories 'secular'

Hagia Sophia, proceeded along with, not at the expense of, the growing involvement of the groups representative of the people of Constantinople and so of the whole empire.[22] I leave for my final section a discussion of the significance of this twofold development. Let us turn now to the west. There is very little evidence concerning royal inauguration rituals among Germanic peoples before the church became involved here. It is possible that in many cases, regular ritual procedures did not exist, in the absence either of permanent political communities or of permanent kingships.[23] The merovingian dynasty, as Grierson has pointed out,[24] was atypical in its relative stability, and yet, sacral features notwithstanding, it seems to have lacked a fixed ritual for the transmission of royal power.[25] More relevant is the absence of any barbarian inauguration ritual exclusive to kingship: rather, the *rex* was a household-lord writ large, whose succession to his inheritance was thus aptly signified when he took his place on the high-seat in the paternal hall or beat the bounds of the paternal property. Similarly, the

---

and 'ecclesiastical'. The term 'ritualization', accommodating religious action both inside and outside the physical location of a church, seems more apt here: *BC* is concerned as much with the one as the other. Treitinger's misconception generated the conclusion that *Liturgisierung* was operative 'only' in the realm of ideas. See p 28, n 84: 'Trotz alledem bleibt . . . der Gedankengehalt der verkirchlichten Riten und Zeremonien *nur gedankliche Haltung* . . ."Verkirchlichung" bedeutet also *nicht praktisch und rechtlich* grösseren Einfluss der Kirche auf den Kaiser.' (my stress.)

[22] See Beck, 'Senat und Volk [von Konstantinopel]', in *SBAW* PhK (1966) pp 18–19.

[23] See E. A. Thompson, *The Early Germans* (Oxford 1965) pp 32 *seq*; [J. M.] Wallace-Hadrill, [*Early Germanic Kingship in England and on the Continent*] (Oxford 1971) pp 7–8. A primitive Indo-European inauguration ritual persisted for Irish kings: see D. A. Binchy, *Celtic and Anglo-Saxon Kingship* (Oxford 1970) pp 11 *seq*; F. J. Byrne, *Irish Kings and High Kings* (London 1973) pp 15 *seq*. The relative scarcity of Germanic evidence is apparent in O. Höfler, 'Der Sakralcharakter des germanischen Königtums', in *Das Königtum. [Seine geistigen und rechtlichen Grundlagen,]* Vorträge und Forschungen 3 (Lindau-Konstanz 1956) pp 85 *seq*, and R. Wenskus, *Stammesbildung und Verfassung* (Cologne/Graz 1961) pp 482 *seq*. Compare W. Baetke, 'Zur Frage des altnordischen Sakralkönigtums', in *Kleine Schriften* (Weimar 1973) pp 146–7.

[24] 'Election and inheritance in early Germanic Kingship', in *CHJ*, 7 (1941) pp 1–22.

[25] [R.] Schneider, [*Königswahl und Königserhebung im Frühmittelalter*] (Stuttgart 1972) pp 190 *seq*, deals very fully with this problem, rejecting the extreme view of K. Hauck, 'Von einer spätantiken Randkultur zum karolingischen Europa', in *Frühmittelalterliche Studien,* 1 (Berlin 1967) pp 30 *seq*, and recognising, p 260, that no *fest verbindliche Schema* existed, though the merovingians clearly had some kind of *Erhebungszeremoniell*. [K.-U.] Jäschke, ['Frühmittelalterliche Festkrönungen?'], in *HZ*, 211 (1970) pp 580 *seq*, argues persuasively against merovingian crown-wearing or (by implication, *a fortiori*) coronation. Enthronement may have been the norm in the seventh century. Schneider, pp 226–7 and 259, discusses possible clerical influence on late merovingian and Lombard *Königszeremoniell* but the relevance of this to inauguration practices remains problematical.

Symbols in context

dux was set up through rituals of shield-raising and investiture with weapons which were common to all lords of military followings.[26] As our concern is with the inauguration of medieval kings as such, we should concentrate on the period when the characteristics of *rex* and *dux* were becoming fused. The transformative role of the Christian church in the production of this synthesis was critical: what D. H. Green has shown of the linguistic evidence on the origins of kingship[27] seems equally true of royal ritual. Just as Christian clergy were responsible for the formulation of a clearly-defined ideology of kingship as office, so they created (in part, from ingredients ready to hand) rituals to inaugurate the officers.[28] Conversion to Christianity in itself did not immediately bring about these consequences. If the delay in the ritualisation of ruler-making in the empire was caused by the persistence of a rival ideology, in the post-Roman west a similar and more prolonged delay occurred for other reasons. One was the barbarians' consciousness of inhabiting, in Hauck's phrase, 'late antique marginal cultures'; another was the existence of an ideological vacuum, filled only, I suggest, when barbarian élites had fully appropriated (and in so doing remoulded) Christianity. This happened in Visigothic Spain precociously in the seventh century, in England and Gaul in the eighth and ninth centuries, and in east Francia in the tenth century. The outcome so far as royal inaugurations were concerned was broadly common to all these realms: the local hierarchy took over the essential procedures of king-making, made of them a liturgical rite whose central act was the anointing, preceded by the acceptance of conditions by the new office-holder (a foreshadowing, this, of the later coronation oath) and followed by an investiture with weapons and other insignia, usually including a crown.[29]

26 [W.] Schlesinger, 'Herrschaft und Gefolgschaft', in *HZ*, 176 (1953) pp 225–75, and 'Über germanisches Heerkönigtum', in *Das Königtum*, pp 105–41, both now reprinted in *Beiträge [zur deutschen Verfassungsgeschichte des Mittelalters]* (Göttingen 1963) especially pp 26, 35 and 80–1. On the usefulness and the limitations of the typological distinction between *rex* and *dux*, see the sensible remarks of Wallace-Hadrill, pp 14 *seq.*

27 *The Carolingian Lord* (Cambridge 1965) especially pp 223 *seq*, 378 *seq.* Green does not refer to the work of F. Graus, who, from a different standpoint, reaches similar conclusions in 'Über die sogenannte germanische Treue', in *Historica*, 1 (Prague 1959) pp 71–121 and 'Herrschaft und Treue', *ibid* 12 (1966) pp 5–44.

28 F. Kern, *Gottesgnadentum und Widerstandsrecht im früheren Mittelalter*, rev ed R. Buchner (Münster 1954) pp 46 *seq*; Wallace-Hadrill, 'The Via Regia of the Carolingian Age', in *Trends in Medieval Political Thought*, ed B. Smalley (Oxford 1965) pp 27 *seq*; [W.] Ullmann, '[Der] Souveränitätsgedanke [in den mittelalterlichen Krönungsordines]', in *Festschrift P. E. Schramm* (Wiesbaden 1964) pp 81–2.

29 E. Müller, 'Die Anfänge der Königssalbung im Mittelalter', in *HJch* 58 (1938) pp 322

This necessarily brief introduction has served to throw into relief the contrast between the inauguration rituals of east and west. For, although the attention of students of western *Staatssymbolik* in this early period has been focussed on eastern influences, on Byzantium as 'schoolmistress' of the west,[30] more fundamental than any east-west borrowings, it seems to me, is the difference between the inauguration rituals practised in the two main areas of Christendom. Here, again, is our problem. But before offering a possible explanation, it is necessary to clear the ground of a misconception according to which a contrast is seen in terms of Byzantine secular ceremonial on the one hand, western ecclesiastical rite on the other. (I prefer to use the term 'ritual'[31] to transcend what seems to me a false distinction in the context of medieval Christendom, western *and* eastern.) The misconception arises from a widely-held interpretation of the Byzantine inauguration as essentially 'secular'. The original constitutive moment, it is held, was the extra-ecclesiastical elective *Augustus*-acclamation at the beginning of the ritual. The Byzantine emperor, on this view, 'never stood in any need of coronation.'[32] And, in any case, this allegedly unnecessary

---

seq; [C. A.] Bouman, [*Sacring and Crowning*] (Groningen 1957); Schneider pp 190 *seq*, and also pp 52 *seq* for developments in the Lombard kingdom cut short in the eighth century. I have attempted a comparative survey in 'National synods, [kingship as office, and royal anointing: an early medieval syndrome]' in *SCH*, 7 (1971) pp 41 *seq*, though I should now take a different view of the English evidence. The best analysis of the structure of these rituals remains A. M. Hocart, *Kingship* (Oxford 1927) pp 70 *seq*. See now also the fine paper of M. Fortes, 'Of Installation Ceremonies', in *Proceedings of the Royal Anthropological Institute for 1967* (London 1968) pp 5 *seq*.

[30] P. E. Schramm, *Herrschaftszeichen und Staatssymbolik*, 3 vols (Stuttgart 1954–6) 1 pp 30 *seq*, and *passim*; J. Deér, 'Byzanz und die Herrschaftszeichen des Abendlandes', in *BZ*, 50 (1957) pp 405 *seq*, and in *BZ*, 54 (1961) pp 58 *seq*; Jäschke, pp 571 *seq*; Schneider pp 232–3, 260. For Schramm's fundamental contribution here, see the interesting historiographical survey of J. Bak, 'Medieval Symbology of the State', in *Viator*, 4 (Berkeley 1973) pp 33 *seq*, especially 59–60.

[31] I distinguish the term 'ritual' from 'ceremonial' along lines suggested by Goody, 'Religion and Ritual: the Definitional Problem', in *British Journal of Sociology*, 12 (London 1961) pp 142 *seq*. The behaviour we are presently concerned with has the public and collective characteristics of ceremonial, but it also has the religious and, from the actors' standpoint, the purposive characteristics of ritual. Compare the careful distinction drawn by S. MacCormack, ['Change and Continuity in Late Antiquity: the Ceremony of Adventus'], in *Historia*, 21 (1972) p 722. [S.] Tambiah, [*Buddhism and the Spirit-cults in North-East Thailand*] (Cambridge 1970) p 35 and *passim*, is an exemplary study of ritual as 'cosmology in action' in the context of another world-religion.

[32] So Treitinger pp 27–8. For similar views, see Sickel pp 524–5; Dölger, *Byzanz* [*und die europäische Staatenwelt*] (Ettal 1953) pp 292–3; [A.] Michel, [*Die Kaisermacht in der Ostkirche*] (Darmstadt 1959) pp 166 *seq*.

Symbols in context

coronation was itself a piece of secular ceremonial, the patriarch acting as the 'foremost Byzantine citizen',[33] or 'the representative of the state'.[34] More recently, Christophilopoulou has advanced a rather different view: she has claimed that the removal of the coronation from such locations as the palace or the Hippodrome to the inside of a church created 'a new constitutional situation'. The coronation now 'assumed a religious character and became remote from legal consequences'.[35] Which interpretation is correct? Both—and neither. The coronation was a constitutive in the sense that it was part of the process which *as a whole* legitimised co-emperor and 'new' emperor alike, a part which, since in practice throughout Byzantine history it was never dispensed with, can be labelled 'dispensable' only at the risk of some artificiality, not to say anachronism.[36] Further, the reality of Byzantine belief and practice (in contrast to illusions which some modern scholars have cherished), and never more so than in the sixth century, makes nonsense of any interpretation that depends on isolating religious and secular ritual components. Might these categories, along with the implicit assumption of their institutionalisation in 'Church' and 'State', represent unconscious imports from later medieval western history? They have little meaning in the contest of early medieval Byzantium.

Of course, the clerical hierarchy existed as a specialist institution in eastern as in western christendom. But in Byzantium it produced no hierocratic theory, laid no claim to monopolise active participation in the church—which in a sociological sense was coterminous with the

[33] Treitinger p 30.

[34] Bury, [*The*] *Constitution* [*of the Later Roman Empire*] (Cambridge 1910) p 12. Compare Ensslin, 'The Emperor and Imperial Administration', in *Byzantium*, ed Baynes and H. St. L. B. Moss (Oxford 1948) p 270; 'The Patriarch officiated . . . not as representative of the Church but as representative of the electors.'

[35] Christophilopoulou pp 61–2. But this view rests on questionable assumptions.

[36] For the coronation as in some sense 'essential', see Ostrogorsky, in *BZ*, 41 (1941) pp 213 *seq*; L. Bréhier, *Les Institutions de l'Empire Byzantin* (2 ed Paris 1970) p 17; J. M. Hussey, *The Byzantine World* (4 ed London 1970) p 83. Compare also the cautious remarks of Baynes pp 34–5, and Guilland, *Études Byzantines* (Paris 1959) p 210. Still valuable are the comments of Bury, *Constitution*, pp 9 *seq*, 35–6. The extreme argument of [P.] Charanis, 'Coronation [and its constitutional significance in the later Roman Empire]', in *B* 15 (1940/1) pp 49 *seq*, claiming a 'constitutive' role for 'the Church', was effectively rebutted by Dölger, in *BZ*, 43 (1950) pp 146–7. C. Tsirpanlis, ['The Imperial Coronation and Theory in "De Cerimoniis"'], in Κληρονομία, 4 (Thessaloniki 1972) pp 63 *seq*, criticises Charanis without using all the recent literature on the subject. He also wrongly asserts that 'the British' have followed 'the German scholars' in accepting Sickel's opinion. This is hardly true of Bury, Baynes or Hussey. But Tsirpanlis here cites only A. E. R. Boak—an American!

community of Christian believers. The divine will was believed to operate directly through all members of this community. Thus sixth-century theorists focussed not on the coronation (which they did not even mention) but on election and consent as the crucial elements in imperial inauguration. And in election and consent, leading officials, senators and people (Aristotle's πολῖται live on in our sixth-century source) are all involved in the expression of the divine choice, and precisely their coincidence generates a 'lawful succession' (ἔννομος ἀνάρρησις).[37] In such an inclusive cosmology, the patriarch took his place without friction alongside other channels of divine communication.

But whence his special qualification to crown 'new' emperors? It is worth stressing the uniqueness of his role here. The physical performance of the coronation in the ambo of Hagia Sophia underlines the fact that there was room for only two real actors in this drama.[38] Other clergy had no active share in the ritual,[39] nor did the priesthood have any collective role either as electors or as guardians of the regalia, which were kept not in a church but in the palace by imperial chamberlains.[40] The patriarch acted alone, and his position here corresponded to that of the emperor himself in relation to the inauguration of a co-emperor. Just as the senior emperor normally occupied a transcendent composite status at the head of both clerical and political hierarchies—an anomalous status expressed, for instance, in

---

[37] Pertusi pp 12 seq.

[38] The ambo of Hagia Sophia (from 563 to 1204) was described in detail by Paul the Silentiary, Ἔκφρασις τοῦ Ἄμβωνος τῆς Ἁγίας Σωφίας ed P. Friedlander (Leipzig/Berlin 1912) pp 257 seq, especially 297-8. J. J. Kreutzer, Paulus des Silentiarers Beschreibung der Hagia Sophia (Leipzig 1875) p 71-2, estimates the base-diameter of the ambo at 12 feet. The rather smaller elevated platform had also to accommodate the chamberlains who invested the 'new' emperor with the chlamys, and the portable table (ἀντιμίσιον) on which the insignia were placed: BC I 38, p 194. Compare the eighth- and twelfth-century ordines printed by [J.] Goar, [Εὐχολόγιον] (2 ed Venice 1730) pp 726 seq. On the manuscripts, see Brightman, Liturgies, pp lxxxvii seq, and 'Coronations' p 378, with the interesting conclusion that the rite itself remained constant 'from at least the end of the eighth century down to the twelfth.'

[39] The only other cleric mentioned in the ordines is the deacon, who recited the collect and summoned to prayer. BC I 38 makes no specific mention of the clergy, but assigns, on the other hand, a major role to the acclaimers: 'ὁ λαός' and 'τὰ μέρη'.

[40] BC I 38, p 194: 'οἱ τοῦ κουβουκλείου' Compare their role at Justin I's inauguration, BC I 93, p 428; and at Justin II's, similarly, fidi ministri, Corippus, II, lines 86-7. BC I 00 p 466 shows how the insignia were looked after in the 'οἰκειακὸν βασιλικὸν βεστιάριον'. See [R. J. H.] Jenkins, Commentary (London 1962) pp 64 seq, [to the De Administrando Imperii of Constantine Porphyrogenitus], ed Jenkins and G. Moravcsik (Washington, D.C., 1967).

the Melchisedech mosaics of Justinian's Ravenna,[41] or in the emperor's performance of certain liturgical functions and participation in certain liturgical privileges of the priesthood[42]—so, if there were no emperor, the patriarch as head of the clerical hierarchy, and at the same time a senior political dignitary, came to occupy for the time being the highest rank in the system.[43] In the act of coronation, the patriarch was not therefore priest as such, but, like the emperor himself, transcended the distinction between empire and priesthood. Bury and Treitinger were right then to regard him as 'representative of' a collectivity of citizens, but wrong in implying that that collectivity was anything less than a total society, religiously – as well as politically – defined. Thus the coronation was a religious act without being essentially ecclesiastical. The patriarch prayed: so did the demes through their acclamations. The Hippodrome no less than Hagia Sophia was a religious location.[44] Both were centres of the cult of the emperor, and through him, of the whole society. If imperial triumph was celebrated in the success of the charioteer, this was because all victory, like the empire itself, was believed to be divinely-authorised: (ἔνθεος βασιλεία, ἔνθεα ὅπλα).[45]

If then the coronation of a Byzantine emperor was a religious act, the contrast between eastern and western practice should no longer be

[41] E. R. Leach, 'Melchisedech and the emperor: icons of subversion and orthodoxy', in *Proceedings of the Royal Anthropological Institute for 1972* (London 1973) pp 5 *seq*, especially 12–13.

[42] Treitinger pp 139–40; Tsirpanlis p 86, n 8.

[43] For the position of the emperor, see B. Sinogowicz, ['Die Begriffe Reich, Macht und Herrschaft im byzantinischen Kulturbereich'], in *Saeculum*, 4 (Freiburg 1956) pp 450 *seq*; Dvornik pp 815 *seq*; D. A. Miller, 'Royauté et ambiguité sexuelle: symbolique de la monarchie à Byzance', in *Annales*, 26 (1971) pp 639 *seq*. The patriarch was of course ineligible for this position. For the role of ineligibles as 'stand-ins and stake-holders', see Goody pp 10–2: 'The stand-in serves as temporary deputy . . . It is as if the kingship cannot be allowed to lie vacant.' I am suggesting that the patriarch's role was analogous to that of the 'neutrals' cited by Goody.

[44] I cannot agree with the suggestion of Guilland, 'Études sur l'Hippodrome', p 264, that a patriarch would have to hurry away from the Hippodrome embarrassed. For the inauguration of a co-emperor here as late as 776, with the patriarch present, blessing the insignia on a portable altar set up in the kathisma, see Theophanes p 450. For the demes in Hagia Sophia, compare n 20 above. *BC* offers many examples of rituals flowing naturally from one location to another, all of them, and not only churches, having religious significance.

[45] *BC* I 63, p 281, and I 68 and 69, pp 303 *seq*, especially 321–2, show the Hippodrome ritual and acclamations. See J. Gagé, 'Σταυρὸς νικοποιός. La victoire impériale dans l'empire chrétien', in *Revue d'Histoire et de Philosophie Religieuses*, 13 (Strasbourg 1933) pp 370 *seq*, esp p 400 on the fusion of 'deux mystiques triomphales.' See now Alan Cameron, *Porphyrius the Charioteer* (Oxford 1973) pp 250 *seq*.

sought in a crude distinction between religious and secular, but rather, in differing conceptions of the sacred and the profane.[46]

I approach the problem now from the opposite side, taking as my entry-point the central feature of western inaugurations lacking in those of the east: the anointing.[47] In the rest of this paper, I consider three levels of meaning in the anointing ritual and try, through these, to explore the contrast between east and west.

1 Anointing in relation to its recipient, as a *rite de passage*.[48] Both western commentators, notably Hincmar of Rheims, and the western *ordines* themselves made clear that the anointing of a king was constitutive.[49] It incorporated the candidate into his office, changing his status. But it also changed the man, transmitting the divine grace by which alone he was enabled to fulfil his royal *ministerium*.[50] In the belief-system of the west therefore, the anointing was conceived in this as in other ritual contexts as dynamic. It performed a specific function, making the *electus* into a *rex*.[51] The coronation in the east, on the other hand, while it demonstrated an emperor's legitimacy in his right to the universally-recognised symbol of monarchy, the diadem,[52] did not confer qualification to rule. It constituted, instead, a recognition that the chosen emperor was already so qualified. For the absence in early medieval Byzantium of any theory of hereditary emperorship, and the continuing adherence to the principle of election, meant that an emperor, like the Dalai Lama, was strictly

---

[46] Compare M. Douglas, *Purity and Danger* (London 1966) and ed, *Rules and Meanings* (Harmondsworth 1973).

[47] Ostrogorsky, 'Zur Kaisersalbung und Schilderhebung', pp 246–9, has argued that Byzantine imperial anointing was a thirteenth-century import from the west. But this was a Comnenian innovation of the twelfth century: see Christophilopoulou pp 142–4, 210–11; Walter, 'Raising on a shield', pp 162, 171. For information on this matter, I am grateful to professor D. M. Nicol, who revises Ostrogorsky's opinion in a forthcoming article in *Byzantine and Modern Greek Studies*, 2 (Oxford 1976).

[48] A. Van Gennep, *The Rites of Passage*, ed and trans M. Vizedom and G. L. Caffee (London 1960).

[49] Ullman, 'Souveränitätsgedanke', p 77; and [*The*] *Carolingian Renaissance* [*and the Idea of Kingship*] (London 1969) pp 71 *seq*; Wallace-Hadrill pp 133 *seq*.

[50] J. Funkenstein, 'Unction of the Ruler', in *Adel und Kirche. Festschrift G. Tellenbach* (Freiburg 1968) pp 6 *seq*. For the gifts conferred through anointing, see the *consecratio*-prayer of Hincmar's *ordo* for Louis the Stammerer in 877, MGH Cap 2, p 461.

[51] Ullman, 'Souveränitätsgedanke', p 77 n 24.

[52] H.-W. Ritter, *Diadem und Königsherrschaft* (Munich 1965); Alföldi pp 263 *seq*; Jäschke pp 572 *seq*.

speaking found rather than made.[53] The electors were channels through whom a divine predetermination was manifested. Where a western king prostrated himself before his inauguration[54] a Byzantine emperor remained standing throughout his acclamation and coronation alike[55]. Thus the coronation, unlike the western anointing, effected no symbolic rebirth, was not dynamic: it was a static representation of a pre-existing fact, an articulated icon. In asserting the timelessness of the empire,[56] it precluded the possibility of true interregna. Hence the exercise of full governmental powers by a 'new' emperor during the time-lag between *anagoreusis* and coronation;[57] and hence also, I suggest, the absence in Byzantium of anything equivalent to the western 'coronation'-oath.[58]

2 Anointing as a liturgical rite, in relation to the performers. In the west, royal inaugurations were taken over by the national élites of ritual specialists, without whose interaction no ruler could thereafter be made. Some members of these élites used their indispensable ritual function to buttress claims to superiority over the secular power: *quod minus est a meliore benedicitur*.[59] The consecration of a king was regarded as a collective act performed by the episcopate as clerical

[53] Guilland, *Études Byzantines*, pp 207 *seq*: 'Le Droit Divin à Byzance', esp p 221. Compare Goody pp 21-2.
[54] 'Frühdeutsch' *Ordo*, ed C. Erdmann, *Forschungen zur politischen Ideenwelt des Frühmittelalters* (Berlin 1951) pp 83-7; 'Edgar' *Ordo*, ed Schramm, *Kaiser, Könige und Päpste*, 4 vols (Stuttgart 1968) 2, pp 233-41. Compare my comments in *SCH*, 11 (1975) p 46. The idea of rebirth was intimately linked with western conceptions of royal anointing: P. Oppenheim, 'Die sakralen Momente in der deutschen Herrscherweihe', in *Ephemerides Liturgicae*, 58 (Rome 1944) pp 42 *seq*; Ullmann, *Carolingian Renaissance*, pp 71 *seq*.
[55] Goar p 727. At the beginning of the *ordo*, the emperor bows his head in prayer. On the iconographical evidence, see A. Grabar, *L'Empereur dans l'art byzantin* (Paris 1936) pp 112 *seq*, and plate XXVII, 2. It is noteworthy that the theme of royal inauguration/ coronation, though not entirely absent from western baptismal liturgies, is particularly stressed in those of the eastern churches: every Christian becomes 'royal.' See T. Michels, 'Die Akklamation in der Taufliturgie', in *Jahrbuch für Liturgiewissenschaft*, 8 (1928) pp 76 *seq*. On the other hand, the Byzantine conception of imperial coronation as a mystic anointing did not essentially involve the idea of rebirth: see A. Michel pp 10 *seq*.
[56] H. U. Instinsky, 'Kaiser und Ewigkeit', in *Hermes*, 77 (Wiesbaden 1942) pp 313 *seq*.
[57] Dölger and J. Karayannopoulos, *Byzantinische Urkundenlehre* (Munich 1968) pp 51-2.
[58] The contrary view of Charanis, 'Coronation', pp 56 *seq*, must be rejected. Compare Treitinger p 30, on the 'obvious difference' between eastern and western practices.
[59] Heb. 7:7. For the claim that the pope was superior to the emperor whom he anointed, see, for example, Innocent III, *Das Register Papst Innozenz III über den deutschen Thronstreit*, ed W. Holtzmann (Bonn 1947) p 29, n 18. For a similar claim by Hincmar, see my paper, 'Kingship, law and liturgy in the political thought of Hincmar of Rheims' (forthcoming).

mediators of grace:[60] any laymen present had a relatively passive role as witnesses only. It can hardly be coincidental that the same period which saw the clergy assume this new function, with such notable long-term implications for medieval politics and society in the west, saw them also asserting their status as a corporate élite of *oratores*, increasingly separated from the laity by their own law, their own education-system, their monopoly of the language of learning and, above all, of liturgy.[61]

Coronation, by contrast, could be performed by non-specialists. In the east senior emperors themselves crowned their junior colleagues, while in the west, before the crucial addition of anointing to the emperor-making ritual as practised by the papacy, Charlemagne could himself make his son co-emperor.[62] But senior emperors were not the only lay crowners in Byzantium: in the very early period, 'new' emperors were crowned by a military commander and a dowager empress, and subsequently there is sporadic evidence down to the late tenth century of coronations of would-be usurpers by demesmen and soldiers.[63]

The Byzantine inauguration ritual was never devised and managed exclusively by clerics. Its details were revised by the emperors themselves, according to Constantine Porphyrogenitus, 'in whatever way each thinks fit.'[64] It was shaped by a range of participants including the acclaimers[65]—officials, senators, demesmen, soldiers: in this context, all were ritual specialists now. The absence of any clerical monopoly may be related to the general position of the clergy in Byzantine society.[66] The eastern priesthood never conceived of itself as a discrete

---

[60] See the rubrics of the early medieval ordines in Bouman pp 165 *seq*.

[61] J. Le Goff, 'Note sur société tripartite, idéologie monarchique et renouveau économique dans la chrétienté du IXe au XIIe siècle', in *L'Europe au IXe au XIe Siècle*, ed T. Manteuffel and A. Gieysztor (Warsaw 1968) pp 63 *seq*; D. B. Loomis, '*Regnum* and *sacerdotium* in the early eleventh century', in *England before the Conquest. Studies presented to D. Whitelock*, ed P. Clemoes and K. Hughes (Cambridge 1971) pp 129 *seq*; and, for further references, my paper, 'National synods', pp 44–9. See also M. Richter, 'The Church and the Latin language: problems of communication in the medieval west' (forthcoming).

[62] The sources are discussed by [C.-R.] Brühl, ['Fränkischer Krönungsbrauch'], in *HZ*, 194 (1962) pp 276–7.

[63] Ensslin, 'Zur Torqueskrönung', pp 271 *seq*, gives evidence on the early cases; for Hypatius (532), see Malalas p 475; for Basil-Tiberius (717), see Nicephorus p 54; for Bardas-Phocas (987), see Skylitzes-Kedrenos, *Historiarum Compendium*, ed I. Bekker (Bonn 1839) 2, p 438. See also Jenkins, *Commentary*, p. 66.

[64] *BC* I 91, p 417.

[65] Treitinger pp 71 *seq*; Kantorowicz pp 156 *seq*.

[66] For much of what follows in this paragraph, I have relied on Michel, pp 27 *seq*, 56 *seq*,

Symbols in context

juristic corporation. A clear distinction was maintained between the canons, governing internal ecclesiastical organisations, and the laws, made and enforced by the emperor and covering a wide range of ecclesiastical affairs, including the formulation of doctrine. The emperor as law-maker directly implemented God's will[67]. There was no notion of the priesthood as unique mouthpiece of the divine law to which earthly law conformed. The Gelasian distinction between *potestas* and *auctoritas* could not even find linguistic equivalents in Greek.[68] In such imperial characteristics as philanthropy and providence, for the Byzantines as for their hellenistic forebears, power and authority were concentrated.[69] Politically, the institutional church revolved in the imperial orbit. The patriarch, who owed his position to 'the divine grace and our empire [derived] from it' (ἡ θεία χάρις καὶ ἡ ἐξ αὐτῆς βασιλεία ἡμῶν),[70] joined the *archontes* as a leading figure at court; and the synods summoned *by* the emperor engendered like-mindedness *with* the emperor rather than a specifically *episcopalis unanimitas* as in the west. Socially, the maintenance of cultural traditions through education remained to a considerable extent in lay hands.[71] Law in particular was laymen's business. The language of the eastern liturgies was intelligible to lay congregations.[72] The parish-priest, like the layman, could be married in law as in fact.[73] In all these

---

etc, and Beck pp 36 *seq*, 62 *seq*. See also D. Savramis, *Zur Soziologie des byzantinischen Mönchtums* (Leiden 1962) pp 81 *seq*, for some interesting perspectives, though important aspects of the subject are left untouched.

[67] For a clear statement, see the prologue to Justinian's Nov. lxxiii: "Ἐπειδὴ τοίνυν βασιλείαν διὰ τοῦτο ὁ θεὸς ἐξ οὐρανοῦ καθῆκεν ἵνα . . . τοὺς νόμους ἀρμόζῃ πρὸς τὴν τῆς φύσεως ποικιλίαν, διὰ τοῦτο ᾠήθημεν χρῆναι καὶ τοῦτον γράψαι τὸν νόμον καὶ δοῦναι ἐν κοινῷ τοῖς ὑπηκόοις.'

[68] There was no translation for *auctoritas* which conveyed the etymological link with *auctor*, or the legal-constitutional overtones of the Latin term. It was translated ἀξίωμα (dignity) in the Greek version of the *Res Gestae Divi Augusti*. In the sixth-century eastern law-schools, *auctoritate* seems simply to have been transliterated as αὐκτορίτατε, etc. See A. Dain, 'La transcription des mots latins dans les gloses nomiques', in *Revue des Études Latines*, 8 (Paris 1930) pp 96, 111.

[69] For φιλανθρωπία, εὐεργεσία, etc, see now D. J. Constantelos, *Byzantine Philanthropy and Social Welfare* (New Brunswick 1968) pp 43 *seq*; [H.] Hunger, *Prooimion*. [*Elemente der byzantinischen Kaiseridee in den Arengen der Urkunden*] (Vienna 1964) pp 84 *seq*, 143 *seq*.

[70] *BC* II 14, p 565.

[71] Beck, 'Konstantinopel', pp 24 *seq*; and 'Bildung und Theologie im frühmittalelterlichen Byzanz', in *Polychronion. Festschrift F. Dölger* (Heidelberg 1966) pp 69 *seq*, esp p 77.

[72] This feature is unusual among the great world-religions: see Tambiah 197–8. Byzantinists hardly seem to have recognised its significance. But for the neglect of Byzantine history by sociologists of religion see the critical remarks of Savramis p 5.

[73] For the social position of the lower clergy, see Beck, 'Konstantinopel', pp 28–9; and 'Kirche und Klerus im stattlichen Leben von Byzanz', in *REB*, 24 (1966) pp 22–3.

ways, the continuity and homogeneity of eastern society produced a firm integration within it of the institutional church which contrasts significantly with the tension endemic in the western situation. The absence of Byzantine imperial anointing should be seen in relation to the range of performers involved in the inauguration: among these, the clergy were naturally included, yet would hardly seek predominance as a sharply-differentiated élite, still less exploit any such role in a political contest. Where anointing presupposed a restricted group of clerical consecrators, coronation and acclamation, in manifesting 'him who reigned with God',[74] affirmed the divine inspiration operating through all the electors, and so expressed the complementarity of theocratic and democratic principles in Byzantine political thought.[75]

3 Anointing as a symbol. The meaning of the western ritual of royal (and imperial) anointing cannot be understood in isolation. Yet there has been a tendency for ecclesiastical historians simply to acknowledge parallels with one or another anointing ritual, for example those of baptism or episcopal ordination,[76] without attempting any kind of comprehensive systematic analysis of their interrelations[77] or social referents. As for the liturgiologists, they have confined themselves to the invaluable, but from this standpoint preliminary, work of collecting and describing the various rituals involving the use of anointing.[78] What has been neglected is the 'positional dimension' in

---

[74] Goar p 726: 'ὁ μέλλων σὺν θεῷ βασιλεύειν.' For the conception of the emperor as 'θεόστεπτος', see Treitinger p 37; Guilland Études Byzantines, pp 216 seq; Hunger, Prooimion, p 56.

[75] On the integration of the two principles, see Pertusi p 13. See also Guilland, Études Byzantines, pp 207 seq, and the important reassessments of Beck, 'Senat und Volk', esp pp 40–2, 51–2, and 'Res Publica Romana. Vom Staatsdenken der Byzantiner', in SBAW (1970) pp 7 seq. Compare the parallel duality in linguistic developments perceived by G. Dagron, 'Aux origines de la civilisation byzantine: langue de culture et langue d'état', in RH, 241 (1969) pp 23 seq, esp pp 49–50 on two tendencies: 'l'une conduisant à une Église hierarchisée et hellenophone, l'autre à une Église moins imperiale, plus diversifiée, cosmopolite et polyglotte.'

[76] [E.] Eichmann, [Königs-und Bischofsweihe'], in SBAW (1928); K. Hoffmann, Taufsymbolik im mittelalterlichen Herrscherbild (Düsseldorf 1968) pp 9 seq, with rich bibliography. The need for a comprehensive approach had already been suggested by Kantorowicz, The King's Two Bodies (Princeton 1957) p 52, n 22, and by Bouman, 'De oorsprong van de rituele zalving der koningen. De stand van een probleem', in Dancwerc, opstellen aangeboden aan D. T. Enklaar (Groningen 1959) pp 64 seq.

[77] But see the valuable, though brief, section, 'Die Personensalbung', in [R.] Kottje, [Studien zum Einfluss des Alten Testaments auf Recht und Liturgie des frühen Mittelalters] (Bonn 1964) pp 94 seq.

[78] See, for example, the rich material in [P.] Hofmeister, [Die heiligen Öle in der morgen- und abendländischen Kirche] (Würzburg 1948); [L. L.] Mitchell, [Baptismal Anointing] (London 1966); [G.] Ellard, [Ordination Anointings in the Western Church] (Cambridge,

which, as V. W. Turner has said, 'we see the meaning of a symbol as deriving from its relation to other symbols in a specific cluster or gestalt of symbols whose elements acquire much of their significance from their position in its structure.'[79] Such a cluster of symbols confronts us in the oil-rituals of the Christian church. Fully to explore the positional dimension of one such ritual is a task far beyond the scope of this paper. I want merely to suggest some lines along which we might start, lines relevant to our present problem in that they etch still more deeply the contrast between eastern and western Christendom.

In the world of antiquity, and especially in the near east, ritual anointing whether applied to things or persons transferred from the category of the profane to that of the sacred,[80] and in so doing defined boundaries. Here our concern is with rituals of personal anointing, and with the social boundaries these define. The prime function of personal anointing in the eastern church in the early medieval period was to initiate Christians.[81] The oil used for the post-baptismal anointing was made and used especially for this purpose. The chrism, a mixture of aromatics and olive oil, made the Christian: *christi dicti a chrismate.*[82] To a Greek-speaker, the linguistic association

---

Mass., 1933); [H. B.] Porter, '[The] Origin [of the Medieval Rite for Anointing the Sick or Dying]' in *JTS*, ns 7 (1956) pp 211 *seq*. [P.] Menevizoglou, [Τὸ Ἅγιον Μύρον ἐν τῇ ὀρθοδόξῳ ἀνατολικῇ ἐκκλησίᾳ] (Thessaloniki 1972), presents useful material on liturgical and doctrinal aspects, but is relatively weak on the early medieval period and neglects nearly all the major work done on this subject by such 'westerners' as Hofmeister and Mitchell.

[79] 'The syntax of symbolism in an African religion', in *PTRSL* no 772, vol 251 (London 1966) p 295. Turner's concept should prove useful to all students of symbolism. For insights into 'the concordance between symbolic and social experience', see M. Douglas, *Natural Symbols* (London 1970) p 64 and *passim*. J. C. Faris, 'Validation in ethnographical description', in *Man*, ns 3 (London 1968) pp 112 *seq*, implies that many anthropologists have yet to be converted to a recognition of the need to set symbols in a total cultural context. Faris also pleads for a diachronic approach.

[80] E. Kutsch, G. Delling and C. A. Bouman, art. 'Salbung', in *RGG* 5, cols 1330–6; [A. S.] Pease, [art. 'Oleum'], in *PW*, 34, cols 2454 *seq*, at 2466–8.

[81] Mitchell pp 37–8, 44, 53–4, 63–4; Menevizoglou pp 41 *seq*, 188 *seq*. Typically, in both eastern and western churches, simple oil was used for the pre-baptismal anointing associated with exorcism, and chrism (μύρον) for the post-baptismal anointing, associated with the gift of the holy spirit: see B. Welte, *Die Postbaptismale Salbung* (Freiburg 1939). An exception was the Syrian rite, which probably down to the fifth century had had only one, pre-baptismal, anointing.

[82] Tertullian, *De Baptismo*, 7, in *CC* 1, p 282. Compare Isidore, *Etymologiae*, VI, 50 in *PL* 82, col 256: 'Chrisma graece, latine unctio nominatur, ex cuius nomine et christus dicitur et homo post lavacrum sanctificatur.' For other liturgical uses of chrism, see [P.] Bernard, [art. 'Chrême'], in *DTC* 2, cols 2395 *seq*. For its composition, in the west from oil and balsam, in the east from these and a long list of additional ingredients, see Menevizoglou pp 29 *seq*. A basic recipe appears in Exod. 30: 23–5.

JANET L. NELSON

was immediately obvious: anointing was the essential ritual of incorporation in Christian initiation. It, if not baptism, had to be repeated when a lapsed member was being readmitted.[83] When the empire became Christian and the *oikoumene* synonymous with Christendom[84] (in thought if not in fact) it was natural for Christian initiation to be identified with membership of the Christian Roman empire. Ullmann has shown how the equation Roman = Christian operated in the carolingian west.[85] Was it not equally basic in a rather different sense, to the Byzantine world-view? The one boundary which that world-view required lay between the Christian and non-Christian worlds.[86] The Christian world participated actively in the *basileia*, ruled by an emperor whom, according to the opening prayer of the Byzantine *ordo* of *c*800, 'the Lord has been pleased to establish as king over the holy race bought by the blood of his son.[87] The non-Christian world passively acknowledged the superiority of Byzantium. The crucial threshold lay between the non-Christian, un-anointed, profane, barbarian outside, and the Christian, anointed, 'holy race' within. By means of chrism, Christian Byzantine society separated itself off from the external world of non-*christi*.

Conversely, the anointed, the Christian Romans, formed a single community, within which the emphasis was not on boundaries but on communications. Characteristic of Byzantine society were rituals of mass participation:[88] the processions of the emperor or of relics or images through the great cities, the *adventus*, the acclamations in the vernacular of the crowds in the hippodromes, and in the great churches the elaborate preparation of chrism by the patriarch 'before all the people.'[89] To the pure, all things are holy. This was a centripetal

[83] Council of Constantinople (381), cap 7, Mansi, 3, cols 563–4; Council *in Trullo* (692), cap 95, Mansi 11, cols 983–4; the Visigothic *Liber Ordinum*, ed M. Férotin (Paris 1904) cols 100 *seq.*

[84] Sinogowitz pp 452–3, Beck 'Christliche Mission und politische Propaganda im byzantinischen Reich', in *Settimane di studio del Centro italiano di studi sull'alto medioevo*, 14 (Spoleto 1967) pp 650 *seq.*

[85] [The] Growth [of Papal Government in the Middle Ages] (2 ed London 1962) pp 105 *seq.* For this equation in an eighth-century Frankish source, see M. Andrieu, *Les Ordines Romani du haut Moyen Age*, 3 (Louvain 1951) p 187 (*Ordo* XVII): 'romani devoti vel boni cristiani.'

[86] Baynes pp 19–20; Dölger, *Byzanz*, pp 70 *seq.*

[87] Goar p. 726: 'ὃν εὐδόκησας καταστῆσαι βασιλέα ἐπὶ τὸ ἔθνος σου τὸ ἅγιον, ὃ περιεποιήσω τῷ τιμίῳ αἵματι τοῦ μονογενοῦς σου υἱοῦ'.

[88] For what follows, compare n 45 above. See also Treitinger pp 71–2, 172 *seq*; Hunger, *Reich [der Neuen Mitte]* (Graz/Cologne 1965) pp 184–5; MacCormack pp 746–8.

[89] Theodore Lector, cited in *PG* 86, col 208, describes the practice 'τὸ μυστήριον (=μύρον) ἐν τῇ ἐκκλησίᾳ ἐπὶ παντὸς τοῦ λαοῦ ἁγιάζεσθαι', attributing its origin

Symbols in context

society,[90] integrated without being rigidly stratified, in which some careers at least were open to talent, emperorship remained elective, diverse lines of access, both institutional and personal, linked provinces and centre, and spiritual power was accessible to persons, monks and holy men especially, outside the institutional priesthood. As it came into being in the fifth and sixth centuries, as it evolved from the later sixth century with the 'democratisation' of culture, the growing importance of Constantinople itself, and the more pressing consciousness of struggling against an upsurge of surrounding pagan enemies along its boundaries, this society shaped new symbols. The liturgification of Byzantine public life, centred on the capital, reflected a new-found and increasing confidence, yes, but also and in the long run more fundamentally, a new inclusive social structure cemented by common religious belief and practice. Within this structure, it was relatively unimportant to demarcate individual functionaries or specialist groups as monopolists of spiritual power: hence the absence in the Byzantine world of personal anointings defining exclusive status, such as those of emperor or priest. All children born into this society qualified for anointing with chrism. Other personal anointings in the eastern churches had a similarly universal application. This was obviously so in the case of the anointing of the sick,[91] but such later practices in some eastern churches[92] as the anointing of every member of the congregation on great feastdays, of brides and grooms, of newly-delivered mothers and babies, all exemplify the use of anointing as an inclusive symbol, available to all Christians as such in their natural life-crises.

Turning now to the west, we find a different picture. There too, anointing during the early Christian centuries was associated with

---

to a fifth-century patriarch of Antioch. Theodore wrote in Constantinople in the early sixth century. For this and other evidence, see Menevizoglou pp 45–6.

[90] For the following sketch, I have drawn on the works of Guilland and Beck already cited; also Beck, 'Byzantinisches Gefolgschaftswesen', in *SBAW* (1965); and for the critical formative period, D. Claude, *Die Byzantinische Stadt im 6 Jht.* (Munich 1969) pp 121 *seq*, 156 *seq*; P. Brown, *The World of Late Antiquity* (London 1971) esp cap 14, and 'The Rise and Function of the Holy Man in Late Antiquity', in *JRS* 61 (1971) pp 80 *seq*. Hunger, *Reich*, pp 262 *seq*, gives evidence for the continuing significance of holy men throughout the early Byzantine period. Useful comparative perspectives on aspects of Byzantine society can be found in S. Eisenstadt, *The Political Systems of Empires* (New York 1967) esp pp 238 *seq*.

[91] F. W. Puller, *The Anointing of the Sick in Scripture and Tradition* (London 1904) especially appendix II. In these anointings only blessed oil, not chrism, was used.

[92] For details, see Hofmeister pp 226 *seq*.

Christian baptism, and, by extension, with curative functions.[93] The
critical change came in the various western realms between the seventh
and tenth centuries, when anointing began to be used in the initiation
of two specialised classes of people: clergy and kings.[94] Rome, it is
clear, had nothing to do with the origins of these practices, although
many popes from Stephen II onwards were quick to perceive the
implications of anointing rulers in terms of increased papal leverage.[95]
The origins lie north of the Alps. Scholars have long debated precisely where, and contemporary fashion seems to be veering again
towards identifying a penchant for anointings of various sorts as a
typically bizarre Celtic symptom.[96] (Douglas's 'bog Irish' have a long
pedigree!) But the evidence is very slim, and the whole question needs
re-examining in a broader context. In general, two explanations of
these ritual innovations have been offered. One is that the influence of
the old testament model proved irresistible—an especially popular
interpretation of Pippin's royal anointing in 751.[97] The other is epito-
mised in Andrieu's comment à propos the addition of a physical
anointing to the episcopal ordination just at the point where the
prayer-text reads, *Eum caelestis unguenti flore sanctifica*: 'Prendre ces
expressions au sens materiel et les traduire en acte dut paraitre
naturel,' especially when kings were already being anointed.[98] To
become chary of these explanations, we only have to look at the
Byzantine imperial *ordo* with its reference to David's anointing by
Samuel and its request to the Lord to 'anoint thy faithful servant with
the oil of exultation',[99] and then to recall that the Byzantines never

---

[93] For western baptismal anointings, see J. D. C. Fisher, *Christian Initiation: Baptism in
the Medieval West* (London 1965) pp 18 *seq*, 64 *seq*; Mitchell pp 80 *seq*. For the anointing
of the sick, Porter, 'Origin'; and for the magical properties assigned to chrism by the
laity in the west, Bernard col 2413.

[94] For ordination anointings, see Ellard; Andrieu, '[Le] Sacre [épiscopale d'après Hincmar
de Reims]' in *RHE*, 48 (1953) pp 22 *seq*; D. H. Turner, *The Claudius Pontificals, HBS* 97
for 1964 (1971) pp xxiv–vi. For royal anointings, see the works cited above, n 29, and
Kottje pp 94 *seq*.

[95] Ullmann, *Growth*, pp 67 *seq*, 143 *seq*.

[96] So, Porter, 'Origin'; Bouman pp xi–xii; Kottje pp 98–100; Schneider pp 197–8.
Earlier upholders of this view were Eichmann, pp 24 *seq*, and T. Klauser, reviewing
Ellard, in *JLW*, 13 (1933) pp 350–1.

[97] So, Brühl, p 304 with n 2, giving details of earlier literature.

[98] Andrieu, 'Sacre', p 41, n 5.

[99] Goar, p 726: 'τὸν πιστόν σου δοῦλον . . . χρῖσαι καταξίωσον τῷ ἐλαίῳ τῆς ἀγαλλιάσεως'.
For the influence of the old testament on Byzantine ideology, see Baynes, pp 33 *seq*,
and, especially relevant to the present context, Walter pp 168–72. See also above, n 55,
for the Byzantine conception of mystical anointing—in Walter's terms, an 'ideological'
rather than a 'historical' theme.

drew the allegedly 'natural' conclusion, any more than western christians had before the seventh century. It remains legitimate to ask why western kings and priests began to be anointed as and when they did. The question can be posed in terms of the interpretation I have already suggested for the anointing-ritual itself: why were these categories of person specially and now so emphatically marked off from other members of the *populus christianus*? Why were they alone now the 'twice-born'?[100] Why did the chrism, in the west as in the east long since the symbol of incorporation—*illud unde christo incorporemur et unde omnes fideles sanctificantur*[101]—now acquire the further function of marking off internal boundaries within a Christian society? In the various western realms, this development followed closely, indeed presupposed, the achievement of a permanent political and cultural synthesis between Christian (with all that implied in terms of Roman survivals) and barbarian elements: in Visigothic Spain, in late merovingian Gaul, in eighth-century England, and in Ottonian Germany.[102] The barbarians asserted not only their political independence with the creation of their kingdoms of *gentes*, but also their cultural autonomy within Christendom in the sense that, as well as assimilating something of Roman christianity, they imposed new demands and new interpretations on the religion that was now their own. Barbarian clergy innovated. Rome spoke—and also adapted. For the differentiation of hierarchical grades and functions was congenial enough to the Roman church itself. If the anointing of kings made difficulties for the papacy in the age of the Gregorian reform, the anointing of members of the *sacerdotium*, which Rome had finally imported from the north, was found to provide a very practical instrument of demarcation.[103]

For this, surely, was the significance of anointing: the reinforcement

---

[100] For this conception in Hinduism, see Van Gennep pp 104–6, and L. Dumont, *Homo Hierarchicus*, English trans (London 1970) pp 106–7. The analogous linkage of the ideas of rebirth and hierarchy in western Christendom would repay further investigation.

[101] Council of Tours (461), *Mansi* 7, col 949.

[102] For very perceptive comments on this synthesis, see H. Löwe, 'Von Theoderich der Grossen zu Karl dem Grossen. Das Werden des Abendlandes im Geschichtsbild des frühen Mittelalters', in *DA*, 9 (1952) pp 353 *seq*, and, from a different standpoint, the fine analysis of P. Anderson, *Passages from Antiquity to Feudalism* (London 1974) pp 120 *seq*.

[103] For the imperialist interpretation of the anointings of kings and emperors, see *MGH, Li*, 1, p 467; 1, p 566; 2, p 538. But for sacerdotal anointing as helping to define functional boundaries, compare the argument of cardinal Humbert, *ibid* 1, p 234, on the workings of the holy spirit: 'Ipse sanctum chrisma instituit, ipse clericorum vel ministrorum diversos gradus et officia in ecclesia disposuit'.

of stratification, the sharp delineation of restricted channels of access to supernatural power, the specification of those offices which guaranteed the identity and continuity of new political communities. Ritual, in the hands of barbarian priests, defined the holders of theocratic power. For justification the old testament, for clarification the church's law, lay ready to hand. But these *auctoritates* were servants whose utility depended on their relevance to the makers of ritual. The western societies within which and for which the new rituals were designed differed profoundly from the society of Byzantium. They were at once simpler and more highly stratified, they were self-consciously dynamic, assertive. The anointing of their power-holders on the one hand marked off the dominators from the dominated within, and on the other, through the exegesis of divine grace, legitimised that dominance both within, challenging the pagan ideology of *Adelsherrschaft*,[104] and without, asserting political independence in a world of *regna*.

But, finally, why should this one ritual rather than any other have been used for the purposes I have attributed to it? Why specifically anointing? We must expand the positional dimension. In the mediterranean world, olive oil was (and is) a basic commodity. Like corn and wine it was an essential foodstuff (nearly everything was cooked in it); it was fuel for lamps; and it was also soap, shampoo, cosmetic and every sort of patent remedy for ordinary men and women.[105] Outside the mediterranean zone, in temperate Europe, where even the agriculture of corn and vine was an alien imposition (and Duby has shown the implications of that revolution),[106] the olive simply cannot be cultivated.[107] Here, and so in the heartland of the

[104] For the persistent tension between kingship and nobility, see Hauck, 'Die geschichtliche Bedeutung der germanisch Auffassung von Königtum und Adel', in *XI International Congress of Historical Sciences* (Stockholm 1960) Rapports 3, pp 96 *seq*; Schlesinger, *Beiträge*, pp 28 *seq*. H. Hoffmann, 'Französische Fürstenweihen des Hochmittelalters', in *DA*, 18 (1962) pp 92 *seq*, discusses aristocratic imitations of royal insignia and ritual, but stresses that anointing was the one ritual never thus appropriated.

[105] Pease, 'Oleum', and art. 'Ölbaum', in *PW* 34, cols 1998 *seq*. P. D. King, *Law and Society in the Visigothic Kingdom* (Cambridge 1970) pp 212–24, draws attention to the particularly high penalty for damage to olive trees (as compared with other trees) in Visigothic legislation.

[106] G. Duby, 'Le monachisme et l'économie rurale', in *Il monachismo e la riforma ecclesiastica, 1049–1122*, Atti della IV Settimana internazionale di Studio, Mendola 1968 (Milan 1971) pp 336 *seq*, and *Guerriers et Paysans* (Paris 1973) pp 26–7, on the essential place of the olive also in the new *type d'alimentation 'civilisée'*.

[107] For the frequent use by geographers of the criterion of olive-cultivation in defining the mediterranean zone, see [F.] Braudel, [*La Méditerranée et le Monde Méditerranéen*

new medieval society of the west, there was a permanent oil-crisis. Flesh-renouncing monks had to have special permission to cook their vegetables in lard.[108] The ecclesiastical authorities had to proscribe the substitution of nut-oil, or butter.[109] For north-western Europe olive-oil was like pepper or spice, a luxury item. But it was one that northern churchmen insisted upon,[110] and that northern society was willing to pay for. The barbarians conquered the cultivators of the olive; their adoption of Christianity assimilated them to the oil-users. Their power-holders sealed their and their peoples' God-given domination by claiming an extra share of the oil which was both so potent and so scarce.

Within a single Christendom, a single liturgical tradition, personal anointings thus came to have contrasting significance in east and west. In Byzantium, they were inclusive, universally available; in the west they became, additionally, exclusive, defining internal as well as external boundaries. In each case the oil functioned through ritual as, in Douglas's sense, a natural symbol. The divergent social contexts which, for medieval participants, supplied the symbol's divergent meanings may, for the modern ecclesiastical historian, explain them.

University of London
King's College

à l'Époque de Philippe II] (Paris 1949) pp 139–41. See further R. Grand and R. Delatouche, L'Agriculture au Moyen Age (Paris 1951) pp 315, 365.

[108] Fragmentum historicum about the council of Aix-la-Chapelle (816), in MGH Conc, aevi karolini, 1, pp 831–5, at 833: 'Et quia oleum olivarum non habent Franci, voluerunt episcopi, ut oleo lardivo utantur.' Compare ibid, n 2, for the same problem in the eleventh century. In the present context, it is irrelevant whether this passage of the Fragmentum genuinely represents what happened in 816, or belongs with some eleventh-century special pleading: the ecological exigency was constant.

[109] Bede, PL 91, col 1097; Gregory VII, Register VII, 1. To natives of the mediterranean world, the use of butter appeared a very salient sign of barbarism: see Sidonius Apollinaris, Carmina XII, 7, and Braudel p 201, with n 4, for similar expressions of disgust in the sixteenth century. The symbolism of 'inside' and 'outside' arising from such divergent culinary practices deserves further study: in some ascetic traditions, dairy products are classed with flesh as 'impure', while olive-oil belongs unequivocally to the 'pure' vegetable category.

[110] R. Doehaerd, Le Haut Moyen Age Occidental. Economies et Sociétés (Paris 1971) pp 270–1, 274 with n 7. Compare also the indignant western rebuttals of ninth-century Greek accusations that Latins made chrism with river-water: Nicholas I, writing to the Frankish bishops, in PL 119, col 1155, and Ratramnus of Corbie, in PL 121, col 334. Were the accusations mere Photian canards, or did the Franks protest too much?

DID GREGORY THE GREAT KNOW GREEK?

by JOAN M. PETERSEN

TWO assumptions have been made by generations of scholars, including F. Homes Dudden,[1] Pierre Batiffol,[2] and in more recent times, Pierre Riché;[3] the first is that Gregory the Great, in spite of six years' residence in Constantinople as *apocrisiarius*, knew no Greek; the second, that he was totally ignorant of eastern theological thought.[4]

As we shall see later, there are good grounds for challenging both these assumptions, though it will not be possible in this paper to do more than to indicate the lines upon which the second of them may be answered. However, before we examine them, it would be as well to consider how far Greek was known and studied in Rome during the century and a half which preceded Gregory's birth in about 540, and in his own lifetime.

In the late fourth century the study of Greek in Rome began to decline. Greek studies were kept alive principally by two aristocratic groups. On the one hand there was the circle of Symmachus, Macrobius, and Praetextatus, who represented the old guard of paganism; on the other there was the group led by Jerome, which consisted largely of Christian aristocrats living on the Caelian and Aventine and included a number of devout ladies. The growth of what may be termed 'the translation industry', in which Jerome and his rival and former friend Rufinus[5] were intensely active, suggests that the day of the middle-class Greek scholar was passing, but that there was still some

---

[1] [F.] Homes Dudden, [*Gregory the Great: his Place in History and Thought*,] 2 vols (London 1905) 1, pp 153, 288.

[2] Pierre Batiffol, *Saint Grégoire le Grand* (Paris 1928) p 34.

[3] [Pierre] Riché, [*Éducation et culture dans l'occident barbare, VIe–VIIIe siècles*]. (2 ed Paris 1973) p 189.

[4] Homes Dudden pp 76, 288.

[5] Jerome translated: Didymus, *de spiritu sancto*; Epiphanes of Cyprus, *contra Origenem*; Eusebius, *Chronicle*; *The Canons of the Evangelists*; Origen, *Homilies on Isaiah, Jeremiah, Song of Songs, Luke*; Theophilus of Alexandria, *Anathemata*; probably Pachomius, *Regula*. All this was in addition to his translation of the bible. For the numerous translations by Rufinus, see M. von Schanz, *Geschichte der römischen Litteratur*, 4 vols (2 ed Munich 1914) 4 i, pp 415–23.

appreciation of the intellectual contribution made by Christians in the eastern empire.

Conditions in the period of disturbance and upheaval following the sack of Rome by Alaric and the Visigoths in 410 were hardly conducive to study. As evidence of the decay of Greek studies we may cite the cases of Celestine I (422-32), who had to carry on his correspondence with Cyril and Nestorius[6] with the help of an official Greek interpreter, Marius Mercator, and Leo I (440-62), who needed a Latin translation of the proceedings of the council of Chalcedon.[7]

Conditions for the revival of the study of Greek were lacking until the arrival of more stable government under Theodoric in 493. Once again this study was taken up vigorously by two aristocratic groups. The first was led by the great-grandson of the earlier Symmachus, the senator Symmachus. Its most famous adherent was his son-in-law, Boethius. These people formed a nucleus for the revival of hellenism in Rome itself; though they were themselves Christians, they did not propagate a specifically Christian form of Greek culture. It was far otherwise at the other great centre of hellenic culture, the monastery of Vivarium, near Squillace, which was founded by Cassiodorus in about 550.

Both these groups had a considerable long-term influence. Boethius's *de consolatione philosophiae* became one of the best-known and most influential books in medieval Europe. The activities of Cassiodorus's monastery resulted in translations which were widely read.[8] One wonders, however, whether these two groups had much immediate effect on cultural life in Rome and throughout Italy in their own day. It seems scarcely justifiable to speak of a sixth-century renaissance, as P. Courcelle has done,[9] since this term suggests a widespread movement of intellectual revival, whereas the activities of both Symmachus

---

[6] For the correspondence see *PL* 50 (1863). See also *HL* 2 i (1903) bk 9.

[7] Leo I, *Ep* 113, *PL* 54 (1881) col 1028.

[8] Cassiodorus applied the epithet *vir disertissimus* to two translators at Vivarium, Epiphanius Scholasticus and Mutianus. The most important of their numerous translations were the *Codex Encyclicus* (containing the letters of the bishops consulted by the emperor Leo, in favour of the council of Chalcedon); the three-fold *Historia ecclesiastica* of Socrates, Sozomen, and Theodoret (both the work of Epiphanius); *Thirty-four Homilies* of John Chrysostom on Hebrews (the work of Mutianus). The most famous of the translations produced anonymously was that of the *Jewish Antiquities* of Josephus. A third translator was Bellator, a priest, who besides writing biblical commentaries of his own, translated Origen's *Commentaries on Esdras*. For his possible status, see *RB* 39 (1927) p 228. He may well not have resided at Vivarium.

[9] P. Courcelle, *Les lettres grecques en occident* (Paris 1948) pp 17, 136.

and Cassiodorus, in their own lifetime at any rate, appear to have affected only small groups.

On the other hand, one must also ask the question whether sixth-century Rome really was the cultural desert that it is sometimes represented to have been.[10] There appear to have been at least two kinds of hellenic influence at work there. The evidence for the first of these, which may for convenience be called the western strain, since its principal practitioner was an Italian, would be even stronger if we could discover more about the curriculum of the school of Ravenna. It is difficult to find out much about the state of Greek studies there, but it seems that some instruction was available. Venantius Fortunatus (530–600), who studied there,[11] almost certainly knew a little Greek, though his knowledge was not always accurate.[12] Another former student of Ravenna, who is of greater interest and relevance for our purpose, is the poet Arator (*fl.* sixth century), who is actually mentioned by Venantius Fortunatus in his *Vita* of Martin of Tours:

> Sortis apostolicae quae gesta vocantur et Actus
> Facundo eloquio sulcavit vates Arator.[13]

The reference here is to the famous verse rendering of the Acts of the Apostles, of which Arator gave recitations in the church of St Peter-ad-Vincula.[14] These took place in 544, when Rome was being besieged by Totila, and would seem to have had the character of a solemn, quasi-liturgical function in wartime. Otherwise it would be surprising to us that there was an audience for Arator,[15] considering the pedestrian character of the poem itself. From its text it appears that Arator had some acquaintance with Greek authors, including Gregory

---

[10] For example, Homes Dudden p 56. But there is evidence to the contrary. The popes Pelagius I (555–61) and John III (561–75) were certainly Greek scholars. Pelagius, like Gregory the Great, was a man of senatorial family and, again like him, served as *apocrisiarius* in Constantinople. He has two claims to fame: first, through his knowledge of Greek, he was able to help to bring about the condemnation of Origenism in 543; secondly, he translated into Latin the so-called systematic version of the *Apophthegmata Patrum*, which forms book V of the *Vitae Patrum* (*PL* 73 cols 855–988). The translation of the material which forms book VI (*PL* 73 cols 993–1022), was completed by John III, whose origins are unknown.

[11] Paul the Deacon, *Historia Langobardorum, MGH SRL* (1878) p 79.

[12] Venantius Fortunatus, *Vita Sancti Martini, PL* 88 (1850) *ep praef*, col 363. Nam ἐπιχειρήματα, λέξις [sic], διαίρεσις, παραίνεσις . . . . Among the classical authors whom he mentions are Homer and Menander, the standard textbooks for beginners.

[13] *Ibid, PL* 88, bk 1, cap 22–3, col 366.

[14] In prefaces to numerous MSS. See Arator Subdiaconus, *Actus,* ed A. P. McKinlay, *CSEL* 72 (1951) pp xxviii *seq.*

[15] *Ibid.*

of Nazianzus and Justin Martyr.[16] The passage from Gregory of Nazianzus is from *Orat.* 4, which is not one of those translated by Rufinus, and no Latin translation of Justin Martyr was available until the sixteenth century. Arator's poem may not be to our taste, but at least we have evidence here of the existence of a cultured Christian public in Rome in the troubled times of the mid-sixth century, the period of Gregory's boyhood, who were prepared to attend readings of serious poetry.

Parallel with what we have termed for convenience the western strain in sixth-century hellenism in Rome is the eastern or monastic strain, of which the earliest example is the Scythian monk, Dionysius Exiguus, who had been summoned from Constantinople by pope Gelasius I (492–6) to put into order the collection of canons. During his years in Rome he was active as a translator and was in close touch with Eugippius, founder and abbot of the monastery of Lucullanum, which was noted as a *scriptorium*, and with Cassiodorus.[17]

After the death of Arator there is no representative of the western strain of Greek culture in Rome, apart from John III and then Gregory himself, should we consider him qualified for such a description in the light of further examination. He may, however, have been connected with an interesting representative of eastern monastic culture, Gregory of Agrigentum, who figures in his correspondence and is almost certainly identical with the Greek monk of St Sabas on the little Aventine, whose life was written by Leontius, abbot of the same monastery, in the mid-seventh century.[18]

It is against such a background as this that Gregory the Great's performance as a Greek scholar has to be evaluated. Let us return to the assumption that Gregory knew no Greek at all. This rests chiefly on the evidence of three short passages in his *Letters*, all of which have so far been taken at their face value. In the first of these, addressed to the priest Anastasius in June 597, he protests that he knows no Greek:

[16] *Ibid*, index *Auctores classici*, for details.
[17] The fame of Dionysius Exiguus is largely due to his invention of our present system of dating. Among the works translated by him are the *Vita Pachomii*; the περὶ κατασκευῆς ἀνθρώπου of Gregory of Nyssa. For a touching tribute to him by Cassiodorus, see *Inst[itutiones div[inae]*, ed R. A. B. Mynors (Oxford 1937) bk 1, cap 23, 2–3, p 62.
[18] *Gregorii [Papae] Registrum [Epistolarum]*, ed P. Ewald and L. M. Hartmann, *MGH Epp* 2 vols (1891–9) 1, *Epp*, bk 1, 70, p 89; bk 3, 12, p 171. The *Vita* by Leontius is in *PG* 98 (1865) cols 549–716.

Did Gregory the Great know Greek?

Quamvis Graecae linguae nescius.[19] This is repeated in a letter to Eusebius, bishop of Thessalonica, dated 601, with the apparently otiose information that he has never written anything in Greek *Nam nos nec Graece novimus nec aliquod opus aliquando scripsimus.*[20] Thirdly, a rather earlier letter, addressed to Narses in Constantinople in 593, is often cited; here the recipient is asked to convey Gregory's greetings to the lady Dominica, to whom, however, he is not sending a reply because, although she is Latin-speaking, she writes to him in Greek.[21] A further piece of evidence that is sometimes brought forward is that the writer of the *Liber Pontificalis* does not describe any pope as knowing Greek until Leo II (682–3),[22] after whom three others with this qualification are cited.[23]

There are, however, good grounds for challenging this assumption. These are furnished, in the first place, by Gregory's use of Greek words and phrases in his own writings. Such words and phrases may be said to fall into the following categories:

    1 Greek words in Greek characters.[24]
    2 Greek words transliterated for purposes of explanation.[25]
    3 Latin words of Greek origin.[26]
    4 Names of Greek writers.[27]

Secondly, there are certain passages in Gregory's writings which become more intelligible and significant, once it is established that he had some knowledge of Greek. Two of these have already been noticed. In the letter to Eusebius he makes the curious remark that he

---

[19] *Gregorii Registrum*, I, *Epp*, bk 7, 29, p 746.

[20] *Ibid*, 2, *Epp*, bk 11, 55, p 330.

[21] *Ibid*, 1, *Epp*, bk 3, 62, p 225.

[22] *L[iber] P[ontificalis*, ed L Duchesne], 2 ed with additions and corrections by C. Vogel, 3 vols (Paris 1955–7) I, p 359. But see n 10 above.

[23] The other popes mentioned as knowing Greek are John VI (701–5), *natione Grecus* (*LP*, I, p 383), Gregory III (731–41, *LP*, I, p 415), and Zacharias (741–52, *LP*, I, pp 434–5), the translator of the *Dialogues*. See Riché p 468.

[24] *Moralia, PL* 75 (1849) bk 5, cap 31, col 709; bk 7, cap 28, col 786; bk 9, cap 11, cols 867–8; bk 9, cap 15, col 874; *PL* 76 (1849) bk 29, cap 20, col 498; bk 29, cap 31, col 515; *Hom[iliae] in Evang[elia]*, *PL* 76, bk 1, XIX, 2, col 1155.

[25] *Moralia, PL* 75, bk 7, cap 28, col 786; *Hom in Evang, PL* 76, bk 1, VI, 5, col 1097; *Gregorii Registrum*, I, *Epp*, bk 7, 23, p 468.

[26] *Moralia*, all the following examples are from *PL* 75: *allegoria: ep miss*, 1, cols 512, 515; bk 3, cap 13, col 612; bk 3, cap 14, col 615; bk 3, cap 28, col 627. *hypocrisis*: bk 7, cap 28, col 786; *metacismus*: *ep miss*, 5, col 516. *mysterium*: *ep miss*, 1, cols 512, 515; bk 2, cap 20, col 573; bk 3, cap 13, col 612; bk 3, cap 28, cols 626–7. *mysticus*: *praef* 1, col 517. *prophetia*: bk 3, cap 28, col 627. *typicus*: *praef* 1, col 513. *typus*: bk 3, cap 28, col 626. This list is not, of course, exhaustive.

[27] *Moralia, PL* 75, bk 9, cap 11, col 865.

knows no Greek and has never written anything in it. The implication of this might well be that he can read and speak Greek but cannot write it. Again such an incorrigible punster as we know Gregory to have been,[28] might well enjoy teasing his friends; the written word does not at once convey the nuances of speech.

Once we assume that Gregory knew some Greek, a sentence relating to the superiority of Latin manuscripts as compared with Greek is no longer a manifestation of a narrow chauvinism but becomes a rational judgement based on personal experience.[29] Moreover it is unlikely that anyone who had not at least a reading knowledge of a foreign language (which in Gregory's case could hardly be anything other than Greek) would be able to offer the kind of practical advice on the subject of translations that he does in two instances: in writing to Aristobulus in February 591 he asks his correspondent, should it fall to his lot to translate his letters, not to do so word for word, but to convey the sense;[30] in a letter to Narses, dated June 597, he complains of the poor quality of the translators in Constantinople, who, when Latin is dictated to them, lack skill in turning it into Greek; they pay attention to the words but they do not grasp their sense, so that the translation is unintelligible.[31]

Gregory's concern at the difficulty of recruiting good translators suggests that he is aware of the difficulties involved in translation, of which he writes to Eulogius, patriarch of Alexandria in August 600, again complaining of the failure of the translators to grasp the sense of a passage.[32]

Finally a passage in one of the *Homiliae in Ezechielem* suggests that he may have been able to compare the original text of the septuagint with various translations.[33]

The argument from the evidence provided by the *Liber Pontificalis* does not really carry much weight. After all, the earliest popes must have known Greek, but this is never mentioned because it was well-known that the first Christians in Rome were Greek-speaking. In fact the writer of the *Liber Pontificalis* shows little interest one way or the other in the linguistic achievements of the popes until the great renaissance of hellenic studies at the end of the seventh century, which

[28] For example, Paul the Deacon, *S. Gregorii Magni Vita*, PL 75, cap 17, 18, cols 50–1.
[29] *Gregorii Registrum*, 1, *Epp*, bk 6, 14, p 393.
[30] *Ibid*, 1, *Epp*, bk 1, 28, p 41.
[31] *Ibid*, 1, *Epp*, bk 7, 27, p 474.
[32] *Ibid*, 2, *Epp*, bk 10, 21, p 258.
[33] *Homiliae in Ezechielem*, PL 76, bk 1, VII, col 852.

was so remarkable that it could not be passed over without notice.[34]

Yet the objection may well be raised that Gregory did, after all, himself say on at least two occasions that he knew no Greek. Why did he do so, if this was not the case? Or was his knowledge so superficial that it could be regarded as negligible?

The answer to the first of these questions lies in the practice which began in the fourth century, became widespread in the fifth and sixth centuries, and continued into the early middle ages, of using a self-deprecatory statement, known as a *confessio humilitatis*, in which the speaker or writer laid claim to a total lack of knowledge of a subject about which he nevertheless possessed at any rate a modicum of information. It is precisely this attitude which Gregory is adopting with regard to his Greek, and there are good precedents and parallels for it.[35] A relevant earlier parallel is found in Augustine's well-known description of his education in *Conf.* I. 13 and 14, where he complains that the difficulty of learning a foreign language rendered the study of Homer bitter to him: *Nulla verba illa noveram.* But the numerous Greek words scattered through his writings show that this was not literally the case.

The extent of Gregory's actual knowledge of Greek must now be considered. Here again a comparison with Augustine may be helpful, since both make similar use of such knowledge as they possess. In the first place, both are in the habit of using technical terms of Greek origin. Gregory's use of such words has already been noted. Augustine, writing three generations earlier, feels it necessary to apologise for this practice, another instance of a *confessio humilitatis*.[36] Both Gregory and Augustine are capable of using Greek words to illustrate shades of meaning which it is difficult to convey in Latin. The best-known example of this is to be found in the *de Trinitate*, where the exact meaning of the ambiguous word *vita* is being discussed: *quam vitam Graeci non ζωὴν sed βίον vocant.*[37]

There is only one parallel to this recorded in Gregory's works. In *Hom. in Evang.*, bk I, XIX, he is representing the hours at

[34] See Riché pp 393–6, 468 *seq.*

[35] Among the numerous examples of this *topos* may be cited: Ausonius, *Parentalia, PL* 19 (1846) *praef,* cols 841–2; Sedulius, *Carmen Paschale, PL* 19, *dedic,* cols 534–5; Venantius Fortunatus, *Miscellanea, PL* 88, bk 2, 13, col 102; Ennodius, *Epp, PL* 63 (1882) bk 7, cap 12, cap 17, cols 119, 122; bk 8, cap 36, col 145.

[36] For example, *de utilitate credendi, PL* 42 (1886) bk 3, cap 5, col 68.

[37] *de Trinitate, PL* 42, bk 12, cap 7, 11, col 1004.

which the labourers are hired (Matt. 20. 1–10) as the various stages in human life. The eleventh hour is the period of old age, and to demonstrate the honour in which the aged should be held, he employs Greek: *Undecim vero hora est aetas quae decrepita vel veterana dicitur. Unde Graeci valde seniores, non* γέροντας *sed* πρεσβυτέρους *appellant, ut plus quam senes insinuent quos provectiores vocant.*[38]

It is difficult to know to what Greeks Gregory is referring here, but it is worth noticing that πρεσβύτερος is used by Gregory of Nyssa to describe persons who are advanced in piety.[39] This forms a good parallel with *quos provectiores vocant*. The *Homiliae in Ecclesiastem*, where this use of πρεσβύτερος occurs, have never been translated into Latin, which suggests that Gregory the Great may have been acquainted with the Greek text.[39a]

The examples in the works of Augustine of Greek words cited in the text and of etymologies and 'explanations' are by far the more numerous and only a very few can be quoted here. Some of the Greek words are straight forward translations, such as *servitutem religionis, quam* λατρείαν *Graeci vocant.*[40] A typical Augustinian etymology is *platea a latitudine . . . quoniam Graece* πλατύ *latum.*[41]

Since the parallel examples in the works of Gregory the Great are fewer in number, it will be possible to examine all of those so far discovered. There are five etymologies of words written in Greek characters and three 'explanations' of transliterated words. One of the etymologies and two of the 'explanations' are derived from other writers; like Augustine, Gregory was prone to pass on secondhand material.[42]

The secondhand etymology is to be found in *Moralia*, bk VII. 28, where Gregory is making a comment on Isaiah 34. 13–14. The English of his Latin text is: 'There shall be a bed for dragons and pastures for ostriches. Demons shall meet with ass-centaurs and one satyr shall call

---

[38] *Hom in Evang, PL* 76, bk 1, XIX, col 1155.

[39] *Homiliae in Ecclesiastem, PG* 44 (1863) 1, col 629.

[39a] A further indication that Gregory the Great may have been acquainted with the works of Gregory of Nyssa is a reference to an incident described in the latter's *Vita* of Gregory Thaumaturgus in the *Dialogues. Dialogues, PL* 77 (1849) bk I, cap 7, col 184. See also *PG* 46 (1863) col 917.

[40] *de civ*[itate] *Dei, PL* 41 (1845) bk 5, cap 21, col 167.

[41] *Enarratio in Psalmos, PL* 37 (1845) 118, 10, 6, col 1527.

[42] A notable example of this practice is to be found in *de civ Dei*, bk 15, cap 23, col 563, where Augustine admits that he has taken over the etymology of Serapis from Varro (who incidentally gives it incorrectly).

to another.'[43] Of the ass-centaur he says: *Quid vero onocentaurum nomine, nisi et lubrici et elati? Graeci quippe* ὄνος *asinus dicitur et appellatione asini luxuria designatur*, thus following Jerome, who in commenting on the same passage uses the *onocentaur* as the symbol of a debauchee.[44]

One of his secondhand 'explanations' is also to be found in *Moralia*, bk VII. 28. In commenting on the same passage in Isaiah, about the satyrs, Gregory says: *Qui namque alii pilosi appellatione figurantur, nisi hi quos Graeci Panas Latini incubos vocant*. This explanation has been taken over from Augustine himself: *Silvanos et Panas quos vulgo incubos vocant*.[45]

The other secondhand 'explanation' is to be found in *Hom. in Evang.*, bk I. VI, where his explanation of *angelus* as *nuntius* is lifted from Jerome.[46]

It will be convenient to deal with Gregory's other 'explanation' here. In a letter to Theoctista, sister of the emperor Maurice, at Constantinople, he writes of the provision of beds for nuns, *ancillis Dei, quas vos Graeca lingua monastrias dicitis*.[47] His explanation of the word *monastrias* is interesting for our purposes, because in its Greek form it is used by ecclesiastical writers, such as John Chrysostom and John Moschus, and also by Justinian in the *Novellae*, which were originally written in Greek.[48] The same word is retained in transliteration in the Latin version.

We now turn to Gregory's etymologies. Two of these, which are to be found in *Moralia*, bks IX and XXIX respectively, may be cited as examples of his interest in natural phenomena. In both cases he is

---

[43] In places Gregory's Latin text of the book of Job is different from the original Hebrew and consequently from that of the AV and of modern English versions of the bible, which are based upon it. The *NEB* version of this passage is: 'It shall be rough land fit for wolves, a haunt of desert-owls. Marmots shall consort with jackals, and he-goat shall encounter he-goat.'

[44] Jerome, *In Isaiam*, PL 24 (1845) bk 6, cap 13, col 215. See also *Liber contra vigilantium*, PL 23 (1883) bk 1, col 339.

[45] *de civ Dei*, bk 15, cap 23, col 468.

[46] *Hom in Evang*, PL 76, bk 1, VI, 5, col 1097. See *In Matthaeum, Opera exegetica*, CSEL 77 (1949) p 79, and *Hieronymi Chronicon, GCS*, 7 (1913) bk 1, cap 18, p 105, together with German trans *ibid*, vol 5 (1911) p 57.

[47] *Gregorii Registrum*, 1, *Epp*, bk 7, 36, p 467.

[48] Justinian, *Novellae*, bk 1, 27 and 44, in *Digest*, ed Schoell and Kroll (Berlin 1899, repr 1954). Gregory's use of a word found in Justinian lends support to the view of Kassius Hallinger that he had studied Justinian and had been influenced by him as regards his conception of monastic rules and organisation. See 'Der Papst Gregor der Grosse und der heilige Benedikt', *SA*, 42 (1957) pp 73–164.

dealing with the origins of the names of the constellations. His derivation of the name of the Hyades appears to be based on Servius's
comment on *Georgics*, bk I, 138: *Hyades* ἀπὸ τοῦ ὑετοῦ; he says that it
comes from the Greek word ὑετός, meaning 'a shower of rain', the
Latin *imber*.[49] He is less successful in his derivation of the name Pleiades,
which he believes to come from ἀπὸ τοῦ πλείστου, *id est, a pluralitate,
vocatae sunt*.[50] (The word probably comes from πλέω = I sail, because
the Pleiades appear in spring, the sailing season.)

Gregory's other two etymologies are not altogether wrong. In
Moralia, bk IX. 16, he is commenting on Job 9. 13. The English of his
Latin text is: 'God whose wrath no one can resist and under whom
those who carry the earth are bent.'[51] He interprets *qui portant orbem*
as 'the kings of the earth'. The Greek for king is βασιλεύς, which he
believes to be derived from βάσις λαοῦ. Thus the kings are, as it were,
the pillars or basis upholding the weight of their people.

Gregory's derivation of *thesaurus* in *Moralia*, bk XXIX. 38, falls
within the same category.[52] Here he is commenting on Job 38. 22–3:
'Have you visited the storehouse of the snow or seen the arsenal where
the hail is stored, which I have kept ready for the day of calamity, for
war and for the hour of battle?' (*NEB*). His interpretation is that the
cold and hard hearts of wicked men are represented by the snow and
hail. Since the elect of God are chosen from among the wicked, God
has them in a *thesaurus*, that is, a storehouse or arsenal, among the snow
and hail. The word *thesaurus*, according to Gregory, is derived from
θέσις, and the object itself is so called because it is in a fixed position.
Gregory is right, in so far as θησαυρός and θέσις both come from
τίθημι, but neither can strictly be said to come from the other.

Both Gregory and Augustine frequently use Latin words of Greek
origin and there is little to be said in this connection, since it was a
normal practice among educated Romans. The only word of this class

[49] See *Moralia, PL* 75, bk 9, cap 15, col 867, for Gregory's derivation of the Hyades. A
common Latin name for this constellation (mentioned by Servius) was *Suculae* = the
piglets, a translation derived from ὗς, gen. ὑός, a pig. The u in this word is short,
as in ὑάδες, whereas the u in ὕω and in the impersonal form ὕει = it rains, is long,
which favours the former explanation.

[50] See *Moralia, PL* 75, bk 9, cap 15, col 868, for Gregory's derivation of the Pleiades.
The Latin name for this constellation is *Vergiliae* (Cicero, [*de*] *n*[*atura*] *d*[*eorum*], bk 2,
cap 44, 112; Isidore of Seville, *Origines*, bk 3, LXX). Isidore and Gregory may both
have seen the scholia of Servius on Aeneid, bk 1 (Hyades ἀπὸ τοῦ ὕειν) and *Georgics*,
bk 1 (Hyades ἀπὸ τοῦ ὑετοῦ) as well as the passage in Cicero, *nd*.

[51] *PL* 75, col 874. The *NEB* version of this verse is: 'God does not turn back his wrath;
the partisans of Rahab lie prostrate at his feet.'

[52] *PL* 76, col 498.

used by Gregory which is worthy of remark is *metacismus*. This occurs
at the end of his dedicatory letter to Leander of Seville at the beginning
of the *Moralia*. Here he is stressing that he has not paid excessive attention to the rules of style and grammar: *Nam sicut huius quoque epistolae
tenor enuntiat, non metacismi collisiones fugio.*[53] In other words, he is not
worrying about 'dotting the Is and crossing the Ts', as we should say.
Metacismus is one of the Latin forms of the Greek term μυτακισμός.
This word is used principally by the grammarians; the only other
instance of its use by a Latin writer, Gregory or a grammarian, appears
to be in the *Institutiones divinae*, where Cassiodorus is urging his readers
to avoid inelegancies of style: *Meotacismos [sic] et hiatus vocalium omnino
derelinque.*[54]

Lastly, there is the question of the names of Greek authors cited by
Gregory and Augustine. The list supplied by the latter looks very
extensive, but as has been pointed out by H. I. Marrou,[55] all of them
were available in Latin translations. Gregory's list is much shorter:
Hesiod, Aratus, and Callimachus.[56] Three translations of the *Phenomena* of Aratus would have been available to him,[57] and Hesiod and
Callimachus are both mentioned in the same chapter of Quintilian,[58]
which he might well have met during the tertiary stage of his studies
under a *rhetor*.

It is against this kind of cultural background and on the evidence of
his own writings that an estimate of Gregory's education and, in
particular, of his knowledge of Greek has to be formed. In point of
fact we know almost nothing of his education. Gregory of Tours tells
us that he was so skilled in grammar and rhetoric that he was second
to none in the entire city.[59] This statement is repeated with some
embroidery by Paul the Deacon; from both these sources we are given
to understand that he was pre-eminently successful in the traditional
course of studies. The stages of a traditional Roman education are
well-known: elementary studies under a *magister*, which included
Greek;[60] secondary studies under a *grammaticus*, and tertiary studies
under a *rhetor*. It is significant that Jerome appears to have been taught

[53] *Moralia, PL* 75, *ep miss,* 5, col 516.
[54] *Inst div,* ed Mynors, bk 1, cap 15, 7, p 45.
[55] H. I. Marrou, *Saint Augustin et la fin de la culture antique* (Paris 1948) p 33.
[56] *Moralia, PL* 75, bk 9, cap 12, col 865.
[57] By Cicero, Germanicus Caesar, and Avienus.
[58] Quintilian, *Institutiones,* bk 10, cap 1.
[59] Gregory of Tours, *Historia Francorum, PL* 71 (1849) bk 10, cap 1, col 479; Paul the
Deacon, *Vita, PL* 75, cap 1, col 42.
[60] *CIL,* 3 33929; Ferrandus, *Vita Fulgentii, PL* 65 (1892) bk 1, cap 4, col 119.

Greek by a *grammaticus* and reports that he learned further Greek during his rhetorical studies,[61] whereas Augustine seems to have had no more than a *magister*.[62] One suspects that Gregory was in the same position, but whereas Augustine was able to improve his Greek later in life, lack of time and pressure of business made it impossible for Gregory to do so.

Naturally it will be asked why a six years' residence as *apocrisiarius* in Constantinople did not help Gregory to improve his Greek. The short answer is that during that period he would have been living in an entirely Latin milieu. Constantinople, since its foundation by Constantine, had been very much 'the new Rome', a Latin-speaking enclave which, it was hoped, would spread Roman civilisation in the east.[63] At the time when Gregory arrived there, the hellenisation of official life was just beginning. Latin was still, and would be for some time to come, the language of the civil service, the military, the fire-brigade, and the church,[64] but in the university Theodosius II had long ago tried to ensure parity between Greek and Latin by decreeing that ten grammar teachers should be appointed for each language.[65] The tendency to learn Latin in order to pursue a successful career, which had been common in the third century, had evidently become less usual by the time of Justinian. Otherwise there would have been no need for him to give official instructions for the city magistrates to attend Latin classes.[66]

Thus Gregory would have been able to carry on all his official

---

[61] For the rhetorical studies, *Ep* XLIX, ed J. Labourt, II (Paris 1953) pp 133–5; for the elementary instruction under a *magister*, *adversus libros Rufini*, *PL* 23, bk 1, cap 30, col 441. The inference is that Jerome had a *grammaticus* for the intermediate stage of his Greek studies.

[62] In *Conf*, *PL* 32, bk 1, cap 13, 20, col 670, Augustine writes of the unsatisfactory teaching of Latin by the *magister*, but describes the pleasure that he found in his later studies. The inference is that in Greek, which on his own admission he disliked as a boy, he did not go beyond the stage of a *magister* as teacher.

[63] For the subject of Latin in Constantinople in general, see G. Dagron, 'Aux origines de la civilisation byzantine: langue de culture et langue d'état', *RH*, 141 (1969) pp 23 *seq*: L. Hahn, 'Zum Gebrauch der lateinischen Sprache in Konstantinopel', *Festgabe für Martinus von Schanz* (Würzburg 1912) pp 173 *seq*. For the social background, see P. Llewellyn, *Rome in the Dark Ages* (London 1972) pp 29 *seq*.

[64] For the army, see citation from the *Strategikon* (attributed to the emperor Maurice) by H. I. Marrou, *Histoire de l'éducation dans l'antiquité* (6 ed Paris 1965) pp 591–2; for the fire-brigade, John of Lydia, *De magistratibus*, *CSHB* (1837) bk 1, cap 50, p 162; for an interesting survival in the church, *Le livre des cérémonies*, bk 2, cap 83 (74), ed A. Vogt, 2 vols (Paris 1935–9), 2 (1939) pp 169–70.

[65] See Hahn p 180.

[66] John of Lydia, *de mag*, *CSHB*, bk 3, cap 29, p 222.

business and correspondence in his own language. His household consisted of Italian monks from his own monastery of St Andrew on the Caelian, and from what we know of his personal character, it seems unlikely that he took part in social life. Thus it seems unlikely that he would have had much intercourse with Greek-speaking people.

Once it is accepted that Gregory the Great knew a little Greek, the second assumption, that he was totally ignorant of eastern theological thought, will require more detailed examination than it can be given here. We have already seen that he may have had some acquaintance with the writings of Gregory of Nyssa, who is important for our purpose, because much of his work was not translated into Latin. Robert Gillet has pointed out that Gregory had read at any rate part of Rufinus's translation of some of the *Orationes* of Gregory of Nazianzus, in particular the *Apologeticus pro fuga (Orat.* 2).[67] This is re-echoed by Gregory's *Regula pastoralis*, where he answers the charge that he had taken to flight to avoid becoming bishop of Rome. Indeed he specifically names Gregory of Nazianzus in the prologue to book III and borrows from him the famous sentence: *Ars est artium regimen animarum.*[68] A careful examination of the translations of Rufinus and the original texts of Gregory of Nazianzus and a comparison of them with the *Regula pastoralis* and *Homiliae in Evangelia* and *in Ezechielem*, together with a comparison of the relevant passages in the *de sacerdotio* of John Chrysostom with Gregory's justification of his flight in the *Regula pastoralis* will surely be worth while. There is also the possibility that Gregory the Great may have read some of the works of Gregory of Nazianzus which have not been translated into Latin. There are certain similarities of style and thought which are suggestive.[69] An important field for comparison will be the treatment of *contemplatio* and θεωρία in both writers. There appear to be certain similarities of thought between, for example, *Moralia*, bk XVIII. 92, and *Orat.* XXVIII. 1–3. It will also be interesting to see whether Gregory the Great was influenced by Basil, by the *Homilies* of John Chrysostom, and by Evagrius Ponticus. Latin translations of some of

---

[67] See art. 'Grégoire le Grand', *DS* 6 (1967) p 877.

[68] *R[egula] P[astoralis]*, *PL* 77 (1849) bk 3, prologue, col 49, and for the famous sentence, *RP*, *PL* 77, bk 1, cap 1, col 14. The original Greek is in *PG* 35 (Turnhout nd) col 425.

[69] For example, the famous account of a storm at sea in *Dialogues*, *PL* 77, bk 3, cap 36, col 304, is generally believed to be based on the equally famous account in *Aeneid*, bk 1, 100 *seq*, but it is in some ways reminiscent of *Carmen de vita sua*, *PG* 37 (1862), 130 *seq*, col 1038.

Basil's works and of some of the *Homilies* were available, and Evagrius could have influenced him either directly or through Cassian.

A second possible source of eastern influence on Gregory's thought lies in the desert. A comparison between the wonder-stories in the *Dialogues* on the one hand, and the *Lausiac History* of Palladius, the *Apophthegmata Patrum*, and the *Pratum* of John Moschus on the other, may be both interesting and rewarding.

In conclusion, Gregory the Great is a figure of extraordinary fascination and significance, fresh aspects of whose life and work will undoubtedly continue to be revealed. We have long been accustomed to see him as a bridge between classical antiquity and the middle ages. It is now time for us to try to see him as a bridge between eastern and western Christian culture and civilisation.

University of London
Westfield and King's Colleges

PURE AIR AND PORTENTOUS HERESY

by ROSALIND M. T. HILL

ANYONE who studies the works of those western historians who wrote contemporary chronicles of the first four crusades must surely be struck by one curious fact. Almost without exception, these writings show a complete lack of interest in the teachings and practices of any branch of the Christian church except that of the Roman west. The Nestorians and Jacobites whom the crusaders encountered in Syria aroused in them neither surprise nor interest, nor is there any sign that these people were regarded as more incorrect in their beliefs than were the orthodox Greeks. Although the schism between the eastern and western churches was not yet half a century old when the first crusade reached the walls of Constantinople, and although it was an affair of theological scholarship and high-powered ecclesiastical politics, it seems already to have interposed a complete barrier between the ordinary Frank and his Greek counterpart. The political acrimony displayed a hundred years earlier by Liutprand of Cremona had found a safe anchor in religious prejudice.

The crusaders, although certainly stirred by that *valida motio* which the author of the *Gesta Francorum* describes as the prime reason for the first crusade,[1] were not as a rule given to theological speculation. They could manifest a simple, and probably quite sincere, devotion when they thought that they were going to die, but in happier moments they seem to have lived by the rule

> that he should take who has the power
> And he should keep who can.

They drew a distinction between the Christians and heretics whom they met in Europe on the way to Constantinople, regarding the heretics as perfectly fair game for pillage and slaughter,[2] while the more responsible among them, at least, felt that Christians should be spared and their property respected. The author of the *Gesta Francorum* records that some of Peter the Hermit's raffish followers pulled the lead off the roofs of churches in Constantinople and sold it to the

---

[1] *Gesta Francorum*, ed R. Hill (London 1962) p 1.
[2] *Ibid* p 8.

Greeks, behaviour which he describes as 'abominable'.[3] But the only evidence to suggest that he ever entered a Greek church is drawn from his description of a vision seen (not by him) at Antioch, where the appearance of Christ receiving the supplications of Our Lady and Saint Peter recalls a type of ikon fairly common in orthodox churches.[4] Other crusaders did indeed enter church buildings, but apparently rather in the spirit of tourists than in that of worshippers. Fulcher of Chartres was impressed by the beauty and architectural excellence of the churches in Constantinople, and by the great number of relics which they contained.[5] A century later Robert de Clari, remarking engagingly that 'Sancta Sophia in Greek means Holy Trinity in French',[6] inserted into his *History of the Fourth Crusade* a list of all the most notable relics to be found in the city, with notes on the curative properties of each and descriptions of the splendid reliquaries in which they were housed. He marvelled at the great number of chapels contained in the imperial palaces of Boukoleon and Blachernae, at the magnificence and beauty of the churches of St Sophia and the Holy Apostles, and at the multitudes of clerics and monks living in the city,[7] but beyond remarking upon the obvious fact that the Greeks show great reverence for ikons and carry them into battle,[8] he shows not the slightest interest in their religious practices.

It may be argued that crusaders, by definition, had their minds fixed upon the fight for the recovery of the holy sepulchre, and had neither the leisure nor the taste for religious speculation. But this attitude of conscious aloofness was not confined to the time when an actual crusade was in progress. It persisted, as Prawer has shown in a recent lecture, throughout the history of the Latin states. The Franks were keenly interested in some aspects of life in Greece and the Near East— in fortifications and methods of fighting, in buildings and trade and agriculture. In local religion they showed no interest at all. They seem to have classified together in a single lump all those who did not accept the authority of the pope, be they Orthodox Christians, Jacobites, Nestorians, Jews, even on occasion friendly Moslems, and to have treated them rather as the Moslems themselves had treated the

[3] *Ibid* p 3.
[4] *Ibid* pp 47–8.
[5] *PL* 155, pp 833–4.
[6] Robert de Clari, *The Conquest of Constantinople*, ed E. H. MacNeal (New York 1966) p 106.
[7] *Ibid* pp 101–13.
[8] *Ibid* p 89.

dhimmis, 'the people of the book,' as second-class citizens, who were subject to tax, but allowed to go their own way so long as they behaved reasonably. The Franks neither persecuted their subjects nor tried to convert them. Orthodox Christians, like everyone else, were free to worship as they chose. The fact that from the catholic point of view they were merely schismatic while the Nestorians and Jacobites were heretical seems to have made no difference in the eyes of their western rulers. To a Frank, everyone living east of the Adriatic was by definition an inferior being, to be tolerated only so long as he paid his taxes, cultivated his lands and caused no trouble to the soldiers of Christ.

In the west, however, historians had more leisure to reflect upon the problems of theological divergence, and they were not pressed by the immediate need to produce a workable society in a land surrounded by overwhelming numbers of enemies. Such was the historian Guibert de Nogent, who wrote before 1129, basing his work in the matter of factual detail upon the text of the *Gesta Francorum.* Guibert was interested in theology, and added to his work a fairly long and very interesting section dealing with the beliefs of the Greeks and Moslems.[9] He begins by observing, reasonably enough, that the eastern empire has always produced great numbers of heresies, whereas in the west there has arisen one only, that of Pelagius, and he was a Briton. (Almost anything, he thinks, may be expected to come out of the British Isles, which he clearly regards as lying practically outside the civilised world. The power of the crusading spirit, he says, was so great that it stirred up people from the very ends of the earth, even to the Scots in their barbarous kilts.) More civilised parts of the Latin west have produced no heretics worthy of note. In contrast, the east has always abounded in heresiarchs of the most dangerous and pernicious kind. Arius came from Alexandria and Mani, the father of dualism, from Persia; Nestorianism and Apollinarianism grew up from the perversity of teachers in various parts of the eastern empire, and all of them were bad. He attributes this tendency to heresy among the Greeks and their neighbours to the fact that the air in their country is very thin and light, and that they are usually born under a pure and cloudless sky. These circumstances, which one might at first sight suppose to be beneficial, are in fact the reverse. They cause the bodies of the Greeks to be thinner than those of the Latins, and their minds quicker and more volatile. As a result they are inconstant, and unwilling to be

[9] *PL* 156, cols 686–96.

guided either by the authority of their elders or the good advice of their contemporaries. Therefore they have always tended to repudiate tradition and to follow after various kinds of novelty, and thus they fall into heresies. Nor is it true to say that the Greeks have exhibited this peculiarity only in ancient times before the Moslem invasions. Their successors of the present day are just as bad. There seems to be no evidence to suggest that Guibert ever held a serious discussion with a Greek scholar, but he is convinced, largely on the grounds that they refuse to accept the authority of the pope, that they are lightminded in secular affairs and even worse when it comes to their profession of the Christian religion. They are full of 'portentous heresies', resembling, as he rather obscurely remarks 'a congregation of bulls among the kine of the people'. They disparage the Most Holy Trinity by holding the belief that the Holy Ghost is inferior to the Father and the Son. They make a great point of celebrating the eucharist with leavened bread, although it is clear from Holy Scripture that Christ made no special request for bread of this kind, using it simply because it happened to be on the table. Guibert himself rather dislikes the use of leavened bread, which to him savours strongly of Judaism. He takes care to point out that if it were the material used for the institution of the sacrament, it equally constituted the sop which Christ gave at the last supper to Judas, and immediately after Judas had received it, Satan entered into him. The bread, therefore, is merely neutral and can have no natural virtue of its own. Moreover, Guibert asks, how is it possible for the Greeks to claim that they show any proper reverence for the Host, when it is clear that their own priests make no bones about delaying its consecration until after the mid-day meal? As for these priests themselves, each one of them is bound to enter into the state of carnal matrimony, whereas Saint Paul's injunction to a bishop that he should be the husband of one wife is clearly intended to be an injunction binding upon all clergy that each of them should devote himself entirely to his bride the church, the unique spouse of her pastor. They make false claims about relics, impudently declaring that they have in their possession the head of Saint John the Baptist, whereas all right-thinking people know that the true head of the saint is at St Airy in Verdun, *apud Ageriacenses monachos*. Guibert, rather surprisingly for a twelfth century writer, did not wholly approve of the public display of relics, or he could undoubtedly have extended his list of those which were supposed to exist both in the east and the west, since multiplication was common. Undoubtedly some relics, such as the true cross, were capable of extensive sub-division, but others which were not were still apt to turn up in far too many places at once. There were eventually three of Malchus's ears in England alone.

According to Guibert, the incurable levity which the Greeks derive from their pure air contaminates not only their theological understanding and their religious practices but also the propriety of their public behaviour. Their way of life is neither God-fearing nor decent. They buy and sell men and women as if they were brute beasts, selling them even to infidels. This, he says, is contrary to the customs of decent people in the west. (It would not be hard to disprove him, since slaves were being exported from Bristol in the time of bishop Wulfstan of Worcester,[10] and Anselm legislated against the *nefarium negotium* of slave-trading in 1102.)[11] The Greeks according to Guibert do even worse things than slave-trading; they castrate their sons in order to give them a chance of rising high in the imperial service (a fact which was perfectly true, which Fulcher of Chartres, writing at about the same date, records without comment.)[12] They are allowed to sell their daughters to brothels provided that some of the money goes into the imperial treasury. They conduct their public affairs, moreover, in a spirit of disgraceful and improper levity. An example of this is shown by the fact that when the Greek emperor asked for help from the west he added as a kind of bait the information that the women of his own country were more beautiful than those of the Franks. Guibert admits that this may well be true, but he adds that it is a fact unworthy to be considered in the context of serious diplomatic arrangements between responsible Christians. He observes that in the circumstances it is not at all surprising that Mahomet, whom he regards as a *perfidus* or heretic rather than a *paganus* or infidel, was so much horrified by the teachings and behaviour of orthodox Christians in the east that he was driven to renounce the true faith altogether, with results which the Christian church has good cause to regret.

Reading Guibert's work, one is struck anew by the evidence of mutual incomprehension between the Franks and the Greeks. Relations between them grew steadily worse throughout the twelfth century, despite some serious attempts on the part of such men as Baldwin III of Jerusalem and the emperor Manuel Comnenus to improve the situation. The capture of Constantinople in 1204 was no

[10] *Vita Wulfstani*, ed R. R. Darlington (London 1928) pp 43, 91.
[11] Wilkins I, p 383.
[12] *PL* 155, col 834.

unpremeditated act of aggression but the result of a very long period of mutual distrust between two alienated peoples. Nevertheless, it was one of the great tragedies of Christendom, and its shadow lies upon us to this day.

University of London
Westfield College.

THE PAPAL SCANDAL
(PRESIDENTIAL ADDRESS)

by DONALD M. NICOL

THE Greek word *skandalon* means a stumbling-block, an offence. As such it is used frequently in the septuagint and the new testament. In Byzantine texts at least from the eleventh century the word is employed as a collective noun to denote the many obstacles that stood in the way of union between the Greek and Latin churches. In the thirteenth century, however, it is often qualified by the phrase 'relating to or concerning the pope'—τὸ κατὰ τὸν πάπαν σκάνδαλον.[1] It was as if the pope or the papacy had come to be identified as the cause or agent of the stumbling-block that lay in the path of understanding. This is the 'papal scandal' that I have in mind.

If one accepts that the schism between the eastern and western churches was declared on a technicality in 1009, formally and rudely ratified in 1054, aggravated by the early crusades and irreparably transformed into a way of life by the fourth crusade, then one ought to be able to trace the course of Byzantine feeling on the matter by studying the Greek sources available from the eleventh to the thirteenth centuries. To some extent one can, and to some extent the work has been done or is in progress. J. Darrouzès has done most to elucidate and where necessary edit the Greek texts of the twelfth century which illustrate the Byzantine view of the nature of the schism or the scandal. He has clearly shown that there was a significant development in Byzantine opinion in that century.[2] There was a growing feeling that the pope's claim to primacy, or rather supremacy, over the whole church was being pressed to the point where it became a major obstacle. That this feeling was new can be shown by a glance at the anti-Latin literature of the Byzantine church before the twelfth century. The major causes of scandal in those days were thought to be the Latin addition to the creed of the *Filioque* and the Latin use of unleavened bread in the sacrament. The primacy of the see of Rome was a late starter as a scandal.[3]

[1] See, for instance, George Pachymeres, *De Michaele Palaeologo*, pp 359, 366; *De Andronico Palaeologo*, pp 12, 17, 102 (*CSHByz*).

[2] [J.] Darrouzès, 'Les documents [byzantins du XIIᵉ siècle sur la primauté romaine'], *REB*, 23 (1965) pp 42–88.

[3] On the Byzantine view of the primacy of Rome in general see M. Jugie, 'La primauté

In earlier times the Byzantines were content to accept the verdict of their great patriarch Photios who in the ninth century had detected no more than five errors in the Roman creed and ritual. It was left to Michael Keroullarios to extend the list to the number of twenty-three, though he was provoked by the long catalogue of charges against his own church itemised by cardinal Humbert in 1054. Not all his colleagues would agree that the Latins were so multifariously misguided. Peter of Antioch sensibly concluded that most of the twenty-three alleged errors were trivial and probably the result of western ignorance. The two most serious faults were again the addition to the creed and the use of unleavened bread. But neither he nor Keroullarios nor for that matter Photios regarded the primacy of Rome as a scandal.[4]

The encyclical of Keroullarios was the first of many such documents. Lists of Latin errors based upon it were multiplied and circulated; and among ordinary people and the rabble of monks in Byzantium it was the trivia that made the most exciting reading. All were agreed that the addition of the *Filioque* to the creed was wrong, even if few could understand the theological subtleties of the case. But it was easy enough to see that the Latins were at fault in such matters as the marriage of the clergy and all too easy to be persuaded that they christened their infants with saliva, ate the flesh of wolves, drank their own urine and washed their dirty trousers in their cooking pots. A basic text in the development of this form of anti-Latin literature is the so-called *Opusculum contra Francos,* or *Treatise against the Franks and other Latins.* This document, attributed by its manuscript and its editor to Photios, probably dates in reality from the eleventh century. As a disseminator of prejudice it has a lot to answer for. Its twenty-eight sections list a total of thirty-six Latin aberrations. As usual the first two charges, and therefore the most serious, relate to the addition

---

romaine dans l'église byzantine à partir du IXe siècle jusqu'à la dernière tentative d'union avec Rome, au concile de Florence', *DTC*, 13, 1 (1936) cols 357–77; [F.] Dvornik, *The Idea of Apostolicity* [*in Byzantium and the Legend of the Apostle Andrew*], Dumbarton Oaks Studies, 4 (Cambridge, Mass., 1958) and *Byzance et la primauté romaine*, Unam Sanctam, 49 (Paris 1964); [J.] Meyendorff, 'St. Peter [in Byzantine Theology'], in J. Meyendorff, A. Schmemann, N. Afanassief, N. Koulomzine, *The Primacy of Peter in the Orthodox Church* (London 1963) pp 7–29 and, *Byzantine Theology. Historical Trends and Doctrinal Themes* (New York 1974).

[4] The five complaints of Photios are contained in his encyclical to the eastern patriarchs, *PG* 102, cols 721–42. Keroullarios's letter to Peter of Antioch and Peter's reply are in *PG* 120, cols 781–816. See [S.] Runciman, *The Eastern Schism.* [*A study of the papacy and the Eastern Churches during the XIth and XIIth centuries*] (Oxford 1955) pp 52–4, 65–6.

to the creed and to the unleavened bread. But the *Opusculum* has nothing to say about the primacy of Rome.[5]

When and how did the question of the primacy come to rate as a scandal? The Byzantine church had always accorded to the see of Rome a primacy of honour, with pride of place among the five patriarchates, the pentarchy of the oecumenical church, Rome, Constantinople, Alexandria, Antioch and Jerusalem. The twenty-eighth canon of the council of Chalcedon had declared, to the satisfaction of the Byzantines at least, that the privileges of the bishop of Constantinople were equal to those of his colleague in Rome. The exalted rank of both sees was held to derive from the historical contingency that first one and then the other had been the capital city of the Roman empire in which the church was founded and had its being. The apostolic foundation of the church of Rome was accepted as a fact as it was in the case of Antioch, though the apostolic succession of its bishops from saint Peter was another matter. The right of appeal to Rome by other sectors of the church was sometimes allowed, especially when it seemed convenient. But the Byzantines never agreed that the pope had a universal jurisdiction extending over the whole *oikoumene*. The only universal authority in the church was that of an oecumenical council at which all five patriarchs were present or represented. They believed that all bishops were equal. Some might be marginally more equal than others. But neither Rome nor Constantinople had a right to the supereminently unequal status claimed by the papacy.

Photios, who had a normal Byzantine respect for the primacy of the see of Rome, was concerned about the theological and other errors being propagated by its incumbents. If the pope was in error, as in the matter of the *Filioque*, then clearly he must forfeit the respect for his primacy, as well as the respect and recognition of his colleagues in the pentarchy. To later Byzantine theologians the problem became more and more acute as they became aware of the ever more elaborate claims put forward by the reformed papacy. It is no accident that the first Byzantine documents dealing specifically with the primacy of

[5] *Opusculum* [*contra Francos*, ed J. Hergenroether], *Monumenta graeca ad Photium ejusque historiam pertinentia* (Ratisbon 1869) pp 62–71. It was translated into Latin by Hugo Etherianus when he was at the Byzantine court in 1178. The translation was incorporated by the Dominican Bartholomew of Constantinople into his *Tractatus contra Graecos* in 1252. For its probable date and authorship see Beck, p 538; [A.] Argyriou, 'Remarques sur quelques listes [grecques énumérant les hérésies latines'], *BF* 4 (Amsterdam 1972) pp 9–30, esp pp 13–15.

Rome date from the early twelfth century. Previous anti-Latin polemic had concentrated on the points of difference in doctrine, ritual and custom. Such differences were magnified when the crusaders arrived in the east. Their greed, arrogance and contempt for the Greeks were the worst possible advertisement for Latin Christianity. Physical contact with these barbarous foreigners fortified the worst fears and prejudices of the Byzantines. The lists of Latin aberrations grew longer and more detailed. A new complaint was that Roman priests carried arms and took part in war, murdering with one hand and celebrating the sacrament with the other.[6] But the crusades also brought home to the Byzantines the full and tangible significance of the pope's claim to universal supremacy over the church. And it was to counter this claim that their theologians turned to producing what amount to pamphlets *De primatu papae*. Darrouzès has analysed a number of such tracts produced in the twelfth century; and, as he observes, a starting-point for Byzantine criticism of what seemed to be a new Roman conception of the primacy came in the pontificate of Urban II, the prime mover of the first crusade.[7]

In the course of the twelfth century then the question of the primacy of Rome in the church came to worry the Byzantines more than it had ever done before. It came indeed to constitute a major scandal or obstacle to understanding and union. The early crusades stoked the fires of prejudice on both sides. The fourth crusade in 1204 made them almost inextinguishable. Those at the receiving end of the fourth crusade found it hard to believe that its perpetrators were Christians at all. Contemporaries referred to them as 'the Latin dogs', the 'forerunners of antichrist'. The sack of Constantinople, the conquest and dismemberment of the empire coloured all subsequent relationships between Byzantium and the west, political, ecclesiastical and emotional. Fanatical Orthodox propagandists who had always said that the Latins were vicious were triumphantly vindicated. Nor would the Byzantines believe that the crusaders had exceeded the orders of pope Innocent III. For they knew quite well that the pope, though deploring the savagery of his soldiers in Constantinople, regarded the conquest of the city and the establishment of a Latin empire as part of God's plan for the reunification of Christendom

---

[6] Anna Comnena, *Alexiad,* ed B. Leib, 3 vols (Paris 1937–45) bk X, cap 8, 2 pp 218–20. See also the *Opusculum* p 64, § 3. The point may first have been made by Michael Keroullarios, *PG* 120, col 793; but with the crusades it acquired greater force.

[7] Darrouzès, 'Les documents', pp 47–9.

under Rome. The Byzantines were now to be treated to the practical application of the fully developed theory of universal papal sovereignty.

It may be instructive to examine some of the Byzantine statements about the primacy of Rome in and after the thirteenth century to see what impact the disaster of the fourth crusade had on the thinking of its victims. I have consulted some twenty-five Greek documents on or about the subject written between 1204 and 1400. But there is much work to be done in this field. A surprising number of the relevant texts are still in manuscript or only partially edited or printed in Greek and Russian publications of such rarity as to be almost inaccessible. In 1872 the learned Greek archimandrite Andronikos Demetrakopoulos published a book entitled *Orthodoxos Hellas*.[8] This is a sort of *Who's Who* of all the Greeks who committed their anti-Latin arguments to writing from the time of Photios to the end of the eighteenth century. It is a work of patriotic devotion, pious erudition and profound prejudice. It was designed partly as a hellenic counterblast to the enormous compendium of Leo Allatius, *De ecclesiae occidentalis atque orientalis perpetua consensione*, published in 1648.[9] Allatius, as a Greek uniate, had looked for the points of convergence between catholic and orthodox writers through the centuries. Demetrakopoulos looked for the points of divergence and considered Allatius, a Greek from Chios, to have been a traitor to hellenism and a popish lackey. But his book remains a valuable guide through a still relatively unexplored field, for he took great trouble to search the libraries of Europe and often to list the manuscripts of the unpublished works of his anti-latin heroes. It is understandable that many of these works are to be found not in the Vatican but in the libraries of Orthodox countries, Greek, Slav, Roumanian or Russian. Whether *Orthodoxos Hellas* is a proper title for a compendium planned to perpetuate Greek Orthodox bigotry is a matter that I would rather not go into now. I am merely recording my debt to a learned Greek archimandrite who died in Germany just over a hundred years ago.

The fourth crusade was a shocking and bewildering experience for the Byzantines. But they must have seen it coming. The Greek patriarch of Constantinople at the time was John X Kamateros. Just

[8] A. K. Demetrakopoulos, Ὀρθόδοξος Ἑλλὰς ἤτοι περὶ τῶν Ἑλλήνων γραψάντων κατὰ Λατίνων καὶ περὶ τῶν συγγραμμάτων αὐτῶν (Leipzig 1872, repr Athens 1968).

[9] Allatius, [*Leonis Allatii De ecclesiae occidentalis atque orientalis perpetua consensione Libri tres*] (Cologne 1648) repr with an introduction by Kallistos T. Ware (Gregg International Publishers 1970).

before the event, in 1199–1200, he had engaged in a correspondence with pope Innocent III about the primacy of the see of Rome. This in itself is remarkable. Throughout the twelfth century there seems to be only one other personal exchange on the subject between a pope and a patriarch.[10] Innocent's two letters to the patriarch John have long been known.[11] But the patriarch's replies have only recently been published.[12] The second and longer of the two sets out to question the confident proposition that the see of Rome enjoys not only primacy but also plenitude of power and universal jurisdiction as the mother of all churches, to whose fold the Greeks must return or remain outside the ark of salvation. 'Where in the gospels', asks the patriarch, 'does Christ say that the church of the Romans is the head and universal mother of all the churches? . . . There are five great churches which are dignified with patriarchal rank, among which she is the first as among sisters of equal honour. The five patriarchates are like the five senses, each performing a distinct function . . . or like a five-stringed instrument, each string with its own sound but capable of the harmonious music of salvation when struck by the plectrum of the Holy Spirit. . . . The primacy of honour accorded to the church of Rome comes not through Peter having been proclaimed bishop there or having died there, but because the city of Rome was once exalted by the presence of the emperor and the senate, neither of which is to be found there any more'.[13]

There is nothing startlingly new in the patriarch's letters. He makes the following well-worn points: that the true head of the church is Christ; that the church on earth is governed by a pentarchy of patriarchs, among whom the bishop of Rome has a primacy of honour; that this primacy depends upon political and historical circumstances; and that in any event there is a strong case for

---

[10] Correspondence between pope Alexander III and the patriarch Michael of Anchialos in 1173, ed G. Hofmann, 'Papst und Patriarche unter Kaiser Manuel I Komnenos', *EEBS*, 23 (1953) pp 74–82.

[11] Letters of Innocent III of 1198 and 1199, *PL* 214, cols 327–9, 758–65; ed [P. Th.] Haluščynskyj, *Acta Innocentii III (1198–1216)*, P[ontificia] c[ommissio ad] r[edigendum] c[odicem] i[uris] c[anonici] o[rientalis], Fontes ser III, 2 (Vatican City 1944) nos 5, 9, pp 180–2, 187–95.

[12] [A.] Papadakis and [Alice Mary] Talbot, 'John X Camaterus [confronts Innocent III: an unpublished correspondence'], *BS*, 33 (1972) pp 26–41 (Greek text, pp 33–41). See Grumel, *Regestes*, nos 1194, 1196, pp 190–3; [P.] Wirth, 'Zur Frage [eines politischen Engagements Patriarch Johannes' X. Kamateros nach dem vierten Kreuzzug'], *BF*, 4 (1972) pp 239–52, p 244; A. Andrea, 'Latin evidence for the accession date of John X Camaterus', *BZ*, 66 (1973) pp 354–8.

[13] Papadakis and Talbot, 'John X Camaterus', pp 36–7, 40.

counting the church of Jerusalem first in time and rank and the church of Antioch second. All this had been said before. Even the comparison of the pentarchy to the five senses can be found as early as the ninth century, when in fact it was made by a Latin to illustrate the primacy of Rome among the other patriarchates as the first among the senses, the eye of the church.[14] What the patriarch John does politely emphasise to the pope is the difference between Latin and Greek interpretations of the word 'catholic', since in the Orthodox view each of the Christian churches, however humble, possesses the same fulness of grace and catholicity and no one bishop, however important his see, can monopolise the title of catholic for any part of the whole.[15]

Four years after this letter was written the crusaders entered and sacked Constantinople. The patriarch was driven out and his place was taken by a Latin elected by the conquerors. In his exile the patriarch John Kamateros wrote a bitter account of the sufferings of his city and the humiliation of his church. It survives in an anonymous pamphlet entitled 'How the Latin prevailed over us', which recent research has convincingly identified as the patriarch's own composition.[16] He describes himself as a vagrant, without a city and without a throne. He deplores the horror of the conquest as an eye-witness, the plunder of churches and the replacing of Greek priests by Latins. He recalls how he was insulted in his own palace

---

[14] Anastasius Bibliothecarius, *Mansi*, 16, col 7, cited by Dvornik, *The Idea of Apostolicity*, p 277. Compare Peter of Antioch's letter to the patriarch of Aquileia, *PG* 120, cols 757, 760.

[15] Western sources record that in March 1203 the patriarch John with the emperor promised under oath to submit the church of Constantinople to Rome and to go and receive the pallium from the supreme pontiff. Hugh of Saint-Pol, *Chronica regia colonensis*, ed G. Waitz, *MGH, SRG* (Hanover 1880) p 208; Robert of Auxerre, *Chronicon, MGH, SS*, 26, p 270. The story, if not apocryphal, is surely exaggerated. C. M. Brand, *Byzantium confronts the West 1180–1204* (Cambridge, Mass., 1968) pp 243–4, accepts it as evidence that the emperor and the patriarch 'sent their submissions to Innocent III'. But see the more cautious remarks of Grumel, *Regestes*, no 1197, p 193, and Wirth, 'Zur Frage', pp 244–5.

[16] Anonymous, Περὶ τοῦ ὅπως ἴσχυσε καθ᾽ ἡμῶν ὁ Λατῖνος ed archimandrite Arsenij, *Tri stati neizvestnago grečeskago pisatelja načala XIII veka* (Three documents of an unknown Greek writer of the beginning of the thirteenth century for the defence of Orthodoxy and the refutation of the Latin innovations in faith and religion) (Moscow 1892) pp 84–115. For its ascription to the patriarch John Kamateros see Beck p 664, and esp [J. M.] Hoeck and [R.-J.] Loenertz, *Nikolaos-Nektarios [von Otranto Abt von Casole. Beiträge zur Geschichte der ost-westlichen Beziehungen unter Innozenz III. und Friedrich II.]* (Ettal 1965) p 31 and n 6; Wirth, 'Zur Frage', p 246. Extracts from the document are printed in [M.] Jugie, *Theologia dogmatica [christianorum orientalium ab ecclesia dissidentium]*, 4 (Paris, 1931) p 391.

by the pope's legate to Constantinople. But above all he protests against the appointment of a Latin patriarch in his place. There is an irony in this protest, since pope Innocent III too was far from happy about the election of a Venetian prelate as the first Latin patriarch of Constantinople in 1204. But the pope was upset only about the method and the person of the appointment. What bewildered and angered the Greek patriarch was the pope's assumption that he was empowered to make or to ratify such an appointment at all. By what authority could a pope of Rome elect or demote his colleagues in the pentarchy? Brooding on the enormity of this crime the patriarch lost whatever respect he may earlier have expressed for the theory of the primacy of Rome. He denies it categorically and goes further by denying also the primacy of Peter among the apostles. This absolute denial of the primacy of Peter is, as Meyendorff has remarked, an extreme case, unique in all Byzantine literature.[17] To such extremes of irrational bitterness were the Byzantines driven by their treatment at the hands of the Latins. The patriarch will allow to the see and the city of Rome only one mark of primacy and that is the special privilege of being remembered as the city that murdered the holy apostle Peter by hanging him head downwards on a cross.

The Greeks in Constantinople continued to regard John Kamateros as their spiritual head until he died in exile in May 1206. But even under alien rule they saw no good reason why they should not be allowed to appoint a new patriarch of their own faith and language. Their clergy approached the Latin emperor, Henry of Flanders, a tolerant and sensible man. But he could not grant permission unless they first acknowledged obedience to the pope. They therefore wrote a courteous letter to Innocent III asking him to let them elect their own patriarch so that a council of the church could be arranged to discuss the points of dispute between Greeks and Latins. For they had been brought up to believe that a council was the proper and only method of removing scandals in the church, and their case could not be represented until they had a patriarch of their own race and speech.[18]

---

[17] Meyendorff, 'St Peter', p 17. See Dvornik, *Byzance et la primauté*, p 141. On Innocent III's attitude to the election of Thomas Morosini as Latin patriarch see R. L. Wolff, 'Politics in the Latin patriarchate of Constantinople 1204–1261', *DOP*, 8 (1954) pp 223–304.

[18] Letter of the Greek clergy of Constantinople to Innocent III: Greek text in Nicholas Mesarites, *Epitaphios* for his brother John, [ed A.] Heisenberg, *Neue Quellen* [*zur Geschichte des lateinischen Kaisertums und der Kirchenunion*], 1: [*Der Epitaphios des Nikolaos Mesarites auf seinen Bruder Johannes*], *SBAW* (1920) abh 5 pp 63–6.

Shortly afterwards Innocent III received a collective letter from the Greek inhabitants of Constantinople. It followed much the same lines. They accepted the harsh fact of political subjugation to a Frankish emperor, with whom they were quite prepared to co-operate if only for survival. But in spiritual matters they too saw no reason why they should not have a patriarch and bishops of their own appointed in the time-honoured manner; and they called for an oecumenical council for the discussion of common problems, at which their patriarch would answer for them.[19] Pope Innocent III never, it seems, deigned to answer these letters. It has been argued that by ignoring them he lost his chance of winning the allegiance of the church and people of Constantinople by making 'a grand conciliatory gesture'.[20] A new scandal or stumbling-block had now been seen to be erected in the field of ecclesiology, the papal scandal. A new Greek patriarch was in fact elected in 1208 but not at Constantinople. His see was at Nicaea, which was to become the capital of the Byzantine empire and church in exile until its emperor drove the Latins out of Constantinople in 1261.[21]

The primacy, or the overriding authority, of Rome as manifested in the fourth crusade and its consequences became the largest stumbling-block between Greeks and Latins in the years after 1204. In August and September 1206 a series of dialogues took place between the Latin patriarch Thomas Morosini and the brothers Nicholas and John Mesarites. Nicholas, a deacon and later to become bishop of Ephesos, condemned the Latin patriarch's appointment as uncanonical and argued strongly against the pope's power to make such appointments.[22] He refuted the claim that such authority stemmed from saint Peter. For Peter had never been bishop of Rome.

[19] Graecorum ad Innocentium III [P. R. Epistola scripta post captam a Latinis Constantinopolim, regnante Henrico Imperatore], PG 140, cols 293–8 (from J. B. Cotelerius, Ecclesiae Graecae Monumenta (Paris 1677–92) 3, pp 514 seq). For the dating of these letters see Heisenberg, Neue Quellen, 1, pp 13–14; Hoeck-Loenertz, Nikolaos-Nektarios, pp 49–51.

[20] Runciman, The Eastern Schism, pp 154–5. For a different assessment of Innocent III's predicament see [J.] Gill, 'Innocent III [and the Greeks: Aggressor or Apostle?'], in Relations between East and West in the Middle Ages, ed Derek Baker (Edinburgh 1973) pp 95–108. It is significant that it was not until after the appointment of a Latin patriarch in 1204 that Innocent III officially accepted the second rank of Constantinople among the primatial sees of the pentarchy. See the fifth canon of the lateran council of 1215, Mansi, 22, col 990.

[21] See now M. Angold, A Byzantine Government in Exile. Government and Society under the Laskarids of Nicaea, 1204–1261 (Oxford 1975).

[22] Nicholas Mesarites, 'Die Disputation des Nikolaos Mesarites mit dem Kardinallegaten Benedikt und dem lateinischen Patriarchen Thomas Morosini am 30. August 1206',

By trying thus to glorify Peter the Italians merely humiliate him. For they confine the teacher of the whole *oikoumene* to being bishop of one city, thinking to exalt themselves as his successor. Foolish of them, for it shows that they do not know whence or how the see of Rome came by its privileges. It was not through Peter ... but through the fact that Rome was the capital city and contained the senate when the grace of truth first dawned. If you Italians would consult the records you would find this documented and cease to stray from the truth. . . .

Nicholas then proceeds to compare the claims to primacy of Antioch and Jerusalem, though he weakens his case by bringing in the alleged sojourn of saint Andrew in Byzantium and his mythical foundation of the see of Constantinople. 'But', he continues, 'if you come back at me with "Thou art Peter and upon this rock . . .", take note that this was not said of the church of Rome. That is a Jewish way of thinking and debases the grace and divinity of the church by limiting it to districts and countries instead of recognising its working throughout the whole universe'. By confining the meaning of 'the rock' to the church of Rome alone you force yourselves into a narrow interpretation of the promise of Christ and the prophets, that the message of the apostles would reach the ends of the earth and the church be founded on a firm rock, as one catholic and apostolic church inspired by the Holy Spirit—'not a Petrine or Roman church, not a Byzantine or Andreatic or Alexandrine or Antiochene or Palestinian or Asian or European or Libyan or Hyperborean Bosporan church, as empty-headed Roman ignorance would have it, but one extending over all the *oikoumene* to which the voice of the apostles and the power of the gospels' words went out, even to the limits of the world'.[23]

---

ed Heisenberg, *Neue Quellen*, 2: [*Die Unionsverhandlungen vom 30. August 1206. Patriarchenwahl und Kaiserkrönung in Nikaia 1208*], SBAW (1923) abh 2 pp 3–25 (Greek text pp 15–25). Meyendorff, 'St Peter', pp 20–1; Hoeck-Loenertz, *Nikolaos-Nektarios*, pp 41–4.

[23] Much of the text of the latter part of this dialogue (ed Heisenberg, *Neue Quellen*, 2, p 24 lines 1–31) appears, almost verbatim, in an anonymous pamphlet addressed 'To those who say that Rome is the first throne', falsely ascribed to Photios. It has been edited by M. Gordillo, 'Photius et Primatus Romanus. Num Photius habendus sit auctor opuscoli Πρὸς τοὺς λέγοντας ὡς ἡ ʿΡώμη πρῶτος θρόνος?', *OCP*, 6 (1940) pp 3–39 (Greek text pp 11–17); earlier ed by [G.] Rhalles and [M.] Potles, *Syntagma* [Σύνταγμα τῶν θείων καὶ ἱερῶν κανόνων], 4 (Athens 1854) pp 409–15. Its ascription to Photios has been denied by [F.] Dvornik, *The Photian Schism*. [*History and Legend*] (Cambridge 1948) pp 125–7; *The Idea of Apostolicity*, pp 247–53; and *Byzance et la primauté*, p 143; and by Darrouzès, 'Les documents', pp 85–8. Hoeck-Loenertz,

John Mesarites, in his dialogue with the Latin patriarch in September 1206, contended that the pope's jurisdiction was limited territorially like that of the other patriarchs and that he was never authorised to appoint bishops in places not subject to him; and again the plea was made for the right to elect a Greek patriarch of Constantinople.[24] The papal legate who was present protested that it was absurd to imply that the pope's actions could be contrary to the canons. The Roman church, unlike that of Constantinople with its many deviations, had never held a wrong opinion or countenanced a heresy. His Greek audience were then quick to remind him of the case of pope Honorius who had been anathematised by the sixth oecumenical council in 681. This seems to be the first occasion on which the condemnation of Honorius was adduced as an argument against the primacy, or at least the infallibility, of Rome. It was an argument to be used with caution since the eastern patriarchs, as the Byzantines were always ready to admit, were far from blameless in the matter of heresy.[25]

A German chronicler of the fourth crusade records how the armada from Venice put in at Corfu in 1203 on its way to Constantinople and that the bishop of the island invited some of the Latin clergy to dinner. The conversation got round to the primacy of Rome and the Greek bishop gave it as his opinion that he could think of no justification for the see of Rome being specially privileged unless it were that Roman soldiers had crucified Christ.[26] The story may be garbled or apocryphal. But it may well have been the same bishop of Corfu who wrote to pope Innocent III some ten years later. His name was Basil Pediadites. In 1213 Innocent sent out invitations to the fourth lateran council which was to be held in two years time. They went

---

Nikolaos-Nektarios, p 43, still describe it as *warscheinlich photianischen*, but it is probably to be dated to the thirteenth century.

[24] John Mesarites, *Dialogue* between the monks of Propontis and Mount St Auxentios (led by John Mesarites) and the Latin patriarch Thomas and cardinal Benedict, 29 September 1206, ed Heisenberg, *Neue Quellen*, I, pp 52–63 (Greek text). See Hoeck-Loenertz, *Nikolaos-Nektarios*, pp 44–9.

[25] Darrouzès seems to be at fault in writing that 'La première fois . . . que le cas du pape Honorius est invoqué par un Grec comme un argument contre la primauté' was as late as 1357. [J.] Darrouzès, 'Conférence sur la primauté [du pape à Constantinople en 1357'], *REB*, 19 (1961) [=*Mélanges Raymond Janin*] p 82. The case of Honorius is adduced by John Mesarites in 1206 and by the patriarch Germanos II in his letter to the Latin patriarch of Constantinople about 1234. See below p 154.

[26] *Anonymi Halberstadensis De peregrinatione in Graeciam et adventu reliquiarum de Graecia libellus*, ed P. D. Riant, *Exuviae sacrae constantinopolitanae*, I (Geneva 1877) p 14: '. . . nullam aliam causam se scire primatus vel prerogativam sedis romane, nisi quod romani milites Christum crucifixerunt'.

to the archbishops, bishops and abbots, Greek as well as Latin, throughout 'the province of Constantinople'.[27] The only Greek bishop known to have replied was Basil of Corfu. Any doubt about the occasion of his letter (and doubts have been expressed) is resolved on comparing its opening remarks with the text of the pope's invitation to the council. The Greek is a straight translation of the Latin. Basil's letter is little known and therefore perhaps worth quoting at length.[28]

Your letter spoke of driving the beasts out of the vineyard of the Lord of Hosts and of convening an oecumenical council according to the ancient custom of the fathers. . . . And I applauded the intention of your holiness, filled as it is with apostolic zeal. But on considering whether it can be realised my meagre intelligence finds that it is at present impossible. For why I shall tell you. An oecumenical council is composed of a gathering of the five apostolic thrones and their dependent bishops. But if one of the thrones is vacant, and that one of the superior ones, how can such an assembly be called oecumenical? Your holiness surely knows the privileges of the throne of Constantinople . . . that it is granted equal honour and is in no way inferior to that of Rome. If this be so then your council will be substantially deficient if no patriarch of Constantinople is present. Now our see of Constantinople is still widowed; and with no patriarch having been proclaimed how can his synod go to Rome?[29] . . . A regiment of troops cannot join battle

[27] Letter of Innocent III, *PL*, 216, col 826; Haluščynskyj, *Acta Innocentii III*, no 206, p 444.
[28] Basil (Pediadites), *Letter to the pope* (Innocent III), ed Sp. K. Papageorgiou, Ἱστορία τῆς Ἐκκλησίας τῆς Κερκύρας ἀπὸ τῆς συστάσεως αὐτῆς μέχρι τοῦ νῦν (Kerkyra 1920) pp 30–3; earlier ed by A. K. Demetrakopoulos, in Ἐθνικὸν Ἡμερολόγιον (Leipzig 1870) p 187. The *incipit* of the pope's invitations to the council is given in *PL* 216, cols 823–4: 'Vineam Domini Sabaoth multiformes moliuntur bestiae demoliri . . .'. Basil's letter begins thus: Ἔλεγε γὰρ τὰ γράμματα, ὅτι τὸν ἀμπελῶνα Κυρίου Σαβαὼθ παρασκευάζουσι κτήνη ἀποκαθεῖλαι. Gill, 'Innocent III', p 104, suggests that Innocent invited only those bishops from the east who had taken the oath of obedience to him, which implies that Basil of Corfu had done so. The tenor of his letter makes this seem unlikely. There is, however, independent evidence that Basil Pediadites did, for all his protestations and for whatever purpose, visit Rome. Demetrios Chomatianos, ed J. B. Pitra, *Analecta sacra et classica spicilegio solesmensi parata*, 6 (Rome 1891) col 155: . . . ὁ μὲν μακαρίτης Κερκύρας Βασίλειος ὁ Πεδιαδίτης εἰς τὴν πρεσβυτέραν Ῥώμην ἐπεποίητο τὸν ἀπόδημον.
[29] At the time this letter was written (1213 or 1214) there was a patriarch at Nicaea, Michael IV Autoreianos (died 26 August 1214), who was succeeded on 28 September 1214 by Theodore II Eirenikos. But the bishop of Corfu, whose political allegiance lay with the rival Byzantine régime in exile in Epiros, did not recognise the claim of the patriarchs at Nicaea to the title of oecumenical. The Latin patriarchate of

without its colonel . . . and it is the law of the church that bishops cannot act without their metropolitans nor metropolitans without their patriarchs.[30] . . . If then your holiness wishes a council to be canonically convened, let a patriarch first be canonically elected for Constantinople, that is to say by its own synod, just as the other patriarchs are elected and appointed by their own synods. Meanwhile, which of the Greek bishops will come to your council? Those whom your holiness has driven out? Will the metropolitan of Athens come, whom your holiness has expelled from his see and replaced by another? What of the bishops of Thessalonica or Zarnata who have suffered the same from your holiness—not to itemise each of the several bishops whom you have evicted, some of whom are still alive, wandering from place to place like refugees, living monuments of your unlawful behaviour. Thus you have sent adulterers among the undefiled churches of Christ, having divorced them from those to whom the Holy Spirit had united them. . . . So it is not possible for an oecumenical council to be held, since the Greek synod with their patriarch have been cast out by your holiness. . . . The body of Christians has Christ at its head; and the five patriarchs are the five senses around the head. . . . A body deprived of one of its senses is maimed. So also is the church if deprived of one patriarch. And since your holiness spoke of the beasts trying to trample on the vineyard of the Lord of Hosts you might have specified the nature of the beasts . . . For each wild animal has its own form of savagery. Arius fought one way, Sabellios another, Makedonios yet another . . . So also does the man who says that the Holy Spirit proceeds from the Son as well as from the Father, for he is in conflict with the creed as laid down by the seven councils . . .

The taunt at the end of this letter shows that the questions of the primacy of Rome and of the pope's authority had not obscured the oldest scandal of all, the addition of the *Filioque* to the creed. The two matters were indeed inseparably connected. When in 1214 some papal legates asked Nicholas Mesarites what he regarded as the root cause of the schism he replied: 'The cause of the scandals is the fact that your part of the church has chosen to sow tares among the pure

---

Constantinople was vacant from July 1211 (when Thomas Morosini died) until November 1215; but it is improbable that Pediadites had this in mind.

[30] This point is also made in the letter of the Greek clergy to Innocent III, ed Heisenberg, *Neue Quellen*, I, p 65.

wheat of apostolic and patristic doctrine. . . . And if you did not pretend to be deaf you would know that the tares are those which you implanted in the creed . . . by asserting that the Holy Spirit proceeds also from the Son. This is the reason for the division between the churches'.[31]

As time went on the Greek patriarchs at Nicaea confidently claimed the title and the authority of Constantinople. The patriarch Germanos II in 1229 condemns the arrogance of the Latins in setting up the bishop of Rome in the place of Christ as head of all the churches—intolerable vanity in a race of men that has promoted so many crimes and errors, first among which is the addition to the creed.[32] In a letter to some monks in Constantinople (recently published by Gill) Germanos warns them against being deceived into thinking that the heresy of the Latins is of small account, for it is in fact 'almost the recapitulation of all the heresies' that the devil has introduced into the church.[33] Germanos took it upon himself to excommunicate all Greek priests in Constantinople who submitted to the obedience of Rome. But he felt this to be more reasonable than the action of the Latins in imprisoning those clergy who refused to submit. Writing to the Latin patriarch about 1234 Germanos appeals to him to show mercy to those priests incarcerated by his predecessor. 'Prison is for malefactors . . . and they have done no wrong. . . . They have done no more than obey the order of their own church. Either you should set them free or prove that they are violating the canons by not submitting to the church of Rome—the church which has altered the creed by adding to it and which, for that reason alone, the Greeks should shun like the flames'.[34]

[31] Nicholas Mesarites, *Neue Quellen*, 3, [*Die Bericht des Nikolaos Mesarites über die politischen und kirchlichen Ereignisse des Jahres 1214*], *SBAW* (1923) abh 3 p 36.

[32] Germanos II, Second letter to the Orthodox inhabitants of Cyprus, *PG* 140, cols 613C–22B, 617A–B. See Laurent, *Regestes*, no 1250, pp 56–7.

[33] J. Gill, 'An unpublished letter of Germanus, Patriarch of Constantinople (1222–1240)', *B*, 44 (1974) pp 138–51, esp p 143 lines 18–30.

[34] Germanos II, letter to the Latin patriarch of Constantinople (Nicolas de Castro), ed Th. Uspenskij, *Obrazovanie vtorago bolgarskago carstva* (*Organisation of the Second Bulgarian Empire*) (Odessa 1879) appendix, pp 75–8; partial edition by Demetrakopoulos, Ὀρθόδοξος Ἑλλάς, pp 40–3. See Laurent, *Regestes*, no 1277, pp 83–5. See also Germanos II's letters of 1232 to pope Gregory IX and to the cardinals, ed A. L. Tăutu, *Acta Honorii III et Gregorii IX*, PCRCICO, Fontes ser III, 3: (1950) nos 179ᵃ, 179ᵇ, pp 240–9, 249–52. Laurent, *Regestes*, nos 1256, 1257. The Greek version of the latter remains unedited. Germanos there gives a rather optimistic picture of the nations that are in communion with the Greeks: Ethiopians, Syrians, Iberians, Lazi, Alans, Goths, Khazars, Russians and Bulgarians—'et hi omnes tamquam matri nostrae obediunt Ecclesiae, in antiqua orthodoxia immobiles hactenus manentes'.

The Greeks bitterly resented the enforcement upon them of the Latin faith. When writing to Innocent III they had asked: 'Why do you try to bully us like dumb beasts unquestioningly to change our ways rather than allowing us to speak and exchange reasoned argument with you?'[35] It was bad enough for them to be made to take an oath of submission to a foreign patriarch but worse still when that patriarch was answerable to a pope who condoned what they had always thought to be a mistaken if not heretical addition to the creed. This was a matter which fundamentally affected the nature of authority in the church. For, as the Byzantines never tired of reiterating, the *Filioque* had been accepted by one of the five patriarchs alone without the consent of his four colleagues, and the bishop of Rome had no licence to force the whole church to subscribe to an innovation introduced by his authority alone.[36]

Gradually the Byzantines of the thirteenth century were to discover that the church of Rome was responsible for authorising still further innovations or novelties (*kainotomiai*), which was the word regularly used for heresies. After the fourth crusade Greek pamphlets enumerating the errors of the Latins proliferated. Some, especially, those of a more popular nature, make no mention of the primacy of Rome.[37] The longest list is that compiled by Constantine Stilbes, bishop of Cyzicus about 1204, who describes one hundred and four Latin aberrations, malpractices, or novelties.[38] Of particular interest in this work is the detailed catalogue of crimes committed by the crusaders in Constantinople, for all of which, says Stilbes, no penalty was

---

[35] *PG* 140, col 296.

[36] This point is made in the letter of an anonymous patriarch of Constantinople to a patriarch of Jerusalem, ed A. N. Pavlov, *Kritičeskie opyty po istorij drevnješej Greco-Russkoj polemiki protiv Latinjam* (Critical studies on the history of older Greco-Russian polemic against the Latins) [Izvlečeno iz XIX. otčeta o prisuždenij nagrad grafa Uvarova] (St Petersburg 1878), suppl no 6, pp 158–68, p 167: 'There was a time when he (the pope) was our primate, when he was of the same mind and opinion. Let him give proof of his like-mindedness in the faith and he shall have the primacy as of old, when it was the faith that kept the ranks and not force and tyranny. Without this he will never get what he wants from us'. The date and authorship of this letter, which dwells more on the primacy of Peter, is still uncertain. It was formerly attributed to the patriarch Nicholas III writing to Symeon II of Jerusalem about 1085–9. But Darrouzès, 'Les documents', pp 43–51, argued for dating it in the thirteenth century and assigning it to Germanos II writing to Athanasios of Jerusalem between 1229 and 1235. More recently Laurent, *Regestes*, p 109, has argued on internal evidence for placing it in the patriarchate of Joseph I about 1273.

[37] See Argyriou, 'Remarques sur quelques listes', pp 20 *seq*.

[38] [J.] Darrouzès, 'Le Mémoire de [Constantin] Stilbès [contre les Latins'], *REB*, 21 (1963) pp 50–100 (Greek text and translation, pp 61–91).

inflicted upon them by their church. Whence one must conclude that
their hierarchy favour such wickedness and are guilty of abetting it.[39]
On the primacy he is content to say that the Latins 'proclaim and
believe that the pope is not the successor of Peter but Peter himself.
They put him above Peter and all but divinise him declaring him to
be lord of all Christendom; and they demand recognition of his
divinity on oath from the church universal and from every diocese
everywhere'.[40] But Stilbes was the first to record what was to the
Greeks the curious novelty of indulgences. 'The pope and their
hierarchy', he notes, 'absolve murder, perjury and other sins for the
future and in time to come, which amounts to opening the door to
every kind of impropriety for those absolved. And what is even more
laughable, they grant absolution to sinners for stated periods of years
in the future, maybe two or three, or more or less. They play this
game for the past as well, forgiving sins for stated periods of years,
months or days. They cannot cite any justification for this practice in
ecclesiastical law, unless it be perhaps the quantity of gifts paid out to
them by the recipients of this inefficacious absolution'.[41] The same
point was taken up later in the century by Meletios the Confessor in
his still unpublished treatise *Against the Latins*. Meletios marvels at the
claim of the Italian pope to be able to forgive sins not only in the past
but also in the future.[42]

There were other mysterious Latin innovations which only slowly
came to the notice of the Orthodox in the course of the thirteenth
century and for which, when the union of the churches became a
matter of political necessity as it did in the 1270s, they had to invent
Greek words and phrases. The doctrine of purgatory, for instance,
was patiently explained to them by a bilingual Franciscan called
John Parastron; and in the profession of faith submitted to the pope
before the second council of Lyons in 1274 the Greek words
πουργατώριον and καθαρτήριον make almost their first appearance.[43]

[39] Darrouzès, 'Le Mémoire de Stilbès', p 86.
[40] *Ibid* p 61.   [41] *Ibid* p 69.
[42] On Meletios see Beck p 679; D. M. Nicol, 'The Byzantine reaction to the Second
Council of Lyons, 1274', *SCH*, 7 (1971) pp 132–4; Θρησκευτικὴ καὶ Ἠθικὴ
Ἐγκυκλοπαιδεία, 8, col 949; Argyriou, 'Remarques sur quelques listes', pp 23–4.
[43] The Greek and Latin texts of Michael VIII's profession of faith are printed in [A. L.]
Tăutu, [*Acta Urbani IV, Clementis IV, Gregorii X (1261–1276)*], PCRCICO Fontes
ser III, 5, pt 1: (1953) no 41, pp 116–23: p 119: . . . πουργατωρίου, ἤτοι καθαρτηρίου,
καθὼς ὁ ἀδελφὸς Ἰωάννης ἡμῖν διεσάφησε . . . ('. . . purgatorii, hoc est catharterii
quemadmodum frater Johannes [Parastron] nobis notificavit . . .'). Some forty years
earlier George Bardanes, bishop of Corfu, while in Italy engaged in a discussion on the

Similarly, the Greek words μετουσίωσις, μετουσιοῦσθαι were coined (none too happily) at the same time to translate the Latin terms for transubstantiation, another novelty for the Greeks; and the definition of the pope's plenitude of power (*plenitudo potestatis*) had to be clumsily rendered in Greek as τὸ τῆς ἐξουσίας πλήρωμα—for this conception too was to the Greeks a novelty, or a stumbling-block.[44] Every novelty, every innovation that they were obliged to accept heaped the scandal still higher, until it came to be known among them simply as 'the papal scandal'.

In 1261 the Byzantines recovered their capital of Constantinople. The Latin empire and the Latin patriarchate ceased to exist except in title. But almost at once the restored Byzantine empire was faced with the threat of invasion from Italy, of a campaign for the restitution of the Latin régime which, so long as the Greeks remained in schism, could easily be qualified as a crusade. These were the political circumstances that dictated the long negotiations that led to the union of Lyons in 1274. The basis of those negotiations was a document delivered to the Byzantine emperor Michael VIII by pope Clement IV in 1267. This contained a detailed profession of faith which the emperor must endorse before the pope would receive the Orthodox church and people back into the fold of Rome, thereby saving them from a crusade for the forcible salvation of their wayward souls. There were to be no discussions about matters of faith or doctrine. The pope expected the emperor simply to effect the *reductio* of the Greeks to Rome without further ado.[45]

The Byzantines understandably disliked this form of ultimatum. Their objections were clearly expressed by their patriarch Joseph in three documents of 1273: an *apologia* by way of a statement to the emperor, an anti-Latin affidavit, and a profession of faith. It is strange, for all that has been written about the second council of Lyons, that

---

subject of Purgatory with a Franciscan. He left his own account of the discussion, which was probably the first of its kind. Text in M. Roncaglia, *Georges Bardanes, métropolite de Corfou, et Barthélémy de l'Ordre Franciscain, Studi e Testi Francescani*, 4 (Rome 1953) pp 56–71; see also A. Mustoxidi, *Delle Cose Corciresi*, 1 (Corfu 1848) pp 423–7. For the date see Hoeck-Loenertz, *Nikolaos-Nektarios*, p 125.

[44] The first appearance of the Greek word μετουσιοῦσθαι is in Michael VIII's profession of faith in 1274 (see above n 43), ed Tăutu, p 120. Jugie, *Theologia dogmatica*, 3, pp 194–9 ('De voce μετουσίωσις').

[45] Letter of Clement IV to Michael VIII, ed Tăutu no 23, pp 61–9. Compare letter of Gregory X, ed Tăutu, no 32, pp 97–100. See [B.] Roberg, *Die Union [zwischen der griechischen und der lateinischen Kirche auf dem II. Konzil von Lyon (1274)]*, *Bonner Historische Forschungen*, 24 (Bonn 1964) pp 58–9.

only one of these important documents has so far been fully published and properly edited.[46] What is clear from all of them, however, is that the patriarch and his advisers held the first cause of the schism to be the unauthorised addition of the *Filioque* to the creed. So long as the head of the Roman church upheld this distortion of theology and refused to discuss the matter it was impossible to accept his three other basic requirements. These were that the Greek church should acknowledge the primacy of the bishop of Rome, recognise his right of appellate jurisdiction over all the church, and commemorate his name in the liturgy. Joseph's answer to these three propositions was (1) that the pope's primacy is confined to his own ecclesiastical domain and has nothing to do with Constantinople; (2) that he cannot exercise a right of appeal over the whole extent of the pentarchy; (3) that to commemorate his name in the liturgy would be to accept his orthodoxy, which is impossible since he sanctions the corruption of the creed.[47]

Not all the Byzantine objections to the proposed union of the churches in the 1270s were so reasoned. The monks of Constantinople and elsewhere positively courted martyrdom in the defence of their unadulterated faith by disseminating forbidden anti-Latin tracts. The prisons were crowded with the victims of the emperor's persecution. The patriarch Joseph lost his job and was replaced by a more tractable patriarch in the person of John Bekkos, who was prepared to do his

---

[46] The *Apologia* of Joseph I, composed by the monk Job Iasites with the help of the historian George Pachymeres, has been published in part by Demetrakopoulos, Ὀρθόδοξος Ἑλλάς, pp 58–60, and by [J.] Dräseke, 'Der Kircheneinigungsversuch [des Kaisers Michael VIII Paläologos'], *Zeitschrift für wissenschaftliche Theologie*, 34 (Leipzig 1891) pp 332–5. See also C. Chapman, *Michel Paléologue restaurateur de l'empire byzantin* (Paris 1926), pp 110–11; D. M. Nicol, 'The Greeks and the Union of the Churches: The Preliminaries to the Second Council of Lyons, 1261–1274', *Medieval Studies presented to A. Gwynn*, ed J. A. Watt, J. B. Morrall, F. X. Martin (Dublin 1961) pp 468–9; Roberg, *Die Union*, pp 111–12; Laurent, *Regestes*, no 1400, pp 194–7 (where the manuscripts are listed). Joseph's affidavit was published by V. Laurent, 'Le serment anti-latin du patriarche Joseph Iᵉʳ (Juin 1273)', *EO*, 26 (1927) pp 396–407; Laurent, *Regestes*, no 1401, p 197. His profession of faith was printed by Nektarios, patriarch of Jerusalem, Περὶ τῆς ἀρχῆς τοῦ πάπα ἀντίρρησις (Jassy 1682) pp 237–9 (Greek text), and by G. Carelli, *Nuova raccolta di opuscoli scientifici e filologici*, XXIII (Venice 1755) pp 10–23 (Greek and Latin texts). Laurent, *Regestes*, no 1404, pp 199–200. This last is directed against those who were trying to force him into the Latin position; it is mainly about the procession of the Holy Spirit and only indirectly concerned with the primacy of Rome.

[47] It is possible that the letter of an anonymous patriarch of Constantinople edited by A. N. Pavlov was sent by Joseph to his colleague in Jerusalem about 1273. See above, n 36.

emperor's will by promoting the union of the churches. But even among the few unionists the three propositions outlined by Joseph, the pope's primacy, his right of appeal and the commemoration of his name, represented a scandal.[48] The message comes through loud and clear in the Greek documents relating to the council of Lyons which Gill has recently published. 'The very strong impression left after reading these official documents . . . is that the only thing that bothered the Greeks, faced with the question of the union of the Churches, was the canonical position of the pope—the three points, primacy, appeal and commemoration'.[49] Saint Thomas Aquinas, who died on his way to that council, composed the most famous of many Dominican treatises called *Contra errores Graecorum*. It was his opinion that disbelief in the universal primacy of the see of Rome was an error similar to that of disbelief in the procession of the Holy Spirit from the Son.[50]

The union of the churches was in the end proclaimed at Lyons in July 1274. A small Greek delegation there accepted, in the name of their emperor and church, all the basic requirements of the papacy as they had been proposed by Clement IV. There was no argument and no discussion either of theology or of the scandal concerning the pope. The Greeks were simply 'reduced'. The reaction in Byzantium was violent and widespread. As the unionist patriarch John Bekkos later admitted, everyone, man, woman and child, thought the peace in the church to be more a division than a union.[51] But when the danger of invasion from Italy had passed and when the emperor Michael who had forced the issue died in 1282, the union, already disowned by the pope, was solemnly and loudly denounced by the Byzantine church and people. Orthodoxy was restored. Those who had been persecuted in its defence became the heroes of the hour.

---

[48] These were the three capital requirements of the pope (τὰ τρία κεφάλαια) as outlined in the *Apologia* of Joseph, ed Dräseke, 'Der Kircheneingungsversuch', p 333, and elsewhere. See George Pachymeres, *De Michaele Palaeologo*, pp 386–7 (*CSHByz*): πρωτείῳ, ἐκκλήτῳ καὶ μνημοσύνῳ.

[49] J. Gill, 'The Church union of the Council of Lyons (1274) portrayed in Greek documents', *OCP*, 40 (1974) pp 5–45, p 42.

[50] Thomas Aquinas, *Contra errores Graecorum*, ed P. Mandonnet, *S. Thomae Aquinatis Opuscula Omnia*, 3 (Paris 1927) *Opusculum* 27, p 322: Similis autem error est dicentium Christi Vicarium, Romanae Ecclesiae Pontificem non habere universalis Ecclesiae primatum, errori dicentium, Spiritum Sanctum a Filio non procedere. See A. Dondaine, ' "Contra Graecos". Premiers écrits polémiques des Dominicains d'Orient', *AFP*, 21 (1951) pp 387–93.

[51] John Bekkos (Veccus), *De depositione sua*, PG 142 cols 952–3.

One of them, it is worth noting, is to this day commemorated as a confessor in the Orthodox calendar.[52] The union of Lyons was in the short term a political triumph for the emperor Michael VIII and a spiritual triumph for pope Gregory X who convened it. But in the longer term the chief beneficiary was the Orthodox church. For it emerged from its ordeal, as it had emerged from the disaster of the fourth crusade, with a stronger hold than ever on the hearts of its faithful. The prestige of the Byzantine church was immeasurably strengthened and the authority of the patriarchate of Constantinople was soon to extend far beyond the shrinking frontiers of the empire into the Slav and east European countries of the 'Byzantine Commonwealth'.

After the restoration of Orthodoxy in 1282 a generation of Byzantines grew up with the comforting illusion that the church of Rome did not exist. For over forty years there was no direct communication between Constantinople and the papacy. Byzantine theologians immersed themselves in the ever intriguing problems of the Holy Spirit and then, in the fourteenth century, in the questions of the divine light and the energies of God raised by saint Gregory Palamas and the hesychasts. Debates about the primacy of Rome or the authority of the pope were no longer topical. They took place only on the occasions when the emperor made overtures or the pope sent legates to Constantinople to reopen the subject of union. Between 1340 and 1370, for example, seven statements of the Orthodox position were made either in the form of tracts or of dialogues with the Latins. The best known is that by Barlaam of Calabria.[53] This presents the traditional Byzantine case for the collegiality of bishops, the political reasons for the primacy of Rome, the equality of privileges between Rome and Constantinople, the limited jurisdiction of the papacy, the independent appointment of patriarchs, and the proper use of the term catholic, which is not interchangeable with the word Roman. Barlaam's only new contribution is to introduce as an example and a warning the case of 'that shameless woman who became pope'.[54] This is one of the rare Byzantine references to the legend of pope Joan. But then Barlaam was a westerner, a Greek from southern Italy; and in due course, when exasperated by the Byzantines, he went over to Rome and turned his Orthodoxy on its head

---

[52] Meletios the Confessor is commemorated on 19 January.
[53] Barlaam, *Contra Latinos* (Λόγος περὶ τῆς τοῦ πάπα ἀρχῆς) *PG*, 151, cols 1255–80.
[54] Barlaam, *Contra Latinos*, col 1274.

in a treatise in Latin written against the Greeks. The two texts, for and against the primacy of Rome, are printed one above the other in Migne's *Patrology* and might serve as briefs for the defence of either case. Two other short essays by Barlaam on the matter of the primacy, written before his conversion to Rome, remain unpublished.[55]

The alarming success of the Turks, who made their first bridgehead in Europe at Gallipoli in 1354, led some Byzantines, the emperor among them, to look to the Latin west for help. The popes responded by sending emissaries to Constantinople to persuade the Greeks of the advantages of being reduced to Rome, and to assure them that no help could be provided until such reduction had occurred. The Byzantines particularly resented the implication that they were being ravaged by the enemies of the cross like sheep by wolves because they had left the salutary circle of the Roman church. As one of their monks very rightly pointed out to a papal legate in 1357, their enslavement by the Turks was being brought upon them by their own sins and short-comings and had nothing to do with their alleged disobedience to the pope. Had they not in the past scored many a victory over the infidel without submitting to the church of Rome?[56]

Another papal legate, Paul of Smyrna, started the same hare in a discussion with the former emperor John Cantacuzene in 1367. 'The true faith', he said, 'does not exist outside the jurisdiction of the pope. The proof of this fact is that, since you left his communion, the infidel has overcome you and conquered all your land'.[57] It was easy enough for the emperor to reply that the worst damage done to the empire by the infidel, the conquest of Syria and Antioch, had been done long before the schism. He was concerned not to score debating points but to find what were the 'causes of the scandal' and to submit those causes to common discussion in a council of the whole church. 'No one', he said, 'desires union more than I. . . . But what prevents this desire from being accomplished is the fact that never since the

[55] Meyendorff, 'St Peter', p 22, n 47, cites the various manuscripts of the fourteenth and fifteenth centuries. Extracts from one (Paris, Bibliothèque Nationale MS gr. 1218) are printed in Jugie, *Theologia dogmatica*, 4, pp 331 and n 1, 392–3.

[56] Darrouzès, 'Conférence sur la primauté', pp 89–90. It was often rudely said that the Byzantine empire had gone into military decline ever since, and as a result of, the schism. See the statement of the anonymous writer cited by Allatius, cols 785–6: '. . . ever since the patriarch Sergios struck the pope Christopher (*leg* Sergios IV) off his diptychs because of his heretical innovation, you will find that the empire of Constantinople has never prospered in its military ventures'.

[57] [J.] Meyendorff, 'Projets [de concile oecuménique en 1367: un dialogue inédit entre Jean Cantacuzène et le légat Paul']', *DOP*, 14 (1960) pp 147–77, p 174 lines 202–4.

schism have you [the Latins] sought its accomplishment in a friendly and fraternal manner. Always you have adopted a magisterial, authoritarian attitude, never allowing that we or anyone else can contest or contradict what the pope has said or may say in the future, since he is the successor of Peter and therefore speaks with the voice of Christ.'[58] Only at an oecumenical council in the presence of all five patriarchs can the causes of the schism really be resolved, for only thus will the Holy Spirit inform the leaders of the church as it informed the apostles. The claim of the pope to be able to speak for the whole church is the scandal that prevents this.

A few years before this statement Neilos Kabasilas, bishop of Thessalonica, had composed his treatise *On the causes of the dissensions in the church and on the primacy of the pope*.[59] Its Greek title reveals the same sense of where the cause of scandal lay: 'A demonstration of the fact that the only cause of the division which still exists between the church of the Latins and ourselves is the pope's unwillingness to submit the bone of contention to the arbitration of an oecumenical council and his desire to set himself up as the sole judge and master of the controversy, relegating the rest of us to the status of pupils hanging on his words . . .'. Neilos is careful to point out that the dispute is not about the primacy of the see of Rome as it used to be interpreted in the past. It is about the development of that theory to the point where the Romans want to sit in judgment as masters.'The pope, they say, is the supreme bishop and shepherd and father. He has the power to summon councils and also independently to make decisions affecting the whole church'. If this were true then the early councils of the church were superfluous and need never have happened.[60]

The same argument is used by Makarios, bishop of Ankyra, about the year 1400. His essay on the primacy is the most prolix and exhaustive treatment of the subject by a Byzantine writer before the fall of Constantinople. It was printed in Roumania in 1692, is hard to come by and has yet to be properly edited and studied.[61] A nearer

---

[58] Meyendorff, 'Projets', p 172 lines 102–14.

[59] Neilos Kabasilas, [*Nili Archiepiscopi Thessalonicensi libri duo De causis dissensionum in Ecclesia, et de Papae primatu,*] PG 149, cols 683–700, 700–30.

[60] Neilos Kabasilas, cols 685C–88B.

[61] Makarios of Ankyra, *Against the Latins* (Πόνημα, τὸ μὲν καθόλου κατὰ τῆς τῶν Λατίνων κακοδοξίας . . .), ed Dositheos of Jerusalem, Τόμος καταλλαγῆς (Jassy 1692) pp 1–205. The latter part of this work is directed against the heresies of Barlaam and Akindynos in the matter of hesychast theology. Makarios accompanied the emperor Manuel II

contemporary of Neilos Kabasilas was Matthew Angelos Panaretos, a lawyer. Not all of his many works have been published, and his three tracts on the primacy remain in manuscript.[62] The points of emphasis of these three writers vary. But their general conclusions, as expressed by Makarios, are the same, namely that the cause of the separation of the Latins from the other four patriarchates is their uncanonical addition to the creed made on the authority of the pope alone.[63]

But during the last hundred years of Byzantium's existence, before the sins of the Orthodox were finally visited upon them by the Ottoman sultan in 1453, the primacy of Rome was not in the forefront of their minds. For every treatise on the primacy there must be ten on the procession of the Holy Spirit. Every Byzantine theologian worth his salt, lay or cleric, wrote at least one essay on this absorbing problem. As Sir Steven Runciman has written: 'To many pious persons, in the East as well as in the West, it has seemed strange that the unity of Christendom should have been split by a preposition'.[64] Demetrios Kydones, prime minister of several emperors in the fourteenth century, was one such pious person in the east. Kydones was converted to the Roman church by his reading and translations of Thomas Aquinas. It was an intellectual conversion based on reason rather than burning conviction. He felt bound to explain it to his

---

on his celebrated visit to Paris and London in 1400–2. Demetrakopoulos, Ὀρθόδοξος Ἑλλάς pp 88–9; L. Petit, in *DTC*, 9, 2, cols 1441–3; Beck pp 741–2. Some extracts of his statements on the primacy of Rome are printed in Allatius, cols 215, 266, 267, 268, 296, 297, 323, 1127, and in Jugie, *Theologia dogmatica*, 4, pp 396–8. Like Kabasilas, Makarios declared that 'if all bishops had been subject to Rome and the pope could do what he liked then the decrees and canons were in vain and the assemblies of local and oecumenical synods over the ages were superfluous'. Allatius col 296.

[62] [P.] Risso, ['Matteo Angelo Panareto e cinque suoi opuscoli'], *Roma e l'Oriente*, 8 (Rome 1914) pp 91–105, 162–79, 231–7, 274–90; 9 (1915) pp 112–20, 202–6; 10 (1915) pp 63–77, 146–64, 238–51; 11 (1916) pp 28–35, 63–80, 154–60. For his treatises on the primacy see V. Laurent, in *DTC*, 11 (1932) col 1844; Risso, 8 (1914) pp 175–6; 11 (1916) pp 32–3. In general see Laurent, *DTC*, 11 cols 1841–9; Beck, p 745; Jugie, *Theologia dogmatica*, 1, pp 446–8; G. Novak, in Θρησκευτικὴ καὶ Ἠθικὴ Ἐγκυκλοπαιδεία, IX, cols 1118–20.

[63] Makarios of Ankyra, cap XXX, col 1127 (ed Allatius). The same position is stated at length by Symeon of Thessalonica about 1425 in his *Dialogus in Christo Adversus omnes haereses*, PG 155, cols 33–176, caps 19 and 20 (*Adversus Latinos* and *Quaenam sint a Latinis innovata*), especially cols 97–100, 117–121; and also by George Gennadeios Scholarios, notably in his first treatise on the procession of the Holy Spirit, ed L. Petit, X. A. Siderides, M. Jugie, *Oeuvres complètes de Gennade Scholarios*, 2 (Paris 1929) p 234.

[64] S. Runciman, *The Great Church in Captivity. A Study of the Patriarchate of Constantinople from the Eve of the Turkish Conquest to the Greek War of Independence* (Cambridge 1968) p 90.

fellow Greeks in a series of apologies which are among the most remarkable documents of late Byzantine literature.[65] For him the primacy of Rome was a simple matter of logistics to be stated and accepted in legal terms. The church, like an army, needs one single leader whom all will obey. Otherwise anarchy will prevail.[66] He saw the symptoms of such anarchy in the childish squabbles about the minutiae of theology; and he found the endless lucubrations of his Orthodox friends about the Holy Spirit to be tedious and rather absurd.[67]

Kydones was exceptional. His enthusiasm for western culture and scholarship made it possible for him to bridge the gap by ignoring or building above the stumbling-blocks. But more devout and not always less intelligent Greeks sincerely believed that the stumbling-blocks could not be ignored or bypassed, and that only a patient and concerted effort by both sides could roll them away from the path to unity in the church. The first and the last real effort of this nature was made at the council of Florence in 1439. Far more breath was expended on the problems of the Holy Spirit at that council, first in Ferrara and then in eight more sessions at Florence, than on any other subject. The question of the primacy of Rome was comparatively simply resolved, almost as an addendum to the main agenda.[68] Perhaps it did not matter much to the Greeks. Because by that time the status of the patriarchate of Constantinople in the eyes of the Orthodox had changed. The triumph of Orthodoxy out of the ruins of the union of Lyons had reinvigorated the Byzantine church. In the course of the fourteenth century, as the empire sank deeper into its political, economic and military decline, the church came to be seen as the only permanent institution in a dissolving world. The patriarchs of

[65] Demetrios Kydones, *Apologie* [*della propria fede*], I: *Ai Greci ortodossi*; II: *Difesa della propria sincerità*; III: *Il testamento religioso*, ed G. Mercati, *Notizie di Procoro e Demetrio Cidone, Manuele Caleca e Teodoro Meliteniota ed altri appunti per la storia della teologia e della letteratura bizantina del secolo XIV* (Vatican City 1931) pp 359–403, 403–25, 425–35. His fourth *Apologia*, in defence of the authority of the Latin fathers, is unpublished. See R.-J. Loenertz, 'Démétrius Cydonès, I. De la naissance à l'année 1373', *OCP*, 36 (1970) p 55 and n 2.

[66] Demetrios Kydones, *Apologie*, pp 377–9; see also pp 430–1.

[67] *Ibid* p 429.

[68] See J. Gill, *The Council of Florence* (Cambridge 1959) pp 131–269 and 'The Definition of the Primacy of the Pope in the Council of Florence', in *Personalities of the Council of Florence and Other Essays* (Oxford 1964) pp 264–86; D. J. Geanakoplos, 'The Council of Florence (1438–1439) and the problem of union between the Byzantine and Latin Churches', in *Byzantine East and Latin West: Two Worlds of Christendom in Middle Ages and Renaissance* (Oxford 1966) pp 99–109; Runciman, *The Great Church*, pp 106–9.

Constantinople commanded an authority which was more universally, if sometimes grudgingly, respected in the Orthodox world than that of the emperors, not only among the Greeks but also among the Christians of Serbia, Bulgaria, Roumania, Cyprus, Trebizond and Georgia. Though often politically at variance with the temporal rulers of Constantinople they looked on its spiritual head as their primate. Only the Russians, who had not tasted the bitterness of Latin or Turkish occupation, were inclined to go their own way.[69] Even in the parts of the empire under Turkish rule the voice of the patriarch could still be heard. In 1384 the patriarch Neilos, writing to pope Urban VI, corrected the western misapprehension that all letters sent to the patriarchate were opened by the Turks. 'For', he wrote, 'we suffer from the Turks by God's will for our sins, but we have complete freedom to receive and to answer letters, also to appoint, ordain and send bishops wherever we like and to carry on all our ecclesiastical business without hindrance even in the territory of the infidel'.[70]

The primacy of the see of Constantinople in the Orthodox world was increasingly asserted by its patriarchs. As early as 1330 we find one of them describing it as 'the mother of all churches, the promulgator of the sacred doctrine of true religion throughout the *oikoumene*'.[71] The right of Constantinople to hear cases of appeal from other patriarchates was written into Byzantine law in the days of Photios.[72] The fourteenth-century lawyer Matthew Blastares

---

[69] On relations between the Russian church and Constantinople in the fourteenth century, see D. Obolensky, 'Byzantium, Kiev and Moscow: A study in ecclesiastical diplomacy', *DOP*, 11 (1957) pp 21–78; J. Meyendorff, 'Alexius and Roman: A study in Byzantine-Russian relations (1352–1354)', *BS*, 28 (1967) pp 278–88; F. Tinnefeld, 'Byzantinisch-russische Kirchenpolitik im 14. Jahrhunderts', *BZ*, 67 (1974) 359–84.

[70] Neilos, Letter (*pittakion*) to pope Urban VI (September 1384), *MM*, 2, pp 86–7. A very different picture of Christian life under the Turks is, however, conveyed by Matthew, bishop of Ephesos, about 1339. Matthew complains specifically about the interception of his letters by the Turks. D. Reinsch. *Die Briefe des Matthaios von Ephesos im Codex Vindobonensis Theol. Gr. 174* (Berlin 1974) no B 55, p 175 lines 9–11: ὀλίγου γὰρ πρόσθεν, ὡς ἔσχε τὰ καθ᾽ ἡμᾶς, πρὸς σὲ οὐκ οἶδ᾽ ὁπότερον φῷ τραγῳδήσαντες ἢ ἐπιστείλαντες ἔγνωμεν ἀκριβῶς ληφθέντα τοῖς πολεμίοις. See S. Vryonis, *The Decline of Medieval Hellenism in Asia Minor and the Process of Islamization from the Eleventh through the Fifteenth Century* (Berkeley/Los Angeles/London 1971) pp 343–8.

[71] Esaias to the Katholikos of Armenia, *MM*, 1, p 159.

[72] *Epanagoge*, ed J. and P. Zepos, *Jus greco-romanum*, 2 (Athens 1931) tit 3, pp 242–3: Περὶ πατριάρχου § 9. See also A. Pavlov, 'Anonimnaja grečeskaja statja o preimuščestvach konstantinopolskago patriaršago prestola' ['Anonymous Greek treatise on the privileges of the patriarchal throne of Constantinople and an old Slavonic translation of it with two important additions'], *VV*, 4 (1897) pp 143–59.

confirmed that, "while other patriarchs have jurisdiction in their own territories, the bishop of Constantinople is empowered . . . to supervise and judge disputes arising in other patriarchates.'[73] This ruling was cited chapter and verse by the patriarch Neilos to a recalcitrant bishop of Thessalonica in 1382.[74] The traditional concept of a pentarchy, in which the see of Rome held pride of place, was not forgotten. The same Neilos protested to pope Urban VI that the patriarchs of Constantinople were not disputing his primacy, 'for we confess that we hold you to be the first according to the canons of the fathers', provided that the pope was orthodox.[75] But there was a feeling in the fourteenth century that, because the pope was not orthodox, the pentarchy had in any case narrowed down to a tetrarchy. The patriarch Kallistos explained it thus to the clergy of Bulgaria in 1355: 'The five patriarchates were established from the beginning by the catholic and apostolic church of Christ, and so it was as long as the pope of Rome was with us. But since then and until now we are four, united in unbroken communion and in commemoration of each other.'[76]

The title of oecumenical patriarch which in earlier days may have meant no more than bishop of the imperial capital had come in the empire's decline to have a much wider meaning. Patriarchs advise and admonish the secular as well as the spiritual leaders of their Orthodox Slav neighbours with all the assurance of popes. Philotheos, for example, informs the grand duke of Russia in 1370 that he as patriarch is 'set up by God as the common father of all Christians wherever in the world they may be'; and he reminds the bishop of Kiev that the patriarch is 'by God appointed as pastor and teacher of all the universe'.[77] The patriarch Antonios IV writing to the bishop of Novgorod in 1393 calls himself 'father and spiritual lord by God appointed over all Christians in the universe', and 'judge general of the *oikoumene* to whom every Christian may appeal to have his

---

[73] Matthew Blastares, Σύνταγμα, in Rhalles and Potles, *Syntagma*, 6 (1859) p 429.

[74] Neilos to the metropolitan of Thessalonica (July 1382), *MM*, 2, p 40. See also the letter of Kallistos to the patriarch of Antioch, *MM*, 1, p 380.

[75] *MM*, 2, p 87.

[76] Kallistos, exhortation to the clergy of Trnovo (December 1355), *MM*, 1, pp 437–8. For the later development of this theme see Jugie, *Theologia dogmatica*, 4, pp 461–3.

[77] Philotheos, letter ot Dimitri, Grand Duke of Russia (June 1370), *MM*, 1, p 516: κοινὸς πατὴρ ἄνωθεν ἀπὸ θεοῦ καταστὰς εἰς τοὺς ἀπανταχοῦ τῆς γῆς εὑρισκομένους χριστιανοὺς . . . . Philotheos to the metropolitan of Kiev and All Russia (August 1371), *MM*, 1, p 582: . . . ἡ μετριότης ἡμῶν ἐτάχθη παρὰ θεοῦ ποιμὴν καὶ διδάσκαλος πάσης τῆς οἰκουμένης . . . . See also the statement of Neilos (1382), *MM*, 2, p 45.

wrongs righted'.[78] While in his famous letter to Basil, grand duke of Moscow, he claims as patriarch to be 'the catholic teacher of all Christians and to hold the place of Christ'.[79]

Earlier Byzantine political theory had postulated that it was the emperor who was the vice-gerent of God on earth. In the last years of the empire it was the patriarch who claimed and commanded the authority of this high calling, however much he might protest, as Antonios did to the duke of Moscow, that a church without an emperor was unthinkable. Christians acclimatised to such a respect for the see of Constantinople may have thought of the 'scandal concerning the pope' as rather anachronistic or irrelevant. But they had an abiding horror of the scandals and novelties countenanced by the popes in the Latin church, not least of those to do with the Holy Spirit. This may help to explain why it took months of wrangling at Ferrara and Florence to reach a formula about the Holy Spirit and only a matter of days to work out an agreed statement about the primacy of Rome.

Since the fall of Constantinople in 1453 the Orthodox church has shown a phenomenal talent for survival, first under Turkish rule and now under communism. It may not be fanciful to suggest that it learnt some of its earlier lessons in the art of survival through its defiance of the Latins, spiritual and temporal, in the thirteenth century and its defiance also of the Greek emperors who tried to bend its will to their political purposes. In the last centuries of Byzantium, the years of political and military collapse, the Orthodox church built up its spiritual reserves while its patriarchs acquired the international prestige and authority which were to carry their church through long centuries of institutional poverty and physical persecution. Modern Orthodox theologians are sometimes doubtful about dwelling on their Byzantine past. The church should look to the future. I am sure they are right. But it is always worth remembering that after the Turks broke into Constantinople in 1453 the hero of the Byzantine people was not an emperor but a monk. The last emperor had been killed fighting at the walls of his city. Suddenly it was a fact that there was a church without an emperor. The conquering sultan Mehmed II ordained that the patriarch of Constantinople should in

[78] Antonios IV, letter to the bishops, clergy and people of Novgorod (September 1393), *MM*, 2, pp 182, 187: . . . ἐγὼ γάρ εἰμι ὁ καθολικὸς τῆς οἰκουμένης κριτὴς . . . .

[79] Antonios IV, letter to Basil, grand duke of Moscow, *MM*, 2, p 189: . . . καθολικός εἰμι διδάσκαλος πάντων τῶν χριστιανῶν . . . ὁ πατριάρχης ἔχει τὸν τόπον τοῦ Χριστοῦ, καὶ ἐπ' αὐτοῦ κάθηται τοῦ θρόνου τοῦ δεσποτικοῦ . . . .

future be answerable for the conduct of all Christians under Ottoman rule. He knew what he was doing. He knew that the Orthodox church had shown a greater talent for vigorous survival than the Byzantine empire. What he was not to know was that the same church would outlive the Ottoman empire as well.

University of London
King's College

A MISSION TO THE ORTHODOX?
THE CISTERCIANS IN ROMANIA

by BRENDA M. BOLTON

IT has been said that Innocent III shared the popular belief existing at the beginning of the thirteenth century that the world would end in 1284.[1] Perhaps this is the reason why throughout his pontificate he was eager to resolve the divisions facing mankind. These divisions were reflected in the deviations of the heretic, the beliefs of the infidel and the schism of the eastern church. In the first of these Innocent was meeting success, albeit in varying degrees, for example in Languedoc.[2] The second and third needed his further attention. He was of the opinion that a renewed crusading effort in both east and west would be able to achieve mass conversions amongst Jews and Muslims. To this end the fourth crusade of 1204[3], mounted mainly by the Cistercians, came into being.

The unity of the church was also regarded as of paramount importance and therefore had to be included in these last aims. To Innocent, with his grand design for the organisation of a single, united and conforming church,[4] this schismatic situation awaited a 'final solution'. The notorious events associated with 1204 did not deter Innocent from diverting the Cistercians to a mission to the orthodox.

This task was taken up with pride by the Cistercians. One of their chroniclers, Caesarius of Heisterbach, writing in the early years of the thirteenth century stated that 'the vine of Cîteaux had been planted in Greece'. His attribution of this to the Latin emperor Henry of Flanders may have been designed as an historically inaccurate tribute to Henry

---

[1] R. I. Burns, 'Christian-Islamic Confrontation in the West: the thirteenth-century dream of conversion', *AHR* 76 (1971) pp 1386–1412, 1432–34 especially p 1390; R. W. Southern, *Western views of Islam in the Middle Ages* (Cambridge, Mass., 1962) p 42. For Innocent's crusading appeal of April 1213 see *PL* 216 (1855) cols 817–22.

[2] B. M. Bolton, 'Tradition and temerity: papal attitudes to deviants 1159–1216' *SCH* 9 (1972) pp 79–91. [C.] Thouzellier, *Catharisme et Valdéisme [en Languedoc à la fin du xiie siècle]* (2 ed Louvain 1969) pp 183–212 provides a detailed account of the mission to Languedoc.

[3] The events leading up to the fourth crusade are analysed by C. M. Brand, *Byzantium confronts the West 1180–1204* (Cambridge, Mass., 1968) and [A.] Frolow, *[Recherches sur] la déviation de la ive croisade [vers Constantinople]* (Paris 1955).

[4] A. Luchaire, *Innocent III: La Question d'Orient* (Paris 1907) pp 55–75.

but Caesarius was at least correct in noting the expansion of his order in the newly acquired lands of Romania in 1204.[5] To the Cistercians this was one more accepted example that no matter where the boundaries of the Latin world might be extended, there was no country or island where one could not find their order. The church needed them in Spain: they were there. The church needed them in Languedoc: they were there likewise.

Such pride as this, with the accompanying high hopes for success, may have been justified when Caesarius was writing so soon after the event but a clear examination of what actually happened to the Cistercians both during and after the fourth crusade may perhaps suggest that this further planting may have been harmful to the vine.[6] Southern has suggested that the incipient failure of the Cistercian order may have taken place about the year 1200.[7] It may be that the activities of the Cistercians in Romania after 1204 indicate more clearly this failure.

That Innocent should have chosen the Cistercians was only to be expected. Throughout the twelfth century the development of their order and the characteristics of its organisation meant that they filled the gap between two types of order, the military on the one hand and the monastic on the other. The Cistercians had an organisation which was one of the masterpieces of medieval planning.[8] Their military attitude towards their faith was mirrored not only in the discipline of their internal life but also in their practice of it outside their houses. They represented the frontier guards of faith in both a metaphysical and a physical sense. They determined their objectives with absolute rigour and operated to achieve them on both the geographical and spiritual frontiers of orthodoxy. They were ready to attack no matter where these frontiers appeared. Saint Bernard himself had demonstrated the compatibility of military and monastic aims when he praised the *milites christi* who had taken up both the spiritual and the temporal

---

[5] [A.] Manrique, [*Cistercienses seu verius ecclesiastici Annales a conditio Cistercio*] 4 vols (Lyons 1642–1659) 3 p 6. Caesarius writes 'ita ut jam non sit regio vel insula intra metas latinitatis ubi ordo cisterciensis non sit'.

[6] [E.**A.R.**] Brown, ['The cistercians in the latin empire of Constantinople and Greece 1204–1276'] *Traditio* 14 (1958) pp 63–120 especially pp 64–78 for a consideration of Cistercian involvement in events leading up to the fourth crusade.

[7] [R. W.] Southern, *Western Society* [*and the Church in the Middle Ages*] (Harmondsworth 1970) p 269.

[8] *Ibid* p 255.

[9] J. F. O'Callaghan, 'The affiliation of the Order of Calatrava with the Order of Cîteaux', *ASOC* 15 (1959) pp 163–93 especially pp 171–4 and 16 (1960) pp 3–59.

swords to combat the devil and his works. Indeed in another frontier
area, Iberia, the phenomenal growth of the military religious orders
must be attributed to saint Bernard and his followers.⁹ Their example
had led in the second half of the twelfth century to the great Spanish
military orders of Calatrava and Alcantara and to the Portuguese order
of Avis.¹⁰ The appeal of these orders was to the knightly classes,
converted as saint Bernard put it from *the militia mundi* to the *militia
dei*. These orders adopted the severe Cistercian rule, became affiliated
to mother houses and strengthened their links with Cîteaux. Thus on
the western frontier, the exact relationship between knights and
Cistercians was clarified and juridically stated through Cistercian
general chapters. As we shall see, a similar situation did not arise in
the east and it is interesting to speculate on the part which the presence
or absence of land-based internal communications may have played
in this. These were present in Spain but not in Greece.

The Cistercians were regarded as the chief papal agents, and so the
fourth crusade was largely a Cistercian operation planned and
mounted from Cîteaux.¹¹ In addition to the objectives of Innocent III
the Cistercians, who thought that the further intention of any crusade
was certainly to initiate some sort of colonising activity,¹² regarded
the operation in the east as being specifically a colonising expedition.
Innocent wrote of his wish that the order should propagate itself in
any conquered lands there might be.¹³ Already before the crusade,
Innocent considered the orthodox Greeks to be in need of missionary
endeavour. Early in 1204 he had found it necessary to write to his Latin
subjects in Constantinople reminding them of the virtue of obedience
and asking them to work to reunite the Greek and Latin churches 'for
the daughter must return to the mother and all Christ's lambs must
have only one shepherd'.¹⁴

¹⁰ *Ibid* p 176; J. F. O'Callaghan, 'The foundation of the order of Alcantara 1176–1218',
Catholic Historical Review 47 (London 1961–2) pp 471–86; [R. I.] Burns, *The Crusader
kingdom of Valencia: [reconstruction on a thirteenth century frontier]* 2 vols (Cambridge,
Mass., 1967) 1 pp 173–96 and for a comprehensive bibliography [*The*] *Historia Occidentalis [of Jacques de Vitry]* ed J. F. Hinnebusch, *Spicilegium Friburgense* 17 (Fribourg
1972) pp 260–2. Between 1213 and 1221 the knights of Avis adhered to the order of
Calatrava.
¹¹ Brown pp 64, 72–3.
¹² Southern, *Western Society* p 257.
¹³ *PL* 215 (1855) cols 636–8 where Innocent appeals not only to Cistercians but to
Cluniacs, Augustinian canons and other orders, and *PL* 216 (1855) col 594 where the
Cistercians alone are mentioned, 'nos enim volentes ut ordinis Cisterciensis,
religio . . . in Romaniae partibus propagetur'.
¹⁴ *PL* 215 (1855) cols 512–17.

Innocent therefore regarded the task of the Cistercians as being preachers and missionaries on the frontiers of Christianity. They were also to keep the objectives of the crusade firmly before the crusaders. As his main crusade agents and experts in controlling heresy, they had by 1204 already mounted a mission in Languedoc where Innocent regarded them as the most effective instrument for the conversion of the southern French cathars. There their conversion methods involved them in preaching and debating supported by a very powerful papal mandate.[15] He knew that the Cistercians themselves may not have found it so easy to differentiate in practice the partly religious and partly military aspects of their work. Although Innocent was perhaps in advance of his time in wanting as little disruption as possible to accompany the process of conversion, it must be borne in mind that the true interpretation of missionary activity in the medieval sense was for one religion[16] to dominate a subordinate religion. In this the Cistercians had already shown themselves to be eminently suitable at organising large tracts of land of uncertain loyalty. It is likely that Innocent would have thought of them as military police and support troops watching over newly conquered lands, as was their function in Spain. In addition, as a quasi-military monastic order, the Cistercians would have been expected by Innocent to be clear about the objectives of the crusade. It is undoubtedly true that in the case of some crusaders they were successful in this. The dedication of Villehardouin to *simplicitas* might be considered to to be a case in point.[17] Others of course were more concerned with *covoitise* and even abbot Martin of Pairis in his piety did not consider the looting of sacred relics from the church of the Pantocrator to conflict with the idea of *simplicitas*.[18]

It has often been said that the diversion of the fourth crusade to Constantinople meant its complete failure. Arguments on the issue

[15] *Ibid* cols 358–60; Thouzellier, *Catharisme et Valdéisme* p 187.

[16] Burns, *The Crusader kingdom of Valencia*, 1 p 9.

[17] [Geoffrey de] Villehardouin, *La Conquête [de Constantinople]* ed E. Faral (Paris 1938). For a most interesting analysis of Villehardouin's views see [J. M. A.] Beer, *Villehardouin.* [*Epic Historian*], *Études de Philologie et d'histoire,* 7 (Geneva 1968) pp 26–7; C. Morris, 'Geoffrey de Villehardouin and the conquest of Constantinople', *History,* 53 (1968), pp 24–34. For possible influences on Villehardouin, M. R. Gutsch, 'A twelfth century preacher—Fulk of Neuilly', in *The crusades and other historical essays,* ed L. J. Paetow (New York 1928) pp 183–206.

[18] [S.] Runciman, *Byzantine Style and Civilisation* (Harmondsworth 1975) p 158; *Guntherus Parisiensis Historia Constantinopolitana,* ed [P.] Riant in *Exuviae [Sacrae Constantinopolitanae]* 2 vols (Geneva 1875) 1 p 119.

abound.[19] But if the objectives of the crusade included dealing with the 'unorthodoxy' of the orthodox, failure may not have been so complete. This however have may been a casuistic argument presented after the event. No matter which is correct, one of the results of the crusade was the arrival in strength of the Cistercians in Romania.

The question that now has to be asked is whether they were suitable for the tasks which confronted them. The differences between Greeks and Latins could be regarded as a purely jurisdictional matter centering on the recognition of a pope or a patriarch. The Greeks believed that their Roman emperor in Constantinople governed and protected the great society of the Christian faith. The Roman church they thought had strayed far from the paths laid down by the early fathers and councils. Before agreement could be reached, the Latins would have to acknowledge that their kings and emperors were only agents of the one true emperor of the Romans and that their pope was only one of the five patriarchs of the undivided Christian church.[20]

The west for its part regarded the Greeks with revulsion. Their failure to accept the pope's line of succession from Peter and the obstinate way in which they clung to what the Latins considered to be their impure rites only confirmed the view that they were perfidious, hostile to the west and hardened schismatics.[21] Men in western Europe were also concerned about the spiritual wealth of Constantinople. By spiritual wealth they were thinking of the huge store of relics housed in the city. The unworthiness of the Greeks to be the custodians of this sacred treasure was one of the arguments used to justify the crusaders' assault on the city.[22] Both sides, therefore, regarded each other as being worse than the infidel and such mutual incomprehension meant that any mission from the west to the east would at least be difficult if not impossible. The west however regarded the goal of conformity itself as being worth the effort and so undertook missionary activity.

There is no evidence that other orders appeared in Romania until

[19] Among the most recent of the secondary works on the fourth crusade are S. Runciman, *A History of the Crusades* 3 vols (Cambridge 1954) 3 pp 107–31; E. H. McNeal and R. L. Wolff, 'The Fourth Crusade' in *A History of the Crusades* ed K. M. Setton, 2, *The Later Crusades 1189–1311*, ed R. L. Wolff and H. W. Hazard (Philadelphia 1962) pp 153–85; D. M. Nicol, 'The Fourth Crusade and the Greek and Latin Empires 1204–1261' *CMH* 4 pp 275–330 and P. Lemerle, 'Byzance et la Croisade' *Relazioni del X Congresso Internazionale di Scienze Storiche*, 3 (Florence 1955) pp 595–620.
[20] D. M. Nicol, *The Last Centuries of Byzantium 1261–1453* (London 1972) pp 7–8.
[21] Luchaire, *Innocent III: la question d'Orient* p 59.
[22] R. W. Southern, *The Making of the Middle Ages* (London 1967) p 62.

the advent of the mendicants. Even so the Cistercians in addition to the other merits mentioned earlier were the only religious order which could speak with conviction to their orthodox counterparts although there was no Greek name for them as there was later for the Franciscans. As we have seen, the order maintained a severe discipline over its members and also enjoyed a high reputation for the simplicity, austerity and sanctity of its life. It was just these qualities which were the basis for the principal force of monasticism in the east.[23] The life and works of saint Basil were read in the Cistercian foundations of Cîteaux and Clairvaux and so the desire to return to the desert and the recognised value of manual work were elements in Cistercian thought which may have derived from eastern ideas on asceticism. They certainly provide most striking parallels between Cistercian and eastern ideas. If any order was to be heard by the Orthodox, then it was the voice of the Cistercians which many in the west considered to be the one most likely. This was in line with the objective put forward by Innocent III who wanted a vigorous campaign of missionary work among the orthodox which might attract the respect of these schismatic people towards the Latin church. The lay conquerors also supported the Cistercians.[24] These lay benefactors hoped to ensure that they had foundations of great stability and corporate strength, capable of imposing a close supervision on a wide area of country. The leader of the crusade, Boniface of Montferrat who adopted the title of king of Thessalonica was the first to act on behalf on the order. So with the encouragement of pope, emperor and lay lords alike, in the years immediately after the conquest, Cistercian houses were established in Constantinople and Greece to colonise, Christianise and control.

The first Cistercian house to be founded was Chortaitou near Thessalonica, granted in 1205 by Boniface of Montferrat to the

[23] J. LeClercq, 'Les relations entre le monachisme oriental et le monachisme occidental dans le haut moyen âge' in Le Millénaire du Mont Athos 963–1963 2 vols (Chevetogne/Venice 1963–5)2 pp 49–80. Also J. LeClercq, Aux sources de la spiritualité occidentale (Paris 1964) pp 53–64. Another highly stimulating article which illuminates many aspects of the problem is P. McNulty and B. Hamilton, 'Orientale lumen et magistra latinitas: Greek influences on Western Monasticism 900–1100' Millénaire du Mont Athos 1 pp 181–2.

[24] [G.] Millet, [Le monastère de Daphni: Histoire, architecture, mosaïques] (Paris 1899) p 27. They included men such as the emperors Baldwin I (1204–1205) and Henry of Constantinople (1206–1216), Boniface of Montferrat, king of Thessalonica (1204–1207) Otto de la Roche, Megaskyr of Athens (1205–1225) and Geoffrey de Villehardouin, lord of Achaia (1209–1230)

crusader abbot Peter of Locedio.[25] Locedio itself lay in the diocese of Vercelli near Boniface's Lombard lands.[26] By the early 1220s Chortaitou had assumed the responsibilities of a mother house towards the Euboean monastery of St Archangelus in Negroponte.[27] The illustrious Greek monastery of Daphni near Athens was given by Otto de la Roche, a Burgundian knight, and megaskyr of Athens, probably in 1207 to the abbey of Bellevaux near Besançon, with which his family had close connections.[28] The monastery of St Stephen, in or near Constantinople, was occupied after 1208[29] and its Venetian mother house, St Thomas de Torcello, also controlled two monasteries in Crete, Gergeri from 1217 and St Mary Varangorum from 1230.[30] By 1213 or 1214 the house of St Angelus in Pera in Constantinople was affiliated to the abbey of Hautecombe near Geneva.[31] In the following year the community of St Angelus was entrusted with the daughter house of Rufinianai near Chalcedon in Asia Minor, an area won by the Latins only as recently as 1211 or 1212.[32] The location of the monastery of Laurus founded in 1214 remains in doubt[33] and little is known of the community at Zaraca near Corinth occupied by 1225.[34] The convent of St Mary de Percheio in Constantinople contained a community of nuns by 1221,[35] then was taken into papal protection and affiliated to Cîteaux. The convent of St Mary de Verge in Modon appears to have been a later foundation since little is known of it until 1267.[36]

[25] [L.] Janauschek, [*Originum Cisterciensium*] (Vienna 1877) I pp 218–19; Brown p 79 n 83; See also the history of Chortaitou by A. E. Vakalopoulos, in *Epeteris Etaireias Byzantinon Spoudon*, 15 (1939) pp 281–8.

[26] A. Ceruti, 'Un codice del monasterio cisterciense di Lucedio', *Archivio storico italiano*, 4 ser, 8 (Florence 1881) pp 373–8.

[27] Brown p 8.

[28] Janauschek p 214; Millet p 28 n 2.

[29] Janauschek p 215; R. Janin, *La géographie écclesiastique de l'empire byzantin, premier partie: Le siège de Constantinople et le patriarcat oecuménique III: Les églises et les monastères* (Paris 1953) pp 488–93 for evidence of the location of St Stephen.

[30] *Ibid* p 213; L. Santifaller, *Beiträge zur Geschichte des lateinischen Patriarchats von Konstantinopel* (Weimar 1938) pp 95–6; Brown pp 82–5.

[31] *Ibid* p 87, Janauschek p 219.

[32] Brown pp 88–90.

[33] *Ibid* p 95; Janauschek pp 219–20. R. Janin, 'Les sanctuaires de Byzance sous la domination latine 1204–1261'. *Études byzantines* 2 (Paris 1944) p 181 suggests that the monastery was in Constantinople.

[34] Janauschek p 227; Brown pp 93–4 suggests that Zaraca may have been transferred to the Cistercian order on the initiative of Geoffrey de Villehardouin.

[35] Manrique 4 p 240; Brown pp 91–2 nn 152, 153. There is an interesting short section on Cistercian nuns in the east in *Historia Occidentalis*, ed J. F. Hinnebusch, p 268.

[36] Brown p 194 n 164.

What geographical pattern is it possible to see in these foundations? They are all on or near the coastline and bear some relation to a shipping route following a line of ports from Italy all the way round to Constantinople thus showing an external line of communication.

This coastal pattern makes it difficult to equate the foundations in Romania with the usual Cistercian activity on wasteland and frontier. Perhaps because this was an external line of communication their first idea was not to police the area but to establish a line of trading posts as had the Romans in earlier days. If this was so, then it is interesting to note that no trading posts or garrisons were established on the south side of the Black Sea.

Another point which seems strange is that most if not all of the foundations used Orthodox buildings already in existence.[37] There must have been a very large number of vacant Greek monasteries after the conquest only some of which the Cistercians selected for habitation. In this selection instead of following their normal practice of taking wasteland far from habitation, here in Romania they made foundations in the most civilised, developed and populous places.[38] An example is the monastery of Chortaitou which was a rich house with sufficient assets to support two hundred monks.[39] It is true that the Cistercians destroyed the monks' cells, uprooted their olive grove and sold wood and animals belonging to the monastery. Is this simply the viciousness of the Latins of which Nicol has spoken or could this be said to be the deliberate creation of a wasteland at the second stage?[40] Perhaps the terrain of Greece was such that they had no alternative. Of course it must be remembered that the Cistercians were bound to accept these monasteries, coming as they did in the way of gifts from their lay benefactors. Nor is there any evidence that these benefactors provided them with the large tracts of land which they were accustomed to receive in the west.

It is strange that the Cistercians usually such active builders did not themselves create any new houses. But in Constantinople at least, the Latins' reputation was for dismantling and destroying rather than for

---

[37] Millet p 27. Many of the Cistercian foundations were installed in Greek monasteries and kept a deformed version of their former name. Chortaitou, Daphni, St Angelus in Pera, Rufinianai and St Mary de Percheio were imperial houses while the names of Zaraca, Laurus and St Mary de Verge indicate Greek origins.

[38] *Ibid* p 30 n 2. Millet thought it quite natural that the Cistercians should establish themselves in the richest of the imperial monasteries.

[39] *PL* 216 (1855) col 951; Potthast 1 no 4879.

[40] D. M. Nicol, 'The Papal Scandal', *SCH* 13 (1976) above pp 141–68.

building.[41] In the conquered provinces, the Frankish princes preferred to introduce the style that they knew at home and at Daphni a Gothic porch was added to the monastery.[42] More generally, the Cistercians had to adapt their churches to conform to the western tradition with an altar exposed to view. We know for example that the iconostasis in the church at Daphni was destroyed.[43]

While the chroniclers speak of libraries being burnt,[44] some of the monasteries taken over by the Cistercians had large stocks of books of which at least a few must have survived. Did the Cistercians—could they—make use of these books, or were they, as in the west, reluctant to get involved in the work of the schools?[45] We know that Innocent III was very concerned about the libraries in the east and spoke metaphorically of the treasures of learning in Constantinople which he wished to entrust to a group of scholars and masters from Paris if they would start a new university there.[46] It is impossible to say how far the Cistercians heeded Innocent's words or indeed read or spoke Greek themselves. The evidence we have tells us little save that Martin of Pairis learned some words of Greek during his short stay in Constantinople.[47] Possibly like a certain canon of Amiens, he had the patience to spell out Greek words on the frescoes of churches in order to read the inscriptions on the reliquaries he had found.[48]

The organisational links with the mother houses on which the Cistercians prided themselves were also difficult to maintain in far away Romania. Attempts were made to impose the same stringent conditions which pertained to attendance at the curia on these monks going to Greece. This required them to obtain the consent of the abbot of Cîteaux and at least two of the abbots of the first four houses of the

---

[41] Runciman, *Byzantine Style and Civilisation* p 166.

[42] Millet, pp 57–8 and plate VI. The Cistercian additions to the monastery church at Daphni, notably the Gothic exo-narthex, are described by E. G. Stikas in *Deltion tis Christianikis Archaiologikis Etaireias*, ser 4, 3 (Athens 1963) pp 1–43.

[43] *Ibid* p 27. The face of the schismatic Pantocrator was pierced by the crusaders' swords. See also C. N. L. Brooke, 'Religious sentiment and church design in the later middle ages' in *Medieval Church and Society* (London 1971) pp 162–3 for discussion of the differences in church design between east and west.

[44] Runciman, *Byzantine Style and Civilisation* p 158.

[45] Derek Baker, 'Heresy and learning in early cistercianism' *SCH* 9 (Cambridge 1972) p 93.

[46] H. Denifle, *Chartularium Universitatis Parisiensis* 4 vols (Paris 1899) 1 pp 62–3; *PL* 215 (1855) cols 637–38; Southern, *Making of the Middle Ages* p 59.

[47] [P.] Riant, *Des Dépouilles Religieuses* [*enlévées à Constantinople au XIIIᵉ siècle*] (Paris 1875) p 68.

[48] *Ibid* p 67. Walo de Sarton, canon of Picquigny.

order.[49] The importance of the general chapter was further under-
lined by the requirement on all abbots to be present every September at
Cîteaux.[50] Such annual attendance at Cîteaux had already proved to be a
heavy burden for distant houses, and had led to occasional concessions
and in 1216 the general chapter agreed that abbots of Cistercian houses
in Greece should only be required to attend every fourth year.[51] In
1217 they were allowed to attend only every fifth year.[52] There is
however little evidence to tell us how often they went in practice.

It is also interesting to speculate whether the papacy was less concerned with the regulation of Cistercian houses in the east than in the
west. The displaced Greek monks appeared to be a litigious group,
often appealing to the curia to protect them from the misdeeds of the
Cistercians and there are cases in which the curia decided in favour of
the Greeks.[53] This was something that the Cistercians in the west were
not accustomed to, but it is understandable if papal aims are seen to be
the maintenance of the façade at least of a reunited church. This
situation also suggests that the Greeks were using a form of non-co-
operative passive resistance which the Cistercians were not accustomed
to find in their opponents and against which they had little understanding of the correct tactics to use. It may also be true that the papacy's
attitude to the regulation of houses of Cistercian nuns showed less
concern in the east than in the west, an attitude to be expected on a new
frontier.[54] All these points and the fact that the Cistercians do not
appear to have been instructed to call church councils to reform the
clergy, illustrate the fact that the popes appear to have given no very
powerful mandates to the Cistercians in the east as they had done to
those of the order who had gone into Languedoc.

In spite of this the papacy appears to have used Cistercian abbots as
valuable judges and supporters in its struggle with the Latin patriarchs.[55]
The pope appointed the patriarchs either directly or by intervening in

[49] J. M. Canivez, *Statuta Capitulorum Generalium Ordinis Cisterciensis ab anno 1116 ad
annum 1786* 8 vols (Louvain 1933–41) 1 p 65.
[50] *Ibid* 1 p 28.
[51] *Ibid* 1 p 459.
[52] *Ibid* 1 p 468.
[53] PL 216 (1855) cols 594–5 and 951–2. See also Brown, pp 80–1.
[54] *Ibid* p 114. In 1227 the chaplain of the Cistercian convent of St Antony of Paris visited
the nuns of his order in Greece. Compare the suggestion of Manrique (4 p 341) that he
was there to institute their chaplains in their houses and to inspire them, with his
sermons, with the severe attitude taken by the general chapter towards nuns in the west
described by Southern, *Western Society* pp 314–18.
[55] Brown p 96.

disputed elections.[56] Both Innocent III and Honorius III were determined that within Romania papal authority would be supreme. Innocent III in particular had always shown himself to be interested in keeping a very tight control over the higher clergy in the west and continued to try to extend this practice in Romania. The popes believed it to be in their interest to keep the Latin patriarchate weak while the patriarchs fought back to bring their actual position more into accord with their theoretical pretensions. In cases involving the patriarchate in 1217, 1218 and 1223, the abbots of Daphni, Chortaitou and St Angelus in Pera were called upon to act as judges for the pope.[57]

One area of Cistercian activity certainly had no parallel elsewhere. This was the acquisition of relics from Byzantium with which they had become involved from the earliest date.[58] After 1204 the traffic in relics assumed great proportions. The possession of these holy objects may have seemed a certain guarantee of obtaining royal charters of protection or imperial privilege such as that obtained from Philip of Swabia by the abbot of Pairis.[59] Among the sacred objects most sought after by the Latins were fragments of the true cross, any relic of the childhood and passion of Christ, relics of the virgin, the apostles, saint John the Baptist and saint Stephen Protomartyr.[60] The Cistercians had done well out of the division of such religious booty. In 1206 Martin of Pairis returned to his monastery in Alsace loaded with the arms of saints James the Less, Bartholomy and Leo as well as various relics of saints Peter, Thomas, Matthias, Mark, Ignatius Martyr, Blaise, Sebastian, Erasmus, Clement, Suzanne, Amelia and Cyriacus.[61] In 1210, Hugh, abbot of St Ghislain, was charged by the emperor Henry of Flanders with carrying to Clairvaux treasures amongst which were a piece of the true cross and John the Baptist's eyelash.[62] In 1263, the monastery of Daphni played a part in the transmission of relics to

[56] R. L. Wolff, 'The organisation of the Latin Patriarchate of Constantinople 1204–1261: social and administrative consequences of the Latin conquest' *Traditio* 6 (1948) pp 33–60 and 'Politics in the Latin Patriarchate of Constantinople 1204–1261' *DOP* 8 (1954) pp 225–95.

[57] Brown pp 97–108.

[58] Riant, *Des Dépouilles Religieuses* pp 1–30; Frolow, *La déviation de la IVe croisade* pp 7–8, 54–55, 58.

[59] Riant, *Des Dépouilles Religieuses* p 6.

[60] *Ibid* p 27; Frolow, *La déviation de la IVe croisade* pp 59, 65–71 for a discussion of the recrudescence of the Cult of the Passion which stimulated the collection of relics.

[61] Riant, *Des Dépouilles Religiéuses* p 185.

[62] *Ibid* p 184.

Cîteaux.[63] In that year Otto de Cicon, lord of Karystos came into possession of the right arm of John the Baptist from the church at Bucoleon and presented it to Cîteaux. The abbot of Daphni and the abbot of its mother house of Bellevaux who was visiting Greece were to take charge of the transportation of this precious relic.[64] In gratitude the general chapter granted the abbot of Daphni for his lifetime the special privilege usually accorded to abbots in Syria of attending its meetings only every seven years.[65]

We are now ready to pose the question as to how far this mission to the Orthodox, if indeed there was such a mission, was successful. There is no evidence to show that the Cistercians ever preached or that they were in any way able to use the conversion methods which they had used in the western frontiers of Languedoc and Spain. They seem not to have overcome the difficulties of external communications and other difficulties, such as a plentiful supply of monasteries to occupy, Greeks and popes full of duplicity, the need for a new pattern of organisation, and the temptations of abundant religious relics. Indeed these relics may well have been the real cause of failure. Without them the Cistercians might have adapted to the second stage of their mission, finding an inward and outward austerity, which might have led to the hoped-for success. With them, *covoitise*, however disguised, may have as surely corrupted the Cistercians as cupidity for secular treasures corrupted the crusaders.[66]

From 1204 until 1261 when all their houses save Daphni, and possibly the two in Crete, had been lost,[67] Romania presents us with an area in which there is an enormous disparity between the usual Cistercian theory and practice. What is so puzzling is their lack of activity. While in Spain Cistercians had been active in colonial settlement and slow reconquest after military occupation, nothing of this

---

[63] Riant, *Exuviae* 2 pp 144–49; Brown pp 112, 115.
[64] Riant, *Exuviae* 2 pp 147–49.
[65] *Ibid* p 149.
[66] Beer, *Villehardouin* p 24. He regarded *covoitise* as one of the greatest disasters of the expedition. Villehardouin, *La Conquête* p 253 'li uns aporta bien et li autres mauvaisement; que covoitise qui est racine de toz mals, ne laissa: ainz comencierent d'enqui ennavant li covotous a retenir des choses et Nostre Sire les commença mains a amer'. Robert de Clari, *The Conquest of Constantinople*, ed P. Lauer (Paris 1924) pp 101–12, also complains of the crusaders' cupidity for the *quemun de l'ost* got only the leavings of the *rikes hommes*. Also Frolow, *La déviation de la IVe croisade*, p 53.
[67] Rufinianai was probably abandoned soon after 1225 and Chortaitou by 1223 when its daughter house St Archangelus was put directly under the jurisdiction of Locedio. The house at Zaraca was active until 1260 while the nuns of St Mary of Percheio fled to Italy—Brown pp 116–18.

happened in the east. No military religious order emerged, as in Spain, to deal with the situation although in both areas, the knights and crusaders were present in force. It would have been very much in character for Innocent III to have founded such a military order, but it did not happen. It may be that Innocent III took too long to realise the magnitude of the problem. In 1205, he was writing enthusiastically about 'a great part of the eastern church which has in our time changed from disobedience to obedience and from contempt to devotion'.[68] Perhaps when the time came for him to appreciate the real nature of the challenge, it was already too late. Pressed by the hierarchy to tighten the regulations for new orders, harassed by the patriarchs and perplexed by political problems, he was unable to act even though he may have wished to do so. While Cistercian agents quarrelled with the Greeks, collected relics and caused considerable annoyance to subsequent popes, the Latin empire in Greece slipped away from them.

It was to be left to the Franciscans with their particular aptitudes and urban orientation, more representative of the modernity and forward-looking trends of the thirteenth century, to take up the task which the Cistercians had found too much for them.[69] The ageing vine of Cîteaux had perhaps borne too much fruit too quickly on branches which were too far extended from the main stock. In so doing it had become weakened beyond recovery.

University of London
Westfield College.

---

[68] Southern, *Making of the Middle Ages,* p 59.
[69] R.L. Wolff, 'The Latin Empire of Constantinople and the Franciscans', *Tradito* 2 (1944) pp 213-37.

BONAVENTURA, THE TWO MENDICANT ORDERS, AND THE GREEKS AT THE COUNCIL OF LYONS (1274)

by DENO J. GEANAKOPLOS

FOR centuries it has been believed that at the famous council of Lyons, held in 1274 to reunite the Latin and Greek churches,[1] the leading role defending Latin theological views in the debates that presumably took place was played by the great Franciscan theologian, Bonaventura. Recently, however, this view has been seriously called into question,[2] and a re-evaluation of his role and that of other leading protagonists would seem to be in order. Far from being the 'soul of the union,' and the man who 'crushed the Greeks in theological debate,' as has been generally believed,[3] Bonaventura's part in the union seems to have been very limited. It is the purpose of this paper not only to put in clearer light and in its true context the work of Bonaventura with regard to the Greeks at the council, but also to indicate, if only rather briefly, the parts taken by other mendicants, the Franciscans John Parastron and Jerome of Ascoli, and the Dominicans, Albertus Magnus, William of Moerbeke, and their minister general, Peter of Tarentaise. Our aim, then, is to ascertain the relative importance of their respective roles in the preparations for, and the proclamation of, religious union.

This paper will be divided into two sections, the first part dealing

---

[1] Several works have been written, relatively recently, in connection with the problem of religious union at the council of Lyons: see [D.] Geanakoplos, *Emperor Michael [Palaeologus and the West]* (Cambridge, Mass., 1959) caps 11 and 12; [B.] Roberg, [*Die Union zwischen der griechischen und der lateinischen Kirche auf dem II. Konzil von Lyon*] (Bonn 1964); [A.] Franchi, [*Il Concilio II di Lione secondo la Ordinatio Concilii Generalis Lugdunensis*] (Rome 1965); and [H.] Wolter [and H. Holstein, *Lyon I et Lyon II*] (Paris 1965). Pertinent articles on the council, or specific aspects of it, are cited below. We note here only the most recent, that of [J.] Gill (containing some unpublished Greek texts relating to the union), 'The Church Union [of Lyons (1274) Portrayed in Greek Documents],' *OCP* (1974) pp 5–45.

[2] Esp by Franchi pp 158–72. Roberg (see esp p 136, n 9), it seems, had suspected this.

[3] See, for example, R. Menindez, 'Saint Bonaventure, Les Frères-Mineurs et l'Unité de l'église au Concile de Lyon de 1274,' *La France Franciscaine*, 5, 18 (Paris 1935) pp 363–92; also L. Wegemer, *St. Bonaventure the Seraphic Doctor* (New York 1924) pp 1 *seq*; L. De Simone, 'S. Bonaventura al Concilio di Lione II e l'unione con i Greci,' *Asprenas*, 9 (Naples 1962) esp p 125.

with the preparations made by pope Gregory X for two years *before* convocation of the council, together with the parallel, pre-conciliar events in the Byzantine east; and the second part, discussing the activities at the actual conciliar proceedings of the various Franciscan and Dominican, as well as Greek, participants.

No formal acts as such of the conciliar proceedings remain in either Latin or Greek, and the sometimes exaggerated, encomiastic statements of the Franciscan and Dominican sources must be examined with care. But we do have available a precise, if rather brief, account in Latin of the proceedings, a kind of minutes or diary of the council and its liturgical ceremonies. This was formerly entitled, in Mansi and elsewhere, the *Notitia Brevis*. But in the new edition recently prepared by A. Franchi from a more accurate, anonymous Vatican manuscript, it is more correctly entitled *Ordinatio Concilii Generalis Lugdunensis* (*The Order* [or agenda, so to speak] *of the General Council of Lyons*).[4] The famous work of the Dominican Thomas Aquinas, the *Contra Errores Graecorum*, written some years before but not for the use of this council, will not concern us.[5]

On the Greek side, while we have no Syropoulos as at the council of Florence[6] to illuminate the innermost thoughts of the Greek envoys, the lengthy and detailed account of the contemporary historian George Pachymeres tells us much about events in Constantinople before and after the union, though very little about the council itself.[7] Indeed, Pachymeres seems to believe that it was held in Rome. We have, in addition, a short but little-used account on Lyons written by archdeacon George Metochites, a pro-unionist Greek envoy sent to the Roman curia almost immediately after the council in order to help implement its decisions.[8]

---

[4] Franchi pp 67–100, for new ed of Latin text. Compare S. Kuttner, *L'édition romaine des conciles généraux et les actes du premier concile de Lyon* (Rome 1949).

[5] See P. Glorieux, new ed of *Contra Errores Graecorum* (Tournai Paris, 1957); and [A.] Dondaine, [' "Contra Graecos," Premiers écrits polémiques des Dominicains d'Orient,'] *AFP* 21 (1951), pp 320 *seq*.

[6] See excellent new ed of Syropoulos by V. Laurent, *Les Mémoires du Sylvestre Syropoulos sur le concile de Florence (1438–39)* (Paris 1971). Also earlier on Syropoulos see [D.] Geanakoplos, ['The Council of Florence and the Union between the Greek and Latin Churches (1438–39)],' in *Byzantine East* [*and Latin West*] (Oxford 1966) pp 84–111, with bibl cited.

[7] [G.] Pachymeres, [*De Michaele et Andronico Palaeologis,*] ed J. Bekker (Bonn 1835) 1. Compare Geanakoplos, *Emperor Michael*, esp pp 258 *seq*.

[8] For Metochites' text, see C. Giannelli, 'Le récit d'une mission diplomatique de Georges Le Métochite et le Vat. Gr. 1716,' esp pp 419–43, in [H.] Laurent, *Le Bienheureux Innocent V* [(Pierre de Tarentaise) et son temps] (Vatican 1947).

Bonaventura, the two mendicant orders and the Greeks in 1274

In order to understand the context of events in which the council of Lyons took place, we must go back to the early thirteenth century. The destruction of the Byzantine state in 1204, as a result of the fourth crusade and the subsequent erection of a Latin empire in its place, with the forced conversion of the Greek clergy and people to catholicism, had created in Greek minds such a hostility that, even after Constantinople's recovery by the Byzantine emperor Michael VIII Palaeologus in 1261, most Greeks would hear nothing of religious union of the churches. By this time, in fact, fear of the west had created in Greek minds almost a paranoia regarding any future Latin aggression.[9] Thus the principal differences between the two churches, doctrinally the *filioque* (procession of the Holy Spirit from both Father and Son), and, liturgically, use of the *azyma* (unleavened bread) in the holy eucharist, came, after the Latin occupation of Constantinople in 1204, to assume not only religious but ethnic significance as well. Were a Byzantine even to suggest consideration of the *filioque* or *azyma*, he was at once branded by his compatriots with the abusive epithet *Latinophron*. As one imperial Greek envoy, George Metochites, bitterly but meaningfully complained after the council of Lyons: 'Instead of a conflict of words, instead of refutative proof, instead of arguments from the scriptures we [envoys] constantly hear [from the Greek populace] *"Frangos kathestekas"* ("You have become a Frank").' 'Should we pro-unionists,' he continues with acute insight, 'simply because we favour union, be subjected to being called supporters of another nation and not Byzantine patriots? (*alloethneis hemeis all'ou philoromaioi?*)'.[10]

After 1261, the principal enemy of the Byzantine empire was the newly enthroned, highly ambitious king of Sicily, Charles of Anjou. To the Greek emperor Michael Palaeologus the only power able to restrain this grave military threat to Constantinople was Charles's feudal lord for Sicily, the pope. But the papal price for aid was religious union with Rome, meaning in most Greek minds, dogmatic and jurisdictional subordination, once again, of the Greek church to Rome. Nevertheless, despite the intense popular opposition to union, Michael was convinced of the political necessity of union with the

[9] On this 'paranoiac' fear of the Greeks see for example [D.] Geanakoplos, 'Byzantium and the Crusades,' caps 2 and 3 in *A History of the Crusades* (Madison, Wisc., 1975) ed K. Setton, 3 pp 30, 55, and 103; and esp now D. Geanakoplos, *Interaction of the 'Sibling' Byzantine and Western Cultures in Middle Ages and Italian Renaissance (330–1600)* (in the press).

[10] For Greek text see Laurent, *Le Bienheureux Innocent V*, esp pp 424 *seq*.

Roman church.[11] Michael's desire for union was shared, though on other grounds of course, by the new pope Gregory X. Gregory, who had lived long in the holy land, had considerable knowledge of the Greek east. It was in fact his aim, publicly announced soon after his elevation, to convoke a general council not only to bring about much-needed reform in the Latin church, but to effect religious reunion with the Greeks, and then, with Greek aid, to launch a crusade to recover Jerusalem.[12] Writing to emperor Michael, therefore, pope Gregory stated that, if the latter were truly receptive, the pope would send nuncios to Constantinople to discuss religious union and a joint crusade.[13]

But even before dispatching formal ambassadors to Constantinople, the pope, upon receiving a positive reply from the emperor, sent to Constantinople, the Franciscan friar John Parastron in order to instruct Michael in the theological beliefs of the Roman church.[14] His choice of a mendicant for this mission in preference to a member of the secular clergy reflects the long history of Franciscan and Dominican connections with the Greek east. Almost in fact from their foundation, both orders had turned their attention to missionary work in the east in the dual aim of recovering the holy land and bringing about the *reductionem* (return, or perhaps more precisely, 'reduction') of the 'schismatic' Greeks to the Roman church.[15] The choice of John Parastron, a Constantinople-born, Greek Franciscan, to perform the delicate task of instructing Michael proved to be a wise one. For

---

[11] On Charles's and Michael's relations see Geanakoplos, *Emperor Michael*, *passim*; S. Runciman, *The Sicilian Vespers* (Cambridge 1958) *passim*; and now Geanakoplos, 'Byzantium and the Crusades,' pp 33–42. On 31 March 1272 Gregory publicly announced his plans for a general council.

[12] See esp V. Laurent, 'La croisade et la question d'orient sous le pontificat de Grégoire X,' *Revue historique du sud-est européen*, 22 (1945) pp 105 *seq*.

[13] See papal letter in [J.] Guiraud, [*Les registres de Grégoire X*] (Paris 1892–6) no 194, 68b. Compare Geanakoplos, *Emperor Michael*, p 239.

[14] Parastron had earlier been sent to Gregory by Michael. Indeed, already in 1270 Michael had included Parastron in an embassy he had sent to saint Louis of France, in order to restrain Charles of Anjou, at which time Parastron presented Louis with a precious, illuminated Greek new testament. See Geanakoplos, *Emperor Michael*, p 224, n 133, and p 239. On Parastron, see esp G. Golubovich, 'Cenni storici su Fra Giovanni Parastron,' *Bessarione*, 10 (Rome 1906) pp 295 *seq*.

[15] On both Orders' work in the East, see [M.] Roncaglia, *Les frères mineurs* [*et l'église grecque orthodoxe au XIIIᵉ siècle (1221–74)*] (Cairo 1954); more important, G. Golubovich, *Biblioteca bio-bibliografica della Terra Santa e dell'Oriente Francescano*, 2 (Quaracchi 1913); J. Moorman, *A History of the Franciscan Order* (Oxford 1968) pp 226 *seq* and 298–99; also R. Loenertz, 'Les établissements dominicains de Pera-Constantinople,' *EO*, 34 (1935) pp 332–49; and Dondaine.

Parastron soon came to be greatly esteemed not only by Michael but by the Greek populace as well, despite his being a Latinophile and zealous advocate of union. For, unlike the usual convert, he was still favourable to the Greek rites. Viewing the bitter arguments over the question of the Procession of the Holy Spirit as excessive, indeed unnecessary (an attitude remarkable for the time), Parastron, Pachymeres informs us, 'was in the habit of entering into the sanctuaries of the Constantinopolitan churches and, standing at the side of the Greek celebrants, would join in the reading of the offices.'[16] Moreover, at the end of the service, he and other friars (*Frerioi*, as Pachymeres puts it) would join in partaking of the *antidoron* (unconsecrated bread).[17] Significantly, they did not participate in the sacrament of holy communion—doubtless because of the difference in the Greek usage of leavened instead of unleavened bread (*azyma*) in the eucharist.

Parastron became popular even among the Greek clergy, who, if we may believe the later Franciscan chronicler Nicholas Glassberger, at Parastron's death shortly after Lyons, even sought his canonisation from the pope.[18] Parastron's Greek birth, tolerance, and above all, empathy with the Greek mentality, in particular with that of the lesser clergy and common people, made it easier for him to stress that union should be considered more a reversion to the original unity of the church than an acceptance of any new dogmatic beliefs or rites.

The pope's reliance on the Franciscan order was not limited to his use of Parastron's talents. For in the crucial matter of choosing nuncios to send to Michael for discussion of the union, Gregory now turned to his friend and former teacher at the University of Paris, Bonaventura, the minister-general of the Franciscans (he had been instrumental in Gregory's election as pope), and directed him to send four members of his order to Constantinople. Bonaventura thereupon selected the Franciscan friars Jerome of Ascoli, Bonaventura da Mugello, Bonagratia, and Raymond Berengar, who on 24 October 1272 set forth for the Bosporus.[19] Of these four envoys it is certain only that the chief legate, Jerome of Ascoli, knew Greek. To judge, however, as we shall

[16] Pachymeres, I, pp 371–2.
[17] Pachymeres pp 360–1, 368 (compare Geanakoplos, *Emperor Michael*, p 267).
[18] Nicholas Glassberger, *Chronica*, in *Analecta Franciscana*. 2 (Quaracchi 1887) p 88: 'pro eius canonizatione Imperator Graecorum et Praelati Graeciae instanter apud dominum papam laborabant.'
[19] See Roberg pp 102 *seq* and sources cited. Also for date see Geanakoplos, *Emperor Michael* p 239; and the sometimes inaccurate Roncaglia, *Les frères mineurs*, p 125 (compare Pachymeres pp 3–68). On Bonaventura's selection of the envoys see Roberg p 103, n 6, citing a Franciscan source.

see, by certain somewhat inaccurate remarks he made about Greek religious practices in a later report to the pope, Ascoli's Greek must have been considerably less than perfect.[20]

As for the minister-general, Bonaventura, he seems to have known no Greek except perhaps for a few theological phrases. His *Opera Omnia*, to be sure, reveal familiarity with basic Greek theological views, especially of the fourth- and fifth-century Greek fathers. Of the Greek fathers, the names of Chrysostom, the pseudo-Dionysius, and the later John of Damascus appear most frequently in his writings. But they belong, in large part, to the common Christian heritage of the east and west. Nevertheless, several other passages in Bonaventura's *Opera Omnia* indicate more than passing familiarity with current Greek views on the disputed *filioque* and *azyma* questions.[21]

Regarding the *azyma* (use of unleavened bread in communion), after discussing the views of both Latins and Greeks, Bonaventura affirms that, though both had originally received the practice from the Lord, the Greeks had altered the tradition. Therefore, he concludes, 'either the apostles erred or the Greeks invented this' (*finxerunt*)[22]. Elsewhere, he implies that, for the Greeks, the Latin *azyma* was an example of Judaising practices,[23] something that, for the Greeks, was particularly reprehensible. Regarding the *filioque*, it would seem that Bonaventura reflects the common western view that the Greeks were wrong in considering the phrase an unlawful addition to the creed instead of, as the Latins held, a necessary clarification of dogma.[24] His emphasis on prayer and contemplation leading to a kind of mystical union with God (recall the important Byzantine concept of *theosis*),[25]

---

[20] See below text and notes 31–4. Also Wolter p 159, who believes Jerome (the future pope Nicholas IV) knew Greek 'badly.'

[21] See below, next three notes. Compare on his knowledge of the Greek fathers L. Wegemer, *St. Bonaventure the Seraphic Doctor* (New York 1924) p 9.

[22] Bonaventura, [*Opera Omnia*], 4 (Quaracchi 1889), *Sententiarum*, pp 260–1: 'Iuxta hoc quaeritur de controversia Graecorum et Latinorum, unde venerit; et videtur, quod non poterit esse; quia ipsi acceperunt ab Apostolis, et Apostoli ab uno Domino: ergo vel Apostoli erraverunt, vel Graeci finxerunt.'

[23] Bonaventura, 4 p 261, no 5 and p 262, *Conclusio*, no 5.

[24] On the *filioque* see, for example, Bonaventura, 1 (1882), pp 211–23, mentioning, among others, views of John of Damascus, Dionysius, Gregory; see also Geanakoplos, *Byzantine East* pp 99–102.

[25] On 'theosis' see now most recently J. Meyendorff, *Byzantine Theology* (New York 1974) pp 163–4. Compare Bonaventura's famous mystical work, *Itinerarium Mentis ad Deum* on the ascent of the soul to God through faith, reason, and contemplation (see under Bonaventura in *D[izionario] b[iografico degli] I[taliani]*, 11 pp 618–19). The treatise *Teologia Mystica* is now generally believed not to be by Bonaventura but by Hugh of Balma, a late thirteenth-century Carthusian.

his essentially antipathetic attitude to the scholastic, Aristotelian approach of the Dominicans,[26] the Franciscan emphasis on Mariology (despite Bonventura's own denial of the immaculate conception of the Virgin),[27] and the possible Franciscan use of the so-called 'Jesus prayer' —the latter of which apprently had its genesis in the Byzantine East[28]—seem to indicate far greater affinity between his Franciscan type of spirituality and that of the Greeks, than between the Dominican and the Greek. Thus, if any formal dialogue did in fact take place at Lyons, it is reasonable to assume that Bonaventura and the Greek envoys would have got along rather well together. Indeed, one later apostolic notary at the papal court wrote—but this is not corroborated by the original, contemporary sources—that the Greeks called Bonaventura 'Eutychios'[29] (the 'well-fated' or 'fortunate one'). Besides being a literal translation of his name, this appellation might also have carried the implication of a person of affable personality and sympathetic beliefs.

To return to the Franciscan embassy to Constantinople under Jerome of Ascoli, it would seem that Bonaventura, as the immediate superior who had selected the nuncios in the first place, should deserve some credit for its success, however, ephemeral. Bonaventura probably had some communcation with his envoys during their one and one-quarter year sojourn in Constantinople, and on their return to Lyons it is likely that they made a report to him personally as well as to the new Franciscan minister-general, as they did, of course, to the pope.[30] Sometime during their stay in Constantinople, Jerome and his colleagues sent a communication to pope Gregory X. This is especially interesting because it constitutes an illuminating source for contemporary Latin views of Greek religious practices.[31] Thus

---

[26] See *DbI* 11 esp pp 618–19, and 623. Also compare E. Gilson, *History of Christian Philosophy in the Middle Ages* (New York 1955) pp 331–40, who says Bonaventura tried to combine Aristotle and Plato; elsewhere, however, he says that he made little concession to Aristotle.

[27] See *ODCC* under 'Bonaventure.'

[28] See esp article on 'Jesus Prayer' by F. X. Murphy, in *NCE* p 971, and *On the Prayer of Jesus* by Brianchaninov (London 1965) (with little on this point).

[29] Petrus Galesinus, *Sancti Bonaventurae Vita*, ed in St. Bonaventura, *Opera*, I, pp 1–20. On Galesinus see A. Potthast, *Bibliotheca Historica Medii Aevi* (Berlin 1896) p 486. Passage quoted by Franchi p 164, and by Roberg p 136, n 9: 'Hic doctrinae Bonaventurae nomen magnum hic Eutychii, sic enim Graeci illum vocabant . . .'

[30] Franchi p 81, n 25, cites a Vatican source cited by Giannelli, in Laurent, *Le Bienheureux Innocent V*, p 442, on a papal audience then granted to Ascoli, during which Ascoli probably gave Gregory a letter from Joseph, patriarch of Constantinople.

[31] For text of report (which is incomplete) see Roberg pp 229–31, and for discussion, pp 130–4.

Ascoli affirms that the Greeks believe all Latins are excommunicated for rejecting the symbol of faith adopted at Nicaea as the Greeks confess it, and for adding the *filioque* to the creed. Ascoli also states that the Greeks recognize, on the part of the pope, no jursidiction over the entire Christian church without consent of the other four patriarchs, that the Greeks do not consider fornication a mortal sin,[32] that they do not believe in purgatory, that for them the Latin sacraments have no efficacy, and that they [the Greeks] do not admit that the Holy Spirit proceeds from the Son. Differences of rite, Ascoli states, lead the Greeks in fact to re-baptise Latin converts. Ascoli is inaccurate with reference to Greek ecclesiastical practices, however, in saying that the Greeks do not know the four minor orders. (Actually, though the actual titles and functions differed at this time, the Greeks did not lack their own minor orders.)[33] Erroneous, too, is his statement that the Greeks do not practise extreme unction and that they lack the sacrament of confirmation.[34] (Here the Greek practice of confirmation at the same time as baptism may have escaped his notice.)

But the most important result of Ascoli's fifteen-month embassy in Constantinople was to prevail upon Michael and his sixteen-year-old son Andronicus to accept the papal confession of faith sent earlier to the emperor by the pope,[35] and which Parastron explained to Michael. Ascoli obtained the imperial acceptance of the Roman confession at a meeting held in the presence of a pro-unionst group of Greek clergy in February 1274, at the imperial Blachernae palace,[36] that is, shortly before the Franciscan legates' departure with the Greek envoys to attend the council at Lyons.

In this confession, which Michael now sent back to Lyons with his

---

[32] The Greeks in fact do not consider fornication a very serious sin.

[33] See *ODCC* under 'Minor Orders,' listing those for the Latin and for the Greek church.

[34] Latin text in Roberg pp 230–31.

[35] For analysis of this confession of faith (based on pope Clement's letter sent earlier, in 1267, to Michael and the points of which Michael now repeated in his letter to Gregory) see J. Karmires, 'He apodidomene eis ton Michael VIII Palaiologon latinike homologia pisteos tou 1274,' (in Greek) *Archeion Ecclesiastikou kai kanonikou Dikaiou*, 2 (Athens 1947) pp 127 *seq*, who believes it entirely Latin (as I do). Interestingly, Michael's confession of faith sent to pope Gregory contains the first formal enumeration by the Greek church (or emperor) of *seven* sacraments. This seems to be the sole remaining legacy of Lyons in the Orthodox church, see N. Patrinakos, *The Individual and his Orthodox Church* (New York 1970) pp 23–4.

[36] Several studies include a discussion of this episode. Besides Roberg pp 113 *seq*, see [D.] Nicol, 'The Greeks and the Union [of the Churches: Preliminaries to the Second Council of Lyons,]' *Medieval Studies presented to A. Gwynn* (Dublin 1961) pp 463–80.

own ambassadors, the emperor explicitly accepted the *filioque, azyma,* and Roman primacy of ecclesiastical jurisdiction, even the seven sacraments as prescribed and enumerated by Rome[37]—everything to the letter demanded of him by the papacy. At the end of his long letter, Michael, however, begged that 'the Greek church be permitted to recite the creed as it had been before the schism up to our time, and that we remain in observance of the rites we had before the schism— these rites not being contrary to the faith declared above. This is not crucial for your holiness,' Michael wrote, 'but for us it is a matter of vital importance because of the immense multitude of our people.'[38] This latter point attests to the extreme attachment which the mass of the Greek clergy and people felt for their traditional doctrine and especially ritual, in particular the leavened bread of the holy eucharist. To the Greeks their liturgy had by now perhaps come to mean more than any other aspect of their religious life, and, as noted above, they had, since 1204 (whether they consciously realized it or not) come more and more to identify the Byzantine ritual with their ethnic feelings as a people distinct from the Latins.

The letter of Andronicus, the son and heir of Michael, merely repeated what the father had already affirmed. The letter drawn up by the Greek clergy, however, was another matter. What pope Gregory essentially requested of the Byzantine clergy was a profession of faith in the form he prescribed, including explicit acceptance of the *filioque* and *azyma*, along with recognition of Roman primacy of both honour and jurisdiction, that is, the right of appeal to Rome.[39] What evoked the greatest protest in Constantinople, according to the Greek historian Pachymeres, was Michael's insistence on the proclamation of the pope's name in the diptychs, the tablets from which the names of those commemorated at eucharist were publicly read aloud in the liturgy.[40] For mention of the pope's name in the diptychs would signify to the Byzantine clergy that they were already in communion with Rome

---

[37] For Latin translation of Michael's profession see Roberg pp 239–43. French translation of Michael's profession in Wolter pp 276–80.

[38] See French translation of text in Wolter pp 279–80. See also Roberg pp 227–8, for quotation of Michael's request which appears also in Ascoli's letter. Compare below, n 104, citing Beck's view on this matter of Greek rites.

[39] See Pachymeres, pp 386, 395. Also Gregoras, 1 (Bonn 1800) pp 125–6. This demand of Michael about the diptychs was made, possibly, in response to Gregory's instructions to Ascoli. See Geanakoplos, *Emperor Michael*, pp 240–1, for English translation from the papal letter regarding three possible 'verbal' ways submission to Roman primacy could be expressed by the Greeks, text in Guiraud no 194, pp 67–73.

[40] Geanakoplos, *Emperor Michael*, p 264.

and, therefore, that they approved, at least tacitly, of what they considered such Western *kainotomias* ('innovations,' in effect 'heresies') as the *filioque* and the *azyma*, that is, the sacrament of the Holy Eucharist with unleavened bread.

The letter drawn up by the Greek clergy was, for the most part, vaguely composed and fell far short of constituting a profession of faith in the manner required by Rome.[41] The letter in fact lacked the endorsement of most of the Greek clergy, being signed by some forty-odd prelates out of a possible total of one hundred and forty four bishops in the empire.[42] In consequence, though Ascoli had skillfully guided the negotiations with the emperor and his son, he now had to be content with this very weak epistle from the Greek prelates, one which at best indicated only partial submission to Rome.

The Greek clergy did not even mention the crucial theological issues, and the exact forms of papal privilege were left conveniently vague, being referred to only as 'those the pope had enjoyed before the schism.' What the Greek clerics apparently envisaged by this phrase was restoration of the kind of relationship that had existed between the two churches before the schism, presumably meaning 1054—a view which would imply deletion of the *filioque* from the creed and repudiation or annulment of the many papal claims which had burgeoned after that date.[43] Thus the Greek prelates, while leaving it to Michael and his son explicitly to accept everything the pope demanded, submitted, on their part, only an incomplete and ambiguously phrased letter.

Shortly after Michael's acceptance of the papal invitation to send envoys to the forthcoming council, the emperor selected as the Greek representatives three men—as his personal ambassador, the grand logothete (prime minister) George Acropolites, and to represent the

---

[41] For a new Latin ed of the bishops' letter see Roberg pp 235–9. Compare Greek text in Gill, 'The Church Union' pp 28–33. The letter was dated February, 1274.

[42] Thirty five or thirty eight bishops is the calculation of Nicol, 'The Greeks and the Union' p 476, which he changes to '40 odd bishops' in his 'The Byzantine Reaction to [the Council of Lyons],' *SCH* 7 (1971) p 122. More recently Gill, in 'The Church Union' p 6, speaks of 41 signatures. H. Beck, in cap 16, of *From the High Middle Ages to the Eve of the Reformation* (New York 1970) p 126, writes of '44 bishops,' which number seems correct, to judge by the episcopal letter quoted *verbatim* in Roberg pp 235–9. (See also Roberg's views on the ms tradition of this text, pp 255–63.) On the context for this episode, besides the studies mentioned, see the several articles of H. Evert-Kapessova, esp 'Une page des relations byzantino-latines: Byzance et le St.-Siège à l'époque de l'union de Lyon,' *BS* 16 (1955) pp 297–314.

[43] This would show, contrary to some modern views, that the Greeks themselves considered 1054 rather definitive for the schism.

Bonaventura, the two mendicant orders and the Greeks in 1274

Byzantine clergy, the ex-patriarch Germanos III and the archbishop of Nicaea, Theophanes.[43a] Let us look closely for a moment at the leader of the Greek delegation, Acropolites, whose career has not been sufficiently scrutinised with respect to his involvement in this council. Though a civilian official, he was something of a theologian as well.[44] Above all, however, he was a faithful civil servant who understood the necessity of the imperial policy of *economia*—that is, elasticity or flexibility in the administration of ecclesiastical affairs when vital interests of the state were endangered.[45] An extremely learned man, Acropolites taught the philosophy of Aristotle and Plato (note this—a Greek with a good knowledge of Plato in the west two centuries before the famous renaissance figures Chrysoloras and Pletho)[46] as well as the mathematics of Euclid and Nicomachus at the academy (university) of Constantinople, then situated near the church of St. Paul.[47] The modern editor of Acropolites's writings, A. Heisenberg, believes that Acropolites, on his arrival at Capua in southern Italy on his way to Lyons, wrote, at the request of a certain archbishop Marinos of Eboli (who, if not a Calabrian Greek, may at least have been Byzantine-oriented), a work entitled 'On Saints Peter and Paul'— something that would undoubtedly please the pope and which, according to Heisenberg, is still worthy of reading for theological and rhetorical reasons.[48] In this treatise on Peter and Paul and their importance for the Byzantine church, Acropolites terms them the *koryfaei* (chiefs or highest) of the apostles. But this did not at the same

---

[43a] The metropolitan of Philippi was also selected, but he died before departure of the embassy on 11 March 1274.

[44] On Acropolites see esp [A.] Heisenberg's 'Prolegomena' to his [*Georgii Acropolitae, Opera*], 2 (Leipzig 1903) pp iii–xxvi. Also see Beck, p 126: '[Acropolites] lacked theological depth.'

[45] On *economia* see, for example, Geanakoplos, *Emperor Michael*, pp 265, 270, and *Byzantine East* p 77.

[46] It is interesting that in 1271 William of Moerbeke translated from the Greek Proclus' commentary on the *Parmenides* of Plato (Minio-Paluello, p 46—see n 58, below). On Chrysoloras and Pletho see D. Geanakoplos, *Greek Scholars in Venice* (Cambridge 1962) pp 24–8 and 85–6.

[47] See Heisenberg, 'Prolegomena,' p xi; compare S. Runciman, *The Last Byzantine Renaissance* (Cambridge 1970) pp 57–8.

[48] See Heisenberg 'Prolegomena', p xxi. On Marinos of Eboli (apparently archbishop of Capua to 1261) see C. Eubel, *Hierarchia Catholica Medii Aevi* (Regensburg 1898) p 170; and Tafuri, *Scritt Napoli* (Naples 1748) 2¹, p 449–52, listed in U. Chevalier, *Répertoire des sources du Moyen Age, Bio-bibl.* (Paris 1907) 2, col 3082. Also see Franchi p 138, n 27; and F. Schillman's mention of Marino's 'Formulario', in his 'Zur byzantinischen Politik Alexanders IV,' *Römische Quartalschrift*, 22 (Rome 1908) pp 108–31. G. Fedalto's recent *La Chiesa latina in Oriente* (Verona 1973) is unavailable to me.

time mean that he (like other Byzantines) accepted Roman claims to jurisdictional primacy. (This was an attitude common enough in Byzantium but which, according to the Greek historian Syropoulos, at least with respect to saint Peter, was to be a subject of argument on the part of Greeks later at the council of Florence.)[49] It is possible that, if indeed George did find time to write the treatise on his arrival in Italy (something highly unlikely), he did so perhaps as a tribute to the pope, or to convince the papal curia of Michael's sincerity which, for years, had been suspect in western eyes. Another possibility is that Acropolites wrote the work after his return to Constantinople in the aim of supporting Michael's unionist policy among the Greeks, by showing that, from patristic times onward, the Greek church itself had venerated saints Peter and Paul as the *koryfaei* of the apostles.[50]

In still another work, written by Acropolites before Lyons and in which he opposed the *filioque* doctrine, he reveals himself, nevertheless, fairly tolerant of the Latins. He stresses, among other things, that in order to achieve religious union the churches should return to the common views shared in the patristic period—the implication being not only one of common beliefs but that the *filioque* should be deleted from the creed.[51] This, then, was the able diplomat and erudite scholar whom Michael had judiciously chosen as his chief lay ambassador, who, no doubt, had discussions with the pope over political questions and who, at Lyons, took a public, oral oath of allegiance to the pope in the name of Michael and his son.

As for the Byzantine ecclesiastical representatives, ex-patriarch Germanos and archbishop Theophanes, neither could lay claim to any

---

[49] On Syropoulos see Geanakoplos, *Byzantine East*, pp 95–6, relating the disputes over the matter of the Greek clergy's objection to the kissing of the pope's foot, and to the question of the primary rank of saint Peter among the apostles.

[50] See esp [J.] Meyendorff and others, *The Primacy of Peter [in the Orthodox Church]* (London 1963) and his recent *Byzantine Theology* (New York 1974) p 96. Meyendorff, *Primacy of Peter*, esp pp 9, 12, 15, etc shows that the Byzantine attitude toward the primacy and succession of Peter was determined by an 'ecclesiology' different from that of the west. The title *koyrfaeus*, for example, was often given not only to Peter but to other apostles, esp Paul and John. The term did not mean to Byzantines that Peter, and therefore Rome, had jurisdiction over the other apostles or sees. In other words the apostolic and the episcopal functions of Peter were not identical and the Byzantines did not consider a single bishop as the successor of one apostle, as the west did. All bishops are successors of all apostles. Thus the East accepted Peter as chief of the apostles without accepting other Roman claims. (Incidentally, in Acropolites' work there is no mention of Lyons.)

[51] See Heisenberg, 'Prolegomena', 'Logos Deuteros peri tes ek patros tou hagiou pneumatos ekporeuseos,' (in Greek), pp 45–66.

particular distinction, theologically or intellectually. Indeed, Germanos had been removed from office, some years before, by Michael for ineptitude, and Theophanes was apparently not as yet a fully convinced pro-unionist.[52] These three Greek ambassadors, together with the chief imperial interpreter, George Verrhoiotes, and the *Prokathemenos tou Vestiariou* (grand chamberlain) Nicholas Panaretos, together with the Franciscans Ascoli, Bonagratia, and Parastron, now, on 11 March 1274,[53] embarked in two ships for the council in the west. One ship, according to Pachymeres who, besides Ascoli, alone mentions the specific Greek personalities, carried the three principal imperial envoys, as well as Parastron, Ascoli, and Bonagratia, along, of course, with sufficient crewmen to navigate the boat. The second ship, apparently functioning as a supply vessel, carried gifts for the pope and, presumably, servants to minister to the needs of the ambassadors, Greek and Latin. None of those aboard the second ship, except for Verrhoiotes the interpreter and Panaretos, were significant enough to merit mention in Pachymeres's detailed account.[54] Though other names are not mentioned, it is possible, nevertheless, that the ship may also have carried passengers attending to personal business in the west. Off the dangerous coast of Malea (southern Peloponnesus), the latter vessel was lost in a storm, with the interpreter Verrhoiotes, Panaretos, and two hundred and eleven other Greeks aboard,[55] as well as all the lavish gifts for the pope, including golden icons, censers, and the very altar cloth Michael had stripped from the cathedral of St Sophia.[56]

Gregory's preparations for the council were not limited to sending ambassadors to Constantinople. Already as early as 11 March 1273, he

---

[52] See Pachymeres p 384. Compare Nicol, 'The Greeks and the Union' p 477 and esp n 70.

[53] Pachymeres p 385–6. For specific date see Gill p 10.

[54] On the embassy as a whole see esp Pachymeres, pp 384–5 (compare Geanakoplos, *Emperor Michael*, pp 258–9).

[55] Pachymeres pp 396–7; compare Roberg pp 126–7, and Nicol, p 477. Pachymeres p 396, mentions two hundred and thirteen men (*in toto*) as does the report of Ascoli (all civilians, says Franchi, p 136 and p 76). Compare also the late fifteenth-century chroniclers, Peter of Prussia, *Vita B. Alberti*, p 279 and Rudolf of Nijmegen, *Legenda Beati Alberti* (both discussed in Franchi, p 136, n 24), who mention one hundred and twenty persons composing the Greek delegation. But no original source is indicated for their statement. Ascoli's letter to Gregory from cape Leucas also mentions the Greek envoys—the same persons as Pachymeres, but adding the archbishop of Philippi, who died before departure of the embassy: see Ascoli's letter in Roberg pp 227–9; compare also Franchi, p 76, n 22. Ascoli mentions that the lost ship was sunk off Negropont! (Roberg 227–9).

[56] On the gifts, esp the altar cloth, see Pachymeres, pp 384–5.

had asked for the writing of reports or position papers from western scholars with experience of the east.[56a] Especially important was the treatise *Opus Tripartitum*, written by the former Dominican minister-general, Humbert of Romans. His report is in many ways unique, for it avoids the usual polemics and propagandistic approach to the problem of union. Comprehending the need to understand what we would now call the psychology of the Greeks, the dynamics of their hostility, he stresses political as well as dogmatic matters, affirming that the chief political difference reverted to Greek anger at the recreation, in 800, of the Roman empire in the west, by the pope and Charlemagne, despite the already existing Roman (Byzantine) empire in the east. Moreover, with subtlety of understanding, Humbert stressed that no true union could come about unless the Latins and Greeks familiarised themselves with each other's ecclesiastical writings and canons. He even maintained that the pope should not *at once* insist on complete obedience and that the Greeks should be permitted to retain their own ritual—all views that for a Latin were far ahead of his time. To quote from this remarkable work: 'Above all, to further union it is important to study Greek, as was the case in the time of Jerome and Augustine. At the present time knowledge of Greek is so rare in the Roman curia that almost no one can read the language. Indeed, it would be precious for union if Latins could read the theologically important Greek works, the acts of the Greek councils, and diverse canonists [note the mention of Greek canon law which rarely ever interested the west], and their ecclesiastical history. There is too little interest in these writings and too much in philosophy.' (Particularly striking is the latter remark, made by a Dominican at the very height of the western scholastic achievement!) Humbert concludes, equally perceptively, 'It is essential that the Latin fathers be translated into Greek and that they be sent to the Greek east.'[57] Note the emphasis here on the importance of a mutual knowledge of each other's theology and religious practices. Despite his rare perception of Greek attitudes, however, Humbert still regarded the Greeks as 'schismatics' from the Roman church.

Besides the Franciscans mentioned—Jerome of Ascoli, Parastron, and Bonaventura—several Dominicans also played certain roles in the preparation for the council at Lyons. Among these is the famous

---

[56a] See Guiraud n 220, 11 March 1273.
[57] For French transl of important extracts from Humbert's work see Wolter pp 268–76; original Latin text in Mansi 24 cols 125b–32d; compare also Roberg pp 83–95.

translator of Aristotle and Archimedes, William of Moerbeke.[58] As a youth William had been sent to the Greek east where he had learned Greek exceptionally well at the Dominican convent in Pera (Constantinople) and later at that of Thebes in Greece.[59] The Dominican minister-general at the time was none other than Humbert of Romans, who, as just noted, attached special importance to the Latin learning of Greek. In view of Humbert's strong recommendations to the pope on the value of Greek and Moerbeke's long residence in the east, it seems likely that Gregory summoned the latter to Lyons precisely because of his Greek knowledge and, possibly, in order to further other suggestions of Humbert. Indeed, at the council, Moerbeke served in the capacity of interpreter, probably for both sides, since, as we have seen, the official Greek interpreter, Verrhoiotes, along with many others, had drowned on the way to the council.

Another Dominican whose presence at the council and whose relations with the Greeks are generally mentioned by modern authorities but about whom the primary sources seem strangely silent —the *Ordinatio*, for example, does not even cite his name—is the famous but now aged theologian, Albertus Magnus. Though it would appear that he actually was present at the conciliar proceedings, he does not seem to have attended as an official delegate either of the pope or of his own Dominican order. Evidently, Albert was sent to Lyons as a representative of Rudolf of Hapsburg, the new holy Roman emperor, whose candidacy was then in dispute in the curia.[60] Moreover, it is plausible that in the face of strong attacks on the rapidly proliferating mendicant orders, Albert raised his voice primarily on behalf of his own Dominican order, which, with the Franciscan, some of the lay clergy even wished to abolish.

---

[58] On William's translations see esp [M.] Grabmann, [*Guglielmo di Moerbeke il traduttore delle opere di Aristotele*] (Rome 1946) pp 36–51, in *Miscellanea Historiae Pontificiae* (Rome 1946). It has been shown by Grabmann and [L.] Minio-Paluello, [*Opuscula, The Latin Aristotle*] (Amsterdam 1972—reprint of earlier articles) pp 40–56, that Moerbeke translated works of Aristotle much before 1274, and specifically (see Minio-Paluello p 56) that he completed his translation of Aristotle's *Poetics* in 1278 in Viterbo, Italy. (Evidently he remained in Italy after the Lyons council). We know, moreover, that William translated Proclus' *Elementatio Theologica* at the papal court, so he probably went to Lyons from Italy, not from the Byzantine east—compare Minio-Paluello p 36, affirming that 'we do not know exactly when William went to and left [Greece]'. Also, p 36, noting that every year the Dominicans sent monks to Greece for missionary work. Besides Aristotle's *Politics* and *Poetics*, William translated a good part of Archimedes' works (Geanakoplos, *Byzantine East*, p 23).

[59] On William's education see esp Grabmann p 36.

[60] On Albertus at Lyons see Franchi p 129, n 14, and Roberg p 143, n 41 and esp 169–70.

Regarding Albertus's possible connections with the Greek delegation at Lyons, a passage in his *Opera Omnia* contains a curious remark that might seem to link him with the Byzantine delegation: 'And at the council of Lyons the Greeks were forced to admit that fornication, as they do not accept, is a cardinal sin'—the same point, it should be observed, made by Ascoli in his report to the Pope.[61] That Albertus was well aware of the Greek view of the *filioque* question is indicated by several long passages in his writings defending the Latin view against the Greek.[62] Nevertheless, that he actually engaged in formal debate with the Greeks seems, on the basis of the primary sources, as yet undemonstrated, though exchanges on an informal basis certainly cannot be ruled out. Nevertheless, the late fifteenth-century Dominican chronicler Peter of Prussia records that 'In hoc concilio venerabilis frater Albertus plures errores destruxit praecipue Grecorum.'[63] This passage, imprecise as it is, should perhaps rather be taken to refer to *private* or *informal* discussions engaged in by Albertus with one or another of the Greek envoys. Other than this, there seems to be no specific reference to Albertus's involvement at Lyons in the question of religious union.

Having sketched the roles of the leading protagonists, the pope, the Byzantine emperor and his envoys, and the various Franciscan and Dominican intermediaries, let us now focus on the actual conciliar proceedings at Lyons, as set forth expecially in the *Ordinatio*.

The council opened on 4 May 1274, at the cathedral of St John in Lyons. But the Greeks did not appear until seven weeks later. About 20 May, when the letter (already mentioned) of the pope's ambassador to Constantinople, the Franciscan Jerome of Ascoli, was

---

[61] See Albertus's *Opera Omnia*, 18 p 60: 'Graeci qui dicebant quod fornicatio non esset mortale peccatum, in concilio Lugdunensi coacti sunt hoc revocare.' Compare M. Albert, *Albert the Great* (Oxford 1948) p 103: 'Thomas set out for Lyons but the old man (Albertus) arrived there and played a leading part in the proceedings'; also J. Sighart, *Albert the Great of the Order of Friar Preachers* (London 1876) p 372 and W. Hinnebusch, *History of the Dominican Order*, 2 (New York 1973) p 26.

[62] See esp article on Albertus by A. Stohr, 'Der Hl. Albertus über den Ausgang des Heiligen Geistes,' in *Albertus Magnus Festschrift* (Freiburg 1932).

[63] Passage quoted in Franchi (dated 1487) p 171. The Dominican Rudolf of Nijmegen (in 1490) printed his *Legenda Beati Alberti*, which copied Peter of Prussia's biography of Albert printed earlier in 1487. For modern biographies of Albertus, which repeat errors regarding his participation in formal theological debates with the Greeks, see P. von Loé, 'Albert der Grosse auf dem Konzil von Lyon (1274)', in *Kölnische Volkszeitung*, 55 (Cologne 1914) pp 225–6; and D. Lathoud, 'Saint Albert le Grand et l'union des Grecs au second concile de Lyon,' *L'unité de l'église*, 8–10 (Paris 1929–32) pp 461–2 based on erroneous statements of Peter of Prussia) and A. Garreau, *Albert le Grand* (Paris 1932) p 170: 'Lyons was a triumph for the pope *and the Dominicans*.'

received from cape Leucas (near Brindisi in Italy)[64] announcing his
imminent arrival with the Greek ambassadors, the Pope appointed
Bonaventura to deliver a sermon.[65] Bonaventura selected a most
appropriate text for the occasion, from the apocryphal old testament
book Baruch, as he drew an analogy between the Greeks and the
Israelites who had long been in captivity in Babylon. From the Latin
point of view, the Greeks, too—in a symbolic sense captives of heresy
—were now, finally, in general council, returning from the east to the
'true wisdom of the church' in the west. As the text from Baruch reads:
'Arise (*Exsurge*) O Jerusalem [meaning here the entire church] and
stand on high and look about toward the east and behold thy children
gathered together from the rising to the setting sun.'[66]

On the actual arrival, on 24 June, of the Greek representatives
together with Ascoli and Parastron, the *Ordinatio* relates, the entire
community of cardinals, bishops, and abbots with their households,
went forth to meet the Greeks in order to lead them to the pope, who,
with his retinue, was standing awaiting them in the *aula* (hall) of the
papal palace. On their arrival, the pope gave the Greek envoys the
'kiss of peace.'[67] Then, according to the *Ordinatio*, the Greeks, travel-
weary and no doubt still deeply disturbed over the deaths of so many
of their fellow-travellers off cape Malea, after being formally received
by the pope and presenting their credentials—letters with the imperial
gold seal[68]—were escorted to their quarters. No formal discussion of
any kind evidently took place at this time.

Meanwhile, the pope, as we learn from another source, summoned

---

[64] And not from the Greek island of Leucas, as scholars have wrongly believed (compare
Franchi p 76, n 11; and Roberg p 136).

[65] See text in Roberg pp 227–9; compare Franchi pp 75–6.

[66] Text of Baruch (a major new testament prophet) reads: 'Exsurge Jerusalem et sta in
excelso, et circumspice ad orientem, et vide electos filios tuos ab oriente sole usque ad
occidentem in illo sancti gaudentes Dei memoria.' Bonaventura doubtless used the
vulgate version, though the Latin version came from the Greek text.

[67] Franchi pp 79–80, esp.: 'ad pacis osculum honorifice sunt recepti.' Evidently, unlike at
Florence later, the Greeks were not required to kiss the foot of the pope (see
Geanakoplos, *Byzantine East*, pp 64–5); Gregory also was standing, not seated, when he
received the Greeks.

[68] The Greek envoys brought several letters to the pope, among them one each from
Michael and his son, and the letter from the Greek bishops, see [*Acta Urbani IV,
Clementis IV, Gregorii X* ed A.] Tautu (Vatican 1953) nn 43, 45; Roberg p 228.
According to Franchi p 81, n 25, 'the Byzantine legates had two other documents with
them but we are not certain they were presented in this public audience: Andronicus'
letter, read later at the Fourth Session of the Council, a letter from Michael to Gregory
accrediting Germanos and Acropolites to treat of 'mundane negotiations' (doubtless on
the restraint of Charles' ambitions and on the future crusade).

in private session (to which Bonaventura may also have been invited) his envoy Jerome of Ascoli and his companion Bonagratia.[69] (The other two of the original four Franciscan envoys sent to Constantinople had long before returned to the west, dispatched by Palaeologus in order to report to the pope.) Ascoli and Bonagratia now, it seems, presented to pope Gregory special letters from the Greek emperor and his son. Among the letters brought to the pope by the Greek envoys, there were included, it might be noted, a special imperial communication to the pope's nephew. For in this letter Michael stressed (recall that Gregory himself had lived for years in the holy land) that one of his envoys, his relative the ex-patriarch Germanos, had from childhood spent many years in Jerusalem living in Greek monasteries.[70] This remark was no doubt intended as a way of creating a bond between Germanos, and Gregory and his nephew.

Inasmuch as emperor Michael sent no form of oath, questions were apparently rather quickly raised at the council about the official authority of the logothete George Acropolites to swear in the emperor's name. For he presented, it seems, no document specifically authorising him to sign any binding agreement in the emperor's behalf. When queried about this lack, Acropolites claimed that, before he left Constantinople, the emperor had given him authority *viva voce*.[71] And indeed a passage quoting the words of Michael (as repeated in Ascoli's report) would seem to support this contention: 'It is not the habit of the Greeks to take an oath, rather a subscription has the same authority as an oath'[72] (a rather dubious statement, to say the least). In view of this omission and also of the several others in connection with the Greek clergy's letter, serious doubts should have arisen in western minds about flaws and loopholes in the Greek manner of participation in, and acceptance of, religious union. Even the aforementioned letter of the Greek bishops, most fundamental of all, since upon the eastern

---

[69] On Ascoli's papal audience see Franchi p 81, n 25, referring to the report of Metochites (publ by Giannelli, in Laurent, *Le Bienheureux Innocent V*, p 442). At this time Ascoli, believes Roberg p 138, probably consigned to pope Gregory another document, a personal letter from patriarch Joseph of Constantinople.

[70] See text in Roberg p 232. Compare above, n 30.

[71] Franchi p 89, noting that the Greek legates had full powers conferred by Michael, but that one of these powers, that of taking an oath, was based only on oral authorisation from Michael. Compare Tautu, n 47.

[72] Quoted in Franchi p 90, n 40: 'asserens [Michael] hoc non esse consuetudinis apud eos et subscripto habetur pro firmitate etiam juramenti.' A Latin document printed in Tautu indicates that, in order to assuage the suspicions of the Latin canonists at Lyons, Acropolites and the other legates signed a document indicating their acceptance of the papal terms in the name of the emperor.

clergy depended primarily the implementation of union, was but a copy, though it had been signed by the grand chartophylax of St Sophia, John Bekkos, the later pro-unionist patriarch. The original of the letter of the Greek clerics, bearing the signatures of the bishops, was retained in the imperial chancery at Constantinople (*in munimine imperatoris*, as Ascoli put it).[73] Perhaps Michael thought these signatures too precious to risk losing. Or, more probably, Michael thought the sparse number of signatures would look dubious to the pope. Whatever the reason, it seems clear, contrary to the view of some modern historians,[74] that Gregory must have been aware of the shortcomings of the Greek clergy's letter and the lack of unity it reflected. It should be noted here that all medieval popes, and to a certain extent perhaps even Gregory, were imbued with the belief that the emperor, because of what they believed to be his 'caesaropapistic' powers, could with no great difficulty bend the church to his will.[75] This view was certainly strengthened by the fact that it was always the emperor, not the patriarch, who initiated negotiations for union.

Continuing the calendar of events according to the *Ordinatio*—on 29 June, five days after the Greek arrival, the pope, surrounded by all his cardinals, bishops, and other clerics, celebrated mass in the presence of the Byzantine ambassadors. The epistle was read in Latin and Greek, and the gospel chanted, first in Latin by the pope's relative, cardinal Ottobono, then in Greek by a Greek deacon dressed in the habit of his own rite.[76] Bonaventura then delivered a sermon, after which the creed was intoned, first in Latin by the archbishop Erard d'Auxerre and other Latins, and then repeated in Greek by the ex-patriarch Germanos and the Byzantines, along with the Greek bishops of Calabria and the Dominican William of Moerbeke and the Franciscan John [Parastron] of Constantinople, both referred to here as 'penitentiaries' (that is, 'confessors') of the pope. Three times (*ter*) the phrase *ex patre filioque procedit* was chanted.[77] Contrary to what used to be believed by

---

[73] For Latin text see Roberg p 229; compare Franchi p 80, n 24, on the phrase from Ascoli's letter: [the letter with the bishops' signatures had remained] *in munimine* [a safe place=chancery] *imperatoris*.

[74] See, for example, W. Norden, *Das Papsttum und Byzanz* (Berlin 1903) pp 548–62, and HL 6¹ p 175. Compare Geanakoplos *Emperor Michael*, pp 265–6, on Michael's 'dual policy' to the pope and his own clergy.

[75] Compare H. Beck, *Handbook of Church History*, cap 51, 'From the Second Council of Lyons to the Council of Ferrara-Florence', p 488; and Geanakoplos, *Byzantine East* p 94.

[76] *Franchi* p 82 and compare p 110.

[77] *Ibid* p 83 and compare p 111.

historians, the famous story of Theophanes at this moment keeping his mouth shut has recently been shown to be false.[78]

When recitation of the creed was finished, ex-patriarch Germanos, archbishop Theophanes, and logothete Acropolites together all chanted *laudes* (*enkomia*) in Greek in honour of the pope. Thus the mass, with the Greeks standing near the alter (*iuxta altarem*) was completed.[79] There is no mention in the sources that the Greeks then participated in holy communion, which is understandable since the union, though already negotiated in Constantinople, had not yet been formally proclaimed.[80] Subsequently, during the five day interval between 24 June and 29 June, some private conversations, in all probability, did take place between Greeks and Latins. But no formal public debates of any kind on the matter of reunion seem to have transpired. Nor is there any reliable document or other primary source that I can find to contradict this view. There may be one slight exception, however: a little-known source that mentions, if obscurely, that in a letter written after the council by pope Innocent V (formerly the Dominican minister-general, Peter of Tarentaise), to emperor Michael, he made allusion to certain (theological?) exchanges at Lyons 'between Latins and Greeks.'[81] Whether these were formal or private exchanges, or merely conversations, is not clear. It would seem likely, in any event, that Bonaventura and perhaps his envoy Jerome (as happened later with Greek envoys at the council of Florence) may well have been invited to dine with the pope and the three Greek envoys, at which time they surely would have engaged, informally, in some kind of theological or other discussions of opinion, at least off the record. We know that Acropolites was explicitly charged by the emperor to discuss with the pope the political aspects of union, that is, the restraining of Charles, militarily. And pope Gregory, it appears, usually sought to tie such considerations closely to ecclesiastical concessions on the part of the Greeks.

To return to the account of events at the council as recorded in the *Ordinatio*, on the fourth day of July a reception was held by pope

[78] See Nicol, 'The Byzantine Reaction' p 114, n 12, listing authors who have repeated the story about Theophanes. See Franchi p 91, lines 296 *seq*, where Franchi corrects the corrupt text of earlier editions of the *Ordinatio*.

[79] *Franchi* p 83.

[80] Receiving the sacrament of communion would be the main test, if at this time it were a true concelebration of mass. Evidently it was rather a 'pontifical mass' held in the presence of the Greek envoys, who were probably at this time already considered 'Catholics.'

[81] See Franchi, p 46, n 37, citing a Dominican source referring to Innocent's letter.

Gregory for the ambassadors of the great khan of the Tatars (Persians), Abaqa il-Khan, whom the pope hoped to convert to catholicism.[82] This was an extraordinary event which apparently absorbed the attention of all present at Lyons.

Only two days later, on 6 July, during the fourth session of the council, on the feast day of saints Peter and Paul, the actual ceremony proclaiming religious union of the churches took place. After the seating of the Greek envoys, to the right but *behind* the cardinal deacons,[83] the Dominican minister-general, Peter of Tarentaise, rose to deliver a sermon, which, however, like that of Bonaventura, has not survived. Thereupon, the pope delivered an allocution, the original text of which has also been lost. After restating the three aims for his calling of the council—regarding (1) the crusade, (2) union with the Greeks, and (3) correction of abuses in the church—he expressed his jubilation at the conclusion of union between the two churches. As Gregory pointedly emphasised (not without exaggeration), Michael had returned to obedience of the papacy, 'voluntarily and with no other motive than the religious.' (Here the *Ordinatio* steps out of character, as it were, and records 'which was strongly to be doubted').[84] In George Metochites's account there is a passage which would seem pertinent here: describing the pope for whose sincerity, lack of personal ambition, and ability he had genuine admiration, he wrote: 'Gregory even pronounced a public discourse glorifying our Greek nation before an enormous crowd of ecclesiastical dignitaries.' Metochites also speaks of Gregory's great love for the ancient Greek fathers and, strikingly enough, for the necessity to recover Asia Minor for the Byzantines in the coming joint crusade. Praising Gregory's love of union, Metochites compares him to his successor pope (Innocent V), then Peter of Tarentaise, who 'was a dialectician of note and had a profound knowledge of scripture and who desired union but less profoundly than Gregory.' Metochites's report, interestingly, affirms that, in his great zeal for the crusade, Gregory even made plans to meet personally with Michael in the Italian city of Brindisi, or, if the danger from Charles seemed too threatening, in Avlona in the Balkans.[85]

At this point the letters of Michael and his son were read aloud (in Latin translation) in which, in precise and unmistakable language,

---

[82] *Franchi* p 84.
[83] *Ibid* p 85 (compare p 112): 'a latere dextro post cardinales (diaconi).'
[84] *Ibid* p 86 and 112. The *Ordinatio* here reads: 'de quo multum dubitabatur.'
[85] See Laurent, *Le bienheureux Innocent V*, pp 439–40.

Michael declared his adherence to the Roman faith, including acceptance of the *filioque, azyma,* and primacy of papal jurisdiction.
Afterwards, the letter of the Greek prelates was in turn publicly read.
Whereupon in the name of the emperor and his son, the layman
George Acropolites solemnly and publicly abjured the schism.[86] So
far as I can determine from the sources, Acropolites had no authority
to do the same on behalf of the Greek clergy. Nor, apparently, did the
ex-patriarch Germanos or archbishop Theophanes at any time
explicitly and publicly make any such declaration, apart from the
vague letter they brought from the Greek clergy.

After the proclamation of union, the Greek clergy were reseated
in the cathedral, but in a place probably again little to their satisfaction.
For they were placed to the left, but this time behind the cardinal-
presbyters.[87] After this, the symbol of the faith was chanted by the
pope in Latin, together with the entire body of Latins. And, finally,
ex-patriarch Germanos and archbishop Theophanes, along with the
Greek bishops and abbots of the kingdom of Sicily, again chanted
the creed in Greek, during which, according to the *Ordinatio,* the
filioque was this time chanted (only) twice (*bis*).[88]

The next day, at Lyons, on 7 July, the council considered the
important question of reform in the (western) church, especially the
method of papal election and the abuses in the mendicant orders. These
discussions, it would appear, continued among the Latins alone,
until 17 July.

Meantime, during the night between 14 July and 15 July,
Bonaventura suddenly died.[89] One Franciscan chronicler, seeking to
explain the suddenness of his demise, declared that contributory to
his death were his intensive negotiations with the Greeks over union.[90]
But no corroboration seems to exist for this statement, it apparently
having been made for the first time about a century after the fact.
What is more probably referred to here was Bonaventura's intense

---

[86] Franchi pp 81–91. See discussion of Acropolites's oath-taking (and text of the oath
translated into English) in Geanakoplos, *Emperor Michael,* p 262, n 18. Also see text in
Tautu n 48. Acropolites's oath had apparently not been prescribed by Michael in the
form he took it.

[87] Franchi p 91: 'in loco in quo sedebant presbyteri cardinales, post eos.'

[88] *Ibid* p 92. At the conclusion, it is to be noted, on the order of Gregory 'some words
were read aloud from the ancient councils' (*ibid*).

[89] *Ibid* p 95.

[90] See, for example, Roncaglia, p 176, n 8; and esp Franchi, pp 159 and 156, attributing
this to Paolino of Venice, a Franciscan bishop of Pozzuoli, 1324–44: see G. Sbaralea,
Supp script Francisc (Rome 1806) p 574.

preoccupation with the new constitutions of the church, in particular those dealing with the fate of his own beloved Franciscan order.

In the promulgation of these constitutions, which, besides involving the future of the mendicants, concerned, among other matters, a new method of papal election and the doctrine of the procession of the Holy Spirit, the Greeks should have shown keen interest, to say the least. After all, they were now, presumably, an integral part of the 'one united Christian church.' But the Greek envoys, evidently in accordance with instructions given them by Michael himself, took care to avoid presenting any dissenting opinions. And this despite the quite different Greek method of choosing the chief hierarch, and in light of Byzantine religio-political theory, according to which the emperor, not the pope, was vicar of Christ on earth—not to speak, finally, of the polemical Greek attitude toward the vexing *filioque* question. But, again, I find no record in any primary source—Greek, Franciscan, Dominican, or in the *Ordinatio*—of Greek particpation in any of these public discussions despite what one would normally expect.[91]

On 16 July, after baptism of the Tatar ambassador, the new constitutions were read aloud and a eulogy preached over the body of Bonaventura by Peter of Tarentaise, the Dominican minister-general, at which time the Greeks must also have expressed their lament at Bonaventura's demise. Peter's text, a moving one, was taken from David's psalm lamenting the death of 'my brother Jonathan,' certainly another testimonial to the affection felt by the clerics, high and low, for Bonaventura.[92]

On 17 July, at the sixth and final session of the council, two more constitutions were promulgated, only one, however, the *Cum sacrosancta*, concerning the Greek union. After this the council adjourned. Only a few days later, at the end of July, the Greek delegation departed for home accompanied by envoys of the pope. During the last few days, whatever discussions may have taken place with the Greeks very probably concerned how the newly-proclaimed union was to be implemented in Constantinople among the Greek clergy and people. For, as earlier noted, Ascoli and

[91] Even if the legitimate Byzantine patriarch (Joseph) had gone to Lyons, he could not have abjured the schism alone. Byzantine canon law required the presence and assent of *all five patriarchs* at an ecumenical council.

[92] Franchi pp 95–7. On Peter of Tarentaise see Laurent, *Le Bienheureux Innocent V*, [=Peter of Tarentaise], *Studia et documenta* (Rome 1943); and *Innocent Taurisano, Catalogus Hagiographicus ordinis Praedicatorum* (Rome 1918) p 20.

Parastron, and probably even Acropolites, must have informed the pope about the still strong opposition to union of many, if not most, of the Greek people and clerics.

We take note here of only the one constitution, which, besides that on the method of papal election (*Ubi periculum*),[93] must have been of special interest to the Greeks, *Cum sacrosancta*. This, in fact, was read out on 17 July, in the council in the presence of the Greeks.[94] In this constitution it is stated, unquestionably for the benefit of the Greeks, that the Holy Spirit proceeds 'not as from two principles but as from one, not by two spirations but by one unique spiration.' (This, by the way, is a definition in traditional Latin, Augustinian terms.) And it was presumably couched in these terms to answer the perennial Greek accusation of Latin belief in two archic sources, Father and Son, for the Holy Spirit. The constitution concludes: 'This is what the holy Roman church . . . has always professed. It is what comprises the immutable, true doctrine of the Fathers and orthodox doctors, Greek and Latin.[95]

If exchanges did indeed take place at the council between Greeks and Latins, they must have occurred, with few exceptions, through interpreters—through John Parastron and William of Moerbeke who, apparently alone, had a complete and facile knowledge of *spoken* Greek and Latin. As we have seen, Bonaventura had virtually no knowledge of Greek, and the Greek of Albertus Magnus was faulty and limited doubtless to knowledge of the ancient language. To be sure, we should not overlook the still bilingual Greek bishops from southern Italy. (Recall the passages in the *Ordinatio*, that they joined the Greek envoys in chanting the *filioque* in Greek.)[96]

To return once again to the *Ordinatio*, if one carefully examines the

---

[93] On this constitution see B. Roberg, 'Der Konziliare Wortlaut des Konklave-Dekrets "Ubi Periculum" vom 1274,' *Annuarium Historiae Conciliorum* 2 (Amsterdam 1970) pp 231–62, which lists the names of bishops who signed. No Byzantine is included, however.

[94] See Gill pp 10–11. Franchi p 137, believes, I think correctly, that Theophanes and Germanos must have approved the text of '*Cum sacrosancta.*' This occurred probably outside the formal sessions.

[95] '*Cum sacrosancta*' is the same constitution as '*Fideli ac devota*' (text in Roberg p 247, and French translation in Wolter p 286). It was not known until much later that these two canons were the same; see Franchi p 124.

[96] Franchi p 91; compare to this a remark of the fourteenth-century Marino Sanudo, *Istoria del Regno di Romania*, ed C. Hopf, in *Chroniques gréco-romanes* (Berlin 1873) p 143, that 'more Greeks of Calabria and Terra d'Otranto would have been more faithful to Rome if Michael and his patriarch had been more obedient to the pope.' The south Italian Greeks had been united to Rome since the council of Bari in 1098.

events and ceremonies it lists, one wonders where sufficient time could have been found, in the interval from the time of the Greek arrival on 24 June to the public ceremony of union (6 July), for any substantive theological exchanges or formal debates between Greeks and Latins to have taken place. Moreover, the problem of religious union, however important, was frequently not even the primary issue. The council spent long hours discussing the question closest to the pope's heart—the launching of a crusade to Jerusalem. Let us not forget that this involved the heavy taxation of all the usually reluctant western clergy.[97] Even more attention was devoted to the drawing up of new constitutions to correct abuses in the church, notably on the procedure for electing a pope (a method, by the way, still in effect today), and on the excessive proliferation of the many new mendicant orders with their irregularities. It was undoubtedly Bonaventura and Peter of Tarentaise who had to bear the brunt of the attack from the secular clergy, who felt strongly that, on account of the growing abuses of the mendicants, their orders should be curtailed or even abolished.[98] Bonaventura, now a cardinal but still high in Franciscan councils, was always at the side of the pope, as was the Dominican minister-general Peter of Tarentaise. And both were deeply involved in the day-to-day business of the council.

In light of these various considerations, one may justifiably ask again whether adequate opportunity even existed to discuss, much less formally to debate in any extensive, detailed fashion, the burning questions for centuries separating the churches, the *filioque, azyma,* purgatory, and the overriding matter of papal supremacy.[99] Such an argument would, of course, as stressed earlier, not preclude the possibility of informal talks or conversations, for instance at dinner or between formal conciliar sessions. Indeed, we know that ex-patriarch Germanos and George Acropolites were empowered by the emperor

[97] See Franchi pp 98–9, mentioning the pope's pleasure at discussions for a crusade. Indeed, Franchi p 122, lists the crusade as the 'primary' theme of the council. See also the contemporary Venetian M. da Canale, *La cronique des Veniciens*, in *ASI* (1845) pp 670–71 (compare Franchi p 124): 'io so apertamente che grande parlamento sara tenuto colà (Lyons) della Santa Terra.' Plans, among others, were presented to the pope for a crusade by Fidenzio of Padua, then a leading crusader propagandist. On the crusade see also Tautu, n 49.

[98] The *DbI* under 'Bonaventura' (p 617–8) says (correctly) that Bonaventura's principal work at the council of Lyons was in defence of the Franciscan order.

[99] One may recall the interminable discussions, lasting longer than an entire year, at the later council of Florence (1438–9) almost exclusively on the question of the *filioque* (see Geanakoplos, *Byzantine East*, pp 99–103).

to engage in negotiations with pope Gregory over political matters having to do with Charles of Anjou.[99a]

But another view is at the same time plausible and even probable—that neither pope nor emperor even desired any formal discussion on religious union to take place at Lyons. On the papal side, earlier documents reveal that it had been for decades papal policy that the emperor first accept the Roman confession of faith proposed by the pope, and only then would the pope agree to convoke an ecumenical council and grant military aid to the Greeks. As an earlier pope, Clement IV, had intransigently written to Michael: 'The truth of divine dogma can never be put in jeopardy by discussion.'[100] It would seem, therefore, that what pope Gregory really wanted at Lyons was not formal theological exchanges but simply ratification of the union which, in his mind, had already been negotiated at Constantinople—to put the seal, so to say, of an ecumenical council on that which had previously been accepted by Michael, his son, and a segment of unionist-minded clergy in Constantinople in the negotiations with Jerome of Ascoli.

From Michael's side, the argument against formal debate seems even more persuasive. For as Michael was clearly aware, in the face of serious rebellion in his capital against his unionist policy not only on the part of virtually all the common people and monks and of many leading prelates, but even of his own family—not to speak of the pro-Lascarid party—discussion of such sensitive issues would probably provoke bitter debate at the council and jeopardise what, above all, he expected as recompense for the union—papal cooperation to force the papal vassal, Charles of Anjou, to desist from his projected attack on Constantinople. In support of this view, we may cite the fact that, in the document which Jerome of Ascoli had sent to the pope from Byzantium, it was stated that papal primacy and dogma had already been recognised and signed by Michael and his son at a meeting with the Greek clergy and Ascoli in Constantinople.[101] In further support of this theory, let us recall that Michael sent to Lyons not the incumbent patriarch Joseph, but rather a sympathetic ex-patriarch and relative of his, who was willing for the sake of political expediency, or, as Michael put it in ecclesiastical

---

[99a] See Geanakoplos, *Emperor Michael*, p 237-45; and Tautu nos 63-4, where proposals are made by the Greeks to Gregory regarding 'peace with the Latins' (meaning Charles).

[100] Quoted in Geanakoplos, *Emperor Michael*, p 203.

[101] See Franchi text on p 229.

terms, of *economia*, to re-establish religious union with Rome in order to safeguard the Byzantine capital. As Michael in effect said to his prelates, 'For the salvation of the ship of state (that is, the *Basileia*) it is often necessary [in matters of the church] to cast overboard all extraneous cargo.'[102]

Contrary to generally-held modern scholarly opinion, pope Gregory probably comprehended more or less accurately the ecclesiastical situation in Constantinople. For, as observed earlier, Jerome of Ascoli (as certain sources, for example even Pachymeres, indicate) had informed him that the incumbent Greek patriarch, the anti-unionist Joseph, had been forced to withdraw from his post, to be re-installed only if Michael's embassy returned unsuccessfully from Lyons.[103] Moreover, to reiterate once again, Gregory surely must have heard from Ascoli, Parastron, and probably Acropolites of the tremendous pressures against union faced by Michael. (It was in fact to Michael's own interest to have this point emphasised by Acropolites.) This could serve to explain Gregory's apparent leniency, especially his willingness to overlook the Greek clergy's ambiguous acceptance of his directives and their rather serious omissions in their episcopal letter brought to Lyons.

In view of pope Gregory's sincerity, which is praised even by the Greeks Pachymeres and Metochites, his apparent lack of objection—probably even agreement—to Michael's plea for retention of the Byzantine ritual,[104] and lastly, the toleration Gregory exhibited even for the Greek clergy's imperfect letter, it would seem that Humbert of Romans's advice to Gregory in his *Opus Tripartitum*—to advance cautiously but surely[105]—may not have been in vain. Like Humbert, and unlike his papal predecessors, Urban and Clement (who had expected immediate and total capitulation of the Greek clergy to everything they demanded, both confessionally and jurisdictionally), Gregory probably believed that, with patience and a certain tolerance on both sides, the union, already realised (if imperfectly) in Constantinople would in time become a lasting reality.

---

[102] On Michael's speeches stressing *economia* (the concept expressed here) see Geanakoplos, *Emperor Michael*, pp 265 and esp n 28.

[103] See Geanakoplos, *Emperor Michael*, p 262.

[104] Beck, p 126, observes (correctly, I believe) that the question of the *filioque* and of rites 'was presumably arranged, orally but successfully, between the pope and the Greek legates.'

[105] Translation in Wolter p 272.

It would, then, seem likely that, from the viewpoints of both pope Gregory and emperor Michael, the council of Lyons was intended merely to *ratify officially* what had *already been negotiated* in the east by the Franciscan delegation headed by Jerome of Ascoli. This hypothesis would seem to be corroborated by the almost total lack of material in the contemporary sources of the time, relating to theological exchanges, particularly in the principal record of the council's activities, the *Ordinatio*.

In the light of our discussion, we may therefore conclude that, despite the Franciscan Bonaventura's attractive personality, profound learning, and, as we have described, presumably sympathetic attitude toward some Greek theological and mystical beliefs, the traditional western opinion of the key role played by him at the council (and, to a lesser degree, by the Dominican Albertus Magnus) with regard to theological debates with the Greeks, has been grossly exaggerated and even misrepresented. The question, of course, arises: why this exaggeration and why for so many centuries? It is to be attributed, it would appear, not only to contemporary Franciscan writers, but especially, to later Franciscan adherents of Bonaventura who, at the time of his canonisation in 1483 and still more in 1588, when he was officially pronounced a 'Doctor of the Church,' wanted to exalt him even more by terming him 'the soul of the Greek union' and even 'the president of the council of Lyons.'[106] Despite the undeniable magnitude of Bonaventura's contribution to many aspects of the council of Lyons, his greatness would seem to lie in areas other than theological victories over the Greeks.

The real protagonists who deserve credit for the success, however ephemeral, of the religious union proclaimed at Lyons—despite the presence of such brilliant western theologians as Bonaventura, Albertus Magnus, and, so to speak, even of the spirit of the dead Thomas Aquinas, and, on the Greek side, of the able diplomat-scholar Acropolites and bishops Germanos and Theophanes—were the two rather obscure Franciscan friars, John Parastron and Jerome of Ascoli. Through personal instruction of Michael in the theology of the Latin faith, and more particularly through his sympathetic participation in liturgical ceremonies with an initially almost totally hostile Greek

---

[106] On this exaggeration see esp Franchi, pp 158 *seq*. In *Bullarium Franciscanum Sixti IV*, ed J. Pou y Marti, 3 no 1562 (compare Franchi p 160), Bonaventura is termed 'Concilio Lugdunensi Praesidens'—manifestly false, unless it refers to his chairmanship of certain committees for matters other than union.

clergy,[107] Parastron, it may be said, prepared the climate for union among at least some bishops in Constantinople, in the process helping them to come to the realisation that religious union with the Latins was perhaps not so reprehensible after all. Even more significant, perhaps, was the role of the Italian Franciscan Jerome of Ascoli, later pope Nicholas IV. Although to be sure, Ascoli achieved something less than complete success with the Greek hierarchy regarding their letter of submission to the pope, it was certainly his conclusion of negotiations with the emperor and his son, as well as with at least a part of the Greek episcopacy, that permitted union, untenable as it later proved, to be at last formally and publicly proclaimed at Lyons.

A word about the significance of the council in east and west: for the west, with its emphasis on papal authority, Lyons has always been considered a true ecumenical council. For the Greek east, on the other hand, the council has been linked with that of Ephesus II (449) as a 'robber council' (*lestrike synodos*).[108] In explanation of this Byzantine view, two considerations, repeatedly affirmed by subsequent Greek theologians and historians, must be emphasised—both of which, incidentally, have been demonstrated or implied in this paper: first, the lack of any formal theological debate—recall that, unlike later at Florence, the Greek emperor and clergy sent to Lyons no prominent theologian to defend Byzantine doctrinal views[109]—and, second, and of even greater import, the absence of legates representing all four of the orthodox patriarchs. It is these two criteria, fundamental for Byzantine 'ecclesiology,' that still in the mind of eastern Christendom serve to negate the 'ecumenicity' and validity of the council of Lyons.

Yale University

---

[107] Beck p 125: 'A first inventory of the higher clergy yielded only a half-dozen partisans of union.'

[108] See Geanakoplos, *Emperor Michael*, esp p 263, n 20. Also see Geanakoplos, 'Byzantium and the Crusades,' pp 55–6, quoting a letter of the south Italian Greek, Barlaam, to the pope affirming the Greek view of Lyons as a 'robber council,' because only the emperor and not the four eastern patriarchs had been represented at Lyons. See M. Calecas, *Adversus Graecos* (PG 152, col 211), who says the Greeks call Lyons a 'tyrannical council.' Compare Beck p 488: 'Lyons was rejected in the East mainly because it was attended by imperial legates, not by any of the Orthodox church.' But compare his p 125: 'Gregory had ... an unfailing sympathy for the difficult situation of Michael.'

[109] The leading Greek theologians were then probably Gregory of Cyprus, Manuel Holobolos, Job Iasites, and perhaps John Bekkos, but none of these was sent to Lyons.

ROBERT GROSSETESTE AND HIS WORK
OF GREEK TRANSLATION

by KATHRYN D. HILL

ROBERT GROSSETESTE was a scholar of many parts; regarded by contemporaries and later historians alike as the vital figure in the intellectual life of thirteenth-century England, his writings range from the theological and pastoral to philosophical and scientific studies.[1] An important aspect of his scholarship, which provides a link through many of his other fields of study, was his work of translation from Greek texts, and it is with this aspect that this paper will deal. In his early writing Grosseteste's interest in Greek authors, both classical and patristic is clear; indeed he was almost the first western medieval writer to use Greek sources extensively, but it is equally clear that in his citation of authorities he was not working from original texts, but from collections of quotations or earlier Latin translations. It was no easy matter, however, to acquire a knowledge of Greek in England in the early thirteenth century; but Grosseteste remedied this situation, learning the language when he was over sixty years old and thus providing a path for others to follow him more easily. He summoned Greek scholars to England, of whom some remained in his household and he collected Greek manuscripts, although this involved sending far afield to Athens or Constantinople, to find and procure them. It is all the more fascinating that this work was done, not while Grosseteste was at Oxford, when he might perhaps have had time for such study, but when he was most occupied with pastoral and secular affairs, after he had become bishop of Lincoln.

In the twelfth and thirteenth centuries it is difficult to find any traces at all of knowledge of Greek in England.[2] There was certainly a dearth of books, grammars or lexicons which would have aided

---

[1] The major works on Grosseteste, on which this paper is based are: [D. A.] Callus (editor), *Robert Grosseteste*, [*Scholar and Bishop.*] (Oxford 1955), [S. Harrison] Thomson, *The Writings* [*of Robert Grosseteste*] (Cambridge 1940) and Francis S. Stevenson, *Robert Grosseteste, Bishop of Lincoln* (London 1899).

[2] G. R. Stephens, *The Knowledge of Greek in England in the Middle Ages* (London 1933) and [M. R.] James, 'Greek Manuscripts [in England before the Renaissance'], *The Library*, 4 series 7 (London 1927) pp 337–53.

learning, although Greek studies had once flourished in the early Anglo-Saxon period. There were some Englishmen who knew the language, but they were scholars like Adelard of Bath who travelled and worked abroad in Spain and southern Italy.[3] It was to Magna Graecia that anyone desiring to learn Greek would probably travel, rather than to the Byzantine empire. There John of Salisbury, whose interest in the language was greater than his knowledge, learned its rudiments; and thence Nicholas the Greek, one of Grosseteste's major helpers came to England.

How Grosseteste acquired his interest in, or knowledge of Greek is uncertain: like the other details of his education and early career there is a great scarcity of information, owing to the fact that there is no contemporary biography of him. The earliest known reference to Grosseteste is in a charter of saint Hugh of Lincoln, dated between 1186-9, where he appears as the last witness, *Magister Robertus Grosteste*.[4] This is an interesting indication of his age, since he cannot have been born later than 1168 to have become a master of arts by this date. From Lincoln, he is mentioned by Gerald of Wales as being in the household of bishop William de Vere at Hereford.[5] Both Lincoln and Hereford were centres of intellectual activity in the late twelfth century, which must have been an attraction to the young scholar, but there is no evidence that this involved the study of Greek. The next phase in Grosseteste's career is obscure. Probably he returned to Oxford to lecture in the arts school, where his career would have been interrupted by the secession of 1209-14. Many of the masters left Oxford for Paris during these years, and it would have been a normal course for Grosseteste to go there to study theology, although no evidence for this has been found.[6] It could have been at Paris that his first interest in Greek was aroused; perhaps if he was there he met Thomas Gallus, who was a close friend later in his life and who was lecturing at Paris in the early thirteenth century and known already to be interested in the Greek theologians. The tradition that Grosseteste became chancellor of the young university of Oxford is a firm one and he may well have been appointed to this post by 1214, but it is

---

[3] R. W. Hunt, 'English Learning in the Late Twelfth Century' *TRHS* 19 (1936) pp 19-35.

[4] *MA* 5 p 191.

[5] *Giraldi Cambrensis Opera* ed J. S. Brewer, J. F. Dimock and G. F. Warner, *RS* 21, 8 vols (London 1861-91) I p 249.

[6] D. A. Callus, 'The Oxford Career of Robert Grosseteste' *Oxoniensia* 10 (Oxford 1945) pp 49-53.

uncertain for how long he held it.[7] A few years after the Franciscans arrived in Oxford in 1224, he agreed to lecture to them and continued in this task until, when he was almost seventy, he became bishop of Lincoln in 1235.[8]

Much of Grosseteste's writing, his theological work and his commentaries on books of Aristotle already in translation, was completed before 1235, but this does not appear to be the case with his translations from Greek. A number of translations are firmly attributed to him in contemporary manuscripts. The most important of these are the works of saint John of Damascus, *the Testament of the Twelve Patriarchs, the Epistles* of saint Ignatius, the works of pseudo-Dionysius, Aristotle's *Nicomachean Ethics* and parts of the *Suda* or lexicon of 'Suidas'. The translation of these texts would be a lengthy and arduous task at any point in Grosseteste's career, yet Roger Bacon states firmly, *non bene scivit linguas ut transferret nisi circa ultimum vitae suae.*[9] It will be seen that all these translations do appear to date from Grosseteste's episcopate. In his earlier writing, his interest in Greek sources is evident, but confined to those already in translation. In the *Hexameron*, completed in about 1235, there are many Greek authorities cited, but these, even in the case of saint John of Damascus's *De Fide Orthodoxa* which Grosseteste later translated himself, are all from earlier translations. There is indication however, in his use of the septuagint, that he was sometimes giving his own Latin version from a Greek text, when it varied from the vulgate.[10] There is also a thirteenth-century manuscript in the Bodleian which contains the *Hexameron*, with notes in Grosseteste's own hand, including some Greek words in Greek letters.[11] In the *Commentary on the Psalms* there is a similar indication, in the latter part of the work, written in about 1231–5, that Grosseteste's knowledge of Greek was increasing. The first part of the *Commentary*, written before 1231, has far fewer citations of Greek writers; certainly by the time he wrote the second part, Grosseteste must have acquired a Greek catena on the psalms.[12]

Thus it does appear that Grosseteste began his study of Greek before

[7] Callus, *Robert Grosseteste* pp 7–10.

[8] *Fratris Thomae vulgo dicti de Eccleston Tractatus de Adventu Fratrum Minorum in Angliam,* ed A. G. Little (Manchester 1951) p 48.

[9] [*Rogeri*] *Bacon Opera Inedita* [ed J. S. Brewer], RS 15 (London 1859) pp 91, 472.

[10] J. T. Muckle, 'Robert Grosseteste's Use of Greek Sources in his Hexameron' *Medievalia et Humanistica* 3 (Boulder, Cleveland 1945) pp 33–48.

[11] [Beryl] Smalley, ['The Biblical Scholar'], in Callus, *Robert Grosseteste* pp 79–80.

[12] M. R. James, 'Robert Grosseteste on the Psalms' *JTS* 23 (1922) pp 181–5.

he became bishop, although he was not fully proficient at it. In 1231–2 he had a serious illness, *febris acutae* as he described to his sister Juetta, who was a nun.[13] It was after this that he resigned all his preferments, apart from his Lincoln prebend. He may have occupied himself in the enforced leisure of his convalescence with learning the language. When he left Oxford for Lincoln in 1235, he seems to have been getting into his stride as a Greek scholar.[14]

There has been debate however about the proficiency which Grosseteste attained in Greek, some only allowing that he directed a group of translators; this is largely owing to a comment of Roger Bacon, and to the consideration that he must have been far too busy as a bishop to spend his time buried in Greek texts. Both Matthew Paris and Nicholas Trivet agree in stressing Grosseteste's profound learning: the former calling him *vir in latino et graeco peritissimus,*[15] the latter declaring him erudite in Latin, Hebrew and Greek.[16] Yet Roger Bacon, although praising the learning of 'the lord Robert', persists that 'he was not proficient enough in Greek and Hebrew to translate by himself, but he had many helpers.'[17] It is more difficult to provide proof of Grosseteste's knowledge of Hebrew and that is beyond the scope of this paper, but it will be seen that Bacon's appraisal of his former teacher's proficiency in Greek was somewhat ungenerous. It might be added here that Bacon considered there were three degrees to learning a language: the first was to attain the same complete mastery and perfection as in one's native tongue; the second, to be able to translate correctly into the native tongue; the third, to have only as much knowledge of a language as to enable one to understand a text without difficulty. This third grade, he maintained could easily be reached with the help of a teacher, in three days![18] It is this last grade which he considers the limit of Grosseteste's attainment. Boethius is the only person however, apart from himself, whom he will allow to have reached perfection as a translator; all others are condemned in various degrees, Grosseteste at least being conceded an honourable mention for his efforts.

It is Roger Bacon who describes on several occasions how

[13] [*Roberti Grosseteste*] *Epistolae* [ed H. R.] Luard *RS* 25 (London 1861) pp 43–5.
[14] Smalley p 78.
[15] [Matthew] Paris, *Chron[ica] Mai[ora]* [ed H. R. Luard], *RS* 57, 7 vols (London 1872–4) 4 p 232.
[16] [Nicholas] Trivet, *Annales* [ed Thomas Hog] (London 1845) p 243.
[17] Bacon, *Opera Inedita* p 472.
[18] *Ibid* pp 433–4.

Grosseteste gathered scholars and texts around him in his work of translation. The bishop was able to do this once he had been appointed to the large and wealthy diocese of Lincoln, in order to overcome the deficiencies and difficulties which must have hindered him when he began to study Greek during his last years at Oxford. Some of the *multi adiutores* in Grosseteste's circle were Greeks from southern Italy, who seem to have remained in the country long after his death.[19] It is difficult to ascertain just how many assistants there were in the bishop's household, but some of them can be clearly identified.

One of the most important was a *magister* Nicholas Grecus; Matthew Paris records his assistance to Grosseteste in translating the *Testament of the Twelve Patriarchs*,[20] and he appears several times in the Lincoln *Rotuli*.[21] By birth and education master Nicholas was obviously a Greek; in 1239 he was presented to the church of Datchet by the abbot and convent of St Albans, by 1246 he had become a canon of Lincoln and he was still serving there in 1278. His close association with Grosseteste is indicated by the fact that after the bishop's death, Nicholas was sent to Rome to assist in procuring his canonisation from Alexander IV (1254–61). This was of course unsuccessful: the papacy did not look kindly on one who had been its stern critic. Nicholas has been identified tentatively with the Nicholas Siculus who translated the pseudo-Aristotelian treatise *De Mundo*,[22] and is also possibly connected with a remarkable Greek-Latin lexicon which survives at the college of arms. M. R. James considered this an outstanding monument to the study of Greek in thirteenth-century England.[23] It was written in the later part of the century by a native of southern Italy and consists of sixteen thousand words, aimed at someone beginning a study of Greek. The work is linked to the Grosseteste circle by the considerable use made of the *Suda*, apparently from the bishop's own translation. On two occasions the authority of a *magister*

[19] *Ibid* p 434, also Callus, *Robert Grosseteste* pp 39–40.

[20] Paris, *Chron Mai* 4 p 232.

[21] *Rotuli [Roberti] Grosseteste [Episcopi Lincolniensis* ed F. N. Davies], Canterbury and York Society 10 (London 1910–13) pp 395, 354; see also J. C. Russell, 'Dictionary [of Writers of Thirteenth Century England]', *BIHR* spec suppl 3 (1936) p 89, and J. C. Russell, 'The Preferments [and *Adiutores* of Robert Grossteste]', *HTR* 26 (Cambridge Mass., 1933) pp 161–72.

[22] [E.] Franceschini, *Roberto Grossatesta [Vescovo di Lincoln, e le sue Traduzioni Latine]* (Venice 1933) pp 15, p 71 and also L. Minio-Paluello, 'Note sull' Aristotele Latino Medioevale', *Rivista di Filosofia Neoscolastica* 42 (Milan 1950) pp 232–6.

[23] James, 'Greek Manuscripts' p 344 and also M. R. James, 'A Graeco-Latin lexikon of the thirteenth-century' *Mélanges offerts à M. Emile Chatelain* (Paris 1910) pp 396–411.

Nicholas is adduced, and this seems likely to have been the same master Nicholas, who was furnishing some information for the lexicon.

The other Greek mentioned in Grosseteste's *Rotuli* is known only by his name *magister* Robertus Grecus; it can only be supposed that he was also connected with the translation work.[24] A fuller picture can be gained of one of the leading English assistants, John of Basingstoke, who was archdeacon of Leicester from 1235 until his death in 1252.[25] Matthew Paris deals with John's career abroad and his learning in Greek at some length.[26] He studied and taught at Paris, and then, more unusually, moved to Athens. There his teacher was the remarkable Constantia, who was not only less than twenty years old but also the daughter of the Athenian archbishop, and an eminent scholar! In addition to her extraordinary learning she was able to foretell plagues, eclipses and even earthquakes. Doubt is cast upon the story of this remarkable young lady however, by the fact that she was apparently untruthful about her parentage. The only Greek metropolitan of Athens whose office coincided with John's visit to the city, was the celebrated Michael Choniates (1182–1204) and he clearly states that he was not a father and produced no offspring.[27] It was while he was in Athens that John saw the work known as the *Testament of the Twelve Patriarchs* which he later described to Grosseteste, and which the bishop sent for and translated. John of Basingstoke may have collected other manuscripts for Grosseteste; he himself was the compiler of a grammar book, the Greek *Donatus* and according to Matthew Paris, he brought knowledge of Greek numerals to England, the curious significance of which the chronicler recounts in some detail.

Thomas the Welshman, who was archdeacon of Lincoln in 1238 until he became bishop of St David's ten years later, was another member of the household who, according to Roger Bacon, was learned in Greek and Latin, thus he may have been another collaborator.[28] Grosseteste had a papal privilege to have four friars as his permanent companions; Nicholas Trivet describes how he would discuss scriptural problems with them, and it is not impossible that they

[24] *Rotuli Grosseteste* pp 247, 300.

[25] J. C. Russell, 'Dictionary' pp 54–5 and also J. C. Russell, 'The Preferments' pp 168–9.

[26] Paris, *Chron Mai* 5 pp 284–7.

[27] Kenneth M. Setton, 'The Byzantine Background to the Italian Renaissance' *Proceedings of the American Philosophical Society* 100 (Philadelphia 1956) pp 60–2; this article also contains a full bibliography on the knowledge of Greek in England.

[28] Callus, *Robert Grosseteste* p 41.

may also have assisted in translation problems.[29] Finally Adam Marsh, the bishop's close friend must frequently have been of assistance, although the extent of this is impossible to define. Adam's interest in the translation is clear from his letters, where mention of it is made several times.

To what extent Grosseteste relied on these *adiutores* and how much he worked alone is an interesting speculation; and depends on the weight one is prepared to attach to Bacon's assessment of his knowledge of Greek. Franceschini, who is the authority on this whole subject, considers that the uniformity of method and technique in all the translations argue for a unity of purpose and execution, and that they are not the work of many minds.[30] Throughout the works there are marginal notulae on minute details of grammar and etymological points to elucidate the text; in some manuscripts these are attributed to *Episcopus*. Grosseteste was fascinated by etymology, on his death-bed he is reputed to have discussed the source of the word 'heresy', and it is clear that these marginal notes are his own work. It is extremely unlikely that he would have spent such effort explaining and elucidating a translation which was not his own work. As Callus wrote, it is more likely that the assistance rendered by the *adiutores* was oral and that they discussed problems and offered information, yet that the bulk of actual translation is rightly attributed to Grosseteste.[31]

Something of the method in which Grosseteste worked on his translations can be deduced. On the whole they are extremely literal, every word in the Greek text being given its Latin equivalent, even if this made the word order or syntax irreconcilable with Latin idiom or occasionally produced a string of incomprehensible words. Even the Greek μέν and δέ were always rendered by *quidem* and *autem*. This close adherence to the text however, was a characteristic feature of all medieval translators, in case they altered or perverted the meaning of the authority being translated, by adding words of their own. When Grosseteste worked on a translation he did not start afresh if one already existed, instead he would revise and correct the earlier work. This is true in the case of his earliest translation, the *De Fide Orthodoxa* of saint John of Damascus. It had been translated in the mid-twelfth century by Burgundio of Pisa, and Grosseteste used this as his base. In the colophon of a manuscript of the work in Pembroke

---

[29] Trivet, *Annales* p 243.
[30] Franceschini, *Roberto Grossatesta*.
[31] Callus, *Robert Grosseteste* p 43.

College, Cambridge, this process is described: 'Robert Grosseteste, bishop of Lincoln corrected the old translation and also inserted many things which he translated from the Greek as examples, and which were not contained in the old translation.'[32]

Grosseteste seems to have been extremely methodical and meticulous in his work. The fact that the same word in Greek is always rendered by its same Latin equivalent, all through the translations, and that similar explanations occur for the same words in different works, suggest that he had carefully tabulated lists and indexed references ready to hand. This would have greatly facilitated and increased the speed of the translation and such tabulation may have been the sort of work which some of the assistants performed.

As has been mentioned already, Grosseteste's first work of translation appears to have been the *opera* of saint John of Damascus, which occupied the first few years of his episcopate. His skill as a translator can be seen here to be at an early stage, compared with his later translations. The eighth-century theologian's work embodied much of the thought of the early Greek church. Grosseteste's translation of it never achieved a wide circulation however, as it was the earlier version of Burgundio of Pisa which continued to be widely used.

A more important work of translation and commentary was that on the *opera* of pseudo-Dionysius. Here again in translating the *Angelical* and *Ecclesiastical Hierarchies, the Divine Names* and *the Mystical Theology*, Grosseteste was revising a previous version of the text. Callus found a date for this work through skilfully analysing a letter written by Adam Marsh to Thomas Gallus, who also commented on the pseudo-Dionysian corpus.[33] Gallus was the abbot of St Andrews at Vercelli in Piedmont, and a friend of Grosseteste's; it has already been speculated that they might have formed their friendship in Paris in the early years of the century. Adam mentions in his letter that he had sent Gallus a copy of the *Angelical Hierarchy*, most likely to be the translation of Grosseteste, in view of his close association with the bishop; he then remarks that Gallus's own commentary on the *Mystical Theology* has just been completed but that he is still working on the *Divine Names*. It is known that these books were completed and circulated by Gallus in 1241 and 1242 respectively, thus the date

[32] Pembroke College, Cambridge, MS 20 fol 1ʳ.
[33] [D. A.] Callus, 'The Date [of Grosseteste's Translations and Commentaries on Pseudo-Dionysius and the Nicomachean Ethics'], *RTAM* 14 (Louvain 1947) pp 186–200. The letter of Adam Marsh is in *Monumenta Franciscana* ed J. S. Brewer, *RS* 4, 2 vols (London 1858) 1 pp 206–7.

of the letter seems likely to be about 1240–1. Since the *Angelical Hierarchy* was the first of the four works which Grosseteste translated, it seems probable that he was at work on pseudo-Dionysius from about 1239–43, when he moved on to other things. The use of this translation seems to have been widest amongst English Franciscan scholars, which is hardly surprising since Grosseteste left his library to them, but by the mid-fourteenth century it was in use on the continent.

By far the most popular of Grosseteste's translations and the one which seems to have caused enough stir to be mentioned by several chroniclers when it was completed in 1242, was *the Testament of the Twelve Patriarchs*. An indication of this popularity is the list of seventy six manuscripts of the work compiled by Harrison Thomson.[34] These are scattered across Europe and the work was early on translated into vernacular editions. The manuscript which Grosseteste had procured from Greece on the advice of John of Basingstoke, still survives at Cambridge with notes in the bishop's own hand.[35] The Greek text purports to be a version of the original Hebrew, part of the Hebrew scripture, the patriarchs being the twelve sons of Jacob. Matthew Paris, who himself copied the translation for the use of the St Alban's monks, claimed that it had been hidden from Christian eyes for centuries *per invidiam Judaeorum*, for it contained 'most evident and most beautiful prophecies of Christ'.[36] It is ironic that this curious and apocryphal work should be that which won Grosseteste most acclaim. He certainly regarded it as authentic and quoted it in a letter to Henry III. The king had asked him what anointing added to the royal dignity, and Grosseteste used the quotation to show the superiority of the priesthood to the kingly office, by comparing the powers of Judah and Levi.[37]

In the later years of his episcopate Grosseteste turned from the Greek fathers to Aristotle, perhaps this was due to criticisms of his work on pseudo-Dionysius which seem to have genuinely and greatly grieved him,[38] or because these were the texts which he now acquired. The major translation was the *Nicomachean Ethics* with its Greek commentaries, and this was a vast and onerous task. He seems to have begun to work on it in about 1242–3, as from this time there are allusions to it and vague references in correspondence, but it was

[34] Thomson, *The Writings* pp 42–4.
[35] University Library, Cambridge, MS Ff. i 24, fols 203ʳ–62ᵛ.
[36] Paris, *Chron Mai* 4 p 232.
[37] *Epistolae*, Luard p 351.
[38] Callus, *Robert Grosseteste* pp 58–60.

probably not completed until 1247 or later.[39] The translation had an immediate success, and saint Albert the Great was one of the first to make use of it, since he quotes it in the fourth book of his *Sentences*, which was completed in 1249; Aquinas, saint Bonaventure and Kilwardby were a few of the others who profited from it. The last work of translation which Grosseteste undertook was the *De Caelo* of Aristotle, but this was left incomplete; perhaps death prevented him from finishing it or his interests moved elsewhere in his final years.

Thus Grosseteste's Greek studies were of outstanding importance, not only for his actual translations, but for the means and impetus which he gave to others to learn Greek. He is undoubtedly the source of the flowering of Greek knowledge in thirteenth-century England. It was a tremendous work which he completed, when he was in his late seventies and not in particularly good health. In addition he was assiduously fulfilling his pastoral duties as diocesan of the largest English bishopric, playing an active role in public affairs and harassed by disputes at one time or another with his chapter, the archbishop, the king and the pope. Yet in the midst of this, his Greek studies seem to have been a relaxation which he undertook with love. A letter which he wrote to the abbot and monks of Peterborough suggests this, when he describes how in a week when he was resting from the tumults of the outside world, he came across a Greek manuscript on the monastic life and spent a pleasant day translating it for their benefit.[40] Thus it is pleasing to imagine the elderly bishop, after an exhausting day of administration or travel, spending a quiet evening in one of his manor houses, surrounded by his friends and engaged in one of his favourite recreations, an ardent discussion of the finer points of the particular translation then in hand.

University of London
Bedford College

[39] Callus, 'The Date', pp 201–9.
[40] *Epistolae*, Luard pp 173–8. The letter is addressed to the abbot and convent 'de Burgo, Luard considers this to be Peterborough, but Callus translates it as Bury (*Robert Grosseteste* p 67).

NEW LIGHT ON THE VISIT OF GRIGORI TSAMBLAK TO THE COUNCIL OF CONSTANCE

by MURIEL HEPPELL

THE council of Constance, convened by Sigismund, king of the Romans, in 1413 had as its primary aim the reform of the western church in head and members. Its most urgent task, which in fact took almost three years to accomplish, was to end the schism which had divided the western church since 1378; it also took measures to combat the 'Wycliffite heresy', which resulted in the condemnation and burning of John Hus, and later of his friend and supporter, Jerome of Prague. However, the problem of relations with the eastern, or Orthodox church was not forgotten, though it played only a marginal role in the council's activities. This subject was kept before the notice of the council by the presence of delegates from Constantinople, who were among the first to arrive,[1] and by some sermons on the subject.[2] For the Byzantines, some kind of understanding with the western church seemed to offer the only hope of securing effective military aid from the west, which might yet save Constantinople from the Turks; and indeed it was the belief that Sigismund would place this topic on the agenda of the council that induced the emperor Manuel II Palaiologos to send representatives to Constance. Apart from the Byzantines, the only advocates of the urgency of the reunion issue were the Polish delegation, headed by the archbishop of Gnezdo, who represented the views of the king of Poland, Vladislav II, and his cousin Vitovt, grand duke of Lithuania. Their motives for wishing to end the more ancient schism that divided the eastern and western churches were clearly stated in a sermon delivered by a member of the Polish delegation, Andrew Laskaris, bishop of Posen.[3] After condemning

---

[1] [Ulrich von] Richental, *Kronik* [*des Konstanzer Concils, 1414 bis 1418*], ed M. Buck, (Hildesheim 1962) p 47; trans. [L. R.] Loomis, [*The Council of Constance*], *Records of Civilisation, Sources and Studies*, 63 (Columbia university press 1961) p 105.

[2] See [H.] Finke, [J. Hollsteiner and H. Heimpel], *Acta* [*Concilii Constanciensis*], 4 vols (Stuttgart 1896–1928) 2, pp 530, 534, 536; see also J. Gill, *The Council of Florence* (Cambridge 1959) pp 20–3.

[3] From his name he would appear to have been of Byzantine origin; Ulrich von Richental remarks that he was a doctor of theology, but that he did not know German well. (Loomis p 103).

what he describes as the 'evil-speaking against the rites and ceremonies and holy observances of the Roman and universal church' by the Greeks, the bishop says that it is now necessary for the two branches of the church to cease their mutual recriminations and 'come together in the unity of the Spirit', and that Vladislav II and Vitovt wish to offer themselves as intermediaries in this process of reconciliation. They are, he says, particularly suited to this role both because of Vitovt's connection by marriage with the imperial family (that is, the Palaiologoi),[4] and by the geographical location of their dominions, which the bishop describes as 'near to Greece';[5] by this he means the Orthodox Russian principalities. Moreover, there was a considerable Orthodox population in Lithuania itself. 'So vast a Greek population,' says the bishop, 'following the Greek rite, live beneath the dominion of the said lords, king and duke, that a month's time would not suffice to traverse the length and breadth of their territory . . .'[6] It was this pro-reunion policy of the king of Poland and the grand duke of Lithuania which was responsible for the visit to Constance in the spring of 1418 of Grigori Tsamblak, Orthodox metropolitan of Kiev, in his capacity of head of the Orthodox church of Lithuania, in which Kiev was situated at that time.

Grigori Tsamblak's legal and canonical position was in fact somewhat dubious. Born in Turnovo, the capital of the second Bulgarian empire, of an illustrious family, and already well-known in the Orthodox world as a writer of sermons, he had in fact been excommunicated by the patriarch of Constantinople for holding his office without the patriarch's approval.[7] The circumstances of his appointment as metropolitan of Kiev are complex, and lie outside the scope of this paper; it is sufficient to say that he had been elected, somewhat reluctantly, by the Orthodox bishops of Lithuania, under pressure from Vitovt (who was himself a recent convert to catholicism). His appointment resulted in a de facto division of the metropolis of Kiev and All Russia—a policy consistently opposed both by successive patriarchs of Constantinople and princes of Moscow,

---

[4] Andrew Laskaris says that Vitovt's daughter was the wife of the 'son of the emperor of Constantinople,' (Loomis p 503), that is the future emperor John VIII. In fact John VIII's first wife was the daughter not of Vitovt but of Vasili I, prince of Moscow from 1389 to 1425. The confusion may have arisen because Vitovt's daughter was married to Vasili I, so that John VIII's wife was Vitovt's granddaughter.

[5] Loomis p 503.

[6] Ibid.

[7] Russkaya Istoricheskaya Biblioteka (Russian Historical Library), 6 no 40.

then the leading Russian principality. However, patriarchal disapproval did not prevent Grigori Tsamblak from setting out for Constance.

Grigori Tsamblak and his suite arrived in Constance on 19 February 1418.[8] According to Ulrich von Richental, he was accompanied by 'nine clerics of his own faith',[9] two secular princes described as the 'duke of Smolensk' and the 'duke of Red Russia',[10] and 'many heathen from Tartary and Turkey who hold the faith of Mahomet.'[11] Within a week of his arrival, Grigori had an audience with the recently elected pope, Martin V, in full consistory.[12] He was escorted by two Polish bishops, the archbishop of Gnezdo (the leader of the Polish delegation), and the bishop of Plotsk; he was also accompanied by a Czech scholar, a master of theology from Prague known as Maurice of Bohemia, who acted as his interpreter.[13] Grigori first greeted the pope in a reverential manner, bowing three times as he walked towards him, and then took his seat in the part of the hall reserved for speakers, while Maurice of Bohemia made a short introductory speech, in which he stressed the 'long and fixed purpose of the lord archbishop [Grigori] to join the faith and obedience of the Roman church.'[14] He then proceeded to read, on Grigori Tsamblak's behalf, a sermon which he himself had presumably translated into Latin. A summary of the text of this sermon is included in cardinal Fillastre's diary.[15]

The theme of the sermon, as presented by Fillastre, is the desire of the speaker to see the eastern and western churches reunited, a view which is expressed in unambiguous and even impassioned language. Grigori states that he himself 'had long hoped for this sacred union,'[16] and that he felt encouraged to work for it by the support of Vladislav II of Poland and Vitovt. 'The sincere devotion and faith of these most serene princes,' he says, 'inspired me to a burning ardour myself for the holy faith of the church, and to diligent labour with all my strength to bring as many as I could to the same pious mind by preaching and admonition in the Ruthenian [that is Slav] tongue,'[17] He says there are many among the orthodox population of Lithuania who share his

---

[8] Richental, *Kronik* p 136; Loomis p 176.
[9] *Ibid.*   [10] Loomis p 178.   [11] *Ibid* p 176.
[12] Fillastre, *Gesta Concilii Constanciensis* (Fillastre's *Diary*); see Loomis p 434.
[13] Grigori Tsamblak had probably been introduced to Maurice of Bohemia by another member of the Polish delegation, Paul Vladimir, dean of the university of Cracow, who had studied under Maurice. (See Loomis p 465, n 321).
[14] *Ibid* p 434.
[15] *Ibid* pp 435-7. For the Latin text, see Finke, *Acta* 2, pp 164-7.
[16] Loomis p 435.
[17] *Ibid.*

opinion, which also has the support of the patriarch of Constantinople and the Byzantine emperor.[18] The sermon ends with a
suggestion that a general council should be summoned to discuss the
reunion issue.

To anyone familiar with Grigori Tsamblak's career and the circumstances of his visit to Constance, this sermon raises many difficulties.
First of all, it contradicts what is known of Grigori's views of the
western church and its relations with Orthodoxy. From those of his
writings which have been published,[19] he appears to have been a man
of sincere though rather conventional piety, and it is significant that
one of his sermons is an anti-Latin polemical tract.[20] Nowhere does he
express, even cautiously, any opinion in favour of reunion with Rome.
Moreover, some of the facts stated in the sermon about the circumstances of his mission to Constance do not agree with the evidence of
other sources. For example, in the course of the sermon, Grigori says
that he 'chanced to be' at the court of Vitovt before he left for
Constance,[21] though in fact he had probably been more or less continuously in contact with Vitovt since 1409.[22] He also says that he
asked permission from Vladislav II and Vitovt to go to Constance and
expound his views,[23] whereas the account of the origin of his visit in
the official Russian chronicle of the times makes it clear that it was
Vitovt who took the initiative.[24]

[18] *Ibid* p 436.
[19] Grigori Tsamblak's most popular writings were his sermons, which have survived in
numerous manuscripts. They are for the most part still unpublished, though extracts
are available in metropolitan Makary, *Istoriya Russkoy Tserkvi*, [*History of the Russian
Church*] 5, 2 (St Petersburg 1886) repr *Slavica Reprints*, no 17 (Düsseldorf/Vaduz 1969).
He also wrote eulogies of his uncle Kiprian, (metropolitan of Kiev and All Russia from
1389 to 1406) and Evtimi, patriarch of Bulgaria from 1371 to 1393, an account of the
martyrdom of saint John the New (a merchant from Trebizond who was beheaded at
Belgorod, present-day Cetatea Alba, probably some time in the second half of the
fourteenth century), and a biography of Stephen Dečanski, king of Serbia from
1321–31. All these have been published.
[20] A Popov, *Istoriko-literaturnyj obzor drevne-russkich polemičeskich sočinenij protiv latinjan,
XI–XV vv,* [*An historical and literary survey of Old Russian polemical tracts against the
Latins from the eleventh to the fifteenth century*] (Moscow 1875, repr London 1972)
pp 320–5.
[21] Loomis p 435.
[22] It was in that year that he delivered his eulogy of metropolitan Kiprian, the date of
which can be calculated from internal evidence.
[23] Loomis p 435.
[24] *Nikonovskaya ili Patriarshaya Letopis'* [*The Nikon Chronicle*], *Polnoye Sobraniye
Russkikh Letopisey* [*The Complete Collection of Old Russian Chronicles*] 11, ed M. I.
Tikhomirov (Moscow 1965) for the institute of history in the academy of sciences of
the USSR, p 233.

The doubts aroused by the content of Grigori's sermon as reported by Fillastre are increased when it is compared with another sermon of Grigori's, extant only in church Slavonic, which is still unpublished. This sermon is preserved in a sixteenth-century manuscript which formed part of the pre-1917 collection of the Vilno public library, now in the soviet republic of Lithuania. I was fortunate in securing the loan of a microfilm of it through the inter-library loan service.

More than half of his sermon (or address) consists of a diversified list of complimentary epithets addressed to the 'fathers and brothers' assembled at Constance; some of these are elaborately developed metaphors, illustrated by allusions to events and personalities from the old testament; among the simpler expressions, the members of the council are likened to 'experienced pilots, guiding the ship of the church to the quiet harbour of reconciliation,'[25] and to 'wise and skilled physicians, preserving the body inviolate from every disease of evil thoughts, and guiding it on the way to perpetual health.'[26] This long opening section is followed by expressions of regret that the church, which was originally a single and united body, has now become dismembered and divided into two hostile groups, so that it can no longer be truly considered the church of Christ. 'For how can the church be called Christian,' asks Grigori, 'which is no longer one in Christ, for Christ united us by baptism and the gospels . . .'[27] He goes on to plead, though in very general terms, that the two sides will try to become more humble and tolerant: 'I would venture, he says, 'to put before you one small point, if you would grant me grace—not in any spirit of accusation, but constrained by your wish; and I say this not only to you, but to the Greeks [also]. Let not the wise man boast of his wisdom as the famous prophet said, and let not the rich man boast of his wealth; but let him boast and take pride only in the Truth, as our teacher Paul boasted.'[28] The sermon concludes with a plea that both sides may come together in a Council to discuss the question of reunion under the guidance of the Holy Spirit. However Grigori concludes: 'Let us not depart in any respect whatsoever from the dogma handed down to us by our God-inspired fathers.'[29]

Before proceeding to discuss the significance of this unpublished sermon, it is necessary to say a few words about its reliability as a

[25] Vilno Public Library MS 105 fol 41v.
[26] *Ibid.*
[27] *Ibid* fol 43v.
[28] *Ibid.*
[29] *Ibid* fol 44v.

source. Unlike most of Grigori Tsamblak's sermons (which were composed for the church festivals) this one is preserved in only a single manuscript; and as this dates from the sixteenth century, it is in fact a late copy. Moreover, the title is confusing, since it describes the text as an address delivered to the 'council of Florence and Constance.'[30] However in spite of these circumstances, the content, context and above all the very individual stylistic features all suggest that it is a genuine work of Grigori Tsamblak, and its authenticity has so far been accepted by those who have studied his career.[31]

A comparison of the Latin and Slavonic texts at once reveals that the Latin version preserved in Fillastre's diary is not a translation of the unpublished Slavonic sermon. Even allowing for the difficulty of translating Grigori Tsamblak's idiosyncratic and involved style, the content is quite different. The text reproduced by Fillastre represents a quite unequivocal pro-reunion attitude, while the unpublished sermon uses great linguistic artistry to say precisely nothing which could commit the speaker to any definite view. Indeed the only passages in which Grigori expresses any personal opinion are those in which he stresses the need for more tolerance and mutual understanding. These read as though he had at least convinced himself of this, and hoped to convince his audience. Clearly some explanation must be sought for the divergence between the two texts, especially as there is no evidence that Grigori delivered more than one sermon at Constance.

I would like to suggest that the unpublished sermon represents the text which Grigori Tsamblak prepared before his departure to Constance, in which he attempted, by means of verbal dexterity at which he was a master, to reconcile the task imposed on him by Vitovt with his own rather negative, or at least uncommitted views on the subject of the reunion of the eastern and western churches. But when he arrived in Constance, he was unable to deliver this sermon. His sponsors in the Polish delegation were strongly committed to support reunion, and they prevailed upon him to deliver an address which was more in accordance with this policy. It is also possible that even this revised form was further modified by the translator, Maurice of Bohemia. Two arguments can be cited in favour of this interpretation, one textual and the other personal. In the version in Fillastre's diary

---

[30] *Ibid* fol 40ʳ.
[31] A. I. Yatsimirskiy, *Grigoriy Tsamblak: Očerk yego žizni, administrativnoy i knižnoy delyat'nosti* [*Grigori Tsamblak: a sketch of his life and administrative and literary activity*], (St Petersburg 1904) p 198.

The visit of Grigori Tsamblak to the council of Constance

Grigori says that he rejoiced greatly when he heard that the schism in the western church had been ended by the election of Martin V as pope.[32] But Grigori Tsamblak can scarcely have heard this news until after his arrival in Constance, since Martin V was not elected until 11 November 1417, and Grigori arrived in Constance on 19 February 1418, after a journey which must have taken at least two months.[33] This suggests that some change in his sermon was made after his arrival. The other argument is that the known facts of Grigori Tsamblak's career indicate that he was not a man of very strong will in practical affairs; on the contrary, he was rather easily influenced and even coerced by stronger personalities.[34]

But whatever the explanation of the difference in content between the Latin and Slavonic sermons, one thing is clear: the traditional view of Grigori Tsamblak on the reunion issue will have to be modified. On the basis of the sermon included in Fillastre's diary, he has usually been regarded as an enlightened champion of reunion, or a betrayer of Orthodoxy, depending on the point of view from which he was being judged. In view of the opinions expressed—or carefully not expressed—in the Slavonic sermon, this verdict is no longer acceptable.

University of London
School of Slavonic and East European Studies

[32] Loomis p 435.
[33] The Polish delegation left Poland on 27 November 1414—see Dlugossius, *Omnia Opera*, ed Ignatius Z. Pauli (Cracow 1877) 13 p 180—and arrived in Constance at the end of January 1415. (Loomis pp 209, 448 n 20).
[34] I have dealt with this point elsewhere, in a more detailed study of Grigori Tsamblak's career.

EASTERN LITURGIES
AND ANGLICAN DIVINES
1510–1662

by G. J. CUMING

IT would be difficult to form an accurate estimate of the extent to which the eastern liturgies were known in the west before the invention of printing. At the time of the council of Florence, the *Liturgy of St John Chrysostom* was celebrated at Ferrara and at Venice[1]; and someone brought with him what is now the earliest extant manuscript of that liturgy, and left it behind in Florence.[2] In the debates, however, the western delegates professed to have no knowledge of the rite.[3] After the fall of Constantinople, Greek scholars and manuscripts reached the west in much greater numbers than before. In England an important step forward was taken about the year 1510, when Erasmus gave John Fisher, bishop of Rochester, a copy of *St Chrysostom* in Greek, with a Latin translation made by himself.[4] This translation was included in subsequent editions of the saint's works, and in its own field exercised almost as important an influence as Erasmus's edition of the Greek new testament. The first printed edition of the Greek text appeared at Rome in 1526, together with *St Basil*. *St Chrysostom* alone appeared at Venice in 1528, with a Latin translation differing slightly from that of Erasmus.

Cranmer probably used this latter edition, as bishop John Dowden long ago suggested;[5] and he also possessed Erasmus's version in the 1539 printing of Chrysostom's works. By 1545 all the Byzantine service-books were in print. Manuscript copies were still being made, and *St James* in particular seems to have been in demand for polemical purposes. A colourful character called Constantine Palaeocappa sold a number of copies to persons of high rank, including Henry VIII, so that this liturgy also was accessible to Cranmer. (Another way in which Palaeocappa contributed to western knowledge of the east

---

[1] [J.] Gill, [*The Council of Florence*] (London 1959) pp 106, 302.
[2] [F. E.] Brightman, L[*iturgies*] E[*astern and*] W[*estern*] (London 1896) p lxxxix.
[3] Gill p 296.
[4] J. Fisher, *De veritate corporis* (Cologne 1527) p lxiiii.
[5] *Workmanship of the Prayer Book* (London 1902) pp 227–9.

was by forging manuscripts which he attributed to lesser-known fathers.)[6]

Cranmer acknowledged his indebtedness to the eastern liturgies by giving a prayer at the end of his (English) Litany of 1544 the title 'A Prayer of Chrysostome'; and it seems highly probable that some petitions in that litany are borrowed from the deacon's litany found two or three pages earlier in *St Chrysostom*.[7] Soon after, the act of uniformity of 1549 speaks of the compilers of the book of common prayer having 'eye and respect unto' Scripture and 'the usages in the primitive Church'. These indications have naturally led scholars to look for further signs of Greek influence in that book. Three passages have been adduced as evidence of such influence, two in the canon, and one in the prayer of humble access. Each of these can be quite closely paralleled from *St Basil*, though not from *St Chrysostom*.

The most striking parallel occurs in the canon at these words: 'with thy Holy Spirit and word vouchsafe to bless and sanctify these thy gifts and creatures of bread and wine'. At first sight this looks very like an eastern *epiclesis* or invocation of the Holy Spirit upon the elements, such as is found in *St Basil*: 'We beseech thee . . . that thy all-holy Spirit may come upon us and upon these gifts set forth, and bless and sanctify them'. The great liturgical scholar F. E. Brightman at first suggested *St Basil* as the source of Cranmer's phrase, but later retracted this view on the ground that there is no word or idea in the passage which cannot be convincingly paralleled from western services or writers. Modern scholars have tended to follow his later view; and it may be added that in *St Basil* the invocation comes *after* the words of institution, not before (as in 1549), which implies a different theology of consecration. Further, in *St Basil* it is the Spirit himself who is to come and sanctify the elements, whereas the 1549 prayer asks the Father to sanctify them with his Spirit and word. This makes no difference theologically, but is a surprising change if Cranmer was following *St Basil* at all closely.

A later passage in the canon of 1549 runs: 'humbly beseeching thee that whosoever shall be partakers of this holy Communion may worthily receive the most precious body and blood of thy Son Jesus Christ and be . . . made one body with thy Son Jesus Christ, that he may dwell in them and they in him'. Brightman compares a passage

---

[6] See, for example, F. J. Leroy, 'Proclus "de traditione Missae": un faux de C. Palaeocappa', in *OCP* 28 (1962) pp 288–99.

[7] F. E. Brightman, *The English Rite* 2 vols (London 1915) 1, pp lxvi, 178.

in *St Basil* which leads up to the Lord's Prayer: 'that . . . we may be united to the holy body and blood of thy Christ, and, receiving them worthily, may have Christ dwelling in our hearts'. But the context of the 1549 passage is all supplied by the Roman canon and St John's gospel, and the material actually shared with *St Basil* is concerned with the general and not unusual ideas of worthy reception and union with the body of Christ. In any case, the passage was deleted in 1552.

The third instance is taken from the prayer of humble access: 'We do not presume to come to this thy table, O merciful Lord, trusting in our own righteousness, but in thy manifold and great mercies . . .'. This again resembles a passage in the anaphora of *St Basil*: 'Not because of our righteousnesses . . . but because of thy mercies and thy pities which thou hast poured out richly upon us, do we take heart to approach thy holy altar'. But both 1549 and *St Basil* are based on Daniel 9.18, and this is enough to account for the resemblance.[8] Thus none of the suggested parallels is really convincing; and it should be observed that none of the three passages occurs at the same point in both rites.

Indeed, Cranmer did not take every opportunity that offered of using eastern material. Bucer, for example, wrote a preface (in the liturgical sense of the word) in the church order for Cologne which is obviously based on eastern models. But Cranmer, though he used the Cologne order very freely, totally ignored this preface, and made no attempt to follow it by introducing a thanksgiving for creation into his canon. Instead, he abbreviated the preface of the Roman canon.

Once a start had been made, the printing of eastern liturgies went on apace, though not in time to have any influence on the prayer books of Edward VI. In 1544 the Uniat Armenian rite was printed in Cracow; in 1548 the Ethiopic, brought to Rome by an Abyssinian called Tasfa Sion, followed by a Latin translation in 1550; in 1560, *St James*, 1563 *The Apostolic Constitutions*, 1572 a Latin translation of the Syriac version of *St James*, 1583 *St Mark*, 1589 *St Peter*, 1592 the Maronite rite, and in 1604 Latin versions of the three Coptic liturgies, *St Cyril*, *St Basil*, and *St Gregory*.[9] Thus by the end of Elizabeth's reign all the important Orthodox liturgies, whether in current use or not, were

[8] For the 1549 passages, see *Everyman* edition (London 1972) pp 222, 223, 225; for *St Basil*, Brightman, *LEW* pp 329 line 26; 410 line 11; 329 line 16. For references to alternative sources, see E. C. Ratcliff, 'The Liturgical Work of Archbishop Cranmer', in *JEH*, 7 (1956) pp 189–203.

[9] Brightman, *LEW* pp xcviii, lxxii, xlviii, xlvi, lxiii, xci, lvii, lxviii; F. A. Gasquet and E. Bishop, *Edward VI and the Book of Common Prayer* (London 1890) p 187 n.

accessible in print to an eager collector. Most of them were reprinted at regular intervals in collections such as the *Bibliotheca Veterum Patrum* published in Paris in 1624, 1644, and 1654. The only important liturgies which remained unprinted were those of the east Syrian Nestorians or 'Chaldaeans', and some report of them had reached the west, as appears from casual allusions.

The Elizabethan divine most interested in the eastern liturgies appears to have been John Jewel. Already in the famous sermon preached at St Paul's Cross in 1560 he makes a point by point comparison of *St James* with the Roman mass, and it should be noted that it was only that same year that Guillaume Morel issued the first printed edition in Paris. The features in *St James* which appealed to Jewel and are absent from the mass are the use of the vernacular and the reading aloud of the institution narrative; communion is offered to the people, who receive it and not merely behold it, and in both kinds. It is by Christ's institution, not man's; it includes preaching, and is full of knowledge and consolation, whereas the mass displays only ignorance and superstition. This is a slightly rosy-tinted view of *St James*, and one may wonder whether Jewel's knowledge of it was really first-hand. At any rate in his prolonged controversy with Thomas Harding he refers to it much less frequently than to the others.

Here the ground was chosen by his adversary, and Jewel is merely replying to his claims that the eastern liturgies support Roman teaching and practice. Jewel's first response is to question the authenticity of *St Basil* and *St Chrysostom* on the ground that their intercessions mention pope Nicolas and the emperor Alexius, whereas the first bearers of those names date from 857 and 1004 respectively. Jewel must have realised that liturgies are added to in the course of time, and wisely does not press this naive argument. One by one the points that he had already made in the Paul's Cross sermon are applied to the two Byzantine liturgies: the words of institution are said aloud; all are invited to communicate; and all receive. Jewel admits that *St Basil* and *St Chrysostom* teach a presence of Christ in the consecrated elements; but it is an invisible presence, which he can accept. True, in the Byzantine rites the host is elevated, but in order that the people may prepare themselves for communion, not (as in the Roman rite) to be gazed on and adored.

Jewel allows that the Byzantines pray for the dead, but since their prayer includes the Blessed Virgin Mary and the apostles, prophets, patriarchs, and martyrs, it cannot be taken to imply a doctrine of purgatory. The eastern liturgies give no support to the Roman practice of dividing the wafer into three pieces. Textual questions are raised: St Chrysostom's apparent support of images depends on the Latin translation; and it appears that though the present text of St Basil refers to the elements as antitypes *before* consecration, the word originally occurred *after* consecration (Stephen Gardiner had already suggested that the text was disordered).

Jewel has read the fourteenth-century *Interpretation of the Divine Liturgy* by Nicolas Cabasilas; but he is guarded about the *Catecheses* of Cyril of Jerusalem, which were not yet in print, and very scornful of the *Epitome of The Apostolic Constitutions*, which, he says, was 'found very lately in the Isle of Candy . . . and in these countries never heard of nor seen before'. Actually, Jewel had not seen it even then: he got his information from a book published in Cologne. In short, Jewel is not really interested in the eastern liturgies as forms of service, but simply as useful allies in the battle against Roman claims.[10]

With the first stirrings of the Laudian movement, a different attitude becomes apparent. Lancelot Andrewes owned a copy of Morel's *Leitourgiai ton Hagion Pateron* (namely, St James, St Basil, and St Chrysostom), probably the same edition that Jewel used; and also some of the Office books. From these sources he drew very heavily in his *Preces Privatae*. He uses St James most frequently, 'and the rest probably more often than it has been possible to trace', says Brightman; in any case, some material is common to all three liturgies. The intercessory character of the *Preces* naturally causes him to make most use of the detailed petitions of the litanies. Here is one link with Cranmer; and another is the way in which he will slip from one liturgy to another in the course of a sentence, a procedure which suggests reliance on an accurate memory rather than transcription from first one source, then another. The section of the *Preces* on the holy mysteries reproduces a large part of the anaphora of St Basil, perhaps the richest of all the Greek anaphoras.

Andrewes's disciple John Cosin had in his library nearly all the liturgies mentioned above, in the Paris *Bibliotheca* edition. In his writings he quotes freely from St James, St Mark, St Peter, St Basil, St Chrysostom, and The Apostolic Constitutions. Of the latter work, compiled by an anonymous Arian about the year 375, Cosin writes, 'The author, whether he was pope Clement I or someone else, was

---

[10] J. Jewel, *Works*, ed J. Ayre, 3 vols, Parker Society (Oxford 1847–50) 1, pp 23, 24, 111, 114, 116, 486, 511; 2, pp 573, 579, 588, 596, 653, 700; 3, p 651.

contemporary with the apostles themselves': he was aware of the problem of authenticity, but conservative in his approach to it. He has compared *St James* with Cyril of Jerusalem, and *St Mark* with Cyril of Alexandria and the Ethiopic liturgy; and has thus seen how they have been 'reduced into this form wherein they now are, by those diverse changes which several ages have made'. (This insight would have saved Jewel from a very weak argument.) Elsewhere Cosin refers to the Syriac and Armenian liturgies. He too has read Cabasilas, in the Paris edition of 1624; and he knows the twelfth-century canonist Theodore Balsamon, at any rate for the *responsum* in which he condemns *St James* and *St Mark* as illegal, even in their own patriarchates.

But unlike the other divines who appear in this paper, Cosin did not confine his knowledge of the eastern liturgies to studying them in books. During his exile in Paris he 'contracted an acquaintance with the venerable prelate Cyril, archbishop of Trebizond', and had 'frequent conference' with him. On one occasion he 'heard him say *St Chrysostom's Liturgy* in a private chapel at the Louvre . . . before Her Majesty the Queen of England and diverse of her attendants there, that they might see the manner of it'. Cosin himself sat with the duke of York in 'a private closet adjoining to the chapel', and declared 'unto him the several passages of that liturgy', having it in his hand 'and showing him, as the archbishop proceeded, the differences between it and the Roman mass'. Cosin's approach is much more that of the modern liturgical scholar, anxious both to be familiar with the rite in its contemporary practice, and to get back as far as possible to its original form. He lived just too soon to benefit from the work of the great Benedictine liturgists of the later seventeenth century; to a large extent he was a pioneer.[11]

By the middle of the seventeenth century, all divines who have an interest in liturgy display a good knowledge of the eastern rites. Anthony Sparrow, for instance, in his *Rationale upon the Book of Common Prayer* (1655) and Hamon L'Estrange in his *Alliance of Divine Offices* (1659) refer to them naturally and regularly as accepted authorities needing no recommendation or defence. Jeremy Taylor followed Andrewes's lead in his *Collection of Offices* (1658), telling us explicitly in the preface that his services are 'collected out of the Devotions of the Greek Church, with some mixture of the *Mozarabick* and *Aethiopick* and other liturgies . . . and therefore for the material

---

[11] J. Cosin, *Works*, ed J. Barrow, Library of Anglo-Catholic Theology, 5 vols (Oxford 1843–58) 4, pp 466 *seq*; 5, pp 355, 408.

part [they] have great warrant and great authority'. In fact, again as with Andrewes, the communion office is largely taken from *St James*. The high authority accorded to this rite, which had not been in general use for centuries, was due to its attribution to the brother of the Lord, which was still accepted by the majority of scholars, though not without reservations. It was therefore held to be a good deal earlier than *St Basil* or *St Chrysostom*; and the same was true of the liturgy attributed to St Clement of Rome contained in *The Apostolic Constitutions*.

In conformity with this new attitude towards the eastern liturgies, the royal warrant for the Savoy conference of 1661 instructs the commissioners to compare the book of common prayer 'with the most ancient liturgies which have been used in the Church in the primitive and purest times'. However, when the conference met, the presbyterian delegates claimed that they could not find 'any records of known credit . . . within the first three hundred years', only 'some liturgical forms fathered upon St Basil, St Chrysostom, and St Ambrose; but we have not seen any copies of them but such as give us sufficient evidence to conclude them either wholly spurious, or so interpolated that we cannot make a judgement which in them hath any primitive authority'. The choice of the first *three* hundred years neatly rules out any liturgy then known, other than those attributed to one or all of the apostles; and the authenticity of the latter was by no means universally accepted, even at this date. The bishops rejoined that, 'though we find not in all ages whole liturgies, yet it is certain that there were such in the oldest times . . . Though those that are extant may be interpolated, yet such things as are found in them all, consistent to Catholic and primitive doctrine, may well be presumed to have been the first'. The presbyterians come very near to modern ways of thinking about early liturgy when they reply: 'a liturgy indeed, such as we have used while the Common Prayer Book was not used, where the psalms, the words of baptism, and the words of consecration, commemoration, and delivery of the Lord's Supper, and many other, were used in a constant form, when other parts were used as the minister found most meet'; the substance of prayer was 'left to the minister's present or prepared conceptions'. They also pointed to the diversity of liturgies in the primitive times as an argument against the imposition of any one form.[12]

After this, the appeal to antiquity was quietly dropped, and the 1662

---

[12] G. Gould, *Documents relating to the Act of Uniformity of 1662* (London 1862) pp 108, 121, 294–5.

edition of the book of common prayer bears no traces at all of any fresh use of eastern material. The only outcome of the suggestion of the royal warrant was the appearance of a few eastern phrases in the stillborn *Reformation of the Liturgy* composed by Richard Baxter.

From 1662 onwards eastern liturgies were not only studied and quoted, but also served as models for contemporary services. *The Apostolic Constitutions* and *St James* formed the basis of the communion offices of the nonjurors and the Scottish episcopalians; but this period has been definitively treated by W. J. Grisbrooke in his work *Anglican Liturgies of the Seventeenth and Eighteenth Centuries*, and needs no further consideration here. The influence of the eastern liturgies in the nineteenth and twentieth centuries must await another historian.

University of London
King's College

THE SCOTTISH BISHOPS
AND ARCHBISHOP ARSENIUS

by HENRY R. SEFTON

SOME time before July 1716 bishop Archibald Campbell made the acquaintance of Arsenius, archbishop of Thebais, who was in England on a begging mission on behalf of Samuel, patriarch of Alexandria. The circumstances of this mission are described in a fragmentary manuscript preserved in the Jolly Kist[1] at the Edinburgh episcopal theological college. According to this account Samuel was elected patriarch by the clergy of Grand Cairo, Alexandria and Damiata in 1710. The new patriarch resolved to travel to Constantinople, Moldavia and Wallachia to procure some charitable assistance for the support of his church and was about to embark at Alexandria when he was informed by letters from Constantinople that one Cosmo, formerly archbishop of Mount Sinai had by bribery been invested in the patriarchal throne by the grand visier and would shortly be arriving with commands to the Greek nation to acknowledge him. This news obliged the patriarch to return to Grand Cairo to consult with his clergy. They strenuously opposed all thoughts of submitting to the intruder and told Samuel that he ought to stand his ground and make the bashaw a sufficient offer to secure his possession against the pretences of his adversary. Cosmo arrived soon afterwards but Samuel had by this time secured the support of the bashaw and the intruder's designs were defeated. All this was accomplished only at very great expense which had involved the patriarch in borrowing thirty thousand dollars upon high interest from what are described as infidels and foreigners. He was also obliged to sell much of the church plate and to pawn other utensils for the loan and credit of this money. It was therefore decided to send a deputation to several parts of Christendom 'in order to procure the charity and beg the benevolence of princes and other persons disposed to assist the afflicted'. The persons appointed for this errand were Arsenius,

All dates are given in new style. Acknowledgement is made of the kind assistance of the principal and staff of Edinburgh episcopal theological college.

[1] Named after bishop Alexander Jolly (1756–1838) who collected much of the material contained in it.

metropolitan of Thebais and Gennadius, archimandrite of Alexandria who set sail for England with the recommendations of their patriarch and the English consuls at Grand Cairo and Tripoli. Along with their attendants they arrived in London in 1712.[2]

Four years later the deputation from Alexandria were still in England in spite of having had a promise of £300 from queen Anne and a further £100 from her successor. Arsenius and Gennadius, their deacons and domestics made a household of nine and they had run up considerable debts for food and lodging and were constantly applying for help from 'charitable and tender-hearted Christians'.[3] Arsenius had also incurred suspicion as to his real motives. Dr John Covel, master of Christ's College, Cambridge, asserts in a letter that 'it is not unlikely that Thebais comes with this fair pretence, not to restore the true elected Samuel, but to intrude himself, or put what he can get in his pocket'.[4]

According to the Scottish historian, John Skinner, bishop Campbell had 'a scheming turn for everything he thought of general usefulness to the church'[5] and so when he met Arsenius he took occasion to suggest that a union might be entered into by the non-jurors and the Greek church. Arsenius's reaction may have been dictated more by his financial straits than by his theological views but apparently he was not averse to Campbell's enquiry.

The relationship of Campbell and his fellow Scotsman, James Gadderar, to the non-jurors is rather curious. Campbell had been consecrated at Dundee in 1711 by three of the Scottish non-juring bishops but at the request of bishop George Hickes who was determined to continue the English non-juring succession. Campbell, Hickes and a Scottish bishop called Falconar had consecrated Gadderar in London the following year. In 1713 Campbell and Gadderar had joined with Hickes in consecrating Jeremy Collier, Nathaniel Spinckes and Samuel Hawes. But for all that they were links in the chain of the English succession Campbell and Gadderar were regarded as Scottish bishops and 'not seldom as foreigners'.[6] On the other hand, Alexander Rose, the last surviving pre-revolution bishop in Scotland can speak of 'your church' when writing to Gadderar and the reference is clearly to the English non-juring communion.[7]

[2] Jolly Kist, folio mss 4. [3] *Ibid*, folio mss 3.
[4] BM Harleian MS 3778 fol 111 quoted [George] Williams, [*The Orthodox Church of the East in the Eighteenth Century*] (London 1868) p lx.
[5] John Skinner, *Ecclesiastical History of Scotland* (London 1788) 2, p 634.
[6] [Henry] Broxap, [The Later Non-Jurors] (Cambridge 1924) p 12.
[7] Jolly Kist, folio mss 6.

When Campbell put forward his scheme for a union with the Greek church to a meeting of the non-juring bishops in London in July 1716 the proposal did not meet with unanimous approval. One of those present indeed expressed the opinion that the Greeks were more corrupt and more bigoted than the Romanists. However Campbell, Collier and Spinckes met later on and drew up 'A Proposal for a Concordate betwixt the orthodox and catholick remnant of British Churches, and the Catholick and Apostolical Oriental Church' which is dated 18 August 1716. It was signed by Campbell, Collier and Gadderar and translated into Greek by Spinckes with the assistance of a Scottish laird, Thomas Rattray of Craighall.

The document thus prepared contains a curious assortment of proposals. The most remarkable is a suggestion for an alteration in the order of precedence of the eastern patriarchs. The first place was to be accorded to the patriarch of Jerusalem and on behalf of the 'Catholic remnant' of the British churches the signatories acknowledge that they first received their Christianity from 'such as came forth from the Church of Jerusalem before ever they were made subject to the Bishop of Rome and that Church'. The request is made for reciprocal recognition as 'a part of the Catholick Church in communion with the Apostles'. The eighth proposal is that 'the most ancient English Liturgy as more near approaching the manner of the Oriental Church be in the first place restored, with such proper additions and alterations as may be agreed on, to render it still more conformable both to that and to the Primitive Standard'. It was also suggested that a church to be called Concordia should be built in or around London. This would be under the jurisdiction of the patriarch of Alexandria. Should it please God 'to restore the suffering Church of this island' they would endeavour to obtain permission for the occasional celebration of the Greek liturgy in St Paul's Cathedral.

In addition to the proposals there is a clear statement of five matters to which the non-jurors cannot give assent. These are according to the decisions of the ancient general councils the authority of the holy scripture, the worship of the Blessed Virgin Mary, the invocation of the saints, the worship of the Host in the eucharist and the veneration of images.[8]

---

[8] Williams pp 4–12. Jolly Kist, folio mss 1–5 contain the original documents from the east with translations and also copies of the documents sent by the non-jurors with translations into Greek and Latin. There is a catalogue edited by bishop John Dowden in *JTS* 1 (1900) pp 562–8. Williams has the fullest account in English, but for transcriptions in the original languages see *Mansi* 37 cols 369–624.

The Greek version prepared by Spinckes and Rattray and also a Latin version were handed to Arsenius who left England for Moscow, There he engaged the interest of the czar, Peter the Great who commended the proposals to the four eastern patriarchs and also to the Russian church. Meanwhile the translator, Spinckes had taken up a position of unyielding opposition to the replacement of the existing English liturgy and to the introduction of the usages which it was thought would bring the non-jurors' worship into closer conformity with that of the eastern church.

The senior Scottish bishop, Alexander Rose of Edinburgh, had been informed by Campbell of the intended concordat and had seen a copy of the proposals. He thought it very desirable that all Christian churches should be at peace and in communion with one another, but in his view pressing a conformity in rites and usages was not a proper expedient for obtaining that end. All churches should be left in freedom to determine in these matters according to their circumstances. The restoration of practices, however innocent, primitive and useful, which were associated in common estimation with popery could do nothing but harm to their cause in Scotland. Rose also felt that this was not a very prudent way to conduct the negotiations: 'to goe hastily into terms not necessary in themselves & most probably hurtfull, and that too without being well assured from the other side in matters of great moment and without which a Concordat cannot well take effect, seems to me as what cannot well be excused of some degree of rashness.'[9]

In a letter to Spinckes dated 29 July 1718 Rose includes an account which Campbell had sent him of a meeting of the English non-juror bishops on 23 July 1716. This was probably the occasion when Campbell first suggested the concordat with the Greek church but the account is concerned with the restoration of primitive usages. According to Campbell it was agreed without dissent that until Edward VI's first liturgy could be printed and received with suitable alterations, a certain primitive prayer of invocation of the Holy Ghost should be subjoined to the prayer of consecration and used constantly in all congregations 'where they can bear it'. Anointing with oil was to be made available for any sick person who desired it and priests were given permission to omit the words 'militant here on earth' in the bidding to the prayer for the whole state of Christ's church.[10] Spinckes and his party disputed the authenticity of this account claiming that

[9] Jolly Kist folio mss 6.
[10] Ibid.

it was a fabrication by Campbell and denying that they had ever agreed to these decisions. Although appealed to by both sides in the usages controversy Rose is very careful not to take sides and in a letter to Gadderar, later copied for Spinckes, he says:

> What the Church of England shall bear or be easily brought to, her worthy guides ar the best judges; but sure I am, that som of these usages, particularly prayers for the Dead, shall neither goe down with our clergy or people & for us to seek to introduce them wer nothing less than to lose both ourselves, our labour and the most of our communion: Wherefore I presume it much concerns you and Mr Archibald Campbell to be very cautious in this matter . . .[11]

But caution was very far from the minds of either Gadderar or Campbell and they both took a prominent part in the compilation of the non-juror communion office of 1718. This was an attempt to fulfil the eighth proposal in the concordat with the Greek church as is indicated by its full title: 'A Communion Office, Taken partly from Primitive Liturgies, And partly from the First English Reformed Common-Prayer-Book.' Greek and Latin versions of this office were prepared for the benefit of the eastern church. When Campbell was elected bishop of Aberdeen in 1721 both he and Gadderar saw this as an excellent opportunity for promoting the 'usager' cause in Scotland. Rose had died the previous year but the other Scottish bishops were of the same mind as he and they refused to ratify Campbell's election unless he promised not to maintain any doctrines or usages which were without sanction from the canons of the church. This Campbell refused to do and so the bishops informed the clergy of Aberdeen that their choice was not approved. Campbell however considered that he had been canonically elected and he sent Gadderar to Aberdeen to act as his vicar as he had no intention of giving up residence in London.

Gadderar's influence on the clergy of the north-east of Scotland can be judged by the fact that in 1723 the other Scottish bishops thought it necessary to issue an injunction requiring clergy to promise not to introduce the objectionable usages. The mixed chalice and prayers for the dead were particularly mentioned but there was no express reference to the invocation and the oblation which were included in the 1637 Scottish prayer-book which had been authorised by king Charles I.[12]

[11] *Ibid.*
[12] George Grub, *An Ecclesiastical History of Scotland* (Edinburgh 1861) 3, pp 386–91.

Meanwhile, at long last, an answer had been received from the Greek church to the proposals for a concordat. In a letter addressed to Campbell and the other bishops Arsenius is at pains to point out that this delay was occasioned not by contempt but by the careful synodical examination of the proposals. There was an even greater delay in transmission for the reply dated 12 April 1718 did not reach England until 1721 or 1722. It is courteously worded but is quite uncompromising and requires the submission of the non-jurors on all the disputed points. Non-committal letters from the Russian synod suggested that two delegates be sent from Britain to confer with them. The death of the czar terminated the correspondence with the Russians[13] and a letter from the archbishop of Canterbury, William Wake, to the patriarch of Jerusalem cut short the subsequent correspondence with the Greek church. Wake left the patriarch in no doubt as to the 'schismatical' position of the non-jurors.[14]

The discouraging nature of the correspondence with the east does not seem to have cooled the ardour of Campbell and Gadderar for liturgical change in the direction of closer conformity with the eastern church. Campbell's parting gifts to his presbyters and deacons when he resigned the see of Aberdeen in favour of Gadderar in 1725 were copies of the non-jurors' office and of a book of private devotion compiled by a 'Primitive Catholick'. Gadderar later distributed copies of a reprint of the Scottish communion office of 1637 with instructions as to the rearrangement of its different parts. These instructions provided for the consecration and oblation to be followed by the prayer for Christ's church, the Lord's Prayer, the invitation, the confession, the absolution, the comfortable words and the prayer of humble access.[15] Gadderar was a more diplomatic man than Campbell and he was able to secure concordats with the other bishops which gave him permission to use the mixed chalice unobtrusively and general authority for the use of either the English or Scottish liturgies. Apparently the rearrangement of the parts of the communion was not a matter of contention.

But to Gadderar and to Rattray of Craighall the order as well as the content of the liturgy was of great importance as reflecting conformity with primitive practice. Rattray was an unusually well informed layman and had arranged for the non-jurors' office to be used in his private

[13] Broxap p 32.
[14] Williams lv–lviii.
[15] [A. C.] Don, [*The Scottish Book of Common Prayer 1929*] (London 1949) pp 32–9.

chapel at Craighall. He became a priest in mature life and was certainly in orders by 1724. In 1727 he was consecrated as bishop of Brechin by Gadderar and two other bishops and his growing influence in the church is reflected by his election to Dunkeld in 1731 and as *primus* in 1739. This influence he exercised in the direction of closer approximation in worship to the model provided by the eastern churches and particularly by the church of Jerusalem.

The fruit of Rattray's long interest in the worship of the eastern churches and his most important legacy is his edition, published posthumously in 1744, of *The Ancient Liturgy of the Church of Jerusalem, being the Liturgy of St James, Freed from all latter Additions and Interpolations of whatever kind, and so restored to its Original Purity*. The method used to free the *liturgy of St James* from later interpolations was to compare it with the Clementine liturgy, 'which never having been used in any Church since it was inserted into the Apostolical Constitutions has none of those Additions which were afterwards introduced into the other Liturgies'. Rattray's thoroughness is shown by his consideration of the evidence afforded by saint Cyril's sixth mystagogical catechism and the liturgies of saints Mark, Basil and John Chrysostom. Appended to this is an adaptation of the *Liturgy of St James* intended for actual use entitled 'An Office for the Sacrifice of the Holy Eucharist'.

Rattray's office is the high-water mark of eastern influence in Scottish worship. It is doubtful if it was actually used elsewhere than at Craighall but in the opinion of bishop Dowden it is to Rattray's work that the episcopal churches in Scotland and in the United States of America 'owe the most characteristic of the special features of their respective liturgies'.[16] The most important of these is the order of the prayer of consecration in which the recital of the history of the institution immediately precedes the oblation which in its turn precedes the invocation of the Holy Spirit upon the elements. This order was followed in an addition of the communion office issued in 1755 by bishop William Falconar and this in turn served as a model for the communion office of 1764. It was this rite which was used at the consecration of Samuel Seabury at Aberdeen in 1784 and this rite which Seabury promised to commend to his brethren on his return to the United States.[17]

The negotiations with Arsenius and the Greek church may have

[16] [John] Dowden, [*The Scottish Communion Office 1764*] (Oxford 1922) p 74.
[17] Don pp 51–2; Dowden pp 99–110.

borne no immediate fruit but indirectly they enabled later Scottish bishops to give to the American episcopal church what one of her bishops has described as 'a greater boon than the Episcopate', namely the consecration of prayer.[18]

University of Aberdeen

[18] *American Church Review* 39 (New York July 1882) p 18.

THE FIFTH EARL OF GUILFORD (1766–1827)
AND HIS SECRET CONVERSION
TO THE ORTHODOX CHURCH

by KALLISTOS WARE

IN September 1725 archbishop Wake of Canterbury wrote to patriarch Chrysanthos of Jerusalem, warning him that the non-jurors were in schism from the official and established church of England;[1] and so the remarkable correspondence between the non-juring bishops and the patriarchs of the east was suspended without ever coming to any decisive conclusion. Wake's letter marks in many ways the end of an era. During the previous hundred years, from the reign of king James I onwards, there had been a series of surprisingly positive contacts between England and the Orthodox world. Archbishop Abbot, for example, exchanged letters with Cyril Lukaris (1572–1638), patriarch first of Alexandria and then of Constantinople; and as a result of this Cyril not only sent the *Codex Alexandrinus* as a gift to king Charles I in 1628, but also despatched his most promising disciple, Mitrophanis Kritopoulos (1589–1639), future patriarch of Alexandria, to study for five years at Balliol College, Oxford (1617–22). Later in the century Orthodoxy was made known in England through a series of books, such as Thomas Smith's *An Account of the Greek Church*, published in Latin in 1676 and in English four years later, and Paul Rycaut's *The Present State of the Greek and Armenian Churches*, published in 1679. To these should be added John Covel's *magnum opus* entitled *Some Account of the Present Greek Church*, which did not appear until 1722, but which reflects experience gained in the Levant some fifty years before. During 1699–1705 there was even a short-lived Greek College at Gloucester Hall, Oxford. Last but not least, in 1716–25 came the negotiations between the non-jurors and the Orthodox, to which reference has been already made.

In the hundred years following 1725 the situation is strangely different. A century of flourishing contacts is followed by a century of mutual isolation and ignorance. Visiting Constantinople in the 1830s,

---

[1] In G. Williams, *The Orthodox Church of the East in the Eighteenth Century* (London 1868) pp lv–lviii.

Robert Curzon was disconcerted to find that the ecumenical patriarch had never so much as heard of the archbishop of Canterbury.[2] Relations were not effectively renewed until the pioneer visit of William Palmer of Magdalen to Russia in 1840-1.[3] In comparison with the seventeenth and the nineteenth centuries, the eighteenth century—more exactly, the period 1725-1840—appears to be, from an Anglo-Orthodox standpoint, almost entirely a blank.

Yet there were always contacts. On the Isle of Wight, for example, the family of Paleologos-Colnot, whose members claimed to be heirs to the Byzantine throne, possessed at their residence in Strathwell House an Orthodox chapel, with vestments, reliquaries, icons and censers.[4] A number of them maintained an ecclesiastical double life as prince-bishops of the Orthodox church and as incumbents in the established church of England. In 1763 John Wesley had some of his preachers ordained by one Erasmus, claiming to be Greek bishop of Arcadia in Crete; it has been argued that Wesley was duped by an imposter,[5] but the truth of the matter remains uncertain. Rycaut, Smith and Covel found a worthy successor in the person of John Glen King, whose weighty volume on *The Rites and Ceremonies of the Greek Church, in Russia* was published in 1772. But perhaps the most un-expected Anglo-Orthodox happening in the hundred years following 1725 was the secret baptism of the honourable Frederick North during a visit to the island of Corfu.

Frederick North, subsequently fifth earl of Guilford, was born in 1766.[6] He was the third and youngest son of Frederick North, second

---

[2] R. Curzon, *Visits to Monasteries in the Levant*, with an introduction by D. G. Hogarth (London 1916) pp 333-4.

[3] See his highly readable account of this journey, *Notes of a Visit to the Russian Church in the Years 1840, 1841*, ed cardinal Newman (London 1882).

[4] The family was established at Strathwell by 1545; inventories of the chapel survive from the years 1630, 1753 and 1775. The house was sold by the family in 1866, and then or subsequently the contents of the chapel were presumably dispersed. The family name is variously spelt Colnot, Kolnot or Colnett.

[5] See George Tsoumas, 'Methodism and Bishop Erasmus', *The Greek Orthodox Theological Review*, 2, 2 (Brookline 1956) pp 62-73; A. B. Sackett, 'John Wesley and the Greek Orthodox Bishop', *Proceedings of the Wesley Historical Society*, 38 (Chester 1971-2) pp 81-7, 97-102.

[6] The chief account of his life is by [Andreas Papadopoulos-Vretos], *Notizie [Biografiche-Storiche su Federico Conte di Guilford Pari d'Inghilterra, e sulla da lui fondata Universita Ionia]*, text in Italian and Greek on opposite pages (Athens 1846). Papadopoulos-Vretos first met Guilford in 1820, and from 1824 acted as librarian for his personal library as well as for that of the Ionian academy. While detailed and on the whole accurate concerning Guilford's last years and the foundation of the Ionian academy, he provides only vague and sketchy information about Guilford's early life. On Guilford's

A secret conversion to the Orthodox church

earl of Guilford, who as head of the government during 1770-82 failed to prevent the loss of the American colonies. Frederick North the younger, although always weak in health, lived to survive his two elder brothers, succeeding to the earldom in 1817, and dying unmarried in 1827. Because of the extreme delicacy of his constitution, he spent much of his childhood abroad at health resorts, thus laying the basis of his future wide-ranging knowledge of languages. He was at Eton for a short while and went up to Christ Church, Oxford, in 1782. After Oxford he travelled in Europe, visiting Italy and then sailing from Venice to Corfu, where he arrived on 4 January (OS), probably in the year 1792.[7] He was at that time approaching twenty-six; the island was still under Venetian rule.

---

orthodox baptism we have a fascinating first-hand account by his sponsor at the ceremony, [George] Prosalendis; this was edited by [L. S.] Vrokinis and published under the title Ἀνέκδοτα χειρόγραφα [ἀφορῶντα τὴν κατὰ τὸ Δόγμα τῆς Ὀρθοδόξου Ἐκκλησίας βάπτισιν τοῦ ἀγγλου φιλέλληνος Κόμητος Γυΐλφορδ] (Corfu 1879).

Guilford and the Ionian academy form the theme of a special issue of the Athenian periodical Ἑλληνικὴ Δημιουργία (no 3, 1949): see in particular the articles by G. I. Salvanos and V. G. Salvanou, Ἡ Ἰόνιος Ἀκαδημία, ὁ ἱδρυτὴς αὐτῆς Κόμις Γύλφορδ, οἱ καθηγηταὶ καὶ σπουδασταὶ αὐτῆς, and by K. A. Diamantis, Ἡ Ἰόνιος Ἀκαδημία τοῦ Κόμιτος Γκίλφορδ.

In English there is a short account of Guilford's career by J. M. Rigg in DNB 41 (London 1895) pp 164-6, and a fuller presentation in [Z. D.] Ferriman, [Some English Philhellenes. VI. Lord Guilford] (Anglo-Hellenic league, London 1919) pp 75-109.

[7] There is some uncertainty about the date: the year is usually given as 1791, but several factors point to 1792. The evidence in Prosalendis is contradictory. He writes that North arrived in Venice on 2 December 1791, left four days later, and then reached Corfu on January 1791 (p 57). Either the earlier date is a mistake for 2 December 1790, or else Prosalendis dates the beginning of the new year from 25 March, in which case North's arrival at Corfu was in fact on 4 January 1792, by modern methods of dating.

Certain evidence favours the second hypothesis. North stayed on Corfu until 3 February, when he left to spend lent on Levkas, proceeding after easter for short visits to Ithaka and Zante. While at Zante, so Prosalendis states, he heard about the ending of the Russo-Turkish War (p 166). This could be a reference to the preliminary peace signed at Galatz on 11 August 1791, or else to the treaty of Jassy, concluded on 9 January 1792. From Zante North was summoned home by his family: he travelled via Frankfort, attending the coronation of the emperor Leopold (p 167), and reached England just before the death of his father (p 168). Something is wrong here: Leopold was crowned on 9 October 1790, that is, before North's visit to Corfu, whichever year we choose. Perhaps Prosalendis is referring to the coronation of Leopold's successor Francis II on 14 July 1792. North's father died on 5 August 1792. If we assume that North left Corfu on 3 February 1791 and Levkas after easter, it is difficult to fill in the fifteen months between then and his arrival in England shortly before his father's death. But if we place his visit to Corfu and all the subsequent events in 1792, there is a reasonable time sequence.

The account in Notizie pp 5 seq, disagrees at several points with Prosalendis, but is in general imprecise and untrustworthy.

The Greeks of Corfu quickly noted that in behaviour the new visitor was wholly different from the usual young aristocrat making the grand tour. He went constantly to church, following the Greek services with marked reverence. As one Corfiot noted in his diary for 14 January in that year:

He speaks a little modern Greek, but with a difficult pronunciation different from our own. He loves our church services and is closely familiar with the Orthodox ritual. He has attended the liturgy in the churches of the Most Holy Mother of God *Spiliotissa* and of saint Spyridon, and he delights to hear the Constantinopolitan chanting. He repeatedly makes the sign of the cross as if he were a monk, which is scarcely consistent with the outlook and character of the English.[8]

North spent his evenings at the chief coffee-house in the city, conversing with leading Corfiots; and here he met among others a certain George Prosalendis, a layman in his late seventies with a keen interest in religious topics, and a senior member of the local nobility.[9] Prosalendis took every opportunity to speak with the Englishman about the Orthodox church, and was delighted to find that North was already familiar with its theology, having acquired during the earlier part of his travels books by patriarch Dositheos, Meletios Syrigos and Symeon of Thessalonika.[10] Prosalendis accompanied North to church for the Sunday liturgy, and observed with satisfaction how the young nobleman—the *archon*, as the local Greeks called him—made the sign of the cross in the Orthodox way on entering the church, prostrating himself three times to the ground; throughout the service he continued to make profound bows and prostrations.[11]

One evening in the coffee-house North asked whether the Orthodox church accepted the validity of anglican baptism. Prosalendis inquired how the anglicans baptise, and North replied that the priest dips three fingers in water, and with these moistens the forehead of the child, invoking the name of the Holy Trinity. (This is revealing evidence as to the anglican practice at this date.) Prosalendis said that baptism ought strictly to be by threefold immersion, but in cases of illness and emergency it is sufficient to baptise by affusion, pouring water over the candidate's forehead. For this reason, he continued, the

---

[8] Diary of Nicolas Arliotis, cited by Vrokinis in his introduction to Prosalendis, Ἀνέκδοτα χειρόγραφα, p 47.
[9] Vrokinis recounts the life of Prosalendis (1713–95) in his introduction, *ibid* pp 15–36.
[10] *Ibid* p 66.
[11] *Ibid* p 69.

Orthodox receive Roman catholic converts by anointing them with chrism; their Latin baptism, albeit performed by affusion and not by immersion, is accepted as valid. But moistening the child's forehead cannot by any standards be considered genuine baptism, and so an anglican convert must be baptised.[12] A point of interest here is that Prosalendis appears to know nothing of the decree issued at Constantinople in 1755, requiring all Latin and other converts to Orthodoxy to be without exception rebaptised. The 1755 decree takes a Cyprianic stand: regardless of the manner in which the rite is performed, whether by immersion, affusion or otherwise, all non-Orthodox baptism is deemed invalid, because performed outside the church.[13] Although Corfu and the other Ionian Islands were under the jurisdiction of the patriarchate of Constantinople, presumably the 1755 decision was never applied there because of the offence that it would have given to the Venetian authorities.

After this last conversation with Prosalendis, North asked to see him privately, and they had a long conversation about the Orthodox faith.[14] A few days later, on 22 January, North expressed a firm desire to receive Orthodox baptism.[15] He had made up his mind with some speed: he had only arrived at Corfu eighteen days previously, on 4 January, and his first meeting with Prosalendis was not until 10 January;[16] but perhaps the idea of becoming Orthodox was already in his mind some time before this. The matter was referred to the protopope of Corfu, father Dimitrios Petrettinos. The title 'protopope' calls for some explanation: the Venetians did not allow the Orthodox to maintain a hierarchy in the Ionian Islands, and so in each island the bishop's place was taken by a senior married priest—elected, in the case of Corfu, for a five-year period—who was styled the protopope and exercised episcopal jurisdiction, while lacking of course the sacramental power to ordain.[17]

North laid down one condition: the baptism must be performed in strict secrecy. As he explained, perhaps a little naively, to the protopope:

---

[12] *Ibid* pp 74–75.

[13] On the 1755 decree and its background, see [K.] T. Ware, *Eustratios Argenti: A Study of the Greek Church under Turkish Rule* (Oxford 1964) pp 65–107.

[14] Described in great detail by Prosalendis pp 78–143.

[15] *Ibid* p 145.

[16] *Ibid* p 63.

[17] Petrettinos (1722–95) was elected protopope in 1784, and was re-elected in 1789 and 1794, holding office until his death.

For many years I have been convinced, through my study of the old and new testaments, the holy ecumenical councils and the holy fathers, that I find myself in error. But the social and economic circumstances of myself and my family led me to shrink back. Eventually I decided to travel through the world, in the hope that the Lord would show me some way of giving my soul to Him, while still preserving the social status of my family . . . I desire my baptism to be secret, because of the social and economic commitments of my family.[18]

To this request for concealment the protopope agreed. The baptism took place in the late evening of 23 January, in an inner room at the protopope's residence. Apart from North, only four others were present: the priest Spyridon Montesanto, in whose company North had travelled from Venice to Corfu and who was deputed to perform the ceremony; the protopope himself and Prosalendis, who acted jointly as sponsors or godparents (ἀνάδοχοι); and a deacon. Earlier in the day North had submitted to the protopope a profession of faith, written in Italian,[19] and had made his confession to Montesanto.[20] Prosalendis describes the service thus:

The doors of both the outer and the inner rooms were closed, and the nobleman withdrew to the inner bedroom, where the curtains were drawn. Here he removed his outer garments and came out clothed only in his shirt, as the rubrics prescribe. At once father Montesanto began the service, with the protopope standing on the nobleman's right and myself on his left. First the exorcisms were read, and then the questions about renouncing the devil and accepting Christ: the nobleman gave the answers himself and recited the creed three times. The protopope named him by his own name 'Frederick', and I by the other name which he wished to receive (as father Montesanto had told me), 'Dimitrios'. Then, with his two sponsors holding him by the arms and with the priest going in front, he was led unshod to the holy font, and the sacrament of baptism was administered to him. After this he received the seal of the gift of the Holy Spirit through anointing with the holy chrism (μύρον), and all the ceremonies were performed exactly as prescribed by the service book and by the tradition of the holy eastern Orthodox church . . . Afterwards we had a short

[18] Prosalendis pp 11–12.
[19] Full text in *ibid* pp 41–3.
[20] *Ibid* p 150.

talk, at which it was said that this holy action must be kept secret from everyone apart from the five of us . . . If anyone were to question us out of curiosity, while not in any way denying what had been done we should refrain from confirming it; our constant and unvarying response should be simply to profess ignorance.[21]

Very early next morning North attended the liturgy and received communion in one of the churches of Corfu, and he was later given a written baptismal certificate by the protopope.[22] To Prosalendis North stated that 'he would keep the matter secret for the time being, but under no circumstances would he actually deny it'. Prosalendis expressed the hope that the moment for public disclosure would quickly arrive.[23] He also envisaged the possibility that North, on returning home, would serve as a missionary, initiating a crypto-Orthodox movement within the English aristocracy: 'Through the collaboration of this nobleman with other peers of the realm who have become secret Orthodox, there will be an increase of Orthodoxy in that kingdom.'[24]

North left Corfu on 4 February, and does not seem to have returned for more than twenty-five years. He passed lent in a monastery of the island of Levkas, observing the fast with exemplary strictness, and even persuading the monks to celebrate the presanctified liturgy daily, not merely on Wednesdays and Fridays according to the usual custom. He received communion at the start of lent.[25] After brief visits to Ithaka and Zante he then returned to England.

But the hope of Prosalendis that North would quickly make his Orthodox allegiance public was not realized. During 1792–4 he sat as member of parliament for Banbury; it seems unlikely that he could have done this had it been general knowledge that he was no longer anglican. Up to the present day he remains, so far as I am aware, the only member of the Orthodox church to have sat in parliament. He does not seem to have joined the congregation of the Russian embassy chapel in London, the sole Orthodox place of worship in the capital until the opening of the Greek chapel at 9 Finsbury Circus in 1838; had he received the sacraments openly and regularly at the Russian chapel, this would surely have been noticed by his English friends. During his seven years as governor of Ceylon (1798–1805), he had no Orthodox

---

[21] *Ibid* pp 153–4.
[22] *Ibid* pp 156–7.
[23] *Ibid* p 160.
[24] *Ibid* p 149.
[25] *Ibid* pp 160–4.

chaplain in his retinue. Even when he returned to Corfu in 1820, spending the greater part of each year there until his death in 1827, his status as an Orthodox was not generally known to the Greeks, although some of those close to him certainly guessed the truth.[26]

To the British and Greek public of the time, the fifth earl of Guilford was simply one among a number of British philhellenes. They knew him as the author of a Pindaric ode in Greek honouring the empress Catherine of Russia,[27] as president of the 'Society of the Lovers of the Muses' ('Εταιρία τῶν Φιλομούσων) founded at Athens in 1814,[28] as an indefatigable collector of books and manuscripts.[29] They knew him above all as an ever-generous patron of Greek letters, as benefactor to a host of Greek students in western universities, and as chancellor of the Ionian academy founded at Corfu in 1824, almost entirely through his efforts. This academy or university, as it could with some justice claim to be, served as a notable centre of education to the whole Greek nation during the years of the rising against the Turks and in the period immediately following, when the Greeks possessed as yet no other institute of higher learning. The running of the academy was the consuming interest of Guilford's last years. It declined in importance after his death, particularly with the foundation of the university of Athens in 1837.

His English contemporaries found Guilford courteous and

---

[26] Theoklitos Pharmakidis, professor of theology at the Ionian academy during 1824–5, realized that North was orthodox: see his 'Απολογία (Athens 1840) p 125, cited Notizie, p 15. But Pharmakidis is probably inaccurate when he asserts that this was a matter of common knowledge in Corfu at the time.

[27] Entitled Αἰκατερίνῃ Εἰρηνοποιῷ, this was published anonymously, with a Latin translation (no place or date of publication: ?Leipzig 1792). The text and translation were reprinted with an introduction by A. Papadopoulos-Vretos (Athens 1846).

[28] See Notizie pp 27–9, for North's reply in attic Greek, accepting this office; he signs himself πολίτης 'Αθηναῖος, 'an Athenian citizen'.

[29] As he remarked to Papadopoulos-Vretos: 'Ah! my child, if I were not the earl of Guilford I would have liked to be a librarian', Αἰκατερίνῃ Εἰρηνοποιῷ, intro p 4. His vast collection of books and manuscripts was dispersed in a series of sales at London during 1828–35. One of the most interesting items, in the sale beginning on 9 November 1835, is no 1795: 'A very Curious, Valuable and Extensive Collection of Books in the Modern Greek Language . . . in all 627 vol.' The auctioneer rightly appreciated the importance of this collection, stating in the sale catalogue: 'This is the most Extensive Assemblage of Modern Greek Books ever submitted to Public Sale.' It seems that the collection was acquired by the British Museum. Also in the possession of the British Museum are manuscript catalogues of Guilford's modern Greek books (Add MSS 8220, 16572), which show that the greater part of the collection was on theological topics. This is evidence of Guilford's continuing interest in Orthodoxy, although of course he may have collected the books for use in the Ionian academy rather than for his own personal consultation.

exceptionally amiable in manner, generous and gentle, but definitely eccentric. Courtesy marked him from his early years; in his diary for 1788, Sir Gilbert Elliott describes him as 'the only pleasant son of the family, and he is remarkably so'.[30] His acquaintances could not understand his passion for books and education; as captain Robert Spencer remarked, 'I am a friend of the Earl of Guilford and I respect him, but in my judgement his consuming desire to have large numbers of students and professors with him amounts to madness,'[31] 'A queer fish, but very pleasant', commented Charles James Napier after meeting him at a dinner party in 1819; and, alluding to Guilford's wide range of languages, he speaks of him as 'addressing every person in a different language, and always in that which the person addressed did not understand'. His reputation for oddity was enhanced by his practice in Corfu of wearing the dress of classical Greece. 'He goes about', protests Napier, 'dressed up like Plato, with a gold band around his mad pate and flowing drapery of a purple hue.'[32] But Napier and others seem to know nothing of his Orthodoxy.

Yet, hidden though his church membership remained, the earl of Guilford continued faithful to it until the end. In his later years he was certainly a friend of the Russian chaplain in London, father Smirnov, to whom he gave a copy of his Pindaric ode,[33] and when he lay dying at the London house of his nephew, the earl of Sheffield, he sent for the Russian priest. In the words of his biographer Andreas Papadopoulos-Vretos:

> Perceiving that the last moment of his life was near at hand, he repeatedly asked for the chaplain of the Russian embassy chapel, his old friend father Smirnov, and from his hands he received communion, to the great displeasure of his relatives, and especially of his nephew the earl of Sheffield, in whose house he died. The earl of Sheffield tried in every way to prevent him receiving the ministrations of a priest of a foreign dogma, contrary to that of his forefathers.[34]

Sheffield's conduct strongly suggests that he had not known previously that his uncle was Orthodox. Guilford received communion in the

---

[30] Cited in Ferriman p 77.
[31] *Notizie* p 93.
[32] Cited in Ferriman pp 94–5.
[33] The copy of the first edition of Αἰκατερίνη Εἰρηνοποιῷ in the British Museum bears the inscription on the inside cover, 'Reverend J. Smirnove, with the Author's most affectionate Respects', but there is unfortunately no indication of date.
[34] *Notizie* p 145.

presence of two Greeks, his personal doctor from Kephallinia and his valet from Parga; presumably it was from them that Papadopoulos-Vretos learnt the story of his last days. The earl of Sheffield, as Guilford's heir, did his best to suppress all evidence of his uncle's conversion; according to Papadopoulos-Vretos, on learning about the existence of an eye-witness account written by Prosalendis, he paid £400 to the owner of the manuscript, on the understanding that it should not be published.[35] It did not finally appear in print until a half-century later, in 1879.

Such, then, was the fifth earl of Guilford: a British philhellene, but not as the other philhellenes. His devotion to the hellenic tradition extended not only to classical but to Christian Greece. He saw how impossible it is to understand the continuity of Greek history without appreciating the part played by the Orthodox church; nor was he content merely to admire that church from a distance, but himself became a communicant member of it. Even though he never made his action public and so disappointed the hopes of his Corfiot friends that he would initiate an English-Orthodox movement, yet his conversion shows how the Christian east has never ceased to exercise an attraction in the occident, even over members of the eighteenth-century tory aristocracy.

University of Oxford

---

[35] *Ibid* p 13. But Papadopoulos-Vretos is not an unprejudiced witness, since he resented most bitterly the way in which Sheffield, after Guilford's death, had the latter's books removed from the Ionian academy and auctioned in London.

ANTI-CLERICALISM IN
PRE-INDEPENDENCE GREECE *c.* 1750–1821

by RICHARD CLOGG

WRITING in the 1820s, during the Greek war of independence, of his tour of the Peloponnese Sir William Gell noted that there was 'a saying common among the Greeks, that the country labours under three curses, the priests, the cogia bashis, and the Turks; always placing the plagues in this order'.[1] This kind of sentiment is a commonplace of the sources, both Greek and non-Greek, relating to pre-independence Greece and it is clear that anti-clericalism was deeply rooted, and not only among the intelligentsia, but among virtually all classes of Greek society. The prevalence, and indeed, the virulence of anti-clerical attitudes in Greece during the pre-independence period must call into question the view still advanced by authorities on this period that the church played a central role in the forging of the Greek national movement. Sir Steven Runciman, for instance, has written that 'Hellenism survived, nurtured by the Church, because the Greeks unceasingly hoped and planned for the day when they would recover their freedom', while Douglas Dakin has written that 'so closely knit was the national existence of the Greeks with their Church that in their liberation movement there was no hostility to the Greek patriarchate comparable to that which the Italians displayed towards the Papacy'.[2] Views of this kind also constitute the common currency of Greek historiography. D. A. Zakythinos, for instance, has written that 'it is universally admitted that the Church saved the Greek Nation during the dark years of slavery'. But he goes on to say that earlier and more recent historians, the 'healthy minded' among them, as well as those having 'certain special political tendencies', do not subscribe to such a view *in toto*. He quotes the founding father of modern Greek

---

[1] William Gell, *Narrative of a Journey in the Morea*, (London 1823) pp 65–6.

[2] Steven Runciman, *The Great Church in Captivity. A Study of the Patriarchate of Constantinople from the Eve of the Turkish Conquest to the Greek War of Independence*, (Cambridge 1968) p viii and Douglas Dakin, 'The Greek Unification and the Italian Risorgimento Compared', *Balkan Studies*, 10 (Thessaloniki 1969) p 8. See also Peter Hammond, *The Waters of Marah: The Present State of the Greek Church*, (London 1956) p 25: 'during the dark days of oppression every national aspiration was fostered and preserved by the Church'.

historiography, Konstantinos Paparrigopoulos, to the effect that 'the ancestral religion did not cease to constitute one of the principal moral mainsprings of Hellenism, but it did not itself alone constitute Hellenism'.[3]

During the critical decades before 1821 anti-clerical attitudes were prompted by political, cultural and socio-economic considerations. While anti-clerical attitudes were by no means confined to the nascent intelligentsia, which for the most part was in the forefront of the struggle for Greek independence, it is nonetheless true that the bulk of the evidence we have for the existence of such attitudes emanates from educated circles. For obvious reasons the intelligentsia was more articulate in its advocacy of anti-clerical opinions than the unlettered mass of the Greek people, although, as I hope to demonstrate, there is abundant evidence to suggest that anti-clericalism was widespread at a popular level.

The anti-clerical attitudes of such protagonists of Greek independence as Rigas Velestinlis (1757–98) and Adamantios Korais (1748–1833) are well known. They were principally prompted by the political attitudes of the patriarchate and the higher clergy and by what they considered to be the cultural obscurantism of the church. The principal charge levied by men such as Rigas, Korais and many others active in the independence movement was that the hierarchy of the church had identified its fortunes with the continuance of a unitary Ottoman empire, and that it preached a policy of *ethelodouleia*, of willing and blind submission to the powers that be.

One of the best known expressions of this attitude of *ethelodouleia* is contained in the *Paternal Exhortation* (Διδασκαλία Πατρική) of Anthimos, patriarch of Jerusalem. This small pamphlet was one of the first productions (1798) of the newly reconstituted patriarchal press in Constantinople, which was set up to ensure ecclesiastical control over the increasing amount of literature in Greek, much of it regarded as objectionable on moral and political grounds by the ecumenical patriarchate and the Ottoman Porte, that was beginning to circulate in the Ottoman dominions. In a key passage of the *Didaskalia Patriki*, Anthimos writes:

> See how clearly our Lord, boundless in mercy and all-wise, has undertaken to guard once more the unsullied Holy and Orthodox faith of us, the pious, and to save all mankind. He raised out of nothing this powerful empire of the Ottomans, in the place of our

[3] D. A. Zakythinos, Ἡ Τουρκοκρατία, (Athens 1957) p 27.

Roman (Byzantine) empire which had begun, in a certain way, to cause to deviate from the beliefs of the Orthodox faith, and He raised up the empire of the Ottomans higher than any other kingdom so as to show without doubt that it came about by divine will, and not by the power of man, and to assure all the faithful that in this way He deigned to bring about a great mystery, namely salvation to his chosen people . . . The all-mighty Lord . . . puts into the heart of the sultan of these Ottomans an inclination to keep free the religious beliefs of our Orthodox faith and, as a work of supererogation, to protect them, even to the point of occasionally chastising Christians who deviate from their faith, that they have always before their eyes the fear of God.[4]

This uncompromising assertion that the Ottoman empire was truly ordained of God provoked an immediate reaction. Adamantios Korais, the indefatigable mentor of the Greek independence movement, published an immediate rebuttal, the *Adelfiki Didaskalia* or *Brotherly Exhortation addressed to the Greeks throughout the Ottoman dominions. In answer to the Paternal Teaching published pseudonymously in Constantinople in the name of His Beatitude the Patriarch of Jerusalem.*[5] Careful not to offend the religious susceptibilities of his Orthodox readers, Korais buttressed his critique of Anthimos's tract and his defence of liberty and democracy with scriptural references, while he played on their religious prejudices by his attacks on the Latin church. Alluding to the recent French liberation of the papal states, Korais wrote that now the Latins could no longer castrate new-born infants so that they might sing in their churches like the corybantes in the temple of Cybele. Korais's polemic prompted Athanasios Parios, one of the most extreme champions of Orthodox reaction, to pen a counter-rebuttal, the *Neos Rapsakis or a reproach and a denunciation in the form of an apology against the atheistical blasphemies put out by one of the libertines against the pious and highly beneficial Paternal Exhortation, recently published by ecclesiastical providence for all Christians.*[6] Athanasios's

---

[4] Διδασκαλία Πατρικὴ συντεθεῖσα παρὰ τοῦ Μακαριωτάτου Πατριάρχου τῆς Ἁγίας Πόλεως Ἱερουσαλὴμ Κὺρ Ἀνθίμου εἰς ὠφέλειαν τῶν Ὀρθοδόξων Χριστιανῶν νῦν πρῶτον τυπωθεῖσα δι' ἰδίας δαπάνης τοῦ Παναγίου Τάφου. Ἐν Κωνσταντινουπόλει παρὰ τῷ Τυπογράφῳ Πογώς Ἰωάννου ἐξ Ἀρμενίων αψγη (1798) pp 13–14.

[5] Ἀδελφικὴ Διδασκαλία πρὸς τοὺς εὑρισκομένους κατὰ πᾶσαν τὴν Ὀθωμανικὴν ἐπικράτειαν Γραῖκούς, εἰς ἀντίρρησιν κατὰ τῆς ψευδωνύμως ἐν ὀνόματι τοῦ Μακαριωτάτου Πατριάρχου Ἱεροσολύμων ἐκδοθείσης ἐν Κωνσταντινουπόλει Πατρικῆς Διδασκαλίας. Ἐν Ῥώμῃ [Paris], ἐν ἔτει Α' τῆς Ἐλευθερίας αψγη (1798).

[6] Νέος Ραψάκης ἤτοι ἔλεγχος καὶ στηλίτευσις ἐν εἴδει ἀπολογίας γινομένη, πρὸς τὰς παρά τινος τῶν λιμπερτίνων ἀντιθέους βλασφημίας γενομένας κατὰ τῆς εὐσεβῶς καὶ λίαν

polemic was never published as it was filched by two young followers of Korais from the person to whom he had entrusted the manuscript to oversee its publication in Leipzig. The two zealots sent it to Korais as an example, as they put it, of 'the perversity of the wretched monks who, . . . under the pretext of defending religion, seek the perpetual enslavement and ignorance of our nation'. Korais, far from reprimanding these young zealots, thanked them for helping to preserve the honour of the Greek nation.[7]

The furore aroused by the publication of the *Didaskalia Patriki* led to immediate attempts to attribute authorship of the tract to others. Korais, as we have seen, refused to accept Anthimos's authorship, while the contemporary chronicler, and erstwhile director of the patriarchal academy in Constantinople, Sergios Makraios, claimed that the true author was not in fact Anthimos, but the ecumenical patriarch, Grigorios V, against whom Makraios bore a grudge. Grigorios, Makraios claimed, had falsely attributed authorship to Anthimos who had been seriously ill and was not expected to recover.[8] He also claimed that the holy synod, taken aback by the reaction to the tract, ordered the remaining copies to be destroyed. Far from being destroyed, however, the *Didaskalia Patriki* went into a second edition in Constantinople in the same year[9] and moreover was translated into Rumanian as the *Învăţătură părintească alcătuită de prea fericitul patriarh al sfintei cetăţi a Ierusalimului chir Antim spre folosul pravoslavnicilor hristiani* . . . by bishop Meletie of Huşi and printed in Iaşi in 1822 in an effort to dampen the ferment consequent on Alexandros Ypsilantis's invasion of the principalities and the native uprising of Tudor Vladimirescu of the previous year.

Moreover, sentiments such as those expressed by Anthimos, shocking though they were to Korais and his ilk, were by no means

---

λυσιτελῶς, ὑπὸ τῆς ἐκκλησιαστικῆς προνοίας, πρὸς πάντας τοὺς χριστιανούς, προεκδοθείσης πατρικῆς παραινέσεως...

[7] See A. Koumarianou, Ὁ Νέος Ραψάκης, Ὁ Ἐρανιστής, 6 (Athens 1968) pp 5–6. In a letter of 27 January 1807 Korais clearly approved thoroughly of their action in robbing the 'blockhead', Iakovos Rotas, Ἀπάνθισμα ἐπιστολῶν Ἀδαμαντίου Κοραῆ, (Athens 1839) 1 p 118.

[8] See Makraios's Ὑπομνήματα Ἐκκλησιαστικῆς Ἱστορίας (*1750–1800*) in K. N. Sathas, Μεσαιωνικὴ Βιβλιοθήκη, 3 (Venice 1872) p 394.

[9] Dr Frank Walton, director of the Gennadius library, Athens, has conclusively established that the Gennadius copy of this rare tract is a second printing (letter to the author 6 May 1972). Dr Vasileios Phoris of the university of Thessaloniki is preparing for publication an authoritative edition of the *Didaskalia Patriki*.

uncommon during the period of the *Tourkokratia*, nor in most cases can they be attributed to Ottoman pressure, which is a claim that can plausibly be advanced for some official patriarchal pronouncements.[10] Anastasios Gordios (1654–1729) wrote that it was 'better to be tyrannised over bodily and to believe in Christ the true God than to find bodily ease and to believe in the Antichrist Pope'.[11] The archimandrite Kyprianos in his *History of Cyprus* printed in Venice in 1788 noted that the Greeks of the island 'who to a certain extent preferred to be subject to the Ottoman, rather than to a Latin, power, were even glad in all their wretchedness, because so far as concerned their rites and customs, they escaped the tyranny of the Latins'.[12] Moreover, a contemporary of Anthimos of Jerusalem, Nikodimos of the Holy Mountain, advanced similar views in his great *Pidalion* which was published in Leipzig in 1800 and is still regarded as the standard commentary on the canon law of the Orthodox church. During the last days of Christian empire, Nikodimos conceded, the Byzantines had practised *oikonomia* in the matter of the rebaptism of schismatic Latins. This, he argued, was

> because the papacy at that time was in the ascendant, and had all the powers of the kings of Europe in its hands, while our own empire was breathing its last. If *oikonomia* had not been practised then, the pope could have raised up the Latins against the peoples of the east, to take captive, to murder or to do a myriad other wicked things to them. But now such bad things they cannot do to us, since Divine Providence has set up over us such a guard [i.e. the Ottoman empire] that in the end he laid low the brows

[10] One likely proclamation of this kind was the patriarchal encyclical issued in 1806 to accompany the imperial *ferman* urging the destruction of the *klefts*. In 1807, when the English fleet appeared before Constantinople, the patriarch Grigorios V personally helped in the construction of the city's defences, Z. N. Mathas, Κατάλογος Ἱστορικὸς τῶν πρώτων ἐπισκόπων καὶ τῶν ἐφεξῆς Πατριαρχῶν τῆς ἐν Κωνσταντινουπόλει ἁγίας καὶ μεγάλης τοῦ Χριστοῦ 'Εκκλησίας (Athens 1884) p 164.

[11] Astérios Argyriou, *Sur Mahomet et contre les Latins. Une oeuvre inédite d'Anastasios Gordios, religieux et professeur grec (XVIIe–XVIIIes.)* (Strasbourg 1967) pp 81-2, cited in A. Vakalopoulos, Ἡ Τουρκοκρατία, IV (Thessaloniki 1973) p 317. On Gordios, see A. K. Dimitrakopoulos, Ὀρθόδοξος Ἑλλὰς ἤτοι περὶ τῶν Ἑλλήνων τῶν γραψάντων κατὰ Λατίνων καὶ περὶ τῶν συγγραμμάτων αὐτῶν (Leipzig 1872) pp 174-5.

[12] Kyprianos, Ἱστορία χρονολογικὴ τῆς Νήσου Κύπρου (Venice 1788), quoted in C. D. Cobham, *Excerpta Cypria* (Nicosia 1895) p 251. See also [Konstantinos] Koumas, [Ἱστορίαι τῶν Ἀνθρωπίνων Πράξεων,] 12 (Vienna 1832) p 600: Ἦσαν καὶ πολλοὶ θρησκευτικοί, οἵτινες ἐκ ζήλου ἐκκλησιαστικοῦ ἐδίδασκαν, ὅτι ἡ θεία πρόνοια μᾶς ὑπέβαλεν εἰς τὸ Ὀθωμανικὸν σκῆπτρον διὰ νὰ μᾶς φυλάξῃ δι' αὐτοῦ ἀπὸ τὰς αἱρέσεις καὶ ἀπὸ τὴν εἰς χριστιανικάς τινας χώρας ἐμφιλοχωρήσασαν ἀδιαφορίαν περὶ τὰ θεῖα.

of those haughty ones. Now I say, when the fury of the papacy counts as nothing to us, what further need is there of *oikonomia*, for *oikonomia* has its limits . . . [Now] rigour and the canons of the eastern church should have their rightful place.[13]

Such phil-Ottoman sentiments were not always made by ecclesiastics. The Kozaniot doctor Mikhail Perdikaris, for instance, in a manuscript diatribe of 1811 directed against Rigas Velestinlis wrote that it was apparent that throughout the extent of the Ottoman dominions 'the Christians live in peace, quiet and concord, without pride, without vain and fruitless luxury, [while] the Ottoman satraps not only do not threaten their peace and security but moreover protect them, for this race [of the Ottomans] is by nature bountiful and generous'.[14] But in most cases such sentiments were expressed in a religious context and they necessarily aroused the wrath of the active protagonists of Greek independence. The anonymous author, for instance, of the *Elliniki Nomarkhia*, which contains some of the bitterest of contemporary polemics against the hierarchy, castigated the kinds of attitude espoused by Anthimos and those of similar persuasion. 'How', he asked, 'should the Greeks be woken from the fog of tyranny? The preachers, who were under an obligation to show them the truth, do not undertake the task. But how do these worldly automata, these false preachers answer? . . . "Beloved," they say, "God gave us the Ottoman tyranny, to punish us for our sins, chastising us in the present life so that he may liberate us after death from eternal torment".' He went on to reproach preachers in church: 'Do they ever mention the maxim "Fight for faith and country"? [popularly attributed to Constantine XI Palaiologos]. Do they ever explain what is the motherland? . . . Do they ever adduce the examples of Themistocles, of Aristeides, of Socrates, and of a myriad other virtuous and wise men? . . . Have they ever mentioned how the world is governed and what

[13] Nikodimos Agioreitis, . . . Πηδάλιον τῆς νοητῆς νηός, τῆς μίας ἁγίας, καθολικῆς, καὶ ἀποστολικῆς τῶν Ὀρθοδόξων Ἐκκλησίας, ἤτοι ἅπαντες οἱ ἱεροί, καὶ θεῖοι κανόνες, τῶν τε ἁγίων καὶ πανευφήμων ἀποστόλων, τῶν ἁγίων οἰκουμενικῶν συνόδων, τῶν τοπικῶν, καὶ τῶν κατὰ μέρος θείων πατέρων . . . (Leipzig 1800) p 36, quoted in part in T. Ware, *Eustratios Argenti. A Study of the Greek Church under Turkish Rule* (Oxford 1964) p 102. Although printing costs at this period were twice as high in Leipzig as in Venice, there was greater freedom for the publication of anti-Latin books, which may explain why the *Pidalion* was printed there. See the remarks of Polyzois Lambanitziotis in the preface to his edition of Τοῦ μακαρίου Συμεὼν ἀρχιεπισκόπου Θεσσαλονίκης, τὰ ἅπαντα . . . (Leipzig 1791) quoted in D. Russo, *Studii istorice greco-române*, 2 (Bucharest 1939) p 358.

[14] Mikhail Perdikaris, Ῥήγας ἢ κατὰ Ψευδοφιλελλήνων in Βασικὴ Βιβλιοθήκη, ed L. Vranousis, 11 (Athens 1955) p 193.

is the best government?'[15] The anonymous author of a manuscript composed during the first two decades of the nineteenth century with a view to publication and now preserved in the library of the monastery of Panteleimon on Mount Athos even went so far as to accuse the prelates of the Orthodox church of being 'the allies and abettors of the impious tyrants so as to torment the children of Christ. The tyrants with the sword, the prelates with religion have conspired together to rend into pieces mercilessly my most wretched nation.'[16]

The Orthodox hierarchy's identification, along with other élite groups in pre-independence Greek society such as the Phanariots and the *kocabaşīs*, with the Ottoman status quo and its preaching of subservience to the powers that be necessarily incurred the wrath of active protagonists in the struggle for Greece's emancipation. Equally objectionable to the small but influential intelligentsia was the church's cultural obscurantism. For a while some Greeks, among them Rigas Velestinlis and the members of the *Philiki Etairia*, the secret revolutionary society founded in Odessa in 1814 which laid the organisational framework of the 1821 uprising, saw Greece's salvation as lying in armed revolt against the Ottomans, others, Adamantios Korais notable among them, placed their faith in education. It was held that once the Greeks had reached the educational level of the western Europeans then, in some way which was never clearly defined, the Greeks would achieve the emancipation which was held to be their due. When the church was seen to turn against this process of cultural enlightenment, then it is not surprising that anti-clerical attitudes should have become widespread among the intelligentsia.

Despite its earlier encouragement of education (Theophilos Korydalefs, for instance, had been head of the patriarchal academy in Constantinople in the 1620's) the Orthodox church during the eighteenth century appeared to be adopting an increasingly obscurantist line in theological, educational and cultural matters. In 1723, for instance, Methodios Anthrakitis was twice condemned (once in his absence) for heterodoxy by the holy synod in Constantinople. He was

---

[15] Ἑλληνικὴ Νομαρχία [ἤτοι Λόγος περὶ Ἐλευθερίας, δι' οὗ ἀποδεικνύεται, πόσον εἶναι καλλιοτέρα ἡ Νομαρχικὴ Διοίκησις ἀπὸ τὰς λοιπὰς...ὅτι τάχιστα ἡ Ἑλλὰς πρέπει νὰ συντρίψῃ τὰς ἀλύσους της, ποῖαι ἐστάθησαν αἱ αἰτίαι ὁποὺ μέχρι τῆς σήμερον τὴν ἐφύλαξαν δούλην, καὶ ὁποῖαι εἶναι ὁποὺ μέλλει νὰ τὴν ἐλευθερώσωσι...] ('Italy' 1806) reprinted and edited by G. Valetas (Athens 1957) p 174.

[16] Panteleimon Codex 755. I am most grateful to Dr Leandros Vranousis of the Kentron Erevnis tou Mesaionikou kai Neou Ellinismou tis Akadimias Athinon for allowing me to consult his transcript of this important text which he is to publish.

unfrocked, compelled to retract his teaching and his notebooks were burned.[17] In the middle of the century, the *Athoniada Skholi*, founded in 1753 on the initiative of the *proigoumenos* Meletios of Vatopedi, was closed in 1759 following protests about the content of the teaching of the *skholarkhis*, Evgenios Voulgaris, who was later, at the invitation of Catherine the Great, to become archbishop of Slavyansk and Cherson.

To try to contain the flood of what was considered to be seditious and atheistical literature in Greek entering the Ottoman empire the holy synod decided in 1798 to re-constitute the patriarchal press which had briefly flourished in mid-century during the patriarchate of Samouil Khantzeris. The press, which was to print in both *romaika* and *ellinika* books beneficial to sound learning, was controlled by a committee of overseers. This committee consisted of the ecumenical patriarch, the grand dragoman of the Porte (at this time invariably a Phanariot), a bishop, and one of the *prokritoi*, or oligarchs of the Greek community of Constantinople. The committee, besides overseeing the activities of the press was also to licence the distribution of such Greek books printed outside the bounds of the Ottoman empire 'as did no harm, either spiritually or bodily, to those that read them'. In theory, although not always in practice, books printed at the press were imprinted with a licence to print. One such licence, printed on the second page of the 1799 edition of the *Epitomi ek ton Prophitanakt-davitikon Psalmon* records that the book had been submitted to the committee by the *arkhon* Doctor Vasileios 'and as it contains nothing contrary to our holy church or to the civil power, has been judged worthy of publication, and of unrestricted sale in the shops'. The licence is signed by the patriarch Neophytos VII, the grand dragoman Alexandros Soutsos, the metropolitans Samouil of Ephesus and Ioakeim of Cyzicus, Alexandros Panos Khantzeris and the *megas postelnikos* Ioannis Karatzas.[18]

In 1804 Beniamin Lesvios, the *skholarkhis* of the academy of Kydonies

[17] Chrysostomos Papadopoulos, Ἱστορικὰ σημειώματα, γ΄. Μεθόδιος Ἀνθρακίτης, Θεολογία, 4 (Athens 1926) pp 10–17 and Alkis Anghelou, Ἡ δίκη τοῦ Μεθοδίου Ἀνθρακίτη (ὅπως τὴν ἀφηγεῖται ὁ ἴδιος), Ἀφιέρωμα εἰς τὴν Ἤπειρον εἰς μνήμην Χρίστου Σούλη, (Athens 1955) pp 168–82.
[18] See G. Pappadopoulos and G. P. Angelopoulos, Τὰ κατὰ τὸν . . . Γρηγόριον τὸν Ε΄ . . ., 2 (Athens 1865) pp 496–7 and my 'Some Protestant Tracts printed at the press of the Ecumenical Patriarchate in Constantinople: 1818–1820', *Eastern Churches Review*, 2 (Oxford 1968) pp 158–9.

(Ayvalık), at that time perhaps the most advanced educational centre in the Greek world, was condemned by the patriarchate for teaching that the earth revolved around the sun.[19] In 1819 a strongly anti-clerical and anonymously written tract, the *Stokhasmoi tou Kritonos*, was burnt in the courtyard of the patriarchate, apparently at the instigation of Ilarion of Mount Sinai, one of the chief bugbears of the westernising Greek intelligentsia.[20] The burning of offending books by the patriarchate was clearly not a rare phenomenon. The author of the *Elliniki Nomarkhia*, for instance, fully expected that his own book would be burnt.[21] It was apparently Ilarion, at this time *igoumenos* of the *metokhion* of the monastery of St Catherine in Constantinople and overseer of the patriarchal press, who was behind an attempt to set up a kind of index of prohibited books. For a young Greek, Stephanos Kanelos, wrote, shortly after the outbreak of the Greek war of independence, to the German philhellene Karl Iken that Ilarion had not only forced the patriarch Grigorios V to burn the *Stokhasmoi tou Kritonos* but that he had also 'intended to institute a kind of frightful censorship and inquisition against all books coming from Europe'.[22] A whole corpus of literature, much of it written by ecclesiastics, came into existence whose principal object was to counter the ideas of the western enlightenment, ideas which were proving increasingly attractive to the Greek intelligentsia.[23]

---

[19] Alkis Anghelou, Πρὸς τὴν ἀκμὴ τοῦ νεοελληνικοῦ διαφωτισμοῦ (Οἱ διενέξεις τοῦ Λέσβιου στὴν Σχολὴ Κυδωνιῶν), Μικρασιατικὰ Χρονικά, 7 (Athens 1956) pp 1–81.

[20] D. Gkinis, Κρίτωνος Στοχασμοί, Ἔρανος εἰς Ἀδαμάντιον Κοραῆν, (Athens 1965) p 145.

[21] The 1703 edition of Maximos Kallioupolitis's modern Greek version of the new testament had also been burnt, Alexander Helladius, *Status Praesens Ecclesiae Graecae* (?Altdorf/Nürnberg 1714) p 247.

[22] Andronikos Dimitrakopoulos, Ἐπανορθώσεις σφαλμάτων ἐν τῇ Νεοελληνικῇ Φιλολογία Κ. Σάθα, μετὰ καί τινων προσθηκῶν (Trieste 1872) p 51. For a German version of Kanelos' letter see Karl Iken, *Leukothea. Eine Sammlung von Briefen eines geborenen Griechen über Staatswesen, Literatur und Dichtkunst des neueren Griechenlands* (Leipzig 1825) pp 3–12.

[23] Characteristic examples of this fascinating genre are Antonios Manouil, Τρόπαιον τῆς Ὀρθοδόξου Πίστεως . . . (Vienna 1791); Kelestinos Rodios, Ἡ Ἀθλιότης τῶν Δοκησισόφων, ἤτοι ἀπολογία ὑπὲρ τῆς πίστεως τῶν Χριστιανῶν πρὸς ἀναίρεσιν τινῶν φιλοσοφικῶν ληρημάτων (Trieste 1793); Sergios Makraios, Τρόπαιον ἐκ τῆς ἑλλαδικῆς πανοπλίας κατὰ τῶν ὀπαδῶν τοῦ Κοπερνίκου . . . (Vienna 1797); Athanasios Parios, Χριστιανικὴ Ἀπολογία . . . (Constantinople 1802) and Ἀλεξίκακον Φάρμακον ἤτοι πνευματικὸν ἐγχειρίδιον . . . (Leipzig 1818). The whole subject is discussed in detail by Ariadna Camariano in 'Spiritul filosofic şi revoluţionar francez combatut de Patriarhia Ecumenică şi Sublima Poartă, *Cercetari Literare*, 4 (1941) pp 114–36 and *Spiritul Revoluţionar Francez şi Voltaire in Limba Graecă şi Română*, (Bucharest 1946) *passim*.

In addition, the Church adopted a broadly hostile line towards one of the most significant aspects of the eighteenth-century Greek intellectual revival—the Greeks' recovery of a consciousness of their classical heritage. This had manifested itself in a variety of ways, the study, editing and publication of classical texts (it is easy to overlook Korais's stature as a classical philologist in his multifarious activities in the cause of Greek independence), in a renewed emphasis on the teaching of the classics in the schools, in an increasing obsession with the purity of the Greek language, in an interest in the preservation of the physical remains of the ancient world, in an increasing consciousness among the Greeks that they were the lineal descendants of those ancient worthies so much admired in enlightened Europe, an awareness that was reflected in the practice of adopting the names of these worthies in the place of Christian names.[24]

The church looked with disfavour on this development, fearing that a renewed interest in the culture of the ancient world might lead to atheism. In 1784 the Orthodox clergy of Bucharest could only with difficulty be prevailed upon to grant the Athonite monk and learned grammarian, Neophytos Kafsokalyvitis, a Christian burial after he had cried out in the delirious fever that preceded his death that he was about to rejoin the souls of Plato and Demosthenes.[25] Athanasios Parios, in a tract written in 1802 to discourage Greek parents from sending their children to Europe, that 'chaos of perdition', for business, denounced the philosophers of the ancient world as men who paid only lip service to virtue and learning. For good measure he denounced Plato as 'woman-obsessed, a pederast and a parasite'.[26] Konstantinos Koumas, a former teacher at the *Philologikon Gymnasion* in Smyrna, wrote that the patriarch Grigorios V considered that the Platos and Aristotles, the Newtons and the Descartes, triangles and logarithms led

---

[24] See the characteristic injunction of the author of the *Stokhasmoi tou Kritonos* (Athens 1819): Μὴν ὑποφέρετε νὰ διαρκέσῃ, πλέον ἡ πένθιμος ἀβελτηρία τῶν ἀπογόνων, διὰ τὴν ὁποίαν προδίδουν κάθε ἡμέραν τοὺς προγονικοὺς θησαυρούς, πωλοῦν, λέγω, εἰς ἕναν Κλὰρκ τὸν Πλάτωνα, εἰς ἕναν Ἔλγιν τὰ ὑπάρχοντα τῆς Ἀθηνᾶς, καὶ ἴσως μὲ τοῦ Θεμιστοκλέους τὸ μνῆμα κατασκευάζουν τοίχους! p 153.

[25] C. Th. Dimaras, *La Grèce au Temps des Lumières*, (Geneva 1969) p 13, and *Magasin Encyclopédique*, 8 (1803) pp 488–9.

[26] Nathanail Neokaisareos [Athanasios Parios], Ἀντιφώνησις πρὸς τὸν παράλογον 3ῆλον τῶν τῶν ἀπὸ τῆς Εὐρώπης ἐρχομένων φιλοσόφων δεικνύσα ὅτι μάταιος καὶ ἀνόητος εἶναι ὁ ταλανισμὸς ὅπου κάνουσι τοῦ γένους μας καὶ διδάσκουσα ποία εἶναι ἡ ὄντως καὶ ἀληθινὴ φιλοσοφία. Τούτοις προσετέθη καὶ παραίνεσις ὠφελιμωτάτη πρὸς τοὺς ἀδεῶς πέμποντας τοὺς υἱοὺς των εἰς τὴν Εὐρώπην χάριν πραγματείας . . ., (Trieste 1802) pp 15–16.

to indifference in matters divine.[27] He was presumably thinking here, among other texts, of the encyclical of March 1819 issued by Grigorios and the holy synod. This asked of what benefit was it to the young to learn of 'algebra, and cubes and cube roots, and triangles and triangulated tetragons, and logarithms and symbolic logic, and elliptical projections, and atoms and vacuums, and whirlpools, and power and attraction and gravity . . . and a myriad of the same kind and other monstrous things . . . if, as a consequence, in speech they are barbarians, if they are ungrammatical in their writings, ignorant in the things of religion, degenerate and frenzied in morals, injurious to the state, obscure patriots and unworthy of their ancestral calling . . .?'. The encyclical went on to condemn the innovation 'of giving ancient Greek names to the baptised infants of the faithful'. The hierarchy were enjoined to admonish their flocks 'to abandon forthwith this abuse . . . parents and godparents in future are to name at the time of the holy and secret rebirth with the traditional Christian names, to which pious parents are accustomed, the (names) known in Church, and of the glorious saints that are celebrated by it . . .'[28]

In a multitude of ways, then, during the critical decades before 1821, the hierarchy of the church manifested both its political conservatism and its cultural obscurantism. This in itself was more than enough to arouse the hostility of the active protagonists of Greek independence, and particularly of the intelligentsia. But political conservatism and cultural obscurantism were clearly not the underlying causes of the hostility towards the church that was apparently deeply rooted among the mass of the Greek people. For the most part illiterate, the peasantry and poor urban populations were largely indifferent to, even if they were aware of, the intellectual debates that so exercised the intelligentsia. Inevitably anti-clericalism at a popular level is more difficult to document than anti-clericalism among the intelligentsia, for illiterate populations necessarily leave no written remains. But, if relatively rare, such indications of popular anti-clericalism do exist.

One such manifestation of popular anti-clericalism is the satirical poem the *Rossanglogallos*, or the Russian, the Englishman and the Frenchman. This poem was never printed but appears to have enjoyed a widespread manuscript circulation during the first two decades of the nineteenth century. Travellers such as Byron, John Cam Hobhouse

---

[27] Koumas, p 514.
[28] K. Th. Dimaras, Ὁ Κοραῆς καὶ ἡ Ἐποχή του, Βασικὴ Βιβλιοθήκη 9 (Athens 1953) pp 302–4.

and William Martin Leake also came across versions of the poem, which takes the form of a dialogue between a Russian, an Englishman and a Frenchman, making the grand tour of Greece and inquiring of a Greek patriot the reasons for Greece's continued enslavement. They ask in turn a metropolitan, a Phanariot *hospodar* of Wallachia, a merchant and a *kocabaşī* or notable and find them all to be friends to tyranny. The metropolitan answers:

> I do not know of the yoke (of the Turk) . . .
> I eat and drink with pleasure,
> I do not feel the tyranny . . .
> Two things I crave, yes indeed, by the (Holy) Icons
> Lots of money, and nice girls.
> Now as for Hellas, which you mention
> It is of little concern to me if she has been tyrannised. . . .
> We give them spiritual counsel
> To have faith in the ruler
> And respect the primate,
> Not to regret giving money to the Turk . . .[29]

In the *Elliniki Nomarkhia*, a polemical tract clearly intended for popular consumption, the anonymous author employed all his talent for invective to denigrate the hierarchy. Apparently himself an Epirote, the author was particularly harsh in his strictures against the then (c 1806) metropolitan of Ioannina whom he castigated as 'an adulterer and a sodomite, without the least shame'. Moreover, as he had heard from an eye witness, the metropolitan ate two *okas* of yoghourt for breakfast and half an *oka* of filleted sardines in the afternoon. The generality of the archbishops, he wrote, 'eat and drink like pigs . . . they sleep for fourteen hours at night and two hours in the afternoon. They sing the liturgy two times a year, and when they are not eating, drinking and sleeping, then they plot the most shameful and worthless things that anyone could imagine'.[30]

The seeds of popular antagonism towards the ecclesiastical authorities were implicit in the *millet* system through which the Ottoman Porte exercised control over the non-Muslim populations of the empire. For the church authorities were given wide ranging authority in many matters of civil administration and, as a consequence, much of

---

[29] K. Th. Dimaras, Τὸ κείμενο τοῦ Ροσσαγγλογάλλου, Ἑλληνικά, 17 (Thessaloniki 1962) pp 190–1.

[30] Ἑλληνικὴ Νομαρχία, p 168. An *oka* is the equivalent of approximately two and three quarter pounds.

the odium that would otherwise have rubbed off on the Ottoman authorities was experienced by the ecclesiastical authorities. As bishop Theophilos of Kampania wrote in his *Nomikon* of 1788: 'In the days of the Christian empire (alas) . . . prelates administered only the priesthood and ecclesiastical matters and did not intervene in civil matters . . . Now, however, . . . provincial prelates undertake secular lawsuits and trials, in connection with inheritance, with debts and with almost any aspect of the Christian civil law'.[31]

The extension of the church's jurisdiction into a wide area of civil jurisdiction inevitably brought conflict in those parts of the Greek world where a well-defined code of customary law existed, for example Mykonos, Syros, Naxos, Amorgos, Kythnos, Paros, Thira, Zagora and Melnik.[32] An interesting example of an attempt to resolve the conflict of laws between ecclesiastical and community law is contained in the *Compromise of love and common peace* (Συνυποσχετικὸν ἀγάπης καὶ κοινῆς εἰρήνης) signed in 1785 by Grigorios, metropolitan of Smyrna, and the *dimogerondes* or elders of the Greek community of the city, in the presence of the *arkhons, prokritoi* and the *protomaistoroi* of the guilds. Agreement was reached on the respective jurisdictions of the metropolitan and the Greek *koinon* or community. Among other matters payments for *mnymosyna* were regulated, while excommunications were to be made only in the presence of, and after agreement with, representatives of the *dimogerondes*. That excommunications were a form of punishment much feared by the laity is understandable, given the forbidding form of words used: 'We manifest that X . . . is anathematised from God and damned, and unforgiven, indissoluble after death and without the church of Christ and the fellowship of the Christians bag and baggage . . . and no one is to minister to him, or asperse him, or associate with, or eat with or drink with, or greet or do business with, and work with, or speak with him, or in the event of his dying bury and say requiems for him, in suspension and excommunication'.[33]

A more immediate cause of popular resentment against the church than its pretensions in matters of civil law were the financial

---

[31] N. J. Pantazopoulos, *Church and Law in the Balkan Peninsula during the Ottoman Rule* (Thessaloniki 1967) pp 44–5.

[32] *Ibid* pp 107–8.

[33] *Ibid* pp 107–9 and K. S. Papadopoulos, Εἰδήσεις περὶ τῆς Κοινότητος καὶ τῆς Δημογεροντίας Σμύρνης πρὸ τῆς Ἐπαναστάσεως τοῦ 1821 καὶ ἡ τότε κατὰ τόπους ἀνάπτυξις τοῦ Κοινοτισμοῦ καὶ ἡ χειραφέτησις αὐτοῦ ἀπὸ τῆς Ἐκκλησίας, Μικρασιατικὰ Χρονικά, 9 (Athens 1961) pp 11 *seq*. See also Ἑλληνικὴ Νομαρχία, pp 166–7.

impositions it laid on the Orthodox *pliroma*. These impositions were a direct consequence of the institutionalised corruption of the Ottoman system of government. After the Ottoman conquest of Constantinople it soon became the custom for the patriarch to pay a substantial *peşkeş* or 'gift' in return for the imperial *berat* confirming him in office. The payment of this ever increasing *peşkeş* naturally created a vested interest for the Ottoman authorities in a rapid alternation in the holders of patriarchal office and contributed substantially to the extraordinary turnover in holders of the office of patriarch during the *Tourkokratia*. The anonymous author of the *Elliniki Nomarkhia* described the system in the following way:

> The synod purchases the patriarchal throne from the Ottoman grand vizir for a great amount of money, afterwards it sells this to whoever will give the greatest profit, and it nominates the purchaser as patriarch. The latter, then, to get back whatever he borrowed for the purchase of the throne, sells the dioceses, that is to say the archbishoprics, to whoever gives the greatest amount, and thus he appoints the archbishops, who in turn sell to others their bishoprics. The bishops then sell these to the Christians, that is to say they fleece the people, to get back whatever they expended. And this is the way in which the members of the different ecclesiastical ranks are chosen, that is to say for gold.[34]

The author of the *Elliniki Normarkhia* was certainly no friend to the Orthodox hierarchy and was prone to rhetorical exaggeration but his analysis of the system is substantially correct. The disastrous effects of such a system at local level are attested in a document of 1796 which gives a vivid picture of the realities of rural life in provincial Greece during the last decades of the eighteenth century. This document, not written in the same spirit of polemical invective as the *Elliniki Nomarkhia* and to that extent a more reliable source, paints a graphic picture of corruption and oppression as it affected the ordinary members of the Christian flock and for this reason I want to quote extensively from it:

> And when the chief priest of a diocese dies, immediately the lobbying begins in force, some going to the patriarch, some going to the senior clergy, some to the notables and their wives, and often to the magnates, and of the many one is lucky and receives the office. But as much as he succeeds, many expenses follow him, five, ten, fifteen thousand *grosia*. Some of these expenses are

---

[34] Ἑλληνικὴ Νομαρχία, p 164. See also A. K. Ypsilantis, . . . Τὰ Μετὰ τὴν Ἅλωσιν . . . (Constantinople 1870) p 238.

occasioned by gifts to the go-betweens, some to the Porte, some to the higher clergy, all with IOUs. . . . This new bishop, then, without having 50 *grosia* of his own, falls into an abyss of debt. . . . And with this power (an imperial *berat* confirming him in office), immediately he arrives in the diocese, he begins to seek from the villages help for his new high priestly office of from 50 to 100 *grosia*, from the monasteries of from 100 to 200 *grosia*, from the priests, some 10, some 15 *grosia* and so on, all excessive amounts. The poor cannot resist, fearful of excommunications, curses and exclusion from church. The notables are ashamed of the daily coffee and pipes and the gifts. The *ağas* do not object, for he says to them: 'It is the custom, as my predecessor took it so do I want it'.

Apart from the above he has his regular dues: 10 *paras* from each house, at Easter a lamb from each priest and eggs from each village, sometimes 100, sometimes 200 and sometimes 300. At marriages he takes at the first 45 *paras*, at the second 90 *paras*, at the third he seeks 5 or 10 [*grosia*] and if there is the least relationship between the couple he begins by asking 100 *grosia*, so as to take 50 or 30 or whatever he can. If anyone wishes to make a new priest, he begins by asking for 100 so as to take what he can, making a reduction so that the go-betweens, Turkish or Greek, who mediate, will owe him a favour. When anyone dies, he does this. He begins at 50 [*grosia*] and goes down to whatever he can find to take. If perhaps any monk, either from the monasteries of the Holy Mountain of Athos, or from the Holy Sepulchre, or from Mount Sinai comes to his diocese to circulate to seek alms from the poor Christians, first he must take from him 50 or 60 *grosia* so as to give him permission to circulate in the diocese. . . .

Let us suppose a priest has a village of forty families he [the bishop] takes from him 20 *grosia* each year and gives him permission to officiate. A priest has thirty families, he takes from him 15 *grosia* and so on; thus he sells parishes and this gift is called the *emvatikion*. This burden of debt, which they voluntarily bear for their glory, has brought the hierarchy to such a state that, at present, there remains comfort for the poor Greeks only among the *kocabaşis* and higher clergy, and as the *ağas* treat the unfortunate Greeks, so do the *kocabaşis* and the higher clergy.[35]

[35] S. I. Asdrachas, Πραγματικότητες ἀπὸ τὸν ἑλληνικὸ 18 αἰῶνα in Σταθμοὶ πρὸς τὴν Νέα Ἑλληνικὴ Κοινωνία, ed K. Th. Dimaras (Athens 1965) pp 37–40. See also G. A. Antoniadis and M. M. Papaioannou, Ἰωάννου Οἰκονόμου Λαρισσαίου *1783–1842*

Inevitably as rationalist ideas gained an increasing hold on the Greeks the monasteries came under fire as serving no useful purpose. Korais wrote that Christ had not come 'to transform man, that political animal, into a monastic animal'.[36] Daniil Philippidis and Grigorios Konstantas in their *Geographia Neoteriki* of 1791 attacked the monks for living off the alms which they received from Christians: 'this is an endeavour neither monastic, nor Christian, nor even human'. If they were true monks they should not accept alms for 'in a village 200 men can manage to make a living and support their wives and children and they can also pay so many taxes. Two hundred monks in a monastery, on the other hand, without women, without children, with few or no taxes at all, are unable to'.[37] Another cause of monastic unpopularity was that the monks were widely considered to act as informers to the authorities on the movements of the *klefts*, the 'social bandits' who were a persistent thorn in the flesh of the Ottomans. Certainly there was no love lost between the monks and *klefts*, and monasteries were frequently the target of kleftic raids.[38]

For all the bitterness of the attacks against the hierarchy of the church during the pre-independence period it is important to stress that there is very little evidence of actual religious disbelief. Even such a hostile critic as the author of the *Elliniki Nomarkhia* was concerned to make it clear that he was critical of the hierarchy for departing from the pristine purity of the apostolic church. Adamantios Korais, as we have seen, was careful to buttress his rebuttal of Anthimos' *Didaskalia Patriki* with copious scriptural references. As a young man Korais had translated Platon Levshin's Orthodox catechism into Greek—Ὀρθόδοξος Διδασκαλία εἴτουν σύνοψις τῆς Χριστιανικῆς

Ἐπιστολαὶ Διαφόρων (Athens 1964) pp 169 *seq*; Ph. Bouboulidis, Ἡ Ἠθικὴ Στιχουργία τοῦ Ἀλεξάνδρου Κάλφογλου, Ἐπιστημονικὴ Ἐπετηρὶς τῆς Φιλοσοφικῆς Σχολῆς τοῦ Πανεπιστημίου Ἀθηνῶν, 17 (Athens 1966–7) pp 416 *seq*. and William Leake, *Travels in Northern Greece*, 4 (London 1835) p 281.

[36] Adamantios Korais, Πάρεργα 7, p 36 quoted in M. J. Le Guillou, 'Aux sources des mouvements spirituels de l'Eglise Orthodoxe de Grèce: 1. La renaissance spirituelle du XVIIIe siècle', *Istina*, 7 (Brussels 1960) p 112.

[37] Γεωγραφία νεωτερικὴ [ἐρανισθεῖσα ἀπὸ διαφόρους συγγραφεῖς παρὰ Δανιὴλ ἱερομονάχου καὶ Γρηγορίου ἱεροδιακόνου τῶν Δημητρίεων . . .] (Vienna 1791) repr, ed A. Koumarianou (Athens 1970) p 136.

[38] J. W. Baggally, *The Klephtic Ballads in relation to Greek History (1715–1821)* (Oxford 1936) p 10. A factor tending to undermine popular respect for the monastic order was that two of the most powerful motives leading men to the monastic life at this time were poverty and the tyranny of the Turks, P. D. Apostolopoulos, '44 Documents ecclésiastiques inédits du XVIIIe siècle (Du Suppl. Grec. 708 de la Bibliothèque Nationale de Paris)' Ἑλληνικά, 27 (1974) p 87.

Θεολογίας (Leipzig 1782)—while in a letter of 1785 to Grigorios, then metropolitan of Smyrna and later ecumenical patriarch, he commended the middle way 'far from the Scylla of disbelief and from the Charybdis of superstition'.[39] In his brief autobiography, written in 1829 towards the end of his life, Korais concluded by conceding that 'to criticise all the Eastern clergy for the voluptuousness of a few priestly satraps revelling in Constantinople is to compare the whole of the laity with the Phanariots of Constantinople'.[40]

Faced with such manifestations of hostility, if not of irreligion, the hierarchy made some effort to counter this anti-clerical onslaught. Grigorios V and the holy synod in the encyclical of 1819 drew attention to the support he had given to education during his earlier patriarchates, while Hilarion of Mount Sinai, the overseer of the patriarchal press, in a pamphlet published at the press, besides lauding the praises of 'the most compassionate and heroic' sultan Mahmud II, defended the church's record in educational matters and asserted that the views of 'the ecclesiastical and civil protectors of the nation were worthy of praise and joy and not of tears and blame, as some of these fellow countrymen who, to our misfortune are in Europe, unthinkingly maintain'.[41] A more systematic defence of the hierarchy was published in Pisa in 1815[42] by Ignatios, metropolitan of Oungrovlakhia to counter a pamphlet published in Vienna in the same year by Neophytos Doukas.[43]

Ignatios' *Apologia* is a sophisticated and well argued attempt to rebut the charges levelled against the church by the Greek intelligentsia. The author had a dual purpose, to demonstrate that throughout all political

---

[39] Τῆς Σμυρναίων ἐκκλησίας τὸ σκάφος, κυβερνώμενον ἀπὸ προεστῶτα φιλοσόφον καὶ τὴν μέσην ὁδὸν εὐθυνόμενον, μακρὰν καὶ ἀπὸ τὴν σκύλλαν τῆς ἀπιστίας καὶ ἀπὸ τὴν χάρυβδιν τῆς δεισιδαιμονίας, θέλει φθάση εἰς τὸν λιμένα τῆς σωτηρίας, ὅπου καὶ ὁ κυβερνήτης καὶ οἱ κυβερνώμενοι θέλει ἀπολαύσωσι τὴν ἀμοιβήν, ὁ μὲν τῆς καλῆς οἰκονομίας, οἱ δὲ τῆς ὑπακοῆς, letter of 20 November 1785 in ᾿Αδαμάντιος Κοραῆς, *1 (1774–1798)*, ed K. Th. Dimaras (Athens 1964) p 61.

[40] MS Vivliothiki Korai, Chios: 493. Korais's religious beliefs are discussed in D. S. Balanos, Αἱ θρησκευτικαὶ ἰδέαι τοῦ ᾿Αδαμαντίου Κοραῆ, (Athens 1920). See also Γεωγραφία Νεωτερική, p 137.

[41] Μέλισσα ἢ Συλλογὴ ᾿Ελληνική, 3 (Paris 1821) p 262.

[42] ᾿Απολογία [ἱστορικὴ καὶ κριτικὴ ὑπὲρ τοῦ ἱεροῦ κλήρου τῆς ᾿Ανατολικῆς ᾿Εκκλησίας κατὰ τῶν συκοφαντιῶν τοῦ Νεοφύτου Δούκα συγγραφεῖσα παρὰ Κυρίλλου Κ. κατ' ἐπίμονον ζήτησιν τῶν ὁμογενῶν] ([Pisa] 1815). A defence of the clergy of Moldavia was put forward by the Comte d'Hauterive, secretary to the *hospodar* Alexandros Mavrokordatos Phyraris, *Memoriu asupra vechei şi actualei stari a Moldovei presentat lui Alexandru Voda Ipsilante Domnul Moldovei la 1787*, (Bucharest 1902) pp 146–8.

[43] ᾿Επιστολὴ πρὸς τον Παναγιώτατον Πατριάρχην Κύριον Κύριλλον περὶ ᾿Εκκλησιαστικῆς Εὐταξίας τοῦ Νεοφύτου Δούκα (Vienna 1815), continued as Καλόγερος ἤτοι ᾿Επιστολὴ πρὸς Μοναχοὺς προτρεπτικὴ εἰς φιλολογίαν.

changes the Orthodox church had remained firmly orientated towards
the principles which it received from its founder and that the faults that
Doukas imputed to the hierarchy were to be found only in his
imagination and on the tongue of slanderers, that they lacked true
substance. He listed the imposts and dues levied by the church,
emphasising that their legitimacy was recognised by the Christian
pliroma and confirmed through imperial *berats*. Moreover the clergy
themselves were subject to two forms of tax, the *miri* and the *harac*.
He conceded that it was impossible for an ecumenical patriarch to retain
his throne for life, but this was a result of 'the Ottoman political
system' according to which all offices were held temporarily. Even the
grand mufti (*şeyhülislâm*), the head of the dominant religion, was
subject to this system. An indication of the impartiality of the justice
dispensed in the church courts, Ignatios argued, was that other
nationalities, including Turks, often preferred to have recourse to
church courts when they were in dispute with Christians. Because one
prelate was guilty of embezzlement was no reason to denounce the
entire ecclesiastical estate. Talk of ecclesiastical gluttony was ridiculous.
Priests were obliged to keep strict fasts, which they could break only
in cases of serious illness, and even if they wanted to indulge themselves
at table, they had not the money, unlike the ecclesiastics of some other
nations. He rebutted in detail Doukas's charges that the hierarchy was
indifferent to education:

> The holy (metropolitan) of Ephesus Dionysios, he wrote, in leaving
> Larissa to be translated to Ephesus, occasioned inconsolable grief
> to the Christians of that diocese. He is rather a worthy
> metropolitan for the protection which he shows to the educated
> and to the schools, and for his zeal for the progress of the nation
> in learning . . . The holy (metropolitan) of Heraclea, Meletios, for
> all that the revenues of his diocese are small, for that region
> experienced infinite evils from rebels, supports at his expense five
> pupils in the school at Constantinople (the *Megali tou Genous
> Skholi* at Kuruçeşme) . . . The holy (metropolitan) of Methymni,
> Panaretos, made a school of his very metropolis, and since, for
> such time as he can spare, he dedicates himself to lessons, he
> obliged even the clergy, who serve him, likewise to become
> pupils, and to be taught what they should know before they
> undertook the priestly profession.[44]

[44] Ignatios, 'Ἀπολογία, pp 74–5 and *passim*.

While refusing to accept charges that the ignorant are ordained for money, he concedes that while it is always preferable for the clergy to be educated, this cannot in existing circumstances be made an inflexible norm. He considered Doukas's proposal to employ one hundred of the Athonite monks as language teachers to be impractical, but he did believe that each monastery should delegate one of their number to watch over the education of those priests who were to officiate in the secular world. While conceding some faults in the clergy ('prelates are men, and as men they can have certain weaknesses') he asserted that no other nation so respected its prelates 'as the Greeks today revere theirs'. 'It could be said', he continued, 'that the Greeks today worship, not merely revere, their prelates'. In short the affairs of the eastern church are conducted in such a way that 'harmony between the nation and the church and between the church and the government is complete'.[45]

Despite the efforts of men such as Ignatios Oungrovlakhias to counter the attacks on the church and its hierarchy that were becoming increasingly frequent and increasingly bitter the fact remains that anti-clericalism was a phenomenon deeply rooted in almost all strata of pre-independence Greek society and this fact must call into question the traditional view of the church as the nucleus around which the independence movement coalesced. It is significant that, despite the very considerable role played by the church in the civil government of the Greeks during the *Tourkokratia*, no provision was made in the various constitutions adopted by the Greeks during the course of the war of independence for any such role for the church in an independent Greece.[46] Moreover, one of the most important pieces

[45] *Ibid* pp 79, 61, 74. Perhaps the most judicious assessment of the question is that of that most acute observer of pre-independence Greece, colonel William Leake: 'It is a common sentiment among the laity of Greece, that the bishops have been a great cause of their present degraded state, nor have the Greeks in general any higher esteem for their higher clergy, or for the monastic order from which the prelates are promoted. This, however, is in some degree an injustice; for although the clergy are often an instrument of oppression, and a bishop can hardly avoid acting like a Turk in office, the regular clergy have kept the Greek language alive, and have prevented, perhaps, the dissolution of all national union', *Travels*, pp 281–2.

[46] See article 24 of the Troezen Constitution of 1827: 'Ο κλῆρος, κατὰ τοὺς κανόνας τῆς ʿΑγίας καὶ ʿΙερᾶς ἡμῶν ᾿Εκκλησίας, δὲν ἐμπεριπλέκεται εἰς κανένα δημόσιον ὑπούργημα... Πολιτικὸν Σύνταγμα τῆς ῾Ελλάδος, συνταχθέν, ἀνακριθέν, καὶ ἐπικυρωθὲν κατὰ τὴν Γ᾿ἐθνικὴν Συνέλευσιν (Troezen 1827) p 8. Interestingly enough Rigas Velestinlis in his project for a *New Political Constitution of the Inhabitants of Rumeli, Asia Minor, the Archipelago, Moldavia and Wallachia* of 1797, which he intended as the basis of government for the territories of the Ottoman Empire after the Ottoman tyranny had been overthrown, had made no provision for any part to be played by the church in secular government.

of legislation adopted during the regency of the young Otto of Wittelsbach, was the severely Erastian ecclesiastical settlement, sponsored by one of the regents, Georg von Maurer, with the guidance of Theoklitos Pharmakidis.[47] This settlement of 1833, which was to determine the whole future course of church-state relations in independent Greece, severely limited the church's influence in secular affairs, and signified a dramatic curtailment of the privileges enjoyed by the church under Ottoman rule. Despite the signs of incipient class struggle among the Greeks during the early months of the war the Greek war of independence can in no sense be regarded as revolutionary. The internecine struggles that disfigured the Greek cause and so distressed foreign philhellenes were essentially struggles for power within the ruling élites of Greek society, the very same élites that had dominated pre-revolutionary Greek society and were to dominate post-independence society. Of the powers and privileges of the pre-independence élites only those of the Orthodox hierarchy were to be curtailed in the independent state. After 1830 two of the three curses to which Sir William Gell had referred had been effectively eliminated, the priests and the Turks. Only the *kocabaşīs* remained.

University of London
Kings' College

---

[47] A full analysis of Otto's church settlement may be found in Charles Frazee, *The Orthodox Church and Independent Greece* (Cambridge 1969) pp 110–18.

THE RUMANIAN ORTHODOX CHURCH
AND THE WEST

by ERIC TAPPE

THE title of this paper raises a problem at the very outset. What is meant by 'the Rumanian Orthodox church' when one is talking of a period before the notion of 'Rumania' had been conceived? In this paper it will be taken to mean the Orthodox church as it existed in the principalities of Wallachia, Moldavia and Transylvania from the fourteenth century and has continued in those territories to the present day.

A few words first about the prehistory of the Rumanian Orthodox church as thus defined. The Roman province of Dacia had been created by Trajan in AD 106, and the administration had been withdrawn south of the Danube by Aurelian in 271, after which the territories in question were controlled first by the Goths and then by a succession of other invaders for about ten centuries. During this millenium they remain for us in a darkness lit by very few rays. It is therefore not surprising that there is little evidence for church organisation north of the Danube during this period, especially when we remember that the Dacian lands ceased to belong to the empire half a century before Christianity became a tolerated religion. The first church building so far discovered in the lands north of the lower Danube is at Sucidava, a bridgehead held by the Romans after their withdrawal, destroyed by the Huns in 447, and refounded by Justinian in his first years as emperor. This basilica is apparently from Justinian's time, and being in a bridgehead, may be presumed to have depended on a church organisation south of the Danube.[1]

The adoption of old church Slavonic as the language of the church by Christians in the lands which were later to be called Wallachia, Moldavia and Transylvania is dated to the tenth century and suggests that they were dependent on the Bulgarian church, which had episcopal sees at Vidin and Silistra just across the Danube from Wallachia. From 869 the Bulgarian church, which the first Christian tsar Boris had hoped for a while to attach to Rome, remained dependent on the patriarch

[1] I[storia] B[isericii] R[omâne; manual pentru Institutele Teologice], I (Bucharest 1957) pp 99–100.

of Constantinople. Transylvania, on the other hand, in gradual stages between the eleventh and thirteenth centuries, passed into the hands of the Hungarians, who had already adopted catholicism. In the early thirteenth century the Hungarian king Andrew II, in order to defend his territories against raids by the Cumans, who occupied Wallachia and Moldavia, invited the Teutonic Knights to settle in his borderlands. They pushed over into Wallachia and Moldavia, settling on the southern and eastern foothills of the Carpathians. Though the king drove out the knights in 1225, colonies with catholic settlers had been set up by then and remained there. Dominican missionaries converted the khan of Cumania, whose territories included Wallachia and Moldavia, and pope Gregory IV appointed a bishop for the Cumans. The see was named Milcovia, the Milcov being the river dividing what were later the principalities of Wallachia and Moldavia.[2]

In 1234 the pope wrote to prince Bela, son of the king of Hungary, complaining about certain developments in the diocese of Cumania, since the prince was the ruler of the newly colonised territories. The main point of his complaint may be summarised as follows:

> In the diocese of the Cumans there are certain groups called 'Walathi' [it is evidently to Wallachians, the Rumanian-speaking inhabitants, that he is referring], who, despising the Roman church, receive all the sacraments, not from the bishop of Cumania, but from certain pseudo-bishops holding the rite of the Greeks. Moreover some people from the kingdom of Hungary, both Hungarians and Teutons and other orthodox, cross over to them to live with them, and becoming one people with the Wallachians, receive the sacraments with them.[3] Therefore, that the Wallachians may have no grounds for approaching schismatic bishops by reason of the lack of sacraments, we are instructing the bishop of the Cumans to appoint for them a catholic bishop *illi nationi conformem*.[4]

This last phrase presumably implies a Rumanian-speaking bishop. As for the pseudo-bishops Nicolae Iorga regarded them as *chorepiscopi* living in wooden sketes. 'They arose,' he writes, 'uncanonical as they were even for the eastern church, from an organic development of the local population'.[5]

[2] *IBR*, I pp 130–7.
[3] The word 'orthodox' here refers to members of the Roman church, not the eastern.
[4] *Documente privind istoria României, Veacul XI, XII & XIII, C. Transilvania*, I (Bucharest 1951) pp 403–4.
[5] N. Iorga, *Histoire des Roumains et de la romanité orientale*, 3 (Bucharest 1937) p 137.

The Rumanian Orthodox church and the west

After the invasion of the Tartars in 1241 nothing is heard of the see of Milcov for a long time. The kingdom of Hungary had been weakened, the dynasty which ruled it in the second half of the thirteenth century was a feeble one, and the area south and east of the Carpathians was relieved from Hungarian pressure. This facilitated the development of small political organisations in that area, which presently evolved into the principalities of Wallachia and Moldavia. With the accession of the Angevin dynasty to the Hungarian throne in 1308, Hungarian policy became more aggressive. King Charles Robert was, however, severely defeated in 1330 by Basarab, the ruler of the emerging principality of Wallachia, and thereafter pursued his aims by more peaceful means. A report to the papacy probably instigated by him proposed to pope John XXII the restoration of the see of Milcov, that is, of the former bishopric of the Cumans, and the consecration as its bishop of the Franciscan Vitus de Monteferro, the king's chaplain. The pope wrote to the primate of Hungary, empowering him to do this if the report were true. But neither the primate nor the bishop of Transylvania wished to lose jurisdiction over the catholics beyond the Carpathians, since they would also lose their revenues from those parts; so the matter was dropped. In 1347 the new king Louis drove the Tartars from Moldavia and established Hungarian rule there. He then approached pope Clement VI on the subject of the see of Milcov. A bishop was consecrated. Whether this bishop and his successors in fact resided in the diocese is doubtful.[6]

As each principality became established, it was natural that its ruler should desire a metropolitan see of his own. Thus in the 1350s Nicolae Alexandru of Wallachia put this request to the patriarch of Constantinople. In 1359 Iachint, metropolitan of Vicina (this place is thought to have been on the site of the present day Isaccea on the south bank of the Danube), was translated to Argeş, at that time the capital of Wallachia, as first metropolitan of Ungrovlahia.[7] A few years later pope Gregory IX thought of founding a bishopric of Argeş for the catholics of Wallachia, but evidently decided that the see of Milcov would have to do.[8]

In Moldavia, which emerged as a principality in 1359, the papacy seemed to have a better chance of success. The catholic population was larger than in Wallachia. No Orthodox metropolitan was appointed

---

[6] *IBR*, 1, pp 163–7.
[7] *Ibid* pp 147–50.
[8] *Ibid* p 166.

until 1401, the Orthodox Christians depending till then on the metropolitan of Halicz in Poland. The second prince of Moldavia, Laṭcu, struggling to keep his state independent of Hungary, aimed at securing Polish aid. But in 1370 king Louis of Hungary became king of Poland as well. In desperation, Latcu, on the advice of two Franciscans appealed to pope Urban V, offering his own conversion and that of his people, and asking for his capital Siret to be raised to the rank of a city and become the seat of a catholic bishop. So in 1371 a bishop was consecrated. The see was to be independent of Hungary and Poland, and directly dependent on Rome.

However ready Laṭcu himself might be to abandon orthodoxy for catholicism, it was a different matter with his wife, let alone his subjects. No great number of conversions is known to have taken place. Laṭcu did not build a cathedral nor endow the see of Siret, and in the end he was buried in an Orthodox church. The sees of Siret and Milcov could not flourish without proper endowments and with bishops who were usually absentees and did not speak Rumanian. It is probable that the catholics were mostly inhabitants of the towns colonised by Saxons and Hungarians, while the country people remained Orthodox. Nevertheless the Franciscans and Dominicans persisted with their missionary work.[9]

Laṭcu's successor, Petru Muşat, induced the metropolitan of Halicz to consecrate two bishops of Moldavia, one of whom was Iosif, a kinsman of the prince. He then asked Antonius, patriarch of Constantinople, to recognise Iosif as metropolitan of Moldavia. Antonius refused, wishing to appoint a Greek. A conflict arose, and Antonius excommunicated the Moldavians. It was not until there was a change of both prince and patriarch that the matter was settled, Iosif being recognised as metropolitan of Moldavia in 1401.

Thus at the opening of the fifteenth century both the principalities had Orthodox metropolitans of their own. Yet at the council of Constance in 1418 the Wallachian and Moldavian delegates were not prelates but boyars.[10] At the council of Florence in 1438–9 Damian, metropolitan of Moldavia, was present. He opposed the *filioque* clause, but eventually, under pressure from the patriarch of Constantinople, signed the act of union.[11]

The Rumanians of Transylvania in this period could not have a

[9] *Ibid* pp 167–9.
[10] *Ibid* p 226.
[11] *Ibid* p 230.

properly organised church, since the papacy pressed the kings of Hungary to suppress schismatics on their territory. Since there was no Orthodox metropolitan of Transylvania, the metropolitans of Wallachia from the start bore the title of 'exarch of Hungary and the mountains'. Orthodox bishops in Transylvania led a precarious existence. Thus in 1456 Ioan, the Orthodox bishop of Hunedoara, was removed by the papal inquisitor, John Capistrano, and taken to Rome.[12]

After the battle of Mohács in 1526 a large part of Hungarian territory was annexed by the Turks, but Transylvania became, like Wallachia and Moldavia, a principality paying tribute to the Ottoman empire. At about the same time the reformation arrived there. After 1530 many Saxons became Lutherans, many Hungarians Calvinists. In 1556 the Transylvanian diet abolished the Roman see of Alba Iulia and expelled catholic priests, and in the following year it proclaimed freedom of religion. This was during the reign of the younger Zápolya. But when in 1571 under the catholic prince István Báthory the diet recognised four 'received religions', catholic, Lutheran, Calvinist and unitarian, it gave orthodoxy only the status of a 'tolerated' religion. Being Orthodox, the Rumanians found themselves second-class citizens.[13]

The reformation in Transylvania had important results for Rumanian culture. Attempts to convert the Rumanians to protestantism produced the first monuments of the Rumanian language. The manuscripts which contain these early versions of scripture have been the subject of lengthy discussions. One theory is that they were due to the Hussites, who are known to have been active in Transylvania and Moldavia in the fifteenth century. But the prevailing theory is that they were made after the arrival of the reformation in Transylvania in the 1530s. In any case, the first recorded printing in the Rumanian language is a Lutheran catechism of 1544 from Sibiu in Transylvania.[14]

In Moldavia it seems that between 1530 and 1580 the numbers of catholics diminished through conversion to Lutheranism, Calvinism and Orthodoxy. There was even a protestant prince, an adventurer who called himself the 'despot Iacob Heraclid'. Born on the island of Samos, he had made his way to the west and studied in France. He

---

[12] *Ibid* pp 262–3.
[13] *Ibid* p 379.
[14] D. J. Deletant, 'A Survey of Rumanian Presses and Printing in the Sixteenth Century', [*The*] *S*[*lavonic and*] *E*[*ast*] *E*[*uropean*] *R*[*eview*], 53, no 131 (London, April 1975) p 163.

turned Lutheran and came by way of Germany and Scandinavia to Poland, where he was befriended by the protestant noble Albert Laski. He claimed relationship with the wife of the ruling Moldavian prince, Alexandru Lăpușneanu. In 1561 with financial support from the Habsburg emperor Ferdinand who was hostile to Lăpușneanu, and with the help of Laski and Polish troops, the despot drove his opponent from the country. He was a man of vast ambition, but his schemes came to little. In the course of his attempt to convert the Moldavian catholics to protestantism, he imported a Polish protestant, Lusinski, and had him made bishop. Before long the despot alienated his supporters and in 1563 was murdered.[15] Lăpușneanu returned to the throne, but remembering that Ferdinand had helped the usurper, he did nothing for the catholic cause.

Catholicism began to make a come-back in Moldavia in the 1580s. An Albanian named Bartolomeo Brutti, who had come to Moldavia with prince Iancu Sasul and was made his chamberlain, remained in the same post under the succeeding prince Petru Șchiopul. Brutti influenced the prince in favour of catholicism, and Jesuits were sent to Moldavia. In 1588 the prince informed the pope that his envoys Brutti and Ieremia Movilă would make the act of submission to the pope on his behalf before the papal legate in Poland. Nevertheless, the pope supported an intrigue which dethroned Petru.[16] Brutti, complaining that his services to the papacy were unrewarded, claimed to have brought about the reconversion of twenty thousand catholics who had become protestants. Petru's successor was Aron, whose candidature had the support of the English ambassador at Constantinople, Edward Barton. Barton recommended his candidate as 'one more better than the rest and that was supposed to be less Spanishe'.[17] In fact, Aron began negotiating to join the anti-Ottoman coalition which was led by the emperor Rudolf. Nevertheless he did one thing that Barton asked. He restored to the Hungarian Hussites in Moldavia the churches which had been handed over to the Jesuits under Brutti's influence.[18]

Prince Mihai Viteazul [Michael the Brave] of Wallachia was fervent in the cause of the anti-Ottoman coalition. He was thus able in 1599 to seize the throne of Transylvania with the consent of the emperor. He

[15] C. C. Giurescu, *Istoria Românilor*, 2 (Bucharest 1943) pp 196-9.
[16] *IBR*, 1, pp 371-4.
[17] E. D. Tappe, *Documents concerning Rumanian History 1427-1601 collected from British Archives* (The Hague 1964) p 61.
[18] *Ibid* p 62.

asked the emperor as his liege lord to permit Orthodoxy to be a received religion in Transylvania. Rudolf replied that there should be three received religions: Orthodoxy, catholicism and Lutheranism.[19] In return Mihai protected the catholics in Wallachia. Under his rule the Orthodox bishop in Transylvania became metropolitan of Alba Iulia. But with the murder of Mihai in 1601 there was an end of Rumanian hopes that Orthodoxy would be a received religion. Nevertheless, a quarter of a century later a Calvinist prince of Transylvania, Gábor Bethlen, helped the Orthodox clergy by restoration of property and exemption from taxes, and encouraged schooling in Rumanian and printing in the vernacular. In 1627, on the recommendation of the Calvinist superintendent, he appointed as Orthodox archbishop a monk Ghenadie. Ghenadie accepted the following conditions required by the prince: (i) obedience to the Calvinist superintendent, (ii) Rumanian to be the language of services, sermons and printed church books, (iii) superstitions to be rooted out. But further than this Ghenadie would not go. Bethlen accordingly wrote in 1629 to the patriarch of Constantinople Cyril Lucaris, whose *Confession* had just appeared, asking him to assist in the conversion of the Orthodox in Transylvania to Calvinism. Lucaris replied that, though he could do nothing to prevent their conversion, he would be committing an unforgivable sin if he aided it. In the same year Bethlen died and was succeeded by György Rákóczy, who continued Bethlen's policy. He found that Ghenadie would not print Calvanist books, so he got one Rumanian priest to translate a Calvinist catechism and another to print it, without the knowledge of the metropolitan. Ghenadie died in 1640, and Rákóczy looked for a successor who would be willing to carry out his policy. The Calvinist superintendent, reporting to the prince his efforts to find such a man, writes: 'I have not been able to find a candidate who would change his religion fundamentally.'[20] The successor was, in fact, soon thrown into prison for refusing to spread Calvinist teachings. Resistance to Calvinist propaganda had the paradoxical result of an Orthodox metropolitan hiding a Rumanian printing press so as not to have to use it for this purpose.

The confession of faith drawn up by Cyril Lucaris in 1629 has already been mentioned. To counter its protestant tendencies Petru Movilă, metropolitan of Kiev, summoned a synod to consider a confession of

[19] *IBR*, 1, p 403.
[20] *IBR*, 2 (1958), p 27.

Orthodox faith which he himself had compiled. The synod of Kiev could not agree on two points: purgatory and the Epiklesis. Parthenius, patriarch of Constantinople, was then asked to convoke a more representative synod of the whole Orthodox church. But the Turks would have opposed its being held at Constantinople, and the catholic king of Poland its being held at Kiev. So it was in Jassy, the capital of Moldavia, whose prince at that time was the powerful Vasile Lupu, an active supporter of Orthodoxy—in 1641 he had paid the debts of the Constantinopolitan patriarchate—that the synod met. The two disputed points were settled in the sense of the ancient teachings of the Orthodox church, and the confession was forwarded to Constantinople.[21] From Moldavia in 1645 came another weapon in the struggle against Calvinism. The metropolitan Varlaam published a reply to the Calvinist catechism which had been printed in Transylvania in 1640. This reply was issued as from both Wallachia and Moldavia.[22] Wallachia too was at this time ruled by a strong prince, Matei Basarab. The two principalities were becoming important centres of Orthodox culture for the whole Orthodox world within the Ottoman empire. The threat of catholic domination receded.

But in Transylvania the Calvinist threat to Orthodoxy was replaced at the end of the seventeenth century by that of returning catholic power. After the siege of Vienna in 1683 the Turks were on the retreat in south-east Europe. Transylvania passed into the hands of the Habsburgs, and by 1696 ceased to have a prince of its own. The emperor Leopold confirmed the rights of the three nations (Hungarian, Saxon and Székely) and of the four received religions (catholic, Lutheran, Calvinist and unitarian), and left the Rumanians with their Orthodoxy merely a 'tolerated' religion. Jesuits soon set to work to create a Rumanian uniate church. In 1697 the Orthodox metropolitan Teofil was offered freedom from the supervision of the Calvinist superintendent, if he would accept union with the Roman church. However he died that summer and was succeeded in 1698 by Atanasie. When Atanasie went to Wallachia to be consecrated by the metropolitan, he was received with suspicion, but on swearing to preserve Orthodoxy as laid down in Petru Movila's confession of Orthodox faith and to observe other instructions prescribed by Dositheus, patriarch of Jerusalem, he received consecration.[23]

[21] *Ibid* p 22.
[22] *Ibid* p 58.
[23] *Ibid* p 97.

In April 1698 the emperor Leopold issued a diploma to the effect that Rumanian Orthodox priests who united with one of the received religions of Transylvania, would enjoy all the privileges that went with that religion, and in particular that those who acknowledged the pope as the head of the church would enjoy the privileges of the catholic clergy. In June the primate of Hungary, cardinal Kollonics, informed the Rumanian priests of the four points that they would have to accept if they became united: (i) the pope as head of the church, (ii) the use of unleavened bread for the eucharist, (iii) the *filioque* clause in the creed, (iv) the doctrine of purgatory.

In October 1698 thirty-eight Rumanian protopopes signed a document declaring their wish to become uniates. The document has been attacked on the ground that the Latin version contains points not mentioned in the Rumanian text, and that in this way the signatories were made to appear to have accepted the four points, although the Rumanian text contains the condition that none of the customs of the eastern church should be changed.[24] In February 1699 Leopold published a diploma formally establishing the Rumanian uniate church, with tax exemption for its property and that of its priests.

It was the Rumanian priests rather than their flocks that were tempted by the union, even though a diploma of 1701 promised that uniate laymen would have the privileges of catholics. Indeed there was so little acceptance of the union that in 1701 Atanasie was summoned to Vienna to appear before a judicial commission on which Kollonics sat. Under pressure he signed a document in which he undertook to break ties with the metropolitan and prince of Wallachia, to oblige his flock to accept the union, and to receive a catholic theologian as his assistant. Kollonics then re-ordained him priest and re-consecrated him bishop. A second diploma proclaimed that laymen who accepted the union would enjoy the same rights as members of the three 'nations'. This however provoked the diet of Transylvania to protest to the emperor that the Rumanians would in time become too powerful, and so this concession of first class citizenship was withheld.[25]

The metropolitan see of Alba Iulia was transformed into a uniate bishopric, and thereafter there was no Orthodox metropolitan in Transylvania till 1864. The new bishopric was dependent on the

[24] [*M.*] *Păcurariu* [*Istoria bisericii ortodoxe române*] (Sibiu 1972) p 204.
[25] *IBR*, 2, p 150.

primate of Hungary. Protests followed not only from Transylvanian Rumanians. Atanasie was excommunicated by the patriarchs of Constantinople and Jerusalem as well as by the metropolitan of Wallachia. He himself became disillusioned with the union and died in 1713. He was succeeded by Ioan Patachi, who had gone over to the Latin rite. In 1716, since there was already a see of the Latin rite at Alba Iulia, the uniate see was moved to Făgăraş. Patachi had no more success than Atanasie in consolidating the union. After his death in 1727 the synod of uniate priests elected Inochentie Micu. Micu was aged thirty-six and only in his third year of theological studies when he was elected, and was not installed as bishop till 1732. But from the start he showed himself vigorous. He complained to Vienna that the uniate clergy had not been given their promised privileges, and what is more, he claimed the status of 'nation' for his flock. In 1738 he moved the episcopal residence to the little town of Blaj. Continuing his independent line, he summoned a synod in 1744, at which he proposed that the union should be cast off if the imperial promises were not fulfilled. This synod included laymen and even members of the Orthodox church, being a national rather than a uniate gathering. Inochentie was summoned to Vienna to face a judicial commission and reply to eighty-two charges. He slipped away to Rome, where he lived until his death in 1768.[26]

He was succeeded by Petru Pavel Aron, who founded schools in Blaj, so that in time it became a cultural centre for Transylvanian Rumanians and contributed much to the awakening of Rumanian national consciousness in Transylvania, Wallachia and Moldavia. But in Aron's time, as in that of Inochentie, preaching campaigns against the union were conducted by Orthodox monks, and in 1760 Aron had to flee to Sibiu. It is evident that the union was losing ground. Between the years 1716 and 1762 the number of uniate priests dropped from 2747 to 2253, while that of Orthodox priests rose from 456 to 1380.[27] But a measure taken by the empress Maria Theresa countered the decline. It was the creation of militia regiments of Rumanians along the Carpathians to guard the frontier. To enrol as a militiaman brought exemption from serfdom, but an obligation to accept the union. Grigore Maior, the uniate bishop, who strongly supported this measure, claimed in a report to the emperor Joseph II that between 1762 and 1782 the Orthodox had lost 746 churches and 54,697 of their

[26] *Ibid* p 215.
[27] Păcurariu, p 258. Slightly different figures are given in *IBR*, 2, p 227.

flock.[28] But before the report reached Vienna, the emperor signed an edict of toleration. Any confession which had a hundred families could build itself a church, school and hospital. In the following year he permitted the rejection of membership of the uniate church. Many Rumanian uniates began to return to Orthodoxy. To this local authorities reacted by putting obstacles in their way. Finally with the death of Joseph in 1790 his reforms disappeared also.

From 1761 to 1796 those who filled the Orthodox see in Transylvania were Serbs. From 1796 to 1810 it was vacant. The government then allowed the election of Vasile Moga, a Rumanian whom they trusted to obey their stringent conditions. Moga's tenure lasted thirty-five years. When he died in 1845, he was succeeded by a very different sort of man, Andrei Şaguna. Şaguna's opportunity came after the disturbances of 1848 had created strong distrust at Vienna of the Hungarians. He worked for the restoration of the Orthodox metropolitan see in Transylvania. This was attained in 1864 when he became metropolitan with his residence at Sibiu.

Had the Austrian occupation of Oltenia in 1718 lasted longer, that part of Wallachia might also have suffered the same pressures as the Rumanians in Transylvania. But the Austrians withdrew in 1739. In fact there is very little to be said about relations of the Orthodox church in Wallachia and Moldavia with the west in the period 1650–1850. It may however be of interest to say something of the reception which the British and Foreign Bible Society's agent found there in the 1830s.[29]

At Constantinople in 1834 the newly appointed princes, Alexandru Ghica of Wallachia and Mihail Sturdza of Moldavia, invited the society's agent, Benjamin Barker, to visit their territories and point out the defects of their newly established Lancasterian schools. Barker did not at this stage open the subject of scripture translation, because he feared the influence of the Greeks with whom the princes were lodging. Later at Bucharest when he introduced the subject, Ghica was sympathetic and promised to speak to the triumvirate of bishops who were acting during the vacancy of the metropolitan see of Wallachia. The British consul told Barker that only the prince's consent mattered; the clergy could then offer no opposition. When Barker spoke to Sturdza at Jassy on the same subject, the Moldavian prince told him to

[28] *Ibid* p 321.
[29] E. D. Tappe, 'Rumania and the Bible Society until the Crimean War', *SEER*, 46, no 106 (January 1968) pp 91–104.

consult the metropolitan, Veniamin Costachi. The 'venerable old prelate', as Barker calls him, was most helpful and practical; he offered to print the scriptures for the society on his own press. In 1835, hearing rumours of a change of attitude at Bucharest, Barker went there again and found that the triumvirate were postponing their sanction because they feared that the society had some political end in view and that it might not give them a correct version of scripture. Barker therefore proposed that the most correct edition of the Rumanian new testament be reprinted at Smyrna without note or comment and that the sheets be corrected by a Wallachian scholar. This satisfied them. At the end of the interview the bishop of Argeş took Barker aside and said in a low voice smiling: 'The apostles were fishermen—the English are people of the sea—they are throwing their nets and one of these days they will catch also the Wallachians in them.'

The Society's edition of the new testament was printed in 1838. In Wallachia it was welcomed and distributed, the government deciding to make it a classbook in the Lancasterian schools. Not so in Moldavia. At Jassy the prince told Barker: 'Our metropolitan is a little prejudiced against the publications of your society, from what had transpired at Constantinople'. When Barker at last tracked down Veniamin Costachi at the monastery of Neamţu, the metropolitan refused to discuss the subject. Back in Jassy Barker was told by the prince that the metropolitan had received orders from the patriarchs of Constantinople not to permit any publications coming from the society to circulate in Moldavia. And in fact seven years later Barker reported that great efforts were made by the patriarch to stop the society's work in Wallachia.

After the political union of Wallachia and Moldavia in 1859 it was natural that their churches should also merge. A general synod was created in 1864, and the first primate of Rumania was Nifon, metropolitan of Wallachia, 1865. Similarly when the united principalities became a sovereign state, the kingdom of Rumania, as a result of the war of independence of 1877, it was natural that the Rumanian church should also seek independence. The autocephaly of the Rumanian church was recognised by the patriarch of Constantinople in 1885.

After the Habsburg dominions became a dual monarchy in 1867, Transylvania came under Hungarian rule. The Rumanian uniate church, which since 1853 had had a metropolitan of its own, found itself threatened with incorporation into the catholic church (of the Latin rite) in Hungary. The Vatican council of 1870 was used by the metropolitan and his fellow-delegates as an opportunity to put the case for the preservation of the eastern rite.[30] Nevertheless in Transylvania the conflict continued until the end of the century.

In 1918, as a result of the first world war, Transylvania and the Banat were united to the kingdom of Rumania. A year later one of the Orthodox bishops from the new territories, Miron Cristea, bishop of Caransebeş, was elected primate of Rumania. In 1920 he set up a constituent body to reorganise the Rumanian Orthodox church. Its work was completed in 1925, and in the same year Miron Cristea became the first patriarch of the autocephalous church of Rumania.

The greater Rumania created as a result of the first world war included so many catholics not only in Transylvania but in other new territories that a Rumanian legation was established at the Vatican and an apostolic nuncio sent to Bucharest. After several years of negotiation a concordat was signed in 1927.

In 1922 the patriarch Meletios IV of Constantinople informed the archbishop of Canterbury of the patriarchate's decision to recognise the validity of anglican orders. This decision was communicated to the Rumanian church, and in 1925 Miron Cristea answered Meletios' letter on behalf of the Rumanian synod. He asked that the anglican church should clarify its doctrine of the sacraments. Did it consider ordination a sacrament or not? A satisfactory answer was given in 1935. In June 1935 a conference was held at Bucharest between the Rumanian commission of relations with the anglican communion and a delegation of the church of England appointed by the archbishop of Canterbury and led by Nugent Hicks, bishop of Lincoln. In his introductory letter to the printed report Nugent Hicks stated: 'The Holy Synod unanimously approved the Report, and, in so doing, recognised the validity of Anglican orders.'[31] This was a first and notable landmark in the relations of the Rumanian Orthodox church and the church of England. In the following year the patriarch Miron Cristea visited the archbishop of Canterbury.

Already the dark clouds of the second world war were looming up. Taking up the story again in 1948, we find the communist regime firmly installed as a result of the Russian occupation. In the summer the vacancy left by the death of Miron Cristea was filled, Justinian Marina being enthroned as patriarch on 6 June. On 18 July the 1927 concordat

[30] *IBR*, 2, p 544.
[31] *Report of the Conference at Bucarest from June 1st to June 8th, 1935*, SPCK (London 1936).

with Rome was annulled by the state. October saw what is officially known as the 'reintegration' of the uniate church into the Rumanian Orthodox Church. 'The Romanian government decreed . . . that the $1\frac{1}{2}$ million Uniates were to return to the Orthodox fold, and that the Uniate Church in Romania had ceased to exist. Uniate monasteries and seminaries were closed, and parish churches were handed over to the Orthodox Church . . . All six bishops were arrested. By 1960 four bishops had died in prison . . . There is no longer an organised Uniate Church in Romania'.[32]

One may wonder how much this meant to the layman as opposed to the clergy of the uniate church. In a recent manual for theological seminaries of the Rumanian Orthodox church there is reprinted a passage from a book published in 1947 by Nicolae, Orthodox metropolitan of Sibiu. He speaks of a movement in Transylvania of uniates coming over to Orthodoxy and ascribes it to the contact of uniates and Orthodox in the state schools and in military service. Then he continues:

> Anyway the people know nothing of differences; they received no differences in belief when they became uniate . . . Even the priests make no difference. The *filioque* is not read in the creed even in the cathedral church of Blaj. The metropolitan of Blaj celebrates the holy communion just as I do at Sibiu. But the people would not accept the communion in the way the pure catholics do. It has happened in wartime that soldiers in the Austro-Hungarian army who belonged to the uniate church, lying ill in hospital, needed a priest and asked for communion. There being no uniate priest in the vicinity, the officers summoned to the sick man's bed the priest of the cult which they believed closest to the uniate, namely the catholic. When the catholic tried to communicate the Rumanians with the Host, the lads would say: 'Give me the Rumanian communion!' Of purgatory they know nothing, so what is left of the catholic faith? The pope. But the pope is a long way off.[33]

This must be taken with a certain reserve; it is an Orthodox hierarch that is writing, and he is partly drawing on reminiscences of thirty years before.

Not till the death of Stalin was there any hope that the Rumanian Orthodox church might resume relations with western churches.

---

[32] Trevor Beeson, *Discretion and Valour* (London 1974) p 309.
[33] Quoted from N. Balan, *Biserica şi viaţa* (Sibiu 1947) in Păcurariu, pp 348–9.

The Rumanian Orthodox church and the west

Since 1961 it has belonged to the world council of churches. Perhaps more than any other western church the church of England has had good relations with the Rumanian church; witness the visit of archbishop Ramsey to the patriarch Justinian in 1965 and the return visit of the patriarch here in 1966, as well as exchange of theological students and visits by anglican nuns to Rumanian convents. In general, as long as president Ceauşescu maintains his policy of making contacts all over the world—during his state visit to Italy in 1973 he had a meeting with pope Paul VI—it is likely that the Rumanian church will be allowed and even encouraged to maintain and perhaps extend its contacts with western churches.

University of London
School of Slavonic and East European Studies

ANGLICAN INTERVENTION IN THE ELECTION OF AN ORTHODOX PATRIARCH, 1925-6

by STUART MEWS

'I AM very sorry for being the instrument through which some of these unprincipled Greeks, for their own selfish aims, troubled our Archbishop';[1] in March 1926 Llewellyn H. Gwynne, anglican bishop in Egypt had good reason to feel sorry, though perhaps not quite as much reason as his critics supposed. His apparently maladroit intervention in the name of the archbishop of Canterbury in the election of a new Orthodox patriarch of Alexandria had been maliciously exploited to produce results entirely opposite to his intentions and caused serious embarrassment both to archbishop Davidson and to the British government. But his behaviour, though certainly injudicious, was not so entirely incomprehensible as it originally seemed. An examination of the episode in its context will not only explain Gwynne's behaviour but more importantly shed light upon the complex set of circumstances, attitudes and assumptions which have conditioned relations between Greek Orthodoxy and the church of England in the twentieth century. Any such relationship involves also the relations of centre and periphery, of personal ambitions, party objectives, strategic processes and the larger international religious systems of anglicanism and orthodoxy.

Before 1914 anglicans had had little contact with the Greek church, which to outsiders looked conservative, complacent and self-contained. It was the first world war, which threw everything into the melting-pot and created circumstances in both England and Greece which were particularly favourable to the opening of dialogue.[2] It was a dialogue which was promoted on both sides from a mixture of motives. Noble

---

[1] Lambeth [Palace Library]: [J. A.] Douglas MS 34/224 L. H. Gwynne—J. A. Douglas 19 March 1926.

[2] [Nicolas] Zernov, ['The Eastern Churches and the Ecumenical Movement in the Twentieth Century'], in [*A History of the Ecumenical Movement 1517-1948*, ed Ruth] Rouse and [Stephen C.] Neill (London 1954) p 645. For a useful history of the relations between the church of England and the orthodox church: V. T. Istavridis, *Orthodoxy and Anglicanism* (London 1966).

aspirations after church unity coincided, on both sides, with more immediate but less exalted objectives. In England one effect of the war had been to create a climate in which Roman ceremonial and doctrine were spreading rapidly amongst younger Anglo-catholic clergy. Older high churchmen like bishops Gore and Talbot, and Athelstan Riley of the English Church Union, were quick to grasp the opportunities provided by anglican-orthodox rapprochement to counter a development which they found deeply disturbing.[3] In January 1918 Riley pointed out to the archbishop of Canterbury that 'anything approaching reunion between ourselves and the Easterns involving incidentally, but inevitably, the recognition of our Orders by the Eastern Church, would deal Roman propaganda amongst Anglicans, now very active and, as we have abundant reason to know, successful, the most severe blow conceivable. The argument of isolation from Catholic Christendom is one of the most potent now used by Rome.'[4]

In Greece the war and its aftermath provided the opportunity for reformers to take over leadership of the church. The national schism between the supporters of Eleftherios Venizelos and king Constantine over Greek participation in the war affected every part of the nation's life, including the church. It was a dispute which, as Michael Llewellyn Smith has pointed out, originated in 'a radical difference over the issue of war or neutrality, reflecting a broad difference in psychology between those who shared Venizelos's vision of an expanding, dynamic Greece actively associated with England, and those whose attitude to the outside world was narrow, suspicious and defensive'.[5] Clerics who shared Venizelist aspirations had their chance to translate them into reality in the ecclesiastical sphere in the period after 1917 when king Constantine went into exile, pro-royalist bishops were deposed and their sees filled by government supporters. The new metropolitan of Athens, Meletios Metaxakis, was an ardent Venizelist and enthusiast for church reform, a process which he felt would be assisted by contact with the churches of the west. Although some of his reforms aroused passionate popular opposition, the permission given to priests to cut and trim their hair and beards, for example, provoked a debate in the Athens press said to recall 'the great days of Byzantine

---

[3] T. B. Strong—Edward Lyttelton 16 January 1919, Harold Anson, *T. B. Strong* (London 1949) pp 104–6.

[4] [Lambeth: archbishop] Davidson MS: memorandum by Athelstan Riley 1 January 1919 p 8.

[5] [Michael Llewellyn] Smith, [*Ionian Vision: Greece in Asia Minor 1919–1922*] (London 1973) pp 54 *seq.*

ecclesiastical subtleties chronicled by Gibbon and Finlay',[6] he pressed on regardless. In October 1918 Meletios came to Britain, took part in a conference at Oxford, dined at Lambeth palace with the archbishop of Canterbury, and addressed a public meeting at Westminster central hall. This visit created considerable ecumenical goodwill, but was also part of an energetic and pervasive propaganda drive to influence the British government into supporting Greek claims at the forthcoming Paris peace conference, and more specifically to secure the return of Santa Sophia to Christian hands.[7]

In the immediate post-war years relations between anglicans and the more liberal section of Greek Orthodoxy blossomed, and Meletios through all the ups and downs of his career did everything possible to nurture them, even succeeding during his brief reign as ecumenical patriarch to secure the economic recognition of anglican orders by his holy synod in Constantinople in July 1922.[8] It seemed to many to be a precipitate action taken in circumstances which did not provide much opportunity for cool reflection. For Meletios was in despair, his political hopes had crashed, the Turks were at the gate, his own position was being rapidly undermined, the government of Athens recognizing a rival synod in Constantinople: 'It is certain', he wrote to Venizelos, in April, 1922, 'that all of us here and in Smyrna and in Athens are struggling in the dark and hitting out at friends and enemies without any definite aim any more, since we are desperately divided even in our conception of the general interest of the country.'[9] In such circumstances, the recognition of anglican orders, however limited, even though a matter which had been under discussion for some years, could be too easily dismissed as either a thank-offering for past British help, or as an attempt to gain British goodwill and possibly intervention, or as a final attempt to demonstrate patriarchal authority. Whatever the motive, within twelve months Meletios was forced out of Constantinople by the Turks and shortly afterwards resigned as ecumenical patriarch.[10] It looked like the end of a brief but eventful career even though J. A. Douglas the anglican expert on orthodoxy

[6] Davidson MS (copy): Claud Russell—lord Curzon 22 August 1919.
[7] Ronald Jasper, *Arthur Cayley Headlam. Life and letters of a Bishop* (London 1960) pp 156 *seq.*; [G. K. A.] Bell, [*Randall Davidson*], 2 (London 1935) pp 941, 1088; Dimitri Kitsikis, *Propagande et pressions en politique internationale. La Grèce et ses revendications à la Conférence de la Paix (1919–1920)* (Paris 1963) pp 436–52.
[8] Bell pp 1106 *seq.*
[9] Venizelos MS 316: Meletios—E. Venizelos 25 April 1922, Smith p 269.
[10] Harry J. Psomiades, 'The Ecumenical Patriarchate under the Turkish Republic', *Balkan Studies* 2 (Thessalonika 1961) pp 47–70.

insisted in the *Church Times* that it was 'unlikely that so liberal, vigorous and popular a prelate will long remain in retirement'.[11]

Meletios's decision on anglican orders was also accepted in 1923 by the patriarchate of Jerusalem and the church of Cyprus, but not by the remaining patriarchates of Alexandria, Antioch and Russia or the other autocephalous churches. Alexandria was second in rank to Constantinople and its patriarch, the elderly Photios was anti-Venizelist and pro-Constantine, had been thought to favour the Germans during the war, and was a consistent opponent of Meletios and all his works.[12] Photios had been the only patriarch to accept the removal of Meletios as metropolitan of Athens and the restoration of the previous occupant in 1920.[13] He belonged to that party which regarded the election to the ecumenical patriarchate in 1921 as invalid, and consequently insisted that 'any private opinions of Meletios and the Patriarch of Jerusalem did not represent the Orthodox Church as a whole'.[14] In 1925 he told Rennie McInnes, anglican bishop in Jerusalem, that he had been prejudiced against Meletios because he had believed his reforms to have been inspired by anglicans. Although disabused of that idea, Photios nevertheless felt that in both his programme of reform and attitude to anglican orders Meletios had acted wrongly in not having consulted the other patriarchs before publishing his decisions; they were matters for a general synod of the church.[15]

In the years between 1922 and 1925 the patriarch of Alexandria's hostility to the church of England was gradually eroded. Bishop McInnes had assured him that 'no sensible Anglican would be guilty of interference in the affairs of another Church',[16] but the main factor in overcoming suspicion was the Fellowship of Unity set up in Cairo by canon Temple Gairdner and the anglican bishop in Egypt, Llewellyn H. Gwynne, after the latter's return from the Lambeth conference of 1920.[17]

[11] C[hurch] T[imes] 2 November 1923. J. A. Douglas, vicar of St. Luke, Camberwell, had been an enthusiast for anglican-orthodox understanding ever since his brief stay as acting anglican chaplain at Constantinople 1904–5. He was regarded by W. R. Matthews as 'eccentric': *Memories and Meanings* (London 1969) p 311.

[12] Douglas MS 14/8 L. H. Gwynne—J. A. Douglas 12 November 1923; 14/10 L. H. Gwynne—J. A. Douglas 2 November 1923.

[13] CT 15 December 1921.

[14] Douglas MS 14/8 L. H. Gwynne—J. A. Douglas 12 November 1923; 14/10 L. H. Gwynne—J. A. Douglas 2 November 1923.

[15] Douglas MS 34/92 R. McInnes—Mervyn Haigh 25 May 1925.

[16] Ibid.

[17] Zernov p 652; CT 11 September 1925; Constance E. Padwick, *Temple Gairdner of Cairo* (London 1929) pp 266–9.

Llewellyn Gwynne was an evangelical and an imperialist, a man whose philosophy was said to have been determined by 'an intimate study of the Bible and the writings of Rudyard Kipling'.[18] He was also simple and saintly, a humble man with a keen sense of humour. He had been a great success as deputy chaplain-general in the first world war and his experience in France with all sorts and conditions of men had turned him into an active and dedicated supporter of the ecumenical movement. 'We must dare to scrap that which is out of date and effete in our methods', he wrote in 1917, 'so as to be able to mobilise and unify the enormous Christian resources now lying fallow'.[19] Unlike high churchmen in England, Gwynne had no romantic illusions about Greek orthodoxy. In 1922 he had welcomed the statement from Constantinople about anglican orders but pointed out to J. A. Douglas that 'Greek laymen of any standing urge their ecclesiastical representatives to get in touch with the Church of England' in the belief that it 'has a great power and influence with the British government'.[20] In 1924 he explained that in his experience over twenty-four years:

> I find that these Greek ecclesiastics cannot understand our going to them, cap in hand, begging them to acknowledge Anglican Orders . . . They have no missionary spirit. They keep in watertight compartments and are terrified of anyone having any spiritual hold on their people . . .
>
> I honestly believe what one of the suite of Archbishop Doamotakos [*sic*] stated privately during the Lambeth Conference to be true about the Greek Orthodox and other Eastern Churches: 'If', he said, 'England could get St. Sophia for us, we would gladly acknowledge any orders and agree to almost any doctrine', and I am under no misapprehension that one of the chief factors in being able to influence the representatives of the Eastern Churches is that they believe our Church has great political power.

But he added, 'I am content to make use of that lever if by God's grace we can be of any help to them'—fine paternalist sentiments indeed.[21] It is evident that Gwynne's desire was to see the

[18] H. C. Jackson, *Pastor on the Nile; The Life and Letters of Llewellyn H. Gwynne* (London 1960) p 252.
[19] L. H. Gwynne, 'Preface', *The Church in the Furnace*, ed F. B. MacNutt (London 1917) p xx.
[20] Douglas MS 14/13 L. H. Gwynne—J. A. Douglas 3 October 1922.
[21] *Ibid* 14/14 L. H. Gwynne—J. A. Douglas 15 March 1924.

Greek Orthodox church modernised and mobilised so that it could be effectively deployed in the Christian conquest of Egypt and the Sudan.

Gwynne's 'best and most useful Greek Orthodox friend' was Nicolas, metropolitan of Nubia, an enlightened and scholarly man with some knowledge of anglican ways and doctrine.[22] In 1925 Photios and Nicolas were amongst the Orthodox delegates to visit London for the 1,600th anniversary of the council of Nicaea and they then went on to the Stockholm conference on life and work. It was on the way back from Stockholm that patriarch Photios died.[23]

The death of Photios created a difficult and delicate situation. Bishop Gwynne was deeply disturbed by the possibility that the appointment of a new patriarch of conservative inclinations would destroy his careful and patient efforts at bridge-building just when they seemed to be making progress. When contemplating the possible alternatives, his thoughts turned inevitably to Nicolas of Nubia. 'Unless Nubia is made Patriarch—we shall have to begin our work all over again.'[24]

Unfortunately Gwynne was not the man to stand aside and allow events to take their course. 'Having made up my mind that Nicolas was our man . . . I set to, to use all the influence I could to get him elected'.[25] 'As you know', he wrote to J. A. Douglas, 'I hate pulling strings from fear that we may thwart the will of God, but it steems to me that all the reactionary forces are at work while poor Nubia has been engaged in Europe, and we ought to see that Nubia has fair play and his splendid qualifications at least considered'.[26]

There is some doubt about the lengths to which Gwynne was prepared to go. He certainly wrote to the archbishop of Canterbury asking him to see the Greek ambassador in London, and he did approach the British residency in Cairo to ask them to see the resident Greek minister.[27] On 2 December 1925 he was satisfied that 'Nubia is well in the running for the Patriarchate. All the forces we can marshal are being arrayed on his side. Unless anything unforeseen happens (and

[22] *Ibid* 14/1 L. H. Gwynne—J. A. Douglas 22 January 1921; 14/3 L. H. Gwynne—J. A. Douglas 2 March 1922.

[23] Bell pp 1112–14; Nils Ehrenström, 'Movements for International Friendship and Life and Work, 1925–1948', Rouse and Neill pp 546 *seq.*

[24] Douglas MS 34/116 L. H. Gwynne—J. A. Douglas 25 September 1925.

[25] *Ibid* 34/207 L. H. Gwynne—J. A. Douglas 11 February 1926.

[26] *Ibid* 34/116 L. H. Gwynne—J. A. Douglas 25 September 1925.

[27] *Ibid*; PRO FO 371/10911 J. Murray—chaplain of archbishop of Canterbury 15 October 1925.

you never know with these Greek ecclesiastics what may happen) Nicolas will be appointed Patriarch in February'.[28]

The bishop's confidence was, however, misplaced and something utterly unforeseen, at least by Gwynne, did happen, partly due to the emergence of a new candidate with powerful backing, the ex-patriarch Meletios Metaxakis. 'The great man the patriarch Meletios must reenter the activ [*sic*] role', wrote the metropolitan of Mitileni, 'the occasion is here'. In view of the fact that the metropolitan was clearly angling for Lambeth backing for Meletios, as well as that of the *Times* and *Church Times*, it was somewhat ironic that he should have been one of the most vigorous protesters against the so-called anglican intervention in December. He then alleged that bishop Gwynne had informed the president of the Greek community in Cairo that the British administration wanted the election of Nicolas, who was a personal friend of the archbishop of Canterbury, and that his election would be in the best interests of hellenism in Egypt. It was also claimed that when the merits of Meletios were pointed out to the bishop, he had replied, 'Yes, but he is political'.[29]

On 9 December 1925 Meletios himself asked archbishop Germanos, exarch of the ecumenical patriarchate in the west, to draw the archbishop of Canterbury's attention to the 'infelicitous action' of bishop Gwynne, which he felt certain was a purely personal move 'but it was so maladroit as to have already disturbed the consciences of the laity of the Church'. Already one of the other candidates for the vacant see had complained to the Greek government 'and all my letters from Egypt in these days speak with indignation of this interference of foreigners in the affairs of the Church and I am afraid we shall have a popular outburst of such sentiments'. Writing to J. A. Douglas, Meletios claimed to have received many letters speaking of the σκάνδαλον τοῦ 'Επισκόπου Gwyn [*sic*], and that if Nicolas of Nubia was elected he would be denounced as ἐκλεκτὸς τῶν προτεσταντῶν.[30]

Meletios went on to paint a dismal picture of possible future developments. He feared that Gwynne's behaviour would encourage further action by the Egyptian government which had already stepped in to prevent the synod of bishops proceeding to an election in October. Rumours that an election was imminent had produced an outcry from

---

[28] Douglas MS 34/118 L. H. Gwynne—J. A. Douglas 2 December 1925.

[29] *Ibid* 34/118 Takouos—J. A. Douglas 12 September 1925; 34/105 Takouos—J. A. Douglas 14 December 1925.

[30] *Ibid* 34/122 Meletios—Germanos 7 December 1925; 34/125 Meletios—J. A. Douglas 16 December 1925.

the Greek laity who insisted that they should have a voice in this
election as they had had in that of the late patriarch, but there were
suspicions (which were quite unfounded) that the government had
acted on the promptings of a British government which did not like
the look of what might emerge.[31]

It appears that in the synod of bishops, after much conflict, the issue
became narrowed between Meletios as the candidate of the 'advanced
reformers' and republicans, and Chrysostom, metropolitan of
Trebizond, the choice of the royalists and moderate conservatives.
This was not the first time the two men had been in competition. In
1921 Chrysostom had travelled to London in an unsuccessful attempt
to persuade the archbishop of Canterbury that the election of Meletios
as ecumenical patriarch was uncanonical and that he should not be
recognised.

Early in November 1926, archbishop Germanos (who had not been
consulted) was put forward as a compromise candidate, and the synod
was all set to vote on these three names when the government, allegedly
in the interests of the Greek laity intervened.[32] It is, of course, possible
that Germanos was hurriedly brought forward in an attempt to fore-
stall government intervention. There are certainly clear indications
that the leading lights in the Greek community in Alexandria were
appalled by the polarisation between Meletios and Chrysostom which
threatened to bring into the open again the bitter factionalism which
still existed in the Greek colony. Whether it was at Gwynne's
prompting, or an independent decision of their own, it seems that the
lay leaders of the Alexandrian community had come to the conclusion
that Nicolas of Nubia was the safest choice.[33]

The Greek laity had good reason for apprehension. There were
only 62,000 Greeks in Egypt, mostly living in Alexandria and Cairo,
many of them only second generation immigrants, their fathers having
been attracted by the commercial possibilities of the cotton boom of
1861–6. Lord Cromer had divided the colony into two distinct classes:
high class, sophisticated Greeks from families which had prospered
through the cotton trade and who had 'as of old, carried high the torch
of civilisation in their adopted country', and low class Greek usurers,
drink-sellers and general dealers, who were to be found in almost every

---

[31] *Ibid.*
[32] *Ibid* 34/128 memorandum for the archbishop of Canterbury by J. A. Douglas
29 December 1925.
[33] *Le Messager d'Athènes* (Athens) 12 January 1926.

village: 'He tempts the Egyptian peasant to borrow at some exorbitant rate of interest, and then, by a sharp turn of the legal screw, reduces him from the position of an allodial proprietor to that of a serf. He undermines the moral quality of which the Moslem, when untainted by European association, has in some degree a speciality. That quality is sobriety.' This latter class of Greeks, thought Cromer, should be cleared out 'bag and baggage', a sentiment which many Egyptian nationalists extended to the entire Greek colony.[34]

In 1926 the Greeks of Egypt were wise to be cautious. Allenby's 1922 declaration, though giving Egypt a qualified independence, had turned its politics into a triangle of forces in which power was shared in an imprecise way between the British residency, the Turkish king, and the nationalist Wafd.[35] Nationalist aspirations were rising and this was not the time for the Greek minority to draw attention to itself, either by engaging in bitter factionalism or by taking the provocative step of electing a patriarch like Meletios who was persona non grata in the Moslem world. In these circumstances the effect of Gwynne's alleged indiscretions was not obviously counter-productive. Although there were Greeks who loathed the British for regulating the rates of interest which they could exact, most of them recognised what had been clearly demonstrated in 1854, that Britain alone would guarantee their security and safety.[36] There were times when it was prudent to be agreeable to the British residency, and after all, Greeks brought up under the Ottoman empire were used to governments taking an active interest in patriarchal elections. The reply of the Greek minister at Alexandria, Delmouzos, to a request from the residency for support for Nicolas was polite and conciliatory, and predicted his 'practically certain' election, perhaps a reasonable inference in Alexandria where the president of the community, Mike Salvazo, was a leading supporter.[37] Perhaps the mistake of Gwynne and the British residency was in pushing their candidate too hard and so arousing resentment. J. A. Douglas had quietly seen some prominent Greeks in London and

[34] [Gabriel Baer, 'Social Change in Egypt: 1800–1914', *Political and Social Change in Modern Egypt*, ed P. M.] Holt (London 1968) pp 158, 160; E. R. J. Owen, *Cotton and the Egyptian Economy 1820–1914* (Oxford 1969) p 113; [Earl of] Cromer, [*Modern Egypt*], 2 (London 1908) pp 250–2; Steven Runciman, *The Orthodox Church and the Secular State* (Auckland/Oxford 1971) p 77. For a detailed treatment: A. G. Politis, *L'Hellénisme et l'Egypte moderne*, 2 vols (Paris 1928–30).

[35] Tom Little, *Egypt* (London 1958) p 143.

[36] Ahmed Abdel-Rahim Mustafa, 'The breakdown of the monopoly system in Egypt after 1840', Holt p 303; Cromer p 256.

[37] FO 371/10911 A. Delmouzos—A. Wiggin 3 November 1925.

Paris, among them the president of the Greek Khartoum community, 'but while they took careful note . . . they were all emphatic as to the unwisdom of letting it be known that even I in my *humility* . . . had taken even that action'. But Douglas's public show of neutrality was hardly helped by Sidney Dark, editor of the *Church Times*, who 'calmly added a note to an article I wrote for him and which appeared over my initials that Nubia was the probable choice. This caused a flurry in the Near-East and in London Greek circles'.[38]

In a memorandum to the archbishop of Canterbury, Douglas stressed that the election presented not just a little local difficulty. It had aroused the interest of the whole Orthodox world as well as that of the Greek and Egyptian political parties. 'Different strains met in suppressed but acute conflict and the position resembles that of a protracted petty Papal Conclave, in which each interest plays for position and there are many cross currents'. He listed seven of the interests involved: the extreme ecclesiastical reformers, who approved Meletios's *'precipitate* reform Conference of 1923', moderate reformers who wanted to proceed only when general agreement had been reached, and conservatives. On the political side, Greeks were still divided between royalists and their opponents, while in Egypt there were nationalist and Anglophile groups.

The Egyptian government's insistence on the selection of a provisional list of candidates for submission to the synod by an assembly of lay and clerical delegates, representing the various Greek communities and institutions (like chambers of commerce), provided the opportunity for the emergence of new candidates to champion those interests passed over in the synod. Nicolas of Nubia was now brought forward as the choice of the Anglophile Egyptian government-al people, the metropolitan of Tripoli represented the less Anglophile Egyptians, the metropolitan of Leontopolis the very conservative and more Zaglulist Greeks of Egypt, while the ex-patriarch Constantine, Meletios's unfortunate successor as ecumenical patriarch, forced to resign by the Turks in 1924, was the official candidate of the Greek government. Ecclesiastically, Nicolas was reported to be a moderate reformer, though too partial to anglicanism for some, while the other three additional candidates were elderly bishops of limited outlook.[39]

Douglas also hoped that Nicolas would be the new patriarch, though Germanos would be equally acceptable. He feared the effect on the unity of the orthodox church of the election of Meletios. 'Personally,

[38] Douglas MS 34/131 Memorandum.   [39] *Ibid.*

I love the *man* but his brusquerie in self assertion and failure to consult other hierarchs before proposing reforms have created a personal opposition to him which is irreconcilable'.[40] But if Meletios's record seemed to rule him out for any future role as a reconciler of the anglican and Orthodox churches, it was equally possible, as Meletios pointed out, that the manner of Nicolas's election would render him equally useless. The king of Egypt had the right to intervene and strike out the names of unacceptable candidates. If he agreed with Gwynne, and then struck out all the candidates except Nicolas, lasting damage would be done to relations between the churches. And if Nicolas did become patriarch, the circumstances of his election would make any ecumenical initiatives by him look like 'the payment of a personal debt'.[41]

The archbishop of Canterbury was sorely troubled by these developments: 'Gwynne is the best of men, but not perhaps always the wisest or the most discreet as to exactly what he says'.[42] At least the archbishop was prepared to be charitable unlike W. A. Wigram, chaplain to the British legation in Athens who roundly condemned 'fools who rush in where angels fear to tread. Gwynne has acted like an entirely well-meaning and most pious, bull in a china shop'.[43] But what, if anything, was to be done? The archbishop's normal maxim in such circumstances was 'least said, soonest mended', but the possibility of lasting misunderstanding and the alienation of Orthodox church leaders led him to sanction a letter which Douglas proposed sending to Meletios, with copies to several other leading bishops, asserting that Lambeth did not favour any particular candidate.[44] In order to restrain Meletios from publishing it, Douglas referred to the dispute over the election to the ecumenical patriarchate in 1921 and the absurd allegation made by a French Jesuit that the archbishop of Canterbury had on that occasion worked furiously for Meletios's election.[45] Unfortunately this attempt to pour oil on troubled waters had rather the effect of adding petrol to the flames. A re-translated and much garbled version of the letter, under a different date, with the first paragraph removed, was

[40] *Ibid.*
[41] *Ibid* 34/122 Meletios—Germanos 9 December 1925.
[42] *Ibid* 18/318 R. T. Davidson—J. A. Douglas 23 December 1925.
[43] *Ibid* 34/165 W. A. Wigram—J. A. Douglas 1 January 1926. Wigram was a high churchman who had previously worked with the non-proselytising archbishops' mission to the assyrian Christians.
[44] *Ibid* 18/319, 320 R. T. Davidson—J. A. Douglas 29, 31 December 1925; 34/156 J. A. Douglas—R. T. Davidson 31 December 1925.
[45] *Ibid* 34/160 J. A. Douglas—Meletios 3 January 1926.

soon circulating freely in Egypt and the Sudan. Its appearance totally undermined the credibility of bishop Gwynne and the British residency, which cabled frantically to the foreign office for advice.[46]

It is in the foreign office papers that we can see what had really been happening. Gwynne's original letter to the British residency in Cairo had been sent to the foreign office who had contacted archbishop Davidson. The archbishop did not request British intervention, but in a somewhat cautious reply, simply conceded that 'if therefore it is appropriate to use any influence in the matter I should share Bishop Gwynne's desire that it should be used in favour of Nubia'.[47] It was unfortunate that the foreign office misunderstood the archbishop's wishes and telegraphed a rather more emphatic reply to the residency: 'Archbishop of Canterbury would welcome the appointment of the Metropolitan of Nubia. You should accordingly use your discretion as to the means best calculated to promote the election of this candidate'.[48] On the basis of this telegram, both bishop Gwynne and the staff of the residency felt justified in using the archbishop's name, and discreetly canvassing in Nubia's interest, though most of the canvassing was done by the diplomats not the bishop.[49] Both were justifiably annoyed when the letter of Douglas specifically dissociated the archbishop from any use of his name in the election.[50]

When the assembly met in February 1926, Nicolas topped the poll with ninety-seven votes against seventy-three cast for Meletios while eighty-eight votes were cast for the other candidates.[51] The list then went to the Egyptian government, which to the great indignation of the Greeks, returned it minus the names of three of the leading contenders: Meletios and Chrysostom were rejected on political grounds, and Nicolas was removed because of a charge of moral misconduct which had been brought against him in 1911 even though it had been investigated by the synod at the time and dismissed.[52] Various explanations were offered for the government's behaviour, which relied upon Ottoman precedents of some validity in the days when the patriarch possessed enormous political power, but were

[46] FO 371/11595/102 N. Henderson—J. Murray 24 January 1926; FO 371/11595/99 S. Gaselee—N. Henderson 4 February 1926.
[47] FO 371/10911/126 J. Murray—chaplain of the archbishop of Canterbury 15 October 1925; FO 371/10911/129 R. T. Davidson—J. Murray 20 October 1925.
[48] FO 371/10911 cypher telegram—Sir George Lloyd 23 October 1925.
[49] FO 371/11595/102 N. Henderson—J. Murray 24 January 1926.
[50] FO J486/140/16 telegram Sir George Lloyd—foreign office 26 February 1926.
[51] *Times* 12 February 1926.
[52] FO J486/140/16 lord Lloyd—foreign office 26 February 1926.

utterly anachronistic in 1926. It was said by some that the king had been prompted by corrupt Egyptian officials who expected the disqualified candidates to be willing to pay for their restoration, and certainly Gwynne alleged that Nicolas was being blackmailed, but had begun legal proceedings against his traducer.[53]

The Greek community, which a few months before, had been warning against British intervention in the election, now invoked the declaration of 1922 which guaranteed the protection of minorities, to demand it, and J. A. Douglas harried lord Hugh Cecil, MP for the university of Oxford, to get a debate in parliament. But by this time the foreign office was rather tired of Douglas, who was the most convenient scapegoat for their earlier incompetence, and regarded his attempts to publicise the Egyptian government's intervention as counter-productive.[54]

The residency managed to persuade the Egyptian prime minister to hold back the formal letter to the synod,[55] and the matter was considered by the British foreign secretary, Austen Chamberlain. His compromise solution was to suggest the withdrawal of the vetoes against two of the three candidates: 'I do not think that you are called upon to interfere on behalf of Meletios'.[56] But from Cairo, lord Lloyd argued that the removal only of Meletios would mean a certain victory for Nicolas, provided he won his court case. The victory of the British government's candidate in these circumstances, however, would alienate the large following which Meletios undoubtedly had in Egypt and Greece. Lloyd, therefore pressed for the removal of the disqualification on all three candidates, and the Egyptian prime minister agreed, though insisting on their right to vet the list, and the demand that the successful candidate should, if necessary, acquire Egyptian nationality.[57]

[53] Douglas MS 34/210 J. A. Douglas—lord Hugh Cecil 18 February 1926; 34/224 L. H. Gwynne—J. A. Douglas 19 March 1926.
[54] FO J486/140/16 lord Lloyd—foreign office 25 February 1926; Douglas MS 34/210 J. A. Douglas—lord Hugh Cecil 18 February 1926.
[55] FO J486/140/16 lord Lloyd—foreign office 25 February 1926.
[56] *Ibid*. Note by Austen Chamberlain 1 March 1926. Chamberlain's opinion was based on an earlier note by the foreign office's resident pundit on orthodoxy, Stephen Gaselee, who thought that the Egyptians had valid grounds for opposing Meletios: 'He is something of a fire-brand, and a terrific pan-Hellene; his attitude as Patriarch of Constantinople during the Greek invasion of Asia Minor and their subsequent repulse so incensed the Turks that he very nearly brought the Oecumenical Patriarchate entirely to an end, at any rate as resident in Constantinople'.
[57] Douglas MS 34/229 memorandum by J. A. Douglas nd; FO 371/11596/142 lord Lloyd —foreign office 12 March 1926.

Meanwhile Meletios had won golden opinions by nobly announcing the withdrawal of his candidature in the interests of peace.[58] However, when the list was returned with his name still on it, he did not take any active steps to remove it, and the British minister refused to accept the suggestion of the Greek minister that his name should be crossed off on the strength of newspaper reports of his withdrawal.[59] The result was that on 20 May 1926, Meletios Metaxakis was elected patriarch of Alexandria with one hundred and thirty-eight votes against one hundred and twenty-two cast for Nicolas of Nubia, 'a result which', as a foreign office official noted, 'pleases neither us, nor the Egyptian government nor the Greek government, so that our intervention has not been very happy'.[60]

The ecclesiastical consequences could not, however, be described as unhappy. After a decent interval, the patriarchate of Alexandria recognised anglican orders in 1930. Meletios established a good working relationship with Nicolas, who had won his action, and became the patriarch's right-hand man and eventual successor in 1936.[61] When the result was announced in May 1926, the archbishop of Canterbury was too busy following up the initiative he had taken in the general strike to be much interested in Alexandria,[62] but J. A. Douglas took it in his stride, invited Meletios to London, and continued his indefatigable labours for anglican-orthodox understanding. Only bishop Gwynne seemed to have found the whole episode deeply disturbing. 'Whoever sups with the Devil needs a long spoon', he wrote to Douglas in March, 'Never have I come across such roguery and deception as has been displayed by the Greeks in this matter of the Patriarchate'.[63] But the incident required a phenomenological rather than a theological explanation. He would have been better to leave the devil out of the matter and restrict himself to his observation of February that 'the Greeks are very difficult people to understand and their ideas of playing the game are not ours'.[64]

University of Lancaster

[58] *Messager d'Athènes* 12 March 1926.
[59] FO 371/11596 memorandum by A. Wiggin 14 May 1926.
[60] FO J1191/140/16 note by S. Gaselee.
[61] *CT* 16 January 1931, 11 February 1936.
[62] Stuart Mews, 'The Churches', *The General Strike,* ed Margaret Morris (London 1976) pp 318–37.
[63] Douglas MS 34/224 L. H. Gwynne—J. A. Douglas 19 March 1926.
[64] *Ibid* 34/207 L. H. Gwynne—J. A. Douglas 11 February 1926.

THE SIGNIFICANCE OF THE RUSSIAN ORTHODOX DIASPORA AND ITS EFFECT ON THE CHRISTIAN WEST

by NICOLAS ZERNOV

THE enforced emigrations caused by political or religious conflicts have often been an enriching and stimulating factor in the cultural history of mankind.

Lenin's dictatorship based on red terror forced more than a million Russians to flee from their own country and settle down in various parts of the world.[1] The Russian diaspora included a great variety of people, among them many well-known men. It will suffice to mention a few names: Ivan Bunin (1870–1953), Dimitry Merezhkovsky (1865–1941) in literature; Sergy Rachmaninov (1873–1943) and Igor Stravinsky (1882–1971) in music; Vasily Kandinsky (1866–1944) in painting; Fedor Chaliapin (1873–1938) and Anna Pavlova (1881–1931) in the theatre; Mikhail Rostovtsev (1870–1952) and Georgy Vernadsky (1887–1973) in history; Igor Sikorsky (1889–1972) in aviation; Nikolay Menschokov (b. 1900) in geology. All these people made a substantial contribution to the contemporary world of art and learning.

Looking back on the various achievements of the Russian exiles one can say, however, that their greatest and most lasting gift was in the sphere of religious and philosophical thought. At the time when the soviet authorities were sparing no efforts to de-Christianise the population under their control, the exiles contained a remarkable group of outstanding thinkers who analysed the causes of the disintegration of our civilisation and proposed remedies for its recovery. Their writings are of substantial value both for the preservation of Christian culture in their own country and for the church at large.[2] The purpose of this paper is to study the ecclesiastical position of the Russian diaspora, to analyse its message and its reception among western Christians and in Russia itself.

I should like to start with a short description of the Russian church on the eve of the revolution.

[1] According to the statistics of the league of nations, two million one hundred thousand Russians left Russia before 1926.

[2] See [N.] Zernov, [*Russian*] *Emigré Authors* [*on Theology and Orthodox Culture*] (Boston 1973).

I

THE RUSSIAN CHURCH ON THE EVE OF THE REVOLUTION

The Russian Orthodox church at the beginning of the twentieth century was the largest national church in the world. It numbered some eighty-eight million members including more than one hundred thousand clergy and ninety-five thousand monks and nuns distributed among one thousand and twenty-five religious houses. Seventy percent of the inhabitants of the empire belonged to the Russian church.[3] These millions of Orthodox were all baptised, married and buried by the church and the vast majority went to confession, received holy communion and participated in many other ways in the life of this Christian community. It can be said that the entire life of the Russian people was permeated by the rites, customs and traditions of Orthodoxy. Church feasts were national holidays; the fasts were universally observed; the celebration of Christ's resurrection was an event in which the whole population took an active part. Pilgrimages to holy shrines attracted crowds forty to fifty thousand strong. The church could easily have appeared to an outsider as a grandiose edifice crowning the mighty empire, which covered one sixth of the earth's surface.

But behind this impressive façade lurked many distressing signs of decay and disintegration. The upper, westernised classes were alienated from the church, regarding it mainly as part of a picturesque national heritage. The church's worship and teaching seemed to them to be suitable for simple-minded peasants but as having no significance for the educated. The radical wing of the intelligentsia was openly hostile to the church, accusing it of being a mere appendix to the autocratic rule of the tsars and a hindrance to the social and economic progress of the nation.

There was also dissatisfaction with the church among the peasants and artisans whom various sects attracted. Furthermore, many of the most devout Orthodox were 'Old Believers', who had kept apart from the established church since the great schism of the seventeenth century. The Orthodox church was thus a puzzling body. It was at the same time the source of inspiration and purification for many millions of its faithful members and yet it provoked bitter animosity and sharp criticism among other Russians.

[3] For statistics see G. Simon, *Church, State and Opposition in the USSR* (London 1974) pp 4–5.

Superficially the Russian church under the empire was a faithful guardian of traditional Orthodoxy in its teaching, worship and organisation, but in reality its life was distorted by alien elements from protestant sources introduced by the state. This was done deliberately by Peter the Great, who was determined to deprive the church of its authority and freedom and to reduce it to a government department. His ecclesiastical revolution was executed in such a way that, externally, church organisation was preserved, but the traditional canonical order was destroyed and replaced by a bureaucratic administration.

The emperor failed to kill the church: it remained a living, charismatic body, but it was unable to express its own mind and was in many ways paralysed and disfigured. The supreme head of the Russian church was no longer the patriarch, but the synod of bishops; this was only a pseudo-ecclesiastical organ, for its members were not elected by the church but appointed by the state and could debate only those questions which were selected by a lay procurator. The dioceses were still headed by bishops, but these were state officials who were promoted, demoted or moved from one diocese to another by the procurator. Similarly, the parochial clergy were appointed or dismissed utterly arbitrarily by the bishop and his lay assistants. The parishes were no longer self-governing communities; they were deprived of the right to administer their property and to elect their clergy. Only the church wardens were still chosen by the parishioners.

This highly-centralised bureaucratic system was imposed upon the church in order to take away from its members their initiative and freedom of action. Obedience and subordination were demanded from the top to the bottom; but fortunately this bureaucratic machine was inefficient, for it was entrusted to people who were alien to its Germanic spirit. In spite of Peter's reforms some freedom was left to the Russian Christians. The position of the Russian clergy reflected the condition of the church. Praised and admired by some, criticised and even calumniated by others. A Russian priest differed equally from the celibate and authoritative Roman cleric and from the scholarly protestant pastor, teacher of moral duties and of Christian probity. An Orthodox priest is primarily the celebrant of the divine mysteries. At his best he is (though seldom learned) a man of prayer, humility and charity; at his worst, a mere performer of ecclesiastical sacred rites. He was usually a married man and the father of a large family. He had no high social status; in rural area he was often poor, for he depended for his living on the voluntary donations of his parishioners and this could cause tension. In pre-Petrine Russia, the parochial clergy were elected by their flocks and were closely linked with them. But the imperial government tried to use its priests as officials, and imposed upon them various administrative duties. This policy gradually created a closed clerical caste. In the nineteenth century a parish priest as a rule was the son of a priest and this professionalism conflicted with his pastoral vocation, undermined his authority and unfavourably affected relations with his parishioners.

Yet the Russian priest, in spite of state pressure, remained a dedicated person[4] set apart for divine service, whose very presence among his parishioners reminded them of another world where the poor and the oppressed were favoured, and where the mighty and rich sat in the lowest seats at the heavenly banquet.

Externally, the church under the empire enjoyed a privileged position but in reality the state authorities kept a watchful eye on all its movements. Under the pretext of protection, they imposed a rigid censorship over sermons and religious publications. No church councils were permitted and the church could not express its opinion on any major issue concerning the nation. Such submission was resented by the best members of the church and, whenever pressure was relaxed, voices demanding the restoration of traditional Orthodox order were heard. This happened, for instance, in the first decades of the twentieth century when a vigorous movement advocating church reform burst out in the capitals of the empire. Its programme included the abolition of the synod, the re-introduction of self-government, the revival of parish life and the end of the caste system for the clergy.

The government, under this public pressure, agreed to convoke a council, but this took place only after the fall of the empire. The Russian church council of 1917–18 radically re-shaped the entire organisation of the church, introducing the election of the clergy. On November 5 1917 Tikhon Beliavin (1865–1925) was chosen patriarch of all Russia. When Lenin attacked the church the latter was an independent, self-governing body and this strengthened its resistance. The movement for church reform was accompanied by a remarkable religious revival among the intellectual élite of the nation.

The end of the nineteenth century was a particularly drab and uncreative period in the history of Russian culture. Positivism and

---

[4] The martyrdom of Russian clergy under the communists is a proof of their faithfulness. Cases of apostasy were remarkably few.

materialism enjoyed wide popularity among the intellectuals; religion, art and poetry were in decline, utilitarianism was seen as the last word in progressive civilisation. The new century suddenly changed the climate.

The religious and cultural renaissance of the twentieth century[5] affected all aspects of Russian life; gifted poets and creative artists appeared on the scene; interest in religion, philosophy and theology was re-awakened. The church became a strong centre of attraction; its worship and teaching, its icons and music ceased to be simply a part of folk-lore and revealed their intrinsic, permanent values. A number of conversions from atheism and materialism to Orthodoxy took place. This powerful revival, however, was accompanied by the growth of the negative tendencies like the orgiastic elements latent in popular Russian religiosity. They were exemplified in the notorious figure of Rasputin (1872–1916). In the same time reactionary parties sought and found support for their religious and national chauvinism in certain well-known hierarchs.

The Russian church has always had two distinct traditions which periodically clashed. It is impossible to understand Russian Orthodoxy or Russian culture without a proper grasp of this fact. Their first confrontation took place in the fifteenth century when the foundations of the Moscow tsardom were laid. One party became named the Josephians after its spokesman, saint Joseph of Volotsk (1439–1515). It emphasised the significance of ritual, stressed the importance of order and beauty in the celebration of the sacraments and in church architecture. Monarchy was a divine institution and close co-operation between church and state was a guarantee of stability and expansion. The other party, known as the non-possessors, led by saint Nil of Sorsk (1433–1508), emphasised the spiritual freedom of Christian man, stressed the inner purity of the heart, was opposed to the persecution of heretics and regarded monastic possessions as incompatible with religious vocation.

These two tendencies are deeply rooted in Russian Orthodoxy, which is both ritualistic and informal, closely linked with national history and universal, revering the monarchy as sacred and preaching man's freedom. There are few national churches so deeply polarised as the Russian church, yet its two tendencies are complementary and they were reconciled and harmonised in the lives of some of Russia's out-

[5] See [N.] Zernov, [*The Russian Religious*] *Renaissance* [*of the Twentieth Century*] (London 1963).

standing saints: saint Sergius of Radonezh in the fourteenth century and saint Seraphim of Sarov (1759-1833) in the nineteenth.

Such is, in brief, the picture of the Orthodox church of Russia which the refugees brought with them to western Europe and which became their tutor in Christ amidst the sufferings and trials of exile.

II

THE RUSSIAN CHURCH IN EXILE

In the course of 1920-5 the Russian diaspora was born. Most of the refugees fled to western Europe. Their colonies were established in Bulgaria, Yugoslavia, Czechoslovakia, Germany, Belgium and France. The emigration included people from different social strata, of diverse national and religious backgrounds, of conflicting political views and aspirations. The vast majority, however, belonged to the professional classes, including students, officers and soldiers of the defeated anticommunist armies.

Those of the emigrants who were Orthodox soon began to see their church in a new light. They took it for granted before the collapse of the empire, but few of these refugees had participated then regularly in its liturgical life. The horrors of the revolution, the sufferings of the civil war and the uncertainty and deprivations of exile altered their attitude to the church. Indifference was replaced by a widespread return to religion. The church became the source of consolation and inspiration to many of them: its services acquired new significance. The exiled people felt themselves back in their homeland when they heard the familiar chants and saw their icons illuminated by candlelight. The emigrants flocked to the few Russian churches which they found in Europe, but these were insufficient and they started to create new places for worship. Private houses, barracks or garages were used for this purpose. Everywhere parishes were organised, church choirs formed, Sunday schools established. This was a new experience for both clergy and laity, who were not used to selfgovernment. The problem arose of how to find canonical and material bases for the church in the diaspora.

Prior to the revolution there were a few Russian churches in the capitals of Europe and in places frequented by wealthy Russian tourists. These were included in the St Petersburg diocese and were administered by its metropolitan. This provision could obviously not satisfy the needs of a large and dispersed Russian colony, and in the autumn of 1921 a council was convoked in Karlovtsy, the seat of the Servian patriarch, with the purpose of establishing a proper canonical foundation for the Russian church in the diaspora.

Like the Moscow council of 1917–18, the emigrant council was composed of bishops, priests and laity, elected as the representatives of the newly-founded parishes. There were also delegates from the armed forces, and some well-known political leaders were invited as consultants. The council had ninety-three members, including twelve bishops and twenty-two priests. It proved to be a very stormy gathering which revealed the existence of deeply-conflicting tendencies within the emigrant community.

The council's primary task was to organise into dioceses the scattered Russian Orthodox parishes. Those dispersed over western and central Europe were assigned to the care of metropolitan Evlogy (Geogievsky, 1862–1946), who had already been appointed by patriarch Tikhon to supervise them. The parishes which came into existence in the balkans were put under the jurisdiction of the local autocephalous churches, although Russian refugee bishops were allowed to look after them. Metropolitan Anthony (Khrapovitsky, 1863–1936) was elected as the presiding hierarch over all the exiled communities. To assist him, various ecclesiastical organs were created. Thus this part of the council's task was satisfactorily achieved, but it was not the centre of its members' attention. This was the message to be addressed to all the Russian people. It both inspired and divided them. Many of them believed that their mission was to stir the nation to resist the red imposters and to restore the Orthodox monarchy, the sole guarantee of peace and order. A considerable group among them went still further in their aspirations. They wanted, in the name of the council, to recall the Romanovs to their ancestral throne. The discussion about the council's message split its members into two groups—those who insisted on including the Romanov dynasty in the text of the message, and those who considered it outside the competence of an ecclesiastical gathering and an intervention into politics. The victory in the voting fell to the Romanov supporters, but only by a narrow margin. Half of the bishops and three quarters of the clergy abstained from voting.

When the acts of the council reached Moscow, the patriarch declared them null and void. He disbanded the organs of administration created by the council and reasserted his previous decision to entrust all the Russian parishes in western Europe to metropolitan Evlogy and to recognise him as the sole canonical bishop. The latter tried, however, to avoid open conflict with metropolitan Anthony (a staunch monarchist) and thus the Russian church in exile maintained for some time an uneasy peace between the two parties—one emphasising the Josephian tendency, another advocating the political neutrality of the church. A formal split occurred in 1926. The majority of the Russian parishes in western Europe remained under the jurisdiction of metropolitan Evlogy, the majority of the Russians in the balkans, under metropolitan Anthony's care.

A further division took place in 1930 when metropolitan Sergy, the locum tenens of the patriarch of Moscow demanded from metropolitan Evlogy and his clergy the declaration of loyalty to the soviet government. Only a small minority consented to this demand, the rest of the church in diaspora was obliged to suspend canonical dependance on metropolitan Sergy and entered under canonical obedience to the patriarch of Constantinople.

Thus the Russian church in exile became divided into three sections. The first is known under the name of the synod church. After the death of metropolitan Anthony, he was succeeded by metropolitan Anastazy (Gribanovsky, 1873–1965). The present head of this church is metropolitan Philaret who has his seat in New York. That church now has some fifteen bishops in Europe, America and Australia. The second section formerly led by metropolitan Evlogy, has its centre in Paris and is presided over by metropolitan George, assisted by four bishops. A third section of the church in diaspora is under the jurisdiction of the Moscow patriarchate and is presided over by the exarch Nicodim, metropolitan of Leningrad, with seven bishops under him including metropolitan Anthony of Surogh with his seat in London. The two latter jurisdictions are in communion with each other, but the synod church regards the Moscow patriarchate as so deeply compromised politically that it refuses communion with its clergy.

This is, in brief, the external history of the Russian church in the diaspora. Let us turn our attention to its internal problems.

The Russian Christians in exile were faced with two major tasks: relations with fellow-Christians in Russia and their attitude to western Christians. In both spheres, three distinct attitudes have gradually taken shape. According to the belief of the members of synod church they were the only representatives of the Russian church. Its task was to remain faithful to the ideal of Orthodox tsardom and hope for its eventual restoration. Western Christians were treated by them as apostates from the true faith and the world council of churches regarded as a dupe of soviet propaganda. This group of the old emigrants was joined by some displaced persons belonging to the second emigration; newly arrived emigrants from the Soviet Union (the 'third emigrants') also often approve it.

The second attitude is held by those who belong to the Moscow jurisdiction. According to their view the church cannot exist in open opposition to the state and therefore must co-operate even with a hostile state like the soviet one. They believe that Christians in the diaspora have no right to judge those who carry the heavy load of ecclesiastical administration under the soviets and, by remaining in canonical obedience to the Moscow patriarchate, they express their moral solidarity with them. These Russians follow the lead of the Moscow patriarchate, participate in the ecumenical movement and maintain friendly contacts with western Christians.

The third view stresses the fundamental fact of the radical change in relations between church and state which took place as a result of the collapse of the empire. Its adherents advocate complete disestablishment of the church and welcome the birth of Orthodox communities in western Europe which use their own language for worship. These Russians have a strong attachment to their own country and culture, but they realise also the universality of the church and look forward to the time when the Christian east and west will once more enjoy full sacramental communion with each other. These ecumenically-minded Russians have been grouped round the Russian student Christian movement in exile, the theological academy of St Sergius in Paris and the fellowship of St Alban and St Sergius in England. The supporters of this view can be found both in the Moscow and Constantinople jurisdictions.

III

THE RUSSIAN RELIGIOUS RENAISSANCE AND ITS IMPACT ON THE CHURCH IN THE DIASPORA

The Russian religious renaissance, mentioned in part I, had far reaching repercussions in the religious life of the exiled community. One of the characteristics of the first Russian emigration (1920–5), in contrast to the second (1943–6) and the third (1972–6), was the large proportion of young men of student age who were prevented by the first world war and the red terror from pursuing their education. A number of them managed to resume their studies in various European universities; Paris, Berlin, Prague, Belgrade and Sofia became important centres of Russian academic life. The Russian students organised various societies and study circles. Many of them were religiously oriented. The YMCA and the world student Christian federation helped the representatives of these dispersed student groups to meet in Czechoslovakia, in Pŝerov, in the autumn of 1923. Some recently exiled Russian philosophers representing the renewal movement in the church, were also invited to this conference. The result was the formation of the Russian student Christian movement in exile. The conference at Pŝerov produced three important achievements. It helped Russian students to find the inspiration for their missionary work in the eucharistic life of their church; it reconciled two generations—the young men who fought in the ranks of the white armies and their intellectual leaders who had, on the eve of the revolution, exchanged Marxism for Orthodoxy; and it laid the foundation for a fruitful co-operation between Russian and western Christians. As a result, the student movement came for many years to serve as a main channel of communication between the Russian diaspora and the west. Other consequences of the success of the conference were no less significant. The YMCA press was founded in Paris and began to publish theological literature of exceptionally high quality. The St Sergius theological academy was opened in the same city in 1926,[6] and in 1928 the fellowship of St Alban and St Sergius started its work in England. Contacts were established with different branches of the ecumenical movement and Russian professors and students were invited to participate as observers at its conferences.

The leaders and members of the student movement and the majority of the professors at the theological academy in Paris regarded themselves as followers of the non-possessor school of thought. They stood in direct line of succession from those teachers and saints of the church who emphasised the inner freedom of a Christian, the universality of the church, and who were open to the prophetic call of the Holy Spirit.

Saint Tikhon of Zadonsk (1724–83), saint Seraphim of Sarov (1759–1833), archimandrite Makary (Glukharev, 1783–1847), the famous

---

[6] D. A. Lowrie, *Saint Sergius in Paris* (London 1954). Besides St Sergius academy Russians founded the following other theological schools: one in Harbin in Manchuria and three in the United States: St Vladimir seminary near New York and St Tichon seminary, both belonging now to the autocephalous American church, and the seminary of the Holy Trinity in Jordanville, under the jurisdiction of the synod church.

missionary, and Alexey Khomiakov (1804–60) a lay theologian, were some of the best-known representatives of this tradition. The most significant among them for our own time was Vladimir Soloviev (1853–1900), philosopher, poet, theologian and mystic. This friend of Dostoevsky (1821–81) stirred and upset the Russian intellectuals by his unusual personality and original ideas.[7] He foresaw the events of our time, such as ecumenism, totalitarianism, Zionism, which were far removed from his contemporaries who confidently believed in the uninterrupted march of secular civilisation. Soloviev died a lonely and misunderstood man, on the threshold of a new century, but he prepared the ground for that powerful, spontaneous, artistic and religious revival which burst out after his death and was suppressed only by Lenin and his followers.

Among the leaders of this renaissance four men, all ex-Marxists, deserve special mention.[8] They were the sociologist and historian Peter Struve (1870–1944); the theologian Sergy Bulgakov (1871–1944); the religious philosopher Nicolas Berdyaev (1874–1946) and Simeon Frank (1877–1958). They all started their literary careers as atheists and materialists and ended as Orthodox Christians. Their conversions were spectacular and had important consequences. In 1909, eight years before Lenin started his extermination of the liberal intelligentsia, these men predicted the reign of terror which would follow the victory of the revolutionaries. In the symposium called *Signposts* (*Vekhi*) they analysed the ambiguity of secular humanism and convincingly proved that the freedom and dignity of the individual can only be sustained on a Christian basis and has no support in an atheistic and materialistic outlook. After Lenin's victory the same men were able to publish another symposium, *De Profundis*, in which they confirmed the truth of their prophecy. Expelled from Russia in 1922, they assumed leadership in the Russian student movement and became vitally involved in the work of Christian reconciliation.[9] They knew and valued the Christian west and realised that only together can Christians find the right solution of the grave problems confronting them. They were inspired by the belief that the harassing experience of the totalitarian assault on Christianity contained a vital lesson for the whole of Christendom. The leaders of the religious renaissance in

[7] See N. Zernov, *Three Russian Prophets, Khomiakov, Dostoevsky, Soloviev* (London 1944).

[8] See Zernov, *Renaissance*, cap 6 'Four Notable Converts'.

[9] See N. Zernov, *The Reintegration of the Church* (London 1952).

the emigration participated actively in the ecumenical movement. They attended the Lausanne conference in 1927, the Oxford and Edinburgh conferences in 1937, the youth conference in Amsterdam in 1939 and took part in various commissions which prepared these great assemblies. Their status of observers (for the Russian church was crushed and silenced by Stalin's terror) and their small numbers greatly limited the scope of their actions, nevertheless their impact was considerable in spite of these limitations. Their participation in the debates enlarged the field of the doctrinal discussions which had tended to be confined to a restricted field of protestant theology. The other Russian contribution was the introduction of the eucharist of different traditions into the framework of the ecumenical gathering. Previously theological debate was treated as the sole means of achieving reconciliation.

The full scope of the Russian contribution was displayed, however, not so much at these official conferences but in the work of the fellowship of St Alban and St Sergius, an unofficial body created to increase the mutual knowledge first between anglicans and Orthodox, then gradually growing to be an all-embracing ecumenical society. Its conferences had a distinctive liturgical character. Each day started with the celebration of the eucharist, which followed alternatively the eastern and western rite. The members prayed at each others' service, but refrained from taking communion, for intercommunion was not authorised at that time. This method proved to be most efficient and many barriers melted away and genuine unity of belief and common purpose was established.

In 1933 father Sergy Bulgakov outlined a plan for further action. He advocated communion in the sacraments between those eastern and western Christians who reached a real unity of faith. But he insisted that this solemn act of reconciliation should be preceded by corporate repentance sealed by a sacramental blessing bestowed upon these pioneers of unity by their respective bishops.

This proposal provoked heated discussions among the members of the fellowship. It seemed to be revolutionary at the time, when both the Orthodox and Roman catholic churches prohibited any form of intercommunion. At present the situation is different, but the confusion which accompanies the current practice of intercommunion probably could be avoided and much more creative use of it could be secured if church leaders paid more attention to the proposal of the great Russian seer.

The Russian Orthodox diaspora and its effect on the west

Although Orthodox theologians reacted differently to Bulgakov's far-seeing proposal, the religious leaders of the Russian emigration were at one as they opposed uniformity as the structure of church unity; they were sceptical about ecclesiastical diplomacy and mistrusted ambiguous doctrinal statements as the means of bridging gaps between divided Christians.

Thus, as far as the Russian side was concerned, contacts with the west were limited at first to only one section of the exiled community, namely to the leaders of the religious renewal and their younger enthusiastic supporters. The rest of the church in the diaspora remained either indifferent or suspicious of the friendship which sprang up between some Russians and western Christians. Those who supported the synod section of the church had nothing to say to the west, and were not interested in learning anything from the heterodox. The spokesmen of the renaissance, on the contrary, were deeply moved by the possibility of re-starting a dialogue with the west.[10]

IV

THE MESSAGE OF THE RUSSIAN CHURCH IN THE DIASPORA TO THE WEST

The Russian exiles were the witnesses of several catastrophic events which happened simultaneously in their country. These were the moral collapse and bankruptcy of secular humanism, the rise of communist

---

[10] Here I should like to enumerate the most outstanding religious writers in the diaspora and the subjects of their contributions.

Dogmatic theology: archpriest Sergei Bulgakov (1871–1944), metropolitan Anthony Khrapovitsky (1863–1936), archpriest George Florovsky (b. 1893). *Theology and aesthetics:* Nicolas Arseniev (b. 1888), Pavel Evdokimov (1900–1970), Konstantin Mochulsky (1892–1948), archbishop John Shakhovskoy (b. 1902), Vladimir Weidle (1895). *Patristics and liturgiology:* archimandrite Cyprian Kern (1899–1960), archbishop Basil Krivoshein (b. 1900), Abraam Pozov (1890), archpriest Alexander Shmeman (1921). *Byzantology:* archpriest John Meyendorff (1926), Dimitri Obolensky (b. 1918). *Orthodox spirituality:* metropolitan Anthony (Bloom, b. 1914), Nadejda Gorodetskaya (b. 1901), Vladimir Lossky (1903–58), archimandrite Sofrony Sakharov (b. 1896). *Church history:* archpriest Nicolas Afanasiev (1893–1960), George Fedotov (1886–1951), Anton Kartashev (1875–1960), Peter Kovalevsky (b. 1901), Igor Smolich (1898–1970), Nicolas Zernov (b. 1898). *Religious philosophy:* Nicolas Berdyaev (1874–1948), Boris Vysheslavtzev (1877–1954), Simeon Frank (1877–1950), Ivan Ilyin (1891–1974), Lev Karsavin (1882–1952), Nicolas Lossky (1870–1965), Lev Shestov (1866–1938), Feodor Stepun (1884–1965), Lev Zander (1893–1964), archpriest Basil Zenkovsky (1881–1962). Altogether more than three hundred Russian Orthodox authors published their works on various religious subjects during the first fifty years of Russian emigration. For the full list see Zernov, *Emigré Authors.*

totalitarianism and the end of the Constantinian period in the history of the church.

As often happens, only a few outstanding men were able to read properly the significance of these momentous changes and only they had a message to the Christian west, which contained an appeal to draw the necessary conclusions from the Leninist dictatorship in Russia.

On the eve of the revolution the majority of westernised Russians professed a secular humanism and they tried to spread it among the masses. It was sometimes coloured by a sentimental attachment to the church, but more often was imbued with an hostility to religion. It was generally optimistic, believed in the natural goodness of human nature and was confident that man is master of his own destiny and therefore it is in his power to create an order which secures to all justice, peace and material prosperity.

There was a wide spread of the cult of the French revolution, and the use of violence was regarded as the most secure way to achieve a desirable reconstruction of society. For this reason most of them welcomed the fall of the empire and confidently expected that the liberals and socialists would lead the nation towards a bright future of freedom and equality. Lenin's arrival from Switzerland, sponsored by the Germans, was the first challenge to this optimism.

He inflicted a deadly blow upon secular humanism. He not only exterminated his social and liberal rivals; he successfully demonstrated the inconsistency of their position. Communism has revealed those sides of human nature which were ignored by liberal agnostics—man's fear and hatred of God, his lust for power, his irrationality and unwillingness to bear the burden of freedom and responsibility. Totalitarianism has convincingly proved that tyranny and readiness to be enslaved are major factors in human history. Secularism and atheism do not provide any secure ground for a defence of personal freedom and the dignity of the individual. These are rooted in the Christian vision of man as the living image of his Triune Creator.

Lenin and his followers defeated not only liberal humanism,[11] but they also achieved victory over the church, which had been broken down, a large part of it driven underground. The leaders of the religious

[11] A young friend of ours was taken as a hostage in our town in 1918. The commissar of justice promised his mother to release the boy in exchange for a heavy ransom. The mother sold everything, was helped also by friends and brought the money. The commissar took it and declared that her son has been killed the previous night, but that the money would be used for the extension of the red terror.

renaissance movement saw in this humiliation of the church the end of the Constantinian period of church history. The abdication of the last Russian tsar, God's anointed monarch, had been the final act in the drama inaugurated in the fourth century when the close co-operation between church and state, Christianity and paganism, freedom and compulsion, had been brought about. This alliance had provided the church with many advantages, but it had necessitated many compromises and mistaken actions. This epoch having ended, Christians have to stand alone, relying only on their own faith and willingness for sacrifice, rejecting any temptation to use force. The church is not a replica of the state; its task is not to maintain public morals, law and order. The church is called to regenerate its members and to send them into the world as messengers of the kingdom of God.

But the Church itself needs reintegration, a revival of its sacramental life. It suffers from onesidedness in its doctrinal definitions and sectarianism in worship. Christians had lost their sacramental unity through association with the state. At present, when they are gradually recovering their independence, they have a chance of realising their unity, and so deepening their communion in the Holy Spirit.

The convictions of the Russian theologians who represent the movement towards the renewal of the church, and their message, may be summarised under the following headings:

1. Lenin's dictatorship, leading to totalitarian communism, is one of the most decisive turning-points of history. It represents not only an entirely new political and economic system but confronts men with a choice between the Christian and the atheistic vision of life and demonstrates the practical consequences of these two opposed outlooks.

2. The driving power behind totalitarian communism is—man's rebellion against God, his determination to prove his independence and God's impotence to control human affairs. This rebellion feeds a truly demonic desire to dominate the rest of mankind, to impose the party's will upon its fellow men and deprive them of freedom of thought and action. The communists justify this tyranny by their claim that they possess the secret of universal happiness.

3. Marxist-Leninists declare that their main concern is for the well-being of the under-privileged. In reality, they are interested only in their theories, in class struggle and power, being utterly indifferent to real living men. And the result is an accentuation of class privileges, people being systematically sacrificed for the sake of military power and

the supremacy of the party. Ruthless despotism with its mass terror, spying and intimidation accompanied by a deliberate deception reveal that militant atheism is an aberration and that the Christian vision of God and man is the true vision.

4. The relentless drive of the communists against Christianity is not accidental. They resent the believers because only members of the Christian community are capable of resisting the crushing power of an omnipotent state and of retaining their personality and freedom in spite of demands of submission and conformity made by a totalitarian society.

5. European civilisation, with its regard for freedom of thought and its respect for the individual, has its roots in the biblical revelation which recognises man as a son of God, a companion in works with his Creator. Spectacular scientific discoveries are the fruit of eucharistic experience which has taught men to love and care for matter and human labour. The undermining of the Christian basis of our civilisation deprives it of its inner cohesion and vitality and makes it incapable of resisting the pressure of totalitarianism.

6. The future of Christian civilisation depends on the revival of the church, which once more must become a universal eucharistic fellowship consisting of people who are drawn to the encounter with the living God. Christians of the east and west need each other. They are complementary in their achievements and limitations. The trials and martyrdom of Russian Christians are part of the experience of the entire Christian community. The Russians have learned at great cost the true nature of secularism; they hope the Christian west will be spared the ordeal which befell their Orthodox brethren.

Such are the outlines of this message. It was delivered with deep conviction but the west has found it hard to take it seriously.

V

THE CHRISTIAN WEST AND THE
RUSSIAN CHURCH IN THE DIASPORA

The first Russian emigration happened when the west was absorbed in the urgent task of rebuilding its political and economic order after the fratricidal first world war. Optimism prevailed in many quarters: the league of nations was expected to prevent further military conflicts; shattered confidence in social and scientific progress was restored and hopes for a bright future revived. The fall of the St

Petersburg empire was generally welcomed in Europe and America and the news of Lenin's victory was received enthusiastically by radicals and with cautious curiosity by conservatives. Contemporary western comments on the communist revolution displayed almost total ignorance of conditions in Russia. The most incredible stories were spread and believed, whilst reports of the new 'Red' order which refugees brought to the west were lightheartedly dismissed.

The fundamental error of both conservatives and liberals in the west was their association of the new totalitarianism with the old-fashioned, paternal autocracy of the Romanovs. In reality it was an entirely new phenomenon, springing from that failure of secular humanism from which the western world was also suffering.

Western observers saw Leninism as a local event occurring in a backward country, which could in no way be repeated in more advanced states. They did not realise that an unprecedented political system was being born in Russia, which was destined to spread over large parts of Europe and Asia and to become a major threat to the rest of the civilised world. This misjudgement prevented western people from learning from the Russians' experience and from preparing themselves for the hard struggle against totalitarianism which awaited them in the next decades.[12]

The rise of totalitarianism in Germany and the persecution of the church there opened the eyes of some to the new menace, yet Hitler's anti-communist policy increased support for Stalin in left-wing circles. The almost total silence which he was able to impose on his country concealed from the west any idea of the type of red terror which flourished in the land of 'realised socialism'. The abysmal ignorance of western leaders of state and church about the real situation in the Soviet Union was amply illustrated by the glaring mistakes made by them in their negotiations with Stalin during and after the second world war.

There were, however, some bright exceptions among the westerners in the midst of this general illusion. These were a few far-seeing men who understood the importance for the rest of the world of that grim struggle that was going on between the communists and

---

[12] Another illustration of the same fact: in 1963 I published a book in London called *The Russian Religious Renaissance of the Twentieth Century*. Little notice was taken of it in the west, but when a copy of it reached Russia, it immediately attracted attention there and was translated and secretly reproduced in typescript by 'Samisdat'. In 1974 this Russian translation with a preface written in Moscow, explaining the importance of the book to the Russian readers, was published in Paris.

the Christians in Russia. They were also aware of the high intellectual and spiritual quality of some of the Russian churchmen who had sought refuge in the west. Among these friends and supporters of the Russian Orthodox were an American John Mott (1865–1955) and a Swiss Gustav Kullmann (1894–1961), both of the American YMCA, and several anglicans like bishop Walter Frere, C.R. (1863–1938) and the reverend Fynes Clinton (1875–1959). All of them gave both financial and moral support to the Russian theological academy in Paris, the Russian student Christian movement in exile and the fellowship of St Alban and St Sergius.

The exiled Russians were also able to exercise a deep influence on the Roman church, by making friends with two outstanding catholic priests. These were the abbé Paul Couturier (1881–1953) and dom Lambert Beauduin (1874–1960), a friend and inspirer of pope John XXIII. Many ideas of the second Vatican council originated first in the mind of this daring Belgian monk.

The movement for Christian reconciliation acquired far greater momentum after the Vatican council. Joint participation in the eucharist by divided Christians has increased, while at the same time their ties with the state have been loosened; the appreciation of patristic tradition was revived in all those circles where Russian influence was at work.

A further change in relations between the Russian church in the diaspora and the Christian west has taken place in the last ten years. There is an increasing number of protestants and catholics who understand nowadays the seriousness for the rest of the world of the struggle between the Leninists and the Russian Christians. They are prepared to listen to the Russians and take an active part in the studies of this vital conflict.

On one point, however, there remains a grave difference between the views of an influential body of western Christians and the convictions of the Russians involved in the movement for church renewal: the latter insist that from the Christian standpoint the use of violence for promoting even good causes cannot be justified, whilst certain groups in the west show, on the contrary, a readiness to condone or to participate in the killing of their opponents. Evil cannot be destroyed by the extermination of its agents; the willingness of the world council of churches to support, both financially and morally, so-called 'freedom fighters' and other terrorists is a tragic aberration in the opinion of these Russians. They have learned, as the result of their own bitter experience under persecution, to abhor the use of force in ideological conflicts.

The history of the church in the east and west has always been strikingly different. The last half-century deepened still further the gulf between them, but as never before they need to listen to one another and search together for the right Christian answers to the problems of our time.

CONCLUSION

The Russian Orthodox church in the diaspora provides an important chapter in both the history of the Russian church and of the church universal.

Its most obvious achievement was the preservation of the tradition of learning and worship at a time when the Leninists were determined to annihilate it in Russia. But even more important was the demonstration in the Russian church of its vigour and vitality. Under the unfavourable conditions of poverty and uncertainty in exile, after a long period of submission to state control at home and without the previous experience of self-government, the Russian orthodox were able to organise their church life on a sound basis of independence. This revealed the creativity of their theological thought and at the same time, in spite of the originality and prophetic gifts of Russian Christian thinkers, they remained faithful to the Orthodox tradition, proving by this that it can be combined with up-to-date philosophical and theological learning. This inner freedom provided a valuable basis for their penetrating analysis of the causes and consequences of the collapse of the 'sacred' monarchy and of the triumph of Lenin's totalitarianism in Russia.

Unfortunately the divergence of opinion on that very crucial point caused divisions among Russian Orthodox in exile. Painful as they were they did not destroy the fundamental oneness of the Orthodox community in the diaspora, for the majority of church members did not support the extremists who tried by threats of excommunication to impose their will on the rest.

Another significant contribution by the church in the diaspora is its creative attitude towards western Christians. The centuries-long isolation of the Russian church was brought to an end by the exiled community. Russians were able to share their experience with western Christians and establish relations of trust and friendship with some of them. Though they formed a small and materially insecure minority beside the prosperous and well organised western churches, the Russians were neither subdued nor absorbed. On the contrary, they made a marked impression upon their powerful neighbours, opening new avenues of thought to many of them.

Finally a few words have to be said about the relations between the church in the diaspora and in the Soviet Union. The former has always regarded itself as an integral part of the whole Russian church. Its contacts, however, with the episcopate under communist control have often been strained and interrupted.

Since the restoration of the patriarchate in Moscow in 1943, especially after Stalin's death in 1953, which made it possible for the Russian church to join the world council of churches in 1956, contacts between the church in exile and in Russia have greatly increased. They revealed at first the existence of a considerable cultural and intellectual gap between the leaders of the church in the west and those behind the iron curtain. The latter displayed the typical characteristics of men brought up under a totalitarian system: unwillingness to express their own views and undertake responsibility, conformity in thought and action, fear of being denounced and punished for any unguarded remarks. They were people of limited education but men of prayer and dedication, concerned with practical problems. The first years of contacts gave the impression that cultural continuity had been broken in the Russian church and that the riches of theological and philosophical thought created by the leaders of the Russian religious renaissance had evoked no response among the new generation. This impression began to fade out in the sixties. The spread of 'Samisdat' revealed the existence of an audience eager to read religious literature produced in exile. Later, several clandestine works appeared in Russia in direct line of succession to Vladimir Soloviev, Bulgakov, Fedotov and Berdyaev. The beginning of the third emigration in the seventies completed this process of mutual recognition. A number of recent emigrants to the west have shown not only an acquaintance with the literature created by the first emigration but also their ability to pursue ideas which were the centre of attention for their grandfathers.

A few facts will illustrate this restoration of a creative exchange of experience between those who left Russia in the twenties and those who are leaving their country in our own time. *The Messenger*, the organ of the Russian student Christian movement, started in 1926, recently had more articles written in the Soviet Union than in the west. In November 1974 a symposium on religious and philosophical subjects was published simultaneously in typescript in Moscow and in Paris as a printed book. The most impressive side of this unusual literary adventure is that its authors, who include Solzhenitsyn, regard themselves as the successors of the authors of the two previous symposia which discussed the same problem, *Vekhi* (*Signposts*) and *De Profundis*. More than half a century had elapsed before the third volume could be written, but this tragic interval was not wasted. A deeper grasp of the same problems has been revealed by the new book.

So, in conclusion, one can say that if the message of the Russian church in exile had been only partially understood and accepted in the west, it has had a decisive importance for the intellectual élite in Russia. There, it was of inestimable help to Christians, giving them new courage and hope in their lonely stand against the assault of the godless.

The contest between atheistic totalitarianism and the church is universal; on its outcome depends the future of mankind. The Christians under the Leninist yoke are enslaved bodily; their intellectual life is drastically curtailed, but they have won a spiritual victory, for they have discovered the truth of the gospels and the falsehood of the promise of a godless earthly paradise. The Christian west still enjoys its freedom, but its resistance to totalitarianism is weakened by intellectual doubts and by material comforts. The prospects for Christian civilisation are not bright at present. They would be greatly improved if the west took more seriously the harrowing experience of Russian Christians under soviet rule.

Oxford

ABBREVIATIONS

AASRP	*Associated Archaeological Societies Reports and Papers*
AAWG	*Abhandlungen der Akademie [Gesellschaft* to 1942] *der Wissenschaften zu Göttingen*, (Göttingen 1843–)
AAWL	*Abhandlungen der Akademie der Wissenschaften und der Literatur* (Mainz 1950–)
ABAW	*Abhandlungen der Bayerischen Akademie der Wissenchaften* (Munich 1835–)
Abt	Abteilung
ACO	*Acta Conciliorum Oecumenicorum*, ed E. Schwartz (Berlin/Leipzig 1914–40)
ACW	*Ancient Christian Writers*, ed J. Quasten and J. C. Plumpe (Westminster, Maryland/London 1946–)
ADAW	*Abhandlungen der Deutschen* [till 1944 *Preussischen*] *Akademie der Wissenschaften zu Berlin* (Berlin 1815–)
AFP	*Archivum Fratrum Praedicatorum* (Rome 1931–)
AHP	*Archivum historiae pontificiae* (Rome 1963–)
AHR	*American Historical Review* (New York 1895–)
An Bol	*Analecta Bollandiana* (Brussels 1882–)
Annales	*Annales: Economies, Sociétés, Civilisations* (Paris 1946–)
APC	*Proceedings and Ordinances of the Privy Council 1386–1542*, ed Sir Harris Nicolas, 7 vols (London 1834–7)
—	*Acts of the Privy Council of England 1542–1629*, 44 vols (London 1890–1958)
—	*Acts of the Privy Council of England, Colonial Series (1613–1783)*, 5 vols (London 1908–12)
AR	*Archivum Romanicum* (Geneva/Florence 1917–41)
ARG	*Archiv für Reformationsgeschichte* (Berlin/Leipzig/Gütersloh 1903–)
ASAW	*Abhandlungen der Sächsischen Akademie [Gesellschaft* to 1920] *der Wissenschaften zu Leipzig* (Leipzig 1850–)
ASB	*Acta Sanctorum Bollandiana* (Brussels etc. 1643–)
ASC	*Anglo Saxon Chronicle*
ASI	*Archivio storico Italiano* (Florence 1842–)
ASL	*Archivio storico Lombardo*, 1–62 (Milan 1874–1935); ns 1–10 (Milan 1936–47)
ASOC	*Analecta Sacri Ordinis Cisterciensis [Analecta Cisterciensia* since 1965] (Rome 1945–)
ASOSB	*Acta Sanctorum Ordinis Sancti Benedicti*, ed L. D'Achery and J. Mabillon (Paris 1668–1701)
ASP	*Archivio della Società [Deputazione* from 1935] *Romana di Storia Patria* (Rome 1878–1934, 1935–)
ASR	*Archives de Sociologie des Religions* (Paris 1956–)
AV	Authorised Version
AV	*Archivio Veneto* (Venice 1871–): [1891–1921, *Nuovo Archivio Veneto*; 1922–6, *Archivio Veneto-Tridentino*]
B	*Byzantion* (Paris/Boston/Brussels 1924–)
Bale, *Catalogus*	John Bale, *Scriptorum Illustrium Maioris Brytanniae Catalogus*, 2 parts (Basel 1557, 1559)

Bale, *Index*   John Bale, *Index Britanniae Scriptorum*, ed R. L. Poole and
                     M. Bateson (Oxford 1902) *Anecdota Oxoniensia*, medieval and
                     modern series 9

Bale,   John Bale, *Illustrium Maioris Britanniae Scriptorum Summarium*
  Summarium   (Ipswich 1548, reissued Wesel 1549)

BEC   *Bibliothèque de l'École des Chartes* (Paris 1839–   )

Beck   H-G. Beck, *Kirche und theologische Literatur im byzantinischen Reich*
                     (Munich 1959)

BEHE   *Bibliothèque de l'École des Hautes Etudes: Sciences Philologiques et
                     Historiques* (Paris 1869–   )

Bernard   E. Bernard, *Catalogi Librorum Manuscriptorum Angliae et Hiberniae*
                     (Oxford 1697)

BF   *Byzantinische Forschungen* (Amsterdam 1966–   )

BHG   *Bibliotheca Hagiographica Graeca*, ed F. Halkin, 3 vols+1 (3 ed
                     Brussels 1957, 1969)

BHI   *Bibliotheca historica Italica*, ed A. Ceruti, 4 vols
                     (Milan 1876–85), 2 series, 3 vols (Milan 1901–33)

BHL   *Bibliotheca Hagiographica Latina*, 2 vols+1 (Brussels 1898–1901,
                     1911)

BHR   *Bibliothèque d'Humanisme et Renaissance* (Paris/Geneva 1941–   )

BIHR   *Bulletin of the Institute of Historical Research* (London 1923–   )

BJRL   *Bulletin of the John Rylands Library* (Manchester 1903–   )

BL   British Library, London

BM   British Museum, London

Bouquet   M. Bouquet, *Recueil des historiens des Gaules et de la France.
                     Rerum gallicarum et francicarum scriptores*, 24 vols
                     (Paris 1738–1904); new ed L. Delisle, 1–19 (Paris 1868–80)

BQR   *British Quarterly Review* (London 1845–86)

Broadmead   *The Records of a Church of Christ, meeting in Broadmead,
  Records   Bristol 1640–87*, HKS (London 1848)

BS   *Byzantinoslavica* (Prague 1929–   )

Bucer, *Deutsche*   *Martin Bucers Deutsche Schriften*, ed R. Stupperich et al
  Schriften   (Gütersloh/Paris 1960–   )

Bucer, *Opera*   *Martini Buceri Opera Latina*, ed F. Wendel et al
  Latina   (Paris/Gütersloh 1955–   )

BZ   *Byzantinische Zeitschrift* (Leipzig 1892–   )

CA   *Cahiers Archéologiques. Fin de L'Antiquité et Moyen-âge*
                     (Paris 1945–   )

CAH   *Cambridge Ancient History* (Cambridge 1923–39)

CalRev   *Calamy Revised*, ed A. G. Mathews (Oxford 1934)

CalLP   *Calendar of the Letters and Papers (Foreign and Domestic) of the Reign
                     of Henry VIII*, 21 vols in 35 parts (London 1864–1932)

CalSPD   *Calendar of State Papers: Domestic* (London 1856–   )

CalSPF   *Calendar of State Papers: Foreign*, 28 vols (London 1861–1950)

Calvin, *Opera*   *Ioannis Calvini Opera Quae Supersunt Omnia*, ed G. Baum et al,
                     Corpus Reformatorum, 59 vols (Brunswick/Berlin 1863–1900)

Cardwell,   *Documentary Annals of the Reformed Church of England*,
  Documentary   ed E. Cardwell, 2 vols (Oxford 1839)
  Annals

Cardwell,   *Synodalia*, ed E. Cardwell, 2 vols
  Synodalia   (Oxford 1842)

CC   *Corpus Christianorum* (Turnholt 1952–   )

CF   *Classical Folia*, [*Folia* 1946–59] (New York 1960–   )

CH	*Church History* (New York/Chicago 1932–)
CHB	*Cambridge History of the Bible*
CHistS	*Church History Society* (London 1886–92)
CHJ	*Cambridge Historical Journal* (Cambridge 1925–57)
CIG	*Corpus Inscriptionum Graecarum*, ed A. Boeckh, J. Franz, E. Curtius A. Kirchhoff, 4 vols (Berlin 1825–77)
CMH	*Cambridge Medieval History*
CModH	*Cambridge Modern History*
COCR	*Collectanea Ordinis Cisterciensium Reformatorum* (Rome/Westmalle 1934–)
COD	*Conciliorum oecumenicorum decreta* (3 ed Bologna 1973)
CR	*Corpus Reformatorum*, ed C. G. Bretschneider et al (Halle etc. 1834–)
CS	*Cartularium Saxonicum*, ed W. de G. Birch, 3 vols (London 1885–93)
CSCO	*Corpus Scriptorum Christianorum Orientalium* (Paris 1903–)
CSEL	*Corpus Scriptorum Ecclesiasticorum Latinorum* (Vienna 1866–)
CSer	*Camden Series* (London 1838–)
CSHByz	*Corpus Scriptorum Historiae Byzantinae* (Bonn 1828–97)
CYS	*Canterbury and York Society* (London 1907–)
DA	*Deutsches Archiv für [Geschichte, –Weimar 1937–43] die Erforschung des Mittelalters* (Cologne/Graz 1950–)
DACL	*Dictionnaire d'Archéologie chrétienne et de Liturgie*, ed F. Cabrol and H. Leclercq (Paris 1924–)
DDC	*Dictionnaire de Droit Canonique*, ed R. Naz (Paris 1935–)
DHGE	*Dictionnaire d'Histoire et de Géographie ecclésiastiques*, ed A. Baudrillart *et al* (Paris 1912–)
DNB	*Dictionary of National Biography* (London 1885–)
DOP	*Dumbarton Oaks Papers* (Cambridge, Mass., 1941–)
DR	F. Dölger, *Regesten der Kaiserurkunden des oströmischen Reiches (Corpus der griechischen Urkunden des Mittelalters und der neueren Zeit*, Reihe A, Abt I), 5 vols: 1 (565–1025); 2 (1025–1204); 3 (1204–1282); 4 (1282–1341); 5 (1341–1453) (Munich-Berlin 1924–65)
DSAM	*Dictionnaire de Spiritualité, Ascétique et Mystique*, ed M. Viller (Paris 1932–)
DTC	*Dictionnaire de Théologie Catholique*, ed A. Vacant, E. Mangenot, E. Amann, 15 vols (Paris 1903–50)
EcHR	*Economic History Review* (London 1927–)
EEBS	Ἐπετηρὶς Ἑταιρείας Βυζαντινῶν Σπουδῶν (Athens 1924–)
EETS	*Early English Text Society*
EHD	*English Historical Documents* (London 1953–)
EHR	*English Historical Review* (London 1886–)
Ehrhard	A. Ehrhard, *Überlieferung und Bestand der hagiographischen und homiletischen Literatur der griechischen Kirche von den Anfängen bis zum Ende des 16. Jh*, 3 vols in 4, *TU* 50–2 (=4 series 5–7) 11 parts (Leipzig 1936–52)
Emden (O)	A. B. Emden, *A Biographical Register of the University of Oxford to 1500*, 3 vols (London 1957–9)
Emden (C)	A. B. Emden, *A Biographical Register of the University of Cambridge to 1500* (London 1963)
EO	*Echos d'Orient* (Constantinople/Paris 1897–1942)
EYC	*Early Yorkshire Charters*, ed W. Farrer and C. T. Clay, 12 vols (Edinburgh/Wakefield 1914–65)

FGH	*Die Fragmente der griechischen Historiker*, ed F. Jacoby (Berlin 1926–30)
FM	*Histoire de l'église depuis les origines jusqu'à nos jours*, ed A. Fliche and V. Martin (Paris 1935–)
Gangraena	T. Edwards, *Gangraena*, 3 parts (London 1646)
GCS	*Die griechischen christlichen Schriftsteller der erste drei Jahrhunderte* (Leipzig 1897–)
Gee and Hardy	*Documents Illustrative of English Church History* ed H. Gee and W. J. Hardy (London 1896)
Golubovich	Girolamo Golubovich, *Biblioteca bio-bibliografica della Terra Santa e dell' oriente francescano:* series 1, *Annali*, 5 vols (Quaracchi 1906–23) series 2, *Documenti*, 14 vols (Quaracchi 1921–33) series 3, *Documenti* (Quaracchi 1928–) series 4, *Studi*, ed M. Roncaglia (Cairo 1954–)
Grumel, Regestes	V. Grumel, *Les Regestes des Actes du Patriarcat de Constantinople*, I: *Les Actes des Patriarches*, I: 381–715; II: 715–1043; III: 1043–1206 (Socii Assumptionistae Chalcedonenses, 1931, 1936, 1947)
Grundmann	H. Grundmann, *Religiöse Bewegungen im Mittelalter* (Berlin 1935, 2 ed Darmstadt 1970)
HBS	*Henry Bradshaw Society* (London/Canterbury 1891–)
HE	*Historia Ecclesiastica*
HistSt	*Historical Studies* (Melbourne 1940–)
HJ	*Historical Journal* (Cambridge 1958–)
HJch	*Historisches Jahrbuch der Görres Gesellschaft* (Cologne 1880 ff, Munich 1950–)
HKS	Hanserd Knollys Society (London 1847–)
HL	C. J. Hefele and H. Leclercq, *Histore des Conciles*, 10 vols (Paris 1907–35)
HMC	Historical Manuscripts Commission
Hooker, Works	*The Works of . . . Mr. Richard Hooker*, ed J. Keble, 7 ed rev R. W. Church and F. Paget, 3 vols (Oxford 1888)
Houedene	*Chronica Magistri Rogeri de Houedene*, ed W. Stubbs, 4 vols, *RS* 51 (London 1868–71)
HRH	*The Heads of Religious Houses, England and Wales, 940–1216*, ed D. Knowles, C. N. L. Brooke, V. C. M. London (Cambridge 1972)
HS	*Hispania sacra* (Madrid 1948–)
HTR	*Harvard Theological Review* (New York/Cambridge, Mass., 1908–)
HZ	*Historische Zeitschrift* (Munich 1859–)
IER	*Irish Ecclesiastical Record* (Dublin 1864–)
IR	*Innes Review* (Glasgow 1950–)
JAC	*Jahrbuch für Antike und Christentum* (Münster-im-Westfalen 1958–)
Jaffé	*Regesta Pontificum Romanorum ab condita ecclesia ad a. 1198*, 2 ed S. Lowenfeld, F. Kaltenbrunner, P. Ewald, 2 vols (Berlin 1885–8, repr Graz 1958)
JBS	*Journal of British Studies* (Hartford, Conn., 1961–)
JEH	*Journal of Ecclesiastical History* (London 1950–)
JFHS	*Journal of the Friends Historical Society* (London/Philadelphia 1903–)

JHI	*Journal of the History of Ideas* (London 1940–)
JHSChW	*Journal of the Historical Society of the Church in Wales* (Cardiff 1947–)
JIntH	*Journal of Interdisciplinary History* (Cambridge, Mass., 1970–)
JLW	*Jahrbuch für Liturgiewissenschaft* (Münster-im-Westfalen 1921–41)
JMH	*Journal of Modern History* (Chicago 1929–)
JMedH	*Journal of Medieval History* (Amsterdam 1975–)
JRA	*Journal of Religion in Africa* (Leiden 1967–)
JRH	*Journal of Religious History* (Sydney 1960–)
JRS	*Journal of Roman Studies* (London 1910–)
JRSAI	*Journal of the Royal Society of Antiquaries of Ireland* (Dublin 1871–)
JSArch	*Journal of the Society of Archivists* (London 1955–)
JTS	*Journal of Theological Studies* (London 1899–)
Knox, *Works*	*The Works of John Knox,* ed D. Laing, Bannatyne Club/Wodrow Society, 6 vols (Edinburgh 1846–64)
Laurent, *Regestes*	V. Laurent, *Les Regestes des Actes du Patriarcat de Constantinople,* 1: *Les Actes des Patriarches,* IV: *Les Regestes de 1208 à 1309* (Paris 1971)
Le Neve	John Le Neve, *Fasti Ecclesiae Anglicanae 1066–1300,* rev and exp Diana E. Greenway, 1, St Pauls (London 1968); 2, Monastic Cathedrals (1971) *Fasti Ecclesiae Anglicanae 1300–1541* rev and exp H. P. F. King, J. M. Horn, B. Jones, 12 vols (London 1962–7) *Fasti Ecclesiae Anglicanae 1541–1857* rev and exp J. M. Horn, D. M. Smith, 1, St Pauls (1969); 2, Chichester (1971); 3, Canterbury, Rochester, Winchester (1974); 4, York (1975)
Lloyd, *Formularies of faith*	*Formularies of Faith Put Forth by Authority during the Reign of Henry VIII,* ed C. Lloyd (Oxford 1825)
LRS	Lincoln Record Society
LQR	*Law Quarterly Review* (London 1885–)
LThK	*Lexikon für Theologie und Kirche,* ed J. Höfer and K. Rahnes (2 ed Freiburg-im-Breisgau 1957–)
LW	*Luther's Works,* ed J. Pelikan and H. T. Lehman, American edition (St Louis/Philadelphia, 1955–)
MA	*Monasticon Anglicanum,* ed R. Dodsworth and W. Dugdale, 3 vols (London 1655–73); new ed J. Caley, H. Ellis, B. Bandinel, 6 vols in 8 (London 1817–30)
Mansi	J. D. Mansi, *Sacrorum conciliorum nova et amplissima collectio,* 31 vols (Florence/Venice 1757–98); new impression and continuation, ed L. Petit and J. B. Martin, 60 vols (Paris 1899–1927)
MedA	*Medium Aevum* (Oxford 1932–)
MGH	*Monumenta Germaniae Historica inde ab a. c. 500 usque ad a. 1500,* ed G. H. Pertz etc (Berlin, Hanover 1826–)
AA	*Auctores Antiquissimi*
Cap	*Capitularia*
Conc	*Concilia*
Const	*Constitutiones*
Dip	*Diplomata*
Epp	*Epistolae*
Form	*Formularia*
Leg	*Leges*

Lib	*Libelli de Lite*
SS	*Scriptores*
SRG	*Scriptores rerum germanicarum in usum scholarum*
SRL	*Scriptores rerum langobardicarum et italicarum*
SRM	*Scriptores rerum merovingicarum*
MIÖG	*Mitteilungen des Instituts für österreichische Geschichtsforschung* (Graz/Cologne 1880–)
MM	F. Miklosich and J. Müller, *Acta et Diplomata Graeca medii aevi sacra et profana*, 6 vols (Vienna 1860–90)
More, *Works*	*The Complete Works of St. Thomas More*, ed R. S. Sylvester et al, Yale edition (New Haven/London 1963–)
Moyen Age	*Le moyen âge. Revue d'histoire et de philologie* (Paris 1888–)
MS	Manuscript
Muratori	L. A. Muratori, *Rerum italicarum scriptores*, 25 vols (Milan 1723–51); new ed G. Carducci and V. Fiorini, 34 vols in 109 fasc (Città di Castello/Bologna 1900–)
NCE	*New Catholic Encyclopedia*, 15 vols (New York 1967)
NCModH	*New Cambridge Modern History*, 14 vols (Cambridge 1957–70)
nd	no date
NEB	*New English Bible*
NF	Neue Folge
NH	*Northern History* (Leeds 1966–)
ns	new series
NS	New Style
Numen	*Numen: International Review for the History of Religions* (Leiden 1954–)
OCP	*Orientalia Christiana Periodica* (Rome 1935–)
ODCC	*Oxford Dictionary of the Christian Church*, ed F. L. Cross (Oxford 1957), 2 ed with E. A. Livingstone (1974)
OS	Old Style
PBA	*Proceedings of the British Academy*
PG	*Patrologia Graeca*, ed J. P. Migne, 161 vols (Paris 1857–66)
PhK	Philosophisch-historische Klasse
PL	*Patrologia Latina*, ed J. P. Migne, 217+4 index vols (Paris 1841–64)
PO	*Patrologia Orientalis*, ed J. Graffin and F. Nau (Paris 1903–)
Potthast	*Regesta Pontificum Romanorum inde ab a. post Christum natum 1198 ad a. 1304*, ed A. Potthast, 2 vols (1874–5 repr Graz 1957)
PP	*Past and Present* (London 1952–)
PRIA	*Proceedings of the Royal Irish Academy* (Dublin 1836–)
PRO	Public Record Office
PS	Parker Society (Cambridge 1841–45)
PW	*Paulys Realencyklopädie der klassischen Altertumsvissenschaft*, new ed G. Wissowa and W. Kroll (Stuttgart 1893–)
QFIAB	*Quellen & Forschungen aus italienischen Archiven und Bibliotheken* (Rome 1897–)
RB	*Revue Bénédictine* (Maredsous 1884–)
RE	*Realencyclopädie für protestantische Theologie*, ed A. Hauck, 24 vols (3 ed Leipzig, 1896–1913)
REB	*Revue des Études Byzantines* (Bucharest/Paris 1946–)
RecS	Record Series
RGG	*Die Religion in Geschichte und Gegenwart*, 6 vols (Tübingen 1927–32)
RH	*Revue historique* (Paris 1876–)

RHD	*Revue d'histoire du droit* (Haarlem, Gronigen 1923–)
RHDFE	*Revue historique du droit francais et étranger* (Paris 1922–)
RHE	*Revue d'Histoire Ecclésiastique* (Louvain 1900–)
RHEF	*Revue d'Histoire de l'Église de France* (Paris 1910–)
RHR	*Revue de l'Histoire des Religions* (Paris 1880–)
RR	*Regesta Regum Anglo-Normannorum*, ed H. W. C. Davis, H. A. Cronne, Charles Johnson, R. H. C. Davis, 4 vols (Oxford 1913–69)
RS	*Rerum Brittanicarum Medii Aevi Scriptores*, 99 vols (London 1858–1911). *Rolls Series*
RSR	*Revue des sciences religieuses* (Strasbourg 1921–)
RTAM	*Recherches de théologie ancienne et médiévale* (Louvain 1929–)
RSCI	*Rivista di storia della chiesa in Italia* (Rome 1947–)
RStI	*Rivista storica italiana* (Naples 1884–)
RV	Revised Version
S	*Sitzungsberichte*
SA	*Studia Anselmiana* (Rome 1933–)
SBAW	*Sitzungsberichte der bayerischen Akademie der Wissenschaften*, PhH (Munich 1871–)
SCH	*Studies in Church History* (London 1964–)
ScHR	*Scottish Historical Review* (Edinburgh/Glasgow 1904–)
SCR	*Sources chrétiennes*, ed H. de Lubac and J. Daniélou (Paris 1941–)
SGre	*Studi Gregoriani*, ed G. Borino, 7 vols (Rome 1947–61)
SGra	*Studia Gratiana*, ed J. Forchielli and A. M. Stickler (Bologna 1953–)
SMon	*Studia Monastica* (Montserrat, Barcelona 1959–)
Speculum	*Speculum, A Journal of Medieval Studies* (Cambridge, Mass 1926–)
SpicFr	*Spicilegium Friburgense* (Freiburg 1957–)
SS	*Surtees Society* (Durham 1835–)
STC	*A Short-Title Catalogue of Books Printed in England, Scotland and Ireland and of English Books Printed Abroad 1475–1640*, ed A. W. Pollard and G. R. Redgrave (London 1926, repr 1946, 1950)
Strype, *Annals*	John Strype, *Annals of the Reformation and Establishment of Religion . . . during Queen Elizabeth's Happy Reign*, 4 vols in 7 (Oxford 1824)
Strype, *Cranmer*	John Strype, *Memorials of . . . Thomas Cranmer*, 2 vols (Oxford 1840)
Strype, *Grindal*	John Strype, *The History of the Life and Acts of . . . Edmund Grindal* (Oxford 1821)
Strype, *Memorials*	John Strype, *Ecclesiastical Memorials, Relating Chiefly to Religion, and the Reformation of it . . . under King Henry VIII, King Edward VI, and Queen Mary I*, 3 vols in 6 (Oxford 1822)
Strype, *Parker*	John Strype, *The Life and Acts of Matthew Parker*, 3 vols (Oxford 1821)
Strype, *Whitgift*	John Strype, *The Life and Acts of John Whitgift*, 3 vols (Oxford 1822)
sub hag	*subsidia hagiographica*
SVRG	*Schriften des Vereins für Reformationsgeschichte* (Halle/Leipzig/Gütersloh 1883–)
TCBiblS	*Transactions of the Cambridge Bibliographical Society* (Cambridge 1949–)

THSCym	*Transactions of the Historical Society of Cymmrodorion* (London 1822–)
TRHS	*Transactions of the Royal Historical Society* (London 1871–)
TU	*Texte und Untersuchungen zur Geschichte der altchristlichen Literatur* (Leipzig/Berlin 1882–)
VCH	*Victoria County History* (London 1900–)
VHM	G. Tiraboschi, *Vetera Humiliatorum Monumenta*, 3 vols (Milan 1766–8)
Vivarium	*Vivarium: An International Journal for the Philosophy and Intellectual Life of the Middle Ages and Renaissance* (Assen 1963–)
VV	*Vizantijskij Vremennik* 1–25 (St Petersburg 1894–1927), ns 1 (26) (Leningrad 1947–)
WA	D. *Martin Luthers Werke*, ed J. C. F. Knaake (Weimar 1883–) [*Weimarer Ausgabe*]
WA Br	*Briefwechsel*
WA DB	*Deutsche Bibel*
WA TR	*Tischreden*
WelHR	*Welsh History Review* (Cardiff 1960–)
Wharton	H. Wharton, *Anglia Sacra*, 2 parts (London 1691)
Wilkins	*Concilia Magnae Britanniae et Hiberniae A.D. 446–1717*, 4 vols, ed D. Wilkins (London 1737)
YAJ	*Yorkshire Archaeological Journal* (London/Leeds 1870–)
Zanoni	L. Zanoni, *Gli Umiliati nei loro rapporti con l'eresia, l'industria della lana ed i communi nei secoli xii e xiii, Biblioteca Historica Italica,* 2 series, 2 (Milan 1911)
ZKG	*Zeitschrift für Kirchengeschichte* (Gotha/Stuttgart 1878–)
ZOG	*Zeitschrift für osteuropäische Geschichte* (Berlin 1911–35)=*Kyrios* (Berlin 1936–)
ZRG	*Zeitschrift der Savigny-Stiftung für Rechtsgeschichte* (Weimar)
–GAbt	*Germanistische Abteilung* (1863–)
–KAbt	*Kanonistische Abteilung* (1911–)
–RAbt	*Romanistische Abteilung* (1880–)
ZRGG	*Zeitschrift für Religions- und Geistesgeschichte* (Marburg 1948–)
Zwingli, *Werke*	*Huldreich Zwinglis Sämmtliche Werke*, ed E. Egli et al, *CR* (Berlin/Leipzig/Zurich 1905–)

DATE DUE